A HEMISPHERE APART

THE JOHNS HOPKINS SYMPOSIA IN COMPARATIVE HISTORY

The Johns Hopkins Symposia in Comparative History are occasional volumes sponsored by the Department of History at the Johns Hopkins University and the Johns Hopkins University Press comprising original essays by leading scholars in the United States and other countries. Each volume considers, from a comparative perspective, an important topic of current historical interest. The present volume is the fifteenth. Its preparation has been assisted by the James S. Schouler Lecture Fund.

A HEMISPHERE APART

*The Foundations of United States
Policy toward Latin America*

John J. Johnson

The Johns Hopkins University Press
Baltimore and London

The Johns Hopkins University Press
701 West 40th Street, Baltimore, Maryland 21211
The Johns Hopkins Press Ltd., London

The paper used in this publication meets the minimum requirements
of American National Standard for Information Sciences—Permanence
of Paper for Printed Library Materials, ANSI Z39.48–1984.

Library of Congress Cataloging-in-Publication Data

Johnson, John J., 1912–
    Distant neighbors : the foundations of United States policy toward
Latin America, 1815–1830 / John J. Johnson.
        p.   cm. — (The Johns Hopkins symposia in comparative history)
    Includes bibliographical references.
    ISBN 0–8018–3953–X (alk. paper)
    1. Latin America—Foreign relations—United States.   2. United
States—Foreign relations—Latin America.   3. United States—Foreign
relations—1815–1861.   I. Title.   II. Series.
F1418.J753   1990
327.7308—dc20   89–27984
                                                          CIP

To Maurine with Love

CONTENTS

Preface   ix

Introduction   1

1. Domestic Factors I: Industrial Developments, the
   Westward Movement, Catholicism, Monarchism   10

2. Domestic Factors II: Racial and Ethnic Influences   44

3. The Latin American Factor   78

4. The British Impact on United States–Latin
   American Relations   112

5. Weighting the Determinants of Policy   170

Epilogue   187

Notes   209

Bibliographical Sources   247

Index   265

PREFACE

This study reappraises early United States–Latin American relations from an Anglo-American perspective. To explain the pronounced shift from a pro-insurgent view prior to independence to one of limited interest, if not disdain, for the peoples and institutions of the emerging republics by 1830, the book looks beyond the facade of diplomatic events, personalities, and the presumed unity of aspirations toward a common ethos between North and South to underlying domestic factors in the United States, Latin America, and the United Kingdom that were critical in shaping the U.S. view of its (new) southern neighbors. The shadowy and usually neglected subject of ethnic and racial perceptions in the United States and their impact on Anglo-American attitudes toward the alien peoples of Latin America are treated in detail.

The book moves beyond traditional studies in ranking the ingredients that influenced U.S. attitudes according to their relative impact on those attitudes. Whether or not the assessments are in the main sustained—it is assumed that some informed individuals will take exception to them—the approach has the merit of making the examination of the U.S. perspectives on the hemisphere at once more manageable and meaningful.

No claim is made that the determinants of policy during the years 1815 to 1830 would be equally applicable in an earlier or later epoch. Nonetheless, the complexity and confused state of present-day international relations do not conceal that in them one finds more than mere glimmerings of why a cloud of misunderstanding, apprehension, and distrust has overhung hemispheric relations for most of two centuries.

I learned a great deal from the project; I hope that my readers do also.

During the course of my research on this book I became indebted to a number of institutions devoted to the preservation of historical records and to individuals who devote themselves to making research rewarding and pleasurable. Georgette Dorn of the Hispanic Division of the Library of Congress contributed greatly to making several months working in the division profitable. Joan Loftus, David Rozkuszka, Betty Lum, and Marise Morse of Stanford's Jonsson Library of Government Documents knowledgeably and patiently guided me through the library's extensive holdings of U.S. and British official printed documents. I spent considerable time in the United States National Archives before returning to Stanford where I used recently acquired microfilm copies of materials in the (National) Archives under nearly ideal conditions. Mrs. Johnson and I worked side by side during three summers in the Public Record Office, Kew, England. We take special pleasure in expressing our deep gratitude for having had the opportunity to examine the exciting and marvelously preserved records in that fine institution and to benefit from being able to call upon, as necessary, members of its informed and attentive staff. Finally, my sincere thanks to my thoughtful and conscientious copy editor, Jean Toll.

Financial support for the study came at different times from the American Council of Learned Societies, the National Endowment for the Humanities, the Stanford University Emeriti Faculty Development Program, the Andrew W. Mellon Foundation through the Stanford Center for Latin American Studies, and the National Humanities Center. It was as a fellow at the Center during the academic year 1985–86 that I completed research on the project and began the write-up.

In February 1988, at the invitation of the Department of History, The Johns Hopkins University, I delivered the James S. Schouler Lectures. In the lectures I addressed the major themes discussed in the book and received helpful comments from faculty and students for which I am grateful.

INTRODUCTION

The independence of the mainland Iberian colonies in the New World was assured by 1823. Final victory of insurgent groups over the metropolitan powers was accompanied by an easily identified change in the U.S. interest in the region. For a decade and more, while the brutal struggles wore on, public and private opinion in the United States had sided overwhelmingly with the revolutionaries, and concern for their future welfare ran strong. The enthusiasm of Hezekiah Niles, editor of the widely read and influential *Weekly Register*, was such that he dedicated volume 10 of the journal "to the patriots of Mexico and South America contending for liberty and Independence and to all others struggling to obtain civil and religious freedom."[1] In the wake of victory and with the destiny of the ex-colonials in their own hands, interest in them in the United States plummeted, and by the end of the 1820s independent Latin America, Mexico excepted, figured only marginally in the minds of the North American public and in the policy decisions of the national government.

This book, then, deals in chronological terms with the first of the U.S. forays into Latin American affairs that have been followed by indifference. In particular, the volume attempts to answer the question: What were the world conditions and attitudes that in so short a time led to U.S. indifference to the new nations? The United States is the leading actor. The Latin American nations, and especially Great Britain, have major supporting parts. France is cast in a minor, shadowy role.

Independence

The account begins with what many contemporaries in the United States viewed as an unvarnished victory over the Mistress of the Seas. The war that began in 1812, in essence a second War of Independence, had inspired the states to work more closely together than at any time previously. The war, too, had proved the Republic's capacity and determination to survive in a hostile atmosphere. A new spirit of self-reliance marked the beginning of the end of a colonial complex. North Americans ceased to doubt the path of their future or how that path would distinguish their country from other societies. A small-town pastoral society, tenacious of the customary and slow to accept innovation, had given way or was on the brink of giving way to an urban and industrial state, populated by people who shared a faith in the individual, faith in humanity, and faith that perfection not only could be achieved, but could be achieved in the foreseeable future.[2] A revivalist movement that began at the turn of the century had lost its vitality but not before producing a generation of Protestant clergy who came to recognize better the significance of the separation of church and state. The new-minded clergy were not only less concerned than their predecessors with reconciliation of moral virtues with the morals of the marketplace, but in fact became active propagandists for private enterprise and industrial capitalism.

With the war behind it, with the physical security of its western frontier generally assured, and with its economy almost totally free from external pressures, the Republic was at liberty to devote its attention and energies to industrial and infrastructural development and to opening up and securing its claim to an enormously enlarged national domain.[3] A "boomtown" optimism prevailed, nourished first by natural and then by technological abundance.[4] Perseverance, frugality, and an aura of urgency, ebullience, and mission characterized the era. Laborers steeped in the work ethic were resourceful and not easily deterred by difficulties.[5] The cult of the self-made man was universally accepted as was the idea of progress.[6] Abroad, the nation was variously stigmatized as radical, materialistic, utilitarian, a menace, a stirrer of dissension, and its people as rustics given to whiskey imbibing and tobacco chewing, and incapable of achievement in the arts, but these attitudes did little to shake the new society's confidence in itself and its future.[7]

Europe's popular elements, weary of war and taxes and unaware or uncaring about the accounts of travelers who claimed to have been struck by the disparities between the "golden dream" and the vulgar realities of slavery, were by the thousands flocking to its shores, attracted by plenty of land obtainable on a freehold basis.[8] The newcomers were party to transforming a stable and homogeneous society into one of epic change, notable for its mobility and heterogeneity. Some feared that the pride and prosperity that came with independence and the quickening drift toward a secularist society threatened the nation's underpinnings. For the present, however, it was accepted as a self-evident truth that the United States would have a glorious future.

Nationalism, religious activities, physiographic expansion, economic change, and ethnic challenges all influenced the evolution of the nation's foreign policy objectives. By the early Jacksonian era that policy had become so narrowly nationalistic in motivation as at times to give the impression that the rest of the world was unimportant to the nation's welfare. Nowhere was the new view of the world more apparent than in the realm of U.S. relations with the polities being created out of the disintegrating Iberian empires.

The Weakness of the Ex-Colonies

In Latin America, meanwhile, the fruits of victory were bitter. Everywhere a heavy burden of prejudice, custom, and a colonial mentality remained. As the struggles wore on, provincialism and localism destroyed any sense of national unity. The students of the Enlightenment who initially propounded justifications for rebellion were forced to surrender leadership to elite groups composed of the landed aristocracy and their urban constituents, the hierarchy of the Roman Catholic Church, and the officer corps of the various armed forces, who first usurped and then monopolized power. Thus authoritarians born in America replaced authoritarians born in Spain and Portugal. Under the new authoritarians facts prevailed against constitutions. The juridic concept of representative democracy was not repudiated; it was ignored. The Church was encouraged to continue as the interpreter of the social value system. Manual laborers had no sense of their stake in progress and good government; they were left to vegetate on the outskirts of national life. Only cultured elements had any real or permanent standards and traditions, and they were blind to the possible evils that those standards and traditions might bring to societies suddenly left to their own resources.

Elite domination also meant economic victory for the countryside. The rural emphasis forestalled commercial and industrial development. When it became apparent that Latin Americans lacked the capital and the organizational and administrative skills to compete successfully in the North Atlantic trading community foreigners moved in to fill the deficiency. They took over international trade and, thus positioned, used their clout to direct domestic economic development toward production of the commodities that would earn foreign exchange, which could, in turn, be used to purchase imported manufactures.

Overall, then, the prospects for the former colonies appeared indeed bleak. Except for Brazil, they had opted for republicanism rather than monarchy, much to the satisfaction of Washington, but otherwise they had not turned out as the United States had hoped. There were no indications whatever that the republics would soon influence in any significant way the future of the Western world or even learn from it. Taking as cues the region's political instability, its racial mélange, its social inequities, and its economic backwardness, Washington concluded that for the foreseeable future attention to the republics could be safely reduced. That conclusion reinforced the official position that the U.S. future lay in promoting domestic growth while holding foreign nations at arm's length elsewhere in the hemisphere.

The Preeminence of Great Britain

Great Britain had a major influence on the evolution of U.S.–Latin American relations during the 1815–30 epoch. Prior to London's recognition of the republics, beginning in 1824–25, His Majesty's Government's affiliations with Spain and the Holy Alliance were critical to the outcome of Washington's negotiations with Spain over the Floridas, to events leading to U.S. recognition of the new nations, and to the proclamation of President James Monroe in 1823. Following their emancipation the ex-colonials looked to Great Britain, not the United States, as their military protector, as their source of investment capital, manufactured goods, including war matériel, and as arbiter of their disputes, for example, in the conflict between Brazil and Argentina over the Banda Oriental (Uruguay). Although London followed Washington's lead in acknowledging the sovereignty of the new states, because of Great Britain's paramount standing with the republics, in most cases Washington reacted to what London did, or was thought to be doing, in respect to Latin America, rather than the reverse. Washington and London were careful not to take arbitrary stands on such issues as monarchism, republicanism, African slavery, privateering, and trade treaties; had they, it is problematical what the consequences would have been.

There is, however, no doubt whatever that the attempted control of Cuba by one or the other side would have put the two nations on a collision course. In the era of sailing ships, the island's strategic importance was a geopolitical fact no trading nation could ignore. In the hands of a major world power—the United States was already recognized as such—Cuba had the potential to be the key to the commercial and military domination of the entire Caribbean Basin. Its "neutrality" was critical to U.S. strategic defenses and to the growth of the trans-Appalachian West and to Great Britain's trade with its West Indian colonies. Thus between 1815 and 1830 every important move toward Latin America from Washington or London was taken with an eye as to how the other would react regarding Cuba.

Anglo-American Perceptions

The book places considerable emphasis on the perceptions of U.S. private citizens and public officials of themselves and of Latin Americans and their institutions. That aspect of the volume, distinguishing it from other studies requires elaboration.

By perceptions I mean those images that, based on their repeated appearances in the historical records, can be taken to represent, not in a systematic way, but in a general way, the values, beliefs, ideas, and prejudices of a given group. Much like cartoon symbols or clues—dark- or fair-skinned people, firm or receding chins, males or females, adults or children, all of which are loaded with either positive or negative values—perceptions make possible instant, intuitive cognition. They are the mental shortcuts used to assign values to things and peoples. In this study, I have used perceptions/images primarily to establish the ethnocentric attitudes of the opinion elites—those who left written records and who held nearly all economic, social, political, and military power—in the United States, and secondarily of their counterparts in Great Britain. I have not been concerned with the fall of certain perceptions from intellectual respectability. By their very nature perceptions are ambiguous and their influence on societal beliefs or public policy impossible accurately to measure. I have assumed that perceptions provide more than hints, but less than irrefutable pieces of evidence. This is to say, my opinions of how Anglo-Americans reacted to Latin Americans are necessarily largely matters of interpretation. Because of the nature of the discussion in chapter 2, the words *race, racial,* and *race relations* appear frequently in this volume. The words *racist* and *racism,* do not appear at all except in this Introduction and the Epilogue.

Inspired by contacts with "primitive peoples" of the New World, Africa, and Australia, individuals in the United States were intensely interested in racial types that separated mankind. Their opinions about these types could have been informed by a variety of pseudosciences in the public domain by the 1820s—catastrophism, craniology, phrenology, and the study of facial angle and hair texture—in the classification of races. Those pseudosciences became integral to the ideology of racists, defined as groups who have held a correlation between the physical characteristics and moral and intellectual qualities and divided mankind into superior and inferior stocks, and who after

1850 in the United States sought to "prove" the inferiority of racial groups in the degree to which they varied from the "white" norm. Each of the pseudosciences provides strong evidence that in questions of the human race scientific methods were abandoned in the mid-nineteenth century in favor of uncritical speculation.

Anglo-Americans in the early nineteenth century, however, overwhelmingly accepted biblical authority and chronology that man originated from a single pair and was created in a perfect state, and that in the dispersion of mankind after the destruction of the Tower of Babel some tribes had sunk into barbarism. Their views placed Anglo-Americans, a few dissenters to the contrary, squarely on the side of environmentalists and culturalists who explained variations in the human species in terms of climate, food, dress, and modes of living. In sum, they believed in learned behavior rather than in inherited traits. Their perceptions of the main racial groups in Latin America were consistent with that belief.

When treating prejudices and attitudes, as I do in chapter 2, I have chosen to use derivatives of the Greek *ethnos*—ethnic, ethnicity, ethnocentrism. Ethnic attitudes and prejudices have evaluative connotations and serve to identify human beings with their own people as against the rest of humanity. At one level they provide the cement of cultural unity by encouraging thinking in terms of groups rather than individuals. On another level they tend to produce contempt for foreign people, the degree of contempt tending to vary with the degree of contact and the differential elements groups hold to be important. Race, skin color, nationality, language, institutional characteristics, and, to a declining degree, religion have been the most commonly recognized differential factors in peacetime. In wartime or in periods preceding the actual outbreak of hostilities, the criteria for acceptance or rejection may, of course, fluctuate wildly.

The Historical Approach

Some words about substance and sources and certain assumptions. This volume treats the subject of hemispheric relations essentially from the U.S. angle of vision. *It does not presume to treat Latin Americans on their own terms.* My justification for taking that approach is that, throughout the period under review, the initiative of the United States was dominant in U.S.–Latin American relations.

This is not a study in U.S.–Latin American diplomatic relations of the Charles Griffin, Joseph Byrne Lockey, Dexter Perkins, Arthur P. Whitaker, Samuel Flagg Bemis genre. Those distinguished historians constructed their accounts basically around hemispheric "happenings." Those happenings serve mainly as guideposts in this volume. My objective has been not so much to detail the happenings as to establish the context in which they took place. It will become evident to my readers that I have little fascination with sensational events.

I have treated the 1810s and 1820s as a discrete historical period. Attitudes, beliefs, and values held then are not necessarily applicable to any earlier or later time. I believe strongly that the ethical priorities and imperatives of the twentieth century should not be imposed on the patterns of early nineteenth-century thought. I believe, nonetheless, that for at least three reasons ethnic attitudes have a strong tendency to remain a part of an inherited body of cultural experiences. The first is that impressions of foreign peoples are to a large degree formed in childhood and usually in the family group; prejudices, thus, tend to be internalized before adulthood.[9] Second, elites continually recruit from the rank and file and consequently share in its prejudices.[10] Third, whatever a person's private sentiments, his or her public behavior strongly tends to adapt to prevailing climates of opinion.[11]

Examining the Evidence

The scope of this study obliged me to rely in varying degrees on the work of numerous modern scholars. My reliance is particularly apparent in chapter 1, which deals primarily with domestic issues confronting the United States, and in chapter 4, which treats U.S.-British relations as they related to Latin America. I am delighted to acknowledge my indebtedness and I ask the indulgence of those who influenced my thinking, but whom I neither cite not identify. Still, traditional documentary sources—manuscripts and published official materials, contemporary newspapers, journals, textbooks, and travel accounts—provided the core data of the book. Each of those categories, valuable as it was, given the time frame of my undertaking, yielded something less than incontrovertible evidence. Official documents, prepared by agents in the field, I suspect, were often prepared with an eye to what superiors at home wanted to hear. Politicians, whom I consider to be major exemplars of the age, already had a well-developed reputation for being adept at exploiting the common knowledge, traditions, and prejudices of their constituents. Their public pronouncements and theatrics in regard to hemispheric affairs, therefore, have been viewed against a domestic backdrop.

The extent to which newspapers molded public opinion is not easily determined, but that they were widely circulated and mirrored contemporary interests appears evident. So popular were newspapers, the *New York Observer* dared assert that "in no part of the world does the newspaper possess so extensive an influence as in our country. It is estimated that in the whole union, there are at least five hundred newspaper establishments, from which are issued annually more than thirty million sheets."[12] The reading of a representative sample of newspapers from across the nation confirmed, to my satisfaction, the claim of the *New York Commercial Advertiser* of June 29, 1821, that a newsworthy article on Buenos Aires it had previously published had "gone the rounds of most of the papers of the United States."

The spirit of discovery ran strong in the late eighteenth century. Spain, France, and Great Britain each sponsored major scientific expeditions, and those directed by Captain James Cook and Alexander von Humboldt were probably the best known to the English-speaking community. The interests of the scientists tended toward botanical research, but they amassed a great deal of ethnographic data.[13] Nonscientists—adventurers, businessmen, public officials, churchmen—simultaneously joined the race to "discover" what lay in the far corners of the earth. Their interests were more in people, customs, and institutions, less in the natural sciences. The reading public in the United States avidly sought the reports of the latter group because they were easy reading and their contents generally understandable. The *American Quarterly Review* astutely observed: "The press in our day teems with books of travels under the various titles of Journals, Tours, Views, Sketches, Rough Notes, &c. which are all readily bought up by our 'great reading public,' who find themselves thus enabled, with little expense and no hardships to travel at home and perform voyages by the Fireside."[14] Such accounts, however, usually reflected the shock that authors experienced on initial contact with distant lands, "strange" peoples, and unfamiliar surroundings. As a consequence, travel accounts tended to stress the exotic rather than the commonplace.[15] In the case of Latin America, because of the problems of transportation and security, visitors for the most part remained in the major port cities and wrote from that point of view. Life in the agricultural and grazing regions was commonly neglected. Textbook authors consciously promoted the fear of God and love of country. They nearly always judged foreign cultures by U.S. standards, or British standards when British textbooks were published in the United States with but minor substantive changes, a common practice.[16]

That the documents reveal little regarding the views of the general public is regrettable, but not critical. The public, concerned as it was with family and local issues, was essentially inattentive to foreign affairs. When they thought at all about foreign issues their thoughts tended to focus on Europe, where their ancestral ties and economic and security interests were strong, not on Latin America, about which they were only vaguely knowledgeable.[17] Furthermore, as H. Stuart Hughes has, I believe, rightly observed, the fund of ideas available at any particular time to individuals who have received a superior general education are the ideas that eventually inspire government elites.[18]

In summary, I make no claim to having discovered new documentary sources; much is in fact standard fare. I believe that I have read and digested more than a representative number of the traditional materials. I have also read the documents with other than standard purposes in mind and I am confident that I have used them to focus on certain issues that they have not served before. Since the documents I used yielded few reliable enumerative materials, I have made no attempt to quantify the intensity of the feelings and beliefs of Anglo-Americans toward "out-groups."

Despite the ambiguous nature of my evidence I have been basically comfortable with it in establishing how contemporaries in the United States viewed Latin Americans and their institutions. I have not always been comfortable about how my observations on racial attitudes in the United States and Great Britain may be interpreted and used. With that concern in mind I wish at this point to make explicit my objectives in examining racial attitudes. First to explain the waxing and waning of U.S. and British interest in Latin America I had to comprehend, as best I could, the social order being created in those societies, and second, historians of early nineteenth-century hemispheric affairs have largely avoided the role of perceptions as a determinant in those relations. For my part, I believe that impulses, whether rational or irrational, have played a part historically in determining what is "right" and what is "wrong" in international relations; to put it another way, in international affairs opinions are often more influential than truths. As I have already suggested, in bringing up the question of racial attitudes I have had no interest in exposing human frailties or in debunking any people's past or in getting caught up in the niceties of ideological debates. Rather, my sole interest has been to explain a historical condition.

Finally, I hope that I have identified which questions were significant in explaining the sudden changes of interest in the United States toward Latin America in the 1815–30 era. I hope, too, that I have not invented an approach that makes things look smaller the farther away they are, and I hope most of all that I have avoided many of the opportunities to commit logical suicide that impressionistic studies and speculation invite.

1 DOMESTIC FACTORS I
Industrial Developments, the Westward
Movement, Catholicism, Monarchism

The 1815–30 era was, in the United States, an unusually dynamic
and a peculiarly innovative and formative epoch. Concepts that sig-
nally altered the perspective of its people and their place in the Western world were crystallized, energized, or brought to fruition. The
new perspectives were not universally held. Different views of republican government, although fading, still persisted, and conflicting
views over policies with foreign nations caused dissension. Disputes
leading to the Missouri Compromise and the Nullification Acts challenged the powers of the central government as did state's rights and
the rancor born of party differences. Eastern aristocrats who had become Republicans did not quite like the company of frontier Demo-
crats. And the new perspectives were not always reconcilable. One
obvious inconsistency involved the determination of the citizenry to
protect its own liberty, while accepting the institution of African slavery. Traditional moral values, meanwhile, often clashed with emerging practices of capitalism. Society was, nonetheless, an essentially
unified whole and in balance. The future of the nation was no longer
called into question.

Scholars have seldom found an epoch more distinctly marked.
W. B. Cairns, writing in 1898 on literature in the United States, declared the period to be crucial in that field.[1] Frederick Jackson Turner,
publishing in 1906, noted that from the close of the War of 1812 to the
election of Andrew Jackson the nation gave clear evidence that it was
throwing off the last remnants of colonial dependence.[2] In her 1919
article on religious forces in the United States, Martha L. Edwards
limited her study to the years 1815–30.[3] The 1815–30 era is at the
core of John R. Bodo's *The Protestant Clergy and Public Issues, 1812–
1848* (1954). In his Preface Bodo identified three main reasons for selecting 1812 as a starting point: (1) the absence of a real national
feeling prior to that date, (2) the inability of the clergy before that date
to realize the full significance of the separation of church and state,

and (3) the emergence of U.S. nationalism during the War of 1812. Russel Blaine Nye terminated his report on the cultural life of the new nation at 1830.[4] Howard Mumford Jones, writing in 1964, asserted that the administration of John Quincy Adams closed the era in which the classical past was a dynamic force in the nation's political life.[5] Joyce O. Appleby wrote that Jackson's victory in 1828 checked a policy of choosing as chief executive men carefully groomed for leadership; all of his predecessors, except Washington, had established their credentials by serving either as vice president or secretary of state.[6] Douglas Miller, writing in 1970, noted that contemporaries regarded the time as one of rapid change and that repeated historical investigation validated this judgment. Innovation affected almost all aspects of society in the generation after 1812; it was evident that life would "no longer be so simple, self-sufficient, rural, agrarian, decentralized, Anglo-Saxon, and Protestant."[7] Arthur P. Whitaker stated emphatically that, from the point of view of the relations of the United States with Latin America, the period from the close of the eighteenth century to about 1830 possessed unity, completeness, and character in sufficiently high degree to warrant isolating it for special study.[8]

This chapter examines developments in industry, transportation, and physiographic expansion that, I believe, profoundly influenced the course of U.S.–Latin American relations during the 1820s. It also explores attitudes toward Roman Catholicism and monarchical government, issues often considered to have affected hemispheric relations. The ethnic factor in U.S.–Latin American affairs in the 1815–30 era is reserved for separate treatment in the following chapter.

Industrial Development

Technical innovation became the visual centerpiece of the 1815–30 era. Applying technology to factories, transportation, and communications became a game played with enthusiasm and for high stakes. Change became accepted as proof of progress in most quarters. The maxims of Benjamin Franklin's *Poor Richard's Almanac* were embraced and taken to heart. Enterprise was rewarded as never before. Acquisitiveness was raised to the level of a cardinal virtue. Aggressive moneymakers harvested more profit than husbandmen, whom Jefferson had proclaimed the most vigorous, most independent, most virtuous, and most precious part of the states and the rock upon which the Republic must stand.[9] The new entrepreneurs and their modes of economic activism were rationalized in press, pulpit, and classroom. By 1830 the cult of the self-made man—who had already modified laissez-faire as an economic concept by enticing state and municipal governments to grant direct and indirect subsidies—was on the road to universal acceptance.[10] Seven years later Washington Irving coined the expression *the almighty dollar,* which Charles Dickens picked up and gave wide circulation in his *American Notes* (1840).[11] Those in industry and commerce gave more attention to organization, administration, and the costs of raw products than they did to the consequences of the wide-ranging reorientation of individual and social values attendant on industrial capitalism. Material values increasingly won in races with spiritual values. "God's word said increase and multiply. If babies, why not goods, if goods, why not dollars?"[12] For Cairns, "the rights of man occupied thought less and the price of cotton more."[13]

Acceptance of technology had not come naturally or easily. Although the shipbuilding industry had had a long and fruitful history and various small manufacturers had prospered, the United States at the beginning of the nineteenth century was agrarian to the core. Those who were not agriculturist tended toward commerce rather than industry. As Samuel Miller noted, the spirit of the inhabitants had shown itself ominously commercial and had asserted that men of science should expect "little reward either of honour or emolument."[14] The experience of John Fitch tended to confirm that view. He had assembled a successful steamboat in the late 1780s, but the company he founded to promote it floundered in a wave of public indifference.[15] As late as 1803 Benjamin Latrobe, the foremost engineer and architect in the United States, reported only five steam engines in use in the country.[16] Benjamin Franklin was one who contributed to doubts about modern factories. Before 1776 he had eulogized agriculture while declaring that manufacturing was founded on poverty because it required cheap labor.[17] A generation later Theodoric Beck, addressing a society for the promotion of the "Useful Arts" in New York, noted the disease, vice, and other forms of misery in manufacturing centers of England and assumed that no patriot could wish the United States to become, in the strict sense of the word, a manufacturing country.[18]

Beck, however, could not have been unmindful that he was clinging to old ways. As early as 1800 changing international conditions had converted Jefferson, the confirmed agrarian, to at least lukewarm advocacy of domestic manufactures.[19] As Beck spoke, the war-inspired blockade by Great Britain had invigorated the manufacturing sector, first stimulated by the Jeffersonian boycott of foreign trade. Shortly after Beck issued his warning against industry, manufacturers were memorializing Congress to protect domestic manufactures against foreign competition.[20] The debate over whether manufacturing was possible or desirable clearly had swung to the affirmative side.[21] There was no longer any stemming the entrepreneurial ferment transforming the U.S. economy from an agrarian/commercial pattern to a complex economy based upon interregional specialization, and a mechanized future in which the corporation would become the nation's principal economic institution.

The inventor Eli Whitney, more than anyone else, sparked the economic transition. The impact of his cotton gin was felt as much in the textile factories of the Northeast as on the plantations of the South. Cotton production increased by 600 percent and the value of cotton mill production by a like amount during the 1820s. Based upon textile manufacture, dependent on ever-increasing supplies of raw cotton, Lowell, Massachusetts, became the leading industrial center of the time and "Lowell girls," minding the production of cloths, were the most favorably publicized industrial workers in the boom Republic. The inventor's perfection of a system of producing interchangeable parts first revolutionized the munitions industry, but its major import came in the development of machinery needed to spur the manufacture of consumer goods and transportation. Flour milling, meanwhile, was being fundamentally changed by elevators and conveyors, and by cleaning, cooling, and barreling machines. High pressure stationary engines were everywhere making mass production possible.[22]

Little doubt remained about the relationship of manufacturing and national development. The German economist Fredrick List, visiting in the 1820s, was not, but might have been, contrasting the turn-of-the-century rejection of industrial innovation with his observation that the businessmen he had met were quick to adjust to anything new.[23] Author James Kirke Paulding insisted, "The inventors of machinery have caused a greater revolution in the habits, opinions, and morals of mankind, than all the efforts of legislation. Machinery and steam engines have had more influence on the Christian world than Locke's metaphysics, Napoleon's code, or Jeremy Bentham's codification."[24] In 1832 the prestigious *North American Review* declared: "What we claim for machinery is, that it is in modern times by far the most efficient physical cause of human improvement; that it does for civilization what conquest and human labor formerly did, and accomplishes incalculably more than they accomplished."[25] To favor domestic manufactures was quickly becoming a patriotic duty.

Infrastructural Development

Rapid transportation captured a greater share of the nation's collective imagination than did the factory. Fulton's successful trip up the Hudson from New York to Albany (150 miles) in his steamboat, the *Clermont*, triggered a wave of speculation that promised to bring the states together by speeding the movement of people and goods. As early as 1811 steamboats built in the West and adapted to use on shallow inland waterways were plying the Ohio River and before 1830 were a common sight on the Mississippi and its major tributaries. Every major Atlantic port city had its ferry and steam-powered barges.

Before Fulton's memorable voyage alerted the citizenry to the advantages of faster freightage, improved land routes were practically nonexistent. The sixty-two-mile turnpike, completed in 1794, connecting Lancaster, Pennsylvania, and Philadelphia remained the best in the nation. By 1825 there were approximately ten thousand miles of turnpike roads, most of which were in the Northeast and mid-Atlantic states. Sections of the historic Wilderness and Cumberland Gap roads had been opened by 1830 but their completion came in the following two decades. Bridge building, an inevitable adjunct to turnpike construction, had developed into an art in which U.S. engineers excelled. The cost of roadbeds and bridges, however, ran high as did tolls for their use. Anticipated profits from numerous projects proved illusory. In the five-year span before 1830 some turnpikes were abandoned and others would have been had they not been rescued from insolvency by the states.

When turnpikes were unprofitable it was commonly because they could not compete economically with barge canals in moving bulk goods. Canal building had been a little-practiced activity in the United States until the opening of the first section of the Erie Canal in 1819 demonstrated the feasibility of the concept. By the completion of that waterway in 1825 canal digging and lock construction had become the biggest game in town. Mathew Carey, Philadelphia publisher, economist, and social reformer, with little effort enrolled, at an initial fee of $100, hundreds of persons in the Society for the Promotion of Internal Improvement whose purpose was to disseminate accurate information on canals, roads, bridges, railways, and steam engines.[26] Although canal building boomed, none of the enterprises enjoyed the success of the Erie Canal.[27] Like turnpikes, canals had disadvantages. They were not adaptable to all regions and in the North they froze in the winter. And they were overtaken by the railroads in much the same way they had driven turnpikes to the wall.[28]

The vastly increased attention to internal development was in part induced by, and came at a time when, the nation's share of the worldwide carrying trade, following several decades of expansion, was leveling off. For years carriers and traders had profited from a combination of circumstances. As members of the British imperial system they had thrived as reexporters of European products and from direct trade with Great Britain, its Asian markets, and the West Indian colonies. Political independence resulted in a temporarily reduced flow of business with traditional trading partners, but the slack was more than absorbed when U.S. shippers, under the mantle of neutrality, indiscriminately served the European powers engaged in a series of conflicts among themselves during the two decades following 1793. In 1810 only Great Britain exceeded the United States as an ocean carrier. By the 1820s the picture had changed somewhat. Europe found itself at peace and the energies of continental traders, harnessed for a generation, were freed to challenge the near monopoly of trade enjoyed by the United States and Great Britain. And English laws had complicated trading with the West Indies for the United States. These developments, the result of external forces, were a blow to certain Atlantic ports and became a major factor in convincing U.S. investors and public officials that they could best counter the vicissitudes of international trade and the ever-present prospect of naval wars for control of markets and serve the Republic by directing a great share of its energies to domestic manufacture, internal communications, and westward expansion.

Prior to 1830 the South, where a third of the nation's population lived, excluded itself from direct participation in the manufacturing and communications boom the rest of the Republic experienced in the years following the War of 1812. Southern investors chose to sink their surplus and borrowed capital into land along the area's extensive waterways and into slaves. And from a strictly economic perspective their reasoning was sound. By the mid-1820s southern planters had become, in a very real sense, the economic backbone of the nation as cotton replaced shipping as the most important single source of foreign exchange earnings.[29] They readily found buyers prepared to pay reasonable prices for ever-expanding harvests of plantation cotton. Their cotton was the mainstay of the manufacturing industry of the Northeast. Southern cotton and tobacco flooded international markets and earned the foreign currency that other sections used to import the industrial and multifarious items that were giving the new nation its economic muscle and psychological impulses.[30]

Westward Expansion

Following the Battle of New Orleans (1815), the population of the trans-Appalachian West, attracted by cheap land, favorable freight rates, a surging demand for cotton, and markets for staples in industrializing Europe, quickly increased.

Migration to the West had begun well before the East was fully occupied even by colonial standards of population density. Small farmers, land speculators, trappers, and fur traders, counted only in the tens of thousands, made up the vanguard. Prior to the nineteenth century these settlers had pushed the frontier west at an average rate not in excess of two miles annually or a little beyond the western foothills of the Appalachians. Suddenly a tidal wave of settlers swept across the mountains and the occupation of the West became a national obsession. Developments dating from the Treaty of 1783 with Great Britain had opened the West to the flood of settlers. The Pinckney Treaty with Spain in 1795 guaranteed U.S. citizens the right to free navigation of the Mississippi. The Louisiana Purchase, in 1803, added huge stretches to the nation's reservoir of tillable soil. The Lewis and Clark expedition raised continentalism to a national ideology. In the Battle of the Thames (Ontario) in 1813, William Henry Harrison shattered the Shawnee Confederacy. The Treaty of Ghent (1815) relieved pressure from the British by way of Canada. In the Southwest, General Andrew Jackson crushed the insurgent Creeks. Farmers and land speculators proclaiming themselves the agents of progress, which they equated with white settlement, promptly invaded lands overrun by victorious armies.

Meanwhile, between 1800 and 1832, a series of land policy changes made it feasible for financially strapped settlers to obtain title to farm plots. In 1800, the unit of sale had been fixed at a half-section at a minimum price of $2.00 per acre, with four years to complete purchase. By 1832, legislation provided for the sale of public lands in forty-acre lots at $1.25 per acre. These developments were what anthropologists have called "pull factors," and they, in fact, put hundreds of millions of acres of prime farm land, held by the states and the national government, into private hands. There were also "push factors." The thin, unfertile soils of the Northeast offered few inducements for farmers to remain there or for farmers recently arrived from Europe to settle there. Taxes, though not particularly high in the East, were higher than in the West. Soil exhaustion in the cotton and tobacco areas of the South forced farmers to be in constant search of new lands in order to maintain their level of production and keep their slaves in the fields.

In their totality the forces at work remarkably accelerated the pace of population growth in the West. The census of 1800 showed only 387,183 inhabitants in the western states and territories; that of 1810 enumerated 2,419,369.[31] By 1830 the population of the trans-Allegheny West was greater than that of the entire United States at the time of the 1790 census. Other data show that the West contained less than 3 percent of the nation's population in 1790 and 28 percent in 1829. As early as 1821, Indiana, Mississippi, Illinois, Alabama, and Missouri, in that order, had been admitted to the Union. Aware of the population explosion in the West, a writer in the *Quarterly Review* (London) observed:

> What effect may be produced, for good or for evil, when the Western territory shall exceed in population that on the coast of the Atlantic, a period, probably, not so long as that which has passed since the recognition of their independence, when the wealth and intelligence of the country shall be to the East, and the physical force to the West of the Alegany [sic] mountains, it is difficult to calculate, but a confederated republic of such vast extent would be a phenomenon in politics.[32]

The westward march was made in two parallel columns. Southern planters in search of land pushed into the black belt of Alabama and Mississippi and on into Louisiana, Arkansas, and Missouri. In the process, New Orleans replaced Charleston as the cotton capital of the country. Yankee pioneers, meanwhile, overran Ohio, Indiana, and Illinois. By 1830, the vanguard of the southern column had moved into Texas and the northern column, with hardly a pause, had crossed the Mississippi preparatory to leap-frogging to the Pacific.[33]

Pioneers from the South and North differed sharply over institutionalized slavery, but in several respects had much in common. They were one in dynamism, determination, and self-assurance. They wanted land as a means of self-fulfillment. They were willing to take chances. They shared a belief in free trade. This belief placed them in opposition to eastern manufacturers, whom Southerners saw as seeking to industrialize behind tariff barriers detrimental to commercial agriculture, and to merchant capitalists, whom western farmers believed were depriving them of the benefits of industrialization by promoting trans-Atlantic commerce at the expense of trade ties with the hinterland. Both groups were implacable in making their demands and convictions heard in Washington.

Financial Implications

The opening of the trans-Allegheny West influenced U.S.–Latin American relations in three significant ways. (1) Since the enterprise helped to satisfy the psychological needs of an agitated society that sought constantly to overcome a colonial complex and to reaffirm its republicanism and its professed belief in democratic ideals, it made Latin America seem far less important than it had when the future of the Republic was restricted to the farm lands of the Tidewater and Piedmont and overseas commerce seemed to offer the best hope for coastal centers. (2) The West was an undertaking of gigantic proportions for an emerging nation, and the farming competition with industry and transportation for the nation's scarce resources placed such strains on those assets that uncertain ventures lost much of their appeal. (3) Mediating differences between the two systems of production, family farming and slave labor, sharpened by westward expansion, proved to have much greater voter appeal with constituencies little versed in foreign affairs than did championing close ties with remote Latin America.

The financial dimensions of the 1815–30 boom and the opening of the West soon outpaced domestic accumulated capital and led to borrowing abroad. The federal government, controlled by leaders who adhered to a strict constructionist interpretation of the Constitution, John Quincy Adams being the only notable exception prior to 1828, for the most part refrained from direct investment in internal developments.[34] All administrations through Monroe's had appropriated only a million dollars for that purpose. As a consequence of the federal government's policy, the development of the nation's unpreempted resources, the underwriting of industrial enterprises, the construction of turnpikes and canals, and the opening of the West fell heavily on private financiers and the states (municipalities became involved in development projects on only a quite limited scale). Although private capital had accumulated surprisingly fast, many of the projects were too speculative and grandiose or beyond the means of individual investors. It, thus, fell to the separate states to fill the financial void. Several of them, notably Pennsylvania, New York, Ohio, Virginia, and Louisiana undertook major infrastructural projects, either independently or jointly with private investors in what were known as mixed corporations.[35] The sale of public lands and revenues from various taxes and tariffs did not provide sufficient income to meet their commitments to development; to do that they went abroad to raise capital, occasionally to Holland, but almost always to Great Britain.

The states were at first able to borrow on acceptable terms because of the outstanding record the federal government had established in meeting its obligations incurred during the struggle for independence, the purchase of the Louisiana Territory, and the War of 1812. It had, for example, reduced its debts to British bondholders from £5,747,000 in 1805 to £1,271,617 in 1818,[36] and from a high of $90.1 million in 1823 to $82.3 by the end of the decade.[37]

It took the individual states only a short time to establish their own credit standing, and foreign banking houses actually solicited their business.[38] By 1830 Great Britain and the continental powers combined held U.S. securities in the amount of approximately $75 million, nearly all in the name of the states.[39] Private investors, meanwhile, were establishing their credit ratings. After 1826 Baring Brothers and Company of London, one of the most conservative banking houses, began to extend credit to the more stable private companies in the United States. North American merchants and carriers also availed themselves of British credit facilities.[40]

The states' ability to amortize their early loans was generally good (some loans floated abroad did go into default). The favorable standing of the states and the excellent reputation of the federal government made the United States the safest area in the world in which to invest. Still, interest rates in the United States were high (5–7%) compared to what London banks were paying their depositors (2–3%). High interest rates in the United States, combined with maximum safety, were strong inducements for British capital to cross the Atlantic. By the same economic logic the U.S. investors could not export their surplus funds, limited as they were, to Latin America in the form of loans or equities in stock for the same low level of return that the British accepted. North Americans limited their investments in Latin America to small amounts in Mexican mining ventures. They also secured a canal concession across Central America, and made two or three unsuccessful attempts to market loans of Chile, Buenos Aires, and Mexico. Thus, in contrast to what it believed to be its obligations in Central America and the Caribbean some three-quarters of a century later, the United States had little incentive during the 1820s to devote a high level of attention to Latin America in order to protect its investors.

The British investment experience in Latin America provided yet another good reason why U.S. investors had little inducement to cast covetous eyes on the new nations. With so much British capital lying idle after the Napoleonic Wars, financiers and small investors alike were, in the early 1820s, searching for better terms than were available domestically. They consequently listened intently to the siren calls of the new republics, about which the British public knew next to nothing, and to wily mining adventurers, who marketed their shares on the basis of figures meant to be more impressive than precise. Small investors were quickly seduced. A kind of people's capitalism engulfed the British Isles. Between 1822 and 1825 loans subscribed in England on behalf of the Latin American states may have totaled £21 million.[41] By late 1824 the demand for Latin American mining stocks reached such a frenzy as to recall the South Sea Bubble of a century earlier; and the ultimate consequences were the same. Bonds of the new polities almost immediately went into default. Chilean bonds that in 1824 sold as high as 93, by 1827 were going at 30, and were still falling. A Peruvian issue gyrated between 89 and 23.5 during the same period.[42] Most mining ventures, meanwhile, failed to pay dividends and many actually collapsed before beginning operations. Shares of numerous mining companies were being picked up for a shilling or two on the pound. The Latin American experiences of the 1820s in fact shook the British economy for more than a generation.

The credulity of British investors, which gave London financiers the luxury of underwriting inadequately secured Latin American bonds, accounts in considerable part for creating the financial graveyards that the new republics became by 1830.[43] The republics, however, were not without blame for their predicament. Their officials took advantage of the brief but costly financial orgy that British capital spawned to camouflage fiscal irresponsibility and to fund projects without feasibility studies or legislative approval. And with borrowed funds around, those same officials too often permitted the business of government to become confused with the nurture of private fortunes.[44] This is not to suggest that when borrowed money dried up officials bent on lining family pockets did not find other ways of doing so.

A Prospering Nation

Remarkable industrial and infrastructural expansion and the mastery of nature, as best exemplified by the conquest of the West, severely stretched U.S. resources. The results by 1830 seemed worth the price and more. A spirit of unequaled human progress—as defined in terms of those aspects of life contemporaries regarded as valuable—had captured the imagination of the nation. Measured by the historical experiences of Europe, the results of individual achievement within the free population seemed unlimited. The arrival of tens of thousands of immigrants and millions of dollars in the form of loans and investments from Europe confirmed that the United States was the place to be, the spot to invest one's resources, whether in the form of muscle, know-how, or capital. The prospering society had every reason to avoid entangling itself in European conflicts which by some unanticipated turn of events might make it a satellite of a stronger power or an alliance of powers. As for Latin America, it offered no military threat to the United States, but neither did it have anything of a comparable economic nature to attract the average North American and, except for Cuba, still a colony of Spain, increasingly fewer attractions for merchant adventurers.

Contrary to what the discussion thus far might suggest, the nation's early response to independent Latin America was not determined by economic factors alone. Noneconomic variables were also influencing North American reactions to Latin Americans and their institutions. In this chapter I propose to explore two of them—Roman Catholicism and monarchism, leaving others to be examined in succeeding chapters.

Anglo-American Anti-Catholicism

Despite the shocks of the Enlightenment the United States was, in 1815, predominantly a religious-minded nation. For de Tocqueville there was no country in the world where the Christian religion retained greater influence over the souls of men and women than in the United States.[45] Protestantism was indeed a powerful stimulus to the majority of the people. For them only Protestant Christianity was compatible with republican institutions; to be American was to be Protestant. Beneath this rich overlay of Protestantism smoldered an anti-Catholic mood which from time to time provided a rallying point for national unity, though it did not reach maximum force in national life until the 1840s and the 1850s. This section identifies the ingredients of anti-Catholic intolerance in the Union and their influence on hemispheric affairs during the years immediately following the War of 1812.

Anti-Catholicism was very much a part of Anglo-American concerns throughout the colonial era. The original settlers were steeped in antipapal prejudices rooted in the Reformation and Counter-Reformation and kept alive in America by the imperial thrusts of Catholic France and Spain. So general was this anti-Catholic sentiment that by 1700 only in Rhode Island with its liberal statutes, did a Catholic enjoy full civil and religious rights.[46] The persistent fear of the colonists was that "papists" would ally with the French, Spanish, and Indians to disrupt the fur trade and threaten the agricultural ambitions of the seacoast settlers. As the French danger from Canada grew more acute with the outbreak of Queen Anne's War (1702–13) the fear of Catholic-French-Spanish-Indian alliances increased, and some colonies reacted by passing legislation that added obstacles to the free exercise of Catholicism. Much of that legislation remained on the books after the war threat had passed.

A renewal of war with France in the 1750s, accompanied by reports of papist plots and French-Indian alliances, engendered a new and intense outburst of anti-Catholicism which continued after the Peace of Paris ending the French and Indian War (1756–63). With the war fresh in mind, the colonials were in no mood to accept calmly the Quebec Act of 1774, designed by His Majesty's Government to extend toleration to Catholics in Quebec and to include in that province territories in the Ohio country occupied by French settlers. The act was interpreted by the colonial patriot press and skilled propagandists such as Samuel Adams as nothing less than a Catholic coup to establish "popery" on their borders.[47] Distrust of Catholicism and resentment against England over the Quebec Act were in the back of their minds when colonials struck for independence in 1776. Early in the Revolution, the then president of Princeton University, John Witherspoon, believed that a common distrust of popery caused by the Quebec Act united the divergent religious groups in the colonies sufficiently to allow them to wage war.[48]

The War of Independence did much to relieve traditional fear of popery. Charles Carroll, member of a distinguished Catholic family of Maryland and a convinced patriot, signed the Declaration of Independence and later was a member of the Constitutional Convention. France and Spain, the world's two most powerful Roman Catholic nations, and foreign Catholic volunteers such as Count Casimir Pulaski of Poland had fought beside colonials against the Metropolis. Catholics resident throughout the colonies participated in the war in such a way that they were no longer suspected as potential collaborationists. The liberal spirit of the Constitution, meanwhile, brought substantial religious freedom to the nation and resulted in repeated recasting of state constitutions in ways favorable to Catholics. The election of the Unitarian Thomas Jefferson to the presidency in 1800 presaged a further decline in sectarian sentiment.

Despite the trend toward nonsectarianism much state and local legislation continued to disqualify Catholics in various ways when Jefferson left office.[49] Tolerance and mutual understanding between Protestants and Catholics, however, generally prevailed, favored by intimate contact of Catholics and Protestants in the West and Protestants becoming increasingly engrossed in the economic expansion of the country and in the race issue. By 1820, despite a substantial increase in the Catholic population,[50] Protestant-Catholic tension had eased to the point at which anti-Catholic feeling appeared to have vanished.[51]

During the 1820s shrill sectarianism revived as the Catholic Church once again came under suspicion and overt attack as a subversive institution. A wave of condemnatory literature on the Inquisition found its way into newspapers and journals to keep alive in the public mind the use of torture to obtain confessions, the burning of heretics, and the association of the Inquisition with the Roman Catholic Church and the seats of tyrannical power.[52] Immigration, with the Irish making up over 35 percent of the 150,000 newcomers between 1820 and 1830, added to Protestant concerns.[53] By 1830 the Catholic population reached a reported 500,000 in a total population of 12 million.[54] Catholics were more visible than their numbers indicated because they tended to congregate in the large towns and cities.[55] The growing number of priests and nuns, the creations of bishoprics, the construction of churches, the holding of the First Provincial Council in Baltimore in 1829, and the gains made by the Jesuits—the least trusted order of the Catholic establishment—in the Mississippi Valley made manifest the spiritual prosperity of the Church and heightened the suspicions of Protestants.[56]

To the domestic developments that raised questions about Catholicism were added reports from abroad that Protestants found threatening. The return of the Jesuits to France and their seemingly rapid penetration of and influence in the French government put anti-Catholics in the United States on guard.[57] In 1828 a series of lectures by the famous German scholar Friedrich von Schlegel brought the possibility of the expansion of Catholic power close to home. Von Schlegel stressed the connection between monarchy and Catholicism and assailed Protestantism and democracy alike. He labeled the United States the "nursery of revolution" and stated his conviction that Catholic missions in the United States would serve as weapons against republicanism, noxious democratic notions, and heretical doctrines.[58] North Americans interpreted the founding of the Leopold Association in Vienna the following year as evidence of a plot of European despots against United States democracy.[59]

The next year the *Connecticut Observer* kept alive the issue by suggesting that the monarchs of Europe favored promoting Catholicism in the United States as a means of establishing a monarchical system there.[60] Also in 1829, in England, the Emancipation Act which finally removed the general disqualifications of Catholics from holding office or sitting in Parliament produced a profusion of "no-popery" literature in England which quickly found its way across the Atlantic to intensify the forebodings of Protestants.[61]

The renewed fear that an aggressive Catholic Church would subvert the nation's institutions of government, ideals, and way of life was channeled into a number of movements that were more political than spiritual in nature. The movements were not yet able by 1830 to stem the tide of liberalism, but they planted seed for what became the virulent nativist movements of the 1840s and 1850s.[62]

The fear that Catholics might subvert the nation on behalf of an enemy power was but one of the temporal concerns of the anti-Catholic population. For example, the Catholic Church was held to be opposed to political liberty and thus an agency in defense of tyranny against natural law. Jefferson could have been speaking for this anti-Catholic element when he declared, "History, I believe, furnishes no example of a priest-ridden people maintaining a free civil government."[63]

The Church's hierarchical, "authoritarian" organization was considered to be nothing less than the religious equivalent of monarchical despotism. It, thus, stood in apparent contradiction to the democratic American belief that only Protestant Christianity would cultivate personal righteousness and channel the interest and goals of the people into socially acceptable and morally responsible forms of behavior without demanding a slavish submission to authority.[64] The doctrine of the temporal supremacy of the pope was held to be manifestly contrary to republican principles.[65] That Catholics' ultimate loyalty lay beyond the country's frontiers was a deeply disturbing thought to a nation of Protestants whose territorial loyalties were gradually overriding their theological allegiances.[66]

When anti-Catholicism revived after 1820 it assumed a new emphasis on Catholic doctrine and practices. Leading the list of "new" objections to Catholicism on doctrinal grounds were the Church's claim to being the sole custodian of Christian truth and the dogma of the infallibility of the pope, whom the more extremist Protestants saw as the anti-Christ.[67] The Protestants presumed the Church's opposition to progress in contrast to their churches being on the side of the future.[68] By such reasoning the pope became a reactionary despot, hostile both to liberty and progress. That Catholicism was based on oral communication of doctrine and did not encourage the critical reading of religious texts seemed to explain the Church's assumed antiprogressive views on education, its continued countenance of miracles and the worship of idols,[69] and of basing beliefs on faith rather than rational discourse. Protestants attacked auricular confession on the grounds that it was in opposition to the Protestant belief that religion should be an individual experience and that no one's action and intentions could be thrust on any other person. Thus, priests serving as intermediaries between individuals and their God were not only unnecessary, but the clerics' life of prayer and ease added nothing to the common good.[70] The Church's ostentatious ritual and ornate chapels, Protestants argued, were calculated to distract from devotion and to befuddle the minds of the faithful. Music and painting, likewise, were believed to lead the mind away from contemplation.[71] Finally, that so many of the Catholic clergy were foreign born and unacquainted with Anglo-American culture and that they commonly came to the United States with no intention of residing permanently were further cause for Protestant misgivings about the place of Catholicism in the community.

Accounts reaching the United States regarding the Catholic Church in Latin America during the crucial years of the insurgency and postindependence eras were almost uniformly prepared by Protestants. Not surprisingly, their accounts commonly reflected concerns Protestants harbored about the Church in the United States.

Because of the limited number of Catholics in the United States and the restrictions on their participation in politics their share in the resolution of domestic issues was minimal and received far less attention than did the Church's presumed subversiveness. The situation in Latin America was quite the reverse. Though the reporters universally recognized and condemned the Church's hierarchy for seeking to subvert the independence movements in favor of the Iberian powers, their primary concern was with the institution's opposition to republicanism and its immersion in domestic politics. As early as 1813, Agent Joel R. Poinsett, in a report to Secretary of State James Monroe, called attention to the issue: "The clergy whose influence here [Chile] is very great have generally in the confessional and by every secret means in their power, opposed the progress of this country in the system (republican) it has embraced."[72] And in fact as late as 1830 the papal nuncio in Buenos Aires was openly expressing his opposition to both independence and republicanism.[73]

Protestants generally found the Catholic Church in Latin America, in whichever of its roles, in some way a regressive force. At one time they charged it with encouraging superstition, "the worst of all despotisms," belief in miracles, and the worship of idols; at another time with discouraging education because its clergy foresaw "in education and intelligence . . . the decline of their . . . power and a termination of their pernicious influence."[74] "A child which [sic] can repeat the ordinances of the Church, and quantities of orisons to the most popular saint, by rote like a parrot, is considered as being highly gifted."[75] On still other occasions, but for the same presumed reasons, the Protestants found that the church discouraged scientific inquiry and the diffusion of knowledge. The Church's ownership of large rural and urban estates and its activities as a lending agency were contrary to Protestant teachings. That the income of archbishops in Mexico made the hierarchy one of the richest in the world was shocking to Protestants.[76] The Church's numerous saints' days and its sanctioning of spirituous liquors at religious festivals were faulted as having an adverse effect on the per capita output of the large labor force in agriculture.

Nearly all aspects of the Catholic Church in Latin America invited disdain, but none more scorn than did its clergy. Occasionally Protestants paid their respects to specific priests who had befriended them, but as a group the clergy were worthy only of reproach. To begin with, they were reported to come from the "very dregs of the people."[77] They were then turned out of seminaries grossly ignorant, bigoted, and indolent,[78] to be released in society as debauched drones.[79] Their consumption of spirituous liquors occasioned frequent unfavorable comment, as did their participation in such pastimes as gambling, bullfighting, and cockfighting. Their vows of celibacy, it was asserted, were repeatedly violated. They at once exercised their powers with a great deal of leniency and terrified their parishioners by threats of excommunication by the pontiff in Rome.[80] For learning they substituted fanaticism, and their own fanaticism often drove them to direct attacks upon the persons and properties of Protestants.[81] They gave currency to superstition by denying the scriptures to the common people[82] while inculcating the importance of endowing chapels and chaplains.[83] In brief, Protestant reporting was in general agreement with Dr. Francia (José Gaspar Rodríguez), dictator of Paraguay (1814–40), who, in commenting on the teachings of the clergy, reportedly once said, "The priests lead the people to be mindful of the devil and forgetful of God Almighty."[84]

Of the many features that Protestants perceived as distinguishing Anglo-America from Latin America none was so pronounced as the Catholic inspiration that went into the making of Latin American culture, civilization, and society. Given the differing religious influences in the two cultures it would seem reasonable to assume that the "Catholic issue" would figure prominently in their relations at the moment of independence. What actually occurred? Despite the considerable amount of anti-Catholic literature and oratory circulating in the United States, religion did not figure in a significant way in U.S. involvement in Latin American during the 1820s. Furthermore, there were understandable reasons why religion should not have been in any major way injected into the mix that led to Washington's decision to reduce the amount of attention devoted to Latin America as the decade ended. This is not to say that Anglo-America would not have preferred that Latin America be Protestant. We know, for example, that John Q. Adams as president believed that U.S. representation at the Panama Congress of 1826 would offer an opportunity to advance the principle of religious liberty and to make known the opposition of the United States to the "religious bigotry" found in the charters of the new states[85]—positions, incidentally, incompatible with the spirit of the federal Constitution, which provided for the separation of church and state. We know, too, that the United States insisted that treaties with the new nations accord protection to Protestants who wished to worship according to their own beliefs. It is also possible that Protestants consciously or unconsciously may have injected a Catholic variable into their overall assessment of Latin America. For example, rather than simply concluding that Latin America was "backward" some Anglo-Americans may have determined to their own satisfaction that Latin Americans were backward because of their Roman Catholic heritage. I know of no way of factoring the degree that such views may have impacted on relations between North and South out of either the public or official consensus about Latin America. I would speculate, however, that were a method devised accurately to measure the religious variable, the results would be less impressive than has been commonly assumed. Against such examples of anti-Catholicism as those identified a sizable body of evidence can be marshaled to support the contention that, contrary to conventional wisdom, religion probably was a minor factor in early hemispheric affairs.

Any discussion of the relative unimportance of religion as a force in U.S.–Latin American relations must begin with a "brief review of the consequences of the accelerating trend in the United States away from a theocratic and towards a secularist state that characterized the early nineteenth century."[86] Dating from the age of the Enlightenment individuals in the United States had become increasingly rational, intellectual, empirical, and, simultaneously, less reliant on churches to bond society. Deists and Unitarians, small in number but generally well educated, were in the forefront of those who found traditional religious systems incongruent with the nation's increasingly material philosophy. Supplanting the churches were the nation and such voluntary associations as schools, workplaces, markets, which were at once utilitarian in nature and vigilant about their liberties. Collectively, society deified self-fulfillment and accomplishment and rejected universally applied ideal types of behavior that theocrats formerly imposed. "Things were in the saddle and ride mankind."[87] Reflecting the new climate of opinion, the principal purpose of criminal law changed from enforcing moral and religious standards to protecting property and persons.[88] Secular outlooks softened religious friction and turned aggressive impulses to other adversaries. Slavery, for example, replaced religion as an ideological battleground.

Within the increasingly secularist society what groups might be expected to have the greatest say in how religious issues would be reflected in hemispheric affairs? My readings and analysis suggest that there were in fact three such groups: the international business community, public officials, and the Protestant sects themselves. The role of the international business community can be dispensed with rather readily. As a group its members had embraced the secularization of life and values. They thought in essentially temporal rather than spiritual terms. For them cosmopolitanism was a virtue.[89]

Ideological beliefs aside, by the early nineteenth century it was widely accepted that international trade knew no religion. For leading individuals of the international business community to take public stands on religion that conflicted with those of the Latin American majority would have been poor business practice. There was, moreover, at least one other good reason for their suppressing any anti-Catholic feelings they may have had; namely, in Latin America many of those with whom foreigners had to transact business were members of liberal movements whose primary platforms were anticlericalism. Their attack upon the Church fell short of the hopes of Protestant extremists, but the anticlerical elements, nonetheless, were about to make important inroads on the Church's temporal activities and were affecting changes in social thought along the same lines as was the secular movement in the United States, although clearly at a slower pace.

Federal officials who, had they chosen, could have made religion an international bone of contention, despite constitutional restrictions, were little inclined to do so. They were of the gentry; and the Enlightenment ideology had struck deep roots among them. They, for the most part, retained their formal religious affiliations for political purposes, if for no other, but generally remained aloof from religious controversy.[90] Applications or requests from religious organizations, including the Catholic clergy, nearly always received deferential consideration from both elected and appointed officials. Congress, for example, after only minimal debate, granted the Catholic Church the privilege of founding convents and schools in the District of Columbia.[91] Catholics were also commonly named to minor offices in federal departments.[92]

The most conspicuous example of cooperation between the federal government and the Catholic Church was in the home missionary field. The War Department maintained a regular correspondence with the Jesuits, who, along with some Protestant organizations, carried out among the Indians of the Midwest various activities that the federal government was unprepared or disinclined to undertake.

Among services performed by the War Department in support of the Indian missions were providing military protection, and distributing the annual appropriations of upward of $10,000 set aside for "the civilization of the Indians." These awards apparently were made without concern for the tenets of the sects receiving support.[93] Of the Catholic missions the Jesuit establishment at Florisant, Missouri, was most consistently awarded federal funds.[94]

Treaties of friendship, commerce, and navigation negotiated with the new states reflected much the same determination on the part of the federal government to avoid taking sides in religious matters as did its handling of church-sponsored missions among the tribes of the Midwest. In his instructions to Richard Clough Anderson, Jr., minister plenipotentiary to Colombia, Secretary of State Adams stipulated that religious liberty be one of the articles to be incorporated into the commercial treaty that Anderson was to make with the Colombian government. Specifically Anderson's instructions read:

> Among the usual objects of negotiations in treaties of commerce and navigation are the liberty of conscience and of religious worship. . . . Freedom of conscience is in truth, an essential part of the system of American independence. Civil, political, commercial and religious liberty are but various modifications of one great principle founded in the unalienable rights of human nature. As their citizens who may visit or transiently reside with us will enjoy the benefit of religious freedom in its utmost latitude, we are bound to claim for our countrymen who may occasionally dwell for a time with them the reciprocal exercise of the same natural right.[95]

During the negotiations that led to the ratification of a treaty of friendship, commerce, and navigation with Colombia, Anderson submitted to Pedro Gual, secretary of state and foreign relations of Colombia, a draft that included an article, the second section of which stipulated:

> The most perfect freedom of conscience and of worship is granted to the citizens of either party, within the jurisdiction of the other, without being liable to molestation in that respect, for any cause other than an insult on the religion of others. Moreover, when the citizens of one party shall die within the jurisdiction of the other, their bodies shall be buried in the usual burying grounds or other decent and suitable places, and shall be protected from violation or disturbance.

Gual then submitted an amended article:

There is granted to the citizens of Colombia and of the United
States of America the most perfect and entire security of conscience in the countries subject to the jurisdiction of both powers, without being thereby subject to be disturbed or molested
on account of their religious belief so long as they shall respect
the laws and established usages and customs. Likewise the bodies of the citizens of one of the contracting parties who may die
in the territories of the other shall be buried in public, decent,
and adequate burying grounds, and their bodies shall be
protected from violation and disturbance.

Gual's amended article eliminated the phrase "freedom of worship,"
and changed the phrase "freedom of conscience" to "security of conscience." It also substituted the clause "so long as they shall respect
the laws and established usages and customs" for the phrase "for any
cause other than an insult on the religion of others." The amendment
thus omitted two significant words: "freedom" and "worship."

In the final draft of "The General Convention of Peace, Amity,
Navigation, and Commerce between the United States and the Repub-
lic of Colombia," signed by Anderson and Gual on October 3, 1824,
Article XI read:

It is likewise agreed that the most perfect and entire security of
conscience shall be enjoyed by the citizens of both the contracting parties in the countries subject to the jurisdiction of the
one and the other, without their being liable to be disturbed or
molested on account of their religious belief, so long as they
respect the laws and established usages of the Country. Moreover the bodies of the citizens of one of the contracting parties,
who may die in the territories of the other, shall be buried in
the usual burying grounds or in other decent and suitable places
and shall be protected from violation or disturbance.[96]

The article in failing to make an explicit provision for worship
and in substituting "security of conscience" for "freedom of conscience" fell short of Adams's wishes as stated in his instructions to
Anderson. It did provide that the lives and property of U.S. citizens
would not be endangered on religious grounds. The U.S. government
acting under a Constitution that sharply separated church and state
was not compelled to demand more. The treaty was ratified by the
United States on March 7, 1825, and by Colombia on March 27 and
was proclaimed by Adams, by then president, on March 31, 1825.
Anderson defended the treaty on the grounds that it was the best that
could be expected of a strongly Catholic country at that point in time.

In fact, the treaty later served as a model for treaties with all the major countries of Latin America.[97]

Given the very limited interest of the U.S. business community engaged in international commerce in sponsoring Protestantism and the qualified support of Protestants in Catholic Latin America by the U.S. government, it might reasonably be anticipated that the Protestant sects themselves would lead an assault designed to break Rome's grip on the millions of inhabitants of the former Iberian colonies. That is not what happened. No one of the major international societies or the numerous local organizations founded between 1815 and 1830[98] gave sustained attention to missionary activity in Latin America, which "though Christian in name" was "crying out for the living God."[99]

The New Hampshire Bible Society report for 1817 noted minimal Protestant missionary activity in Latin America,[100] and that situation obtained at least until 1829. At a time when U.S. missionary societies were assigning missionaries to the Middle East, Southeast Asia, China, and Pacific Islands they, for all intents, totally neglected Latin America, although the Baptist Missionary Society of Massachusetts showed some interest in Haiti as a missionary field, presumably in the interest of serving blacks who had migrated there from the United States.[101] The Baptists also had but one missionary in Honduras by 1827.[102] The American Bible Society sent two missionaries, John C. Bingham and Theophilus Parvin, to Buenos Aires.[103] Parvin established a school in that city and Bingham returned to the United States by way of the West Coast and Mexico, where he encountered no significant problems in distributing Bibles and tracts. On the basis of his experience some felt that Latin America was ready for Protestant missionary activity.[104]

In 1824 the *Christian Herald* informed its readers, "The whole number of Protestant missionaries in all of South America does not amount to *twenty* [italics in the original], and What are these among so many?"[105] Two years later the *New York Observer* reported, "There is no American missionary in Buenos Aires, nor indeed in South America."[106] A report on U.S. missionary activities around the world appearing in the *Daily National Intelligencer* made no mention of missions in Latin America.[107] Similarly the American Board of Foreign Missions report for 1829 showed forty-seven foreign mission stations (with 224 men and women from the United States) including stations in Bombay, Ceylon, Malta, Beirut, the South Pacific Islands, China, and among the Indians of the Midwest, but none in Latin America.[108]

There does not appear to be any single explanation as to why North American Protestant missionary societies had made only minor forays into Latin America by 1830. There are several explanations of varying plausibility. First, Protestant preachers had grown up in a culture that held that Christianity moved westward not southward from the Holy Lands. Second, through the Louisiana Purchase and terms of the Treaty of Ghent the United States acquired vast tracts of land populated by Indian tribes among whom the Jesuits were experiencing notable success. There, thus, were solid incentives for the Protestant churches to give priority to missionary activity in the newly acquired territory as a way of counteracting Jesuit influence. Third, the Latin American nations, torn by civil disturbances and struggling to retain their independent existence, might not have seemed to offer a favorable climate in which to introduce Protestant missionary activity.[109] Fourth, little support for missionary activity could be anticipated from U.S. citizens resident in Latin America since they were generally indifferent to the prospect of Protestant evangelizing in the new and strongly Catholic societies.[110] Fifth, although Protestants may have faulted Roman Catholic doctrines, practices, and rituals, Roman Catholics, unlike the "heathens" inhabiting the Middle East, Asia, the Pacific Islands, and the Midwest, were Christians, if not of the chosen variety. They, thus, could wait being saved.

To conclude: no influential group or agency in the United States felt obliged to make religion an important determinant in U.S. relations with the emerging nations of Latin America. The merchant class had nothing to gain and conceivably much to lose by raising a religious issue which if advanced was certain to invite controversy. The Constitution of the United States in stipulating the separation of church and state limited the federal government's responsibility to protecting its citizens abroad from transgressions on their religious beliefs while living in a foreign polity. It, in fact, went beyond that responsibility by writing into treaties articles protecting the rights of Protestants to worship according to their conscience and the right to decent burials, and certain agents posted to Latin America sought to influence Latin American leaders in favor of Protestantism or as a minimum to encourage the creation of Catholic churches without ties to Rome. Protestant organizations, including missionary organizations, surrendered any right to a voice in policy making by choosing, for whatever reason, not to expend their energies in Latin America.

Monarchy

It is an axiom of politics that foreign policies are not built on abstractions. It follows that theories of government have little effect on international relations. To put it another way, differences over political theories will not keep two nations apart when their self-interest dictates a contrary course. The following pages examine the monarchical issue in Latin America in terms of that axiom. Specifically they explore the home-grown tendency in favor of monarchy in Latin America, the European-sponsored monarchical projects in the region, and Washington's responses to the challenge they posed for republicanism in the area.

Latin America achieved its political independence in an era of strong reaction to the excesses of the French Revolution and the Napoleonic Wars. Europe, with a vengeance, returned to monarchical systems. The United States was once again an island in a sea of monarchies hostile to republicanism. In such a political climate the United States, ebulliently republican, had reason, it believed, to be apprehensive for its future, especially if the emerging states of Latin America were to come under the sway of European monarchies.

As it turned out, all the former colonies, except Haiti, Brazil, and Mexico, initially opted for the republican system. Throughout much of the 1820s, however, whether monarchism or republicanism would prevail in the region was often in doubt. Several conditions made the new societies likely candidates for monarchical government. In Europe it had become a near truism that monarchy was necessary for *les races latines*. In the New World, Iberian subjects had lived for three centuries under absolute monarchs. The hierarchical nature of the ubiquitous Roman Catholic Church, historically associated with the kingdoms in Europe, inclined toward monarchy. The Catholic clergy believed that the privileges they enjoyed under the Spanish Crown would be better protected by monarchical than by republican regimes. Temporal power in the new polities was vested in the landed aristocracies, composed primarily of the oldest families, whose life styles, strongly influenced by Spanish legislation, conventions, and habits, accustomed them to the outward manifestations of regalism. Their unchallenged authority over their own domains habituated them to monarchical rather than republican practices. As the liberal enthusiasm of the Wars of Independence waned, this element by both political and economic predilection found itself in close affinity with European aristocracy, particularly British aristocracy.

Military leaders and statesmen also ordinarily linked themselves to the aristocracy.[111] José San Martín was one such individual. While in command of revolutionary forces in Peru, he confided that he would look approvingly on a Peruvian kingdom under British protection. The Liberator Simón Bolívar may or may not have entertained accepting a throne—the jury apparently is permanently out on that matter—but there seems to be no doubt that he would have welcomed a British-sponsored monarchy in northern South America. Nor is there doubt that other military heroes of the revolutionary era professed belief in monarchical government.

In Argentina, Manuel Belgrano during the Congress of 1816 held in Tucumán sought to revive the idea of an Incan dynasty, a desire shared by deputies in that assembly. In Brazil, the local aristocracy enthusiastically endorsed Dom Pedro, a scion of the royal house of Portugal, the Braganzas, as the first emperor of an independent Brazil. Furthermore, the initial reaction throughout South America, other than in Paraguay, to the creation of the Brazilian monarchy was officially friendly. Following Rio's formal separation from Portugal, imperial agents, in what proved to be a short-lived show of Latin American solidarity, were readily received by Brazil's neighbors. To the north, although the Mexican Constitution of 1824 contained certain features of the United States Constitution, Foreign Minister Lucas Alamán, a confirmed believer in the royalist idea if there was ever one in Latin America, as late as 1829 sounded a British representative in Mexico, Richard Pakenham, on the feasibility of erecting a Mexican government under a European prince.[112] The historical limitations placed on the participation of the popular elements in the political process and the minimal administrative qualifications of the core of greedy office seekers also added substance to the thought that the new states were better fitted for some form of hereditary rule than for republicanism. Finally the convulsions arising from the passions of electoral candidates strengthened the conviction of those who favored monarchy because of the continuity it supposedly would provide.

Key articles of the Bolivian Constitution of 1826 help to identify the preferences of many leaders of the new nations at the moment of their inception. The handiwork of no less a personage than Simón Bolívar, the document, though essentially republican in nature, contained provisions that suggested the Liberator's ideological love affair with limited monarchy. It secured to the people the enjoyment of all rational and useful liberty, but carefully restricted their political ascendancy by providing for a sort of aristocracy in the form of a body of censors. The heart and soul of the constitution, however, was the executive, an elected president for life, with nearly unlimited power, not subject to removal by the populace, and with the right to name a successor. For its architect, the constitution would at once curb the power of the mob, and pacify the monarchists without betraying the republicans. Bolívar had hoped that the document would serve as a master plan for all of Spanish America. It was, in fact, short lived and fell short of the Liberator's objective. The thinking encapsulated in it, however, lived on and many of its provisions materialized throughout the hemisphere as characteristic of a new extralegal phenomenon, *caudillismo* or strongman government.[113]

To the domestic conditions that induced some Creole aristocrats to favor monarchical government were added allures generated in Europe. Throughout the teens and the early years of the 1820s France was acutely sensitive to the dangers of sacrificing important commercial interests by rigid adherence to the principle of legitimacy, which it strongly favored. It would solve its predicament by erecting Bourbon monarchies in the disrupted Spanish Empire. Such monarchies the Quai d'Orsai, with good reason, believed would be advantageous to French commerce, strengthen bonds of common interest between the New World and France, and serve as a counterpoise to the republicanism favored by Creole liberals and the United States. In pursuit of its objective, France, in 1818, gained the ear of Juan Martín Pueyrredón, supreme director of the Provinces of La Plata, who expressed to French officials an interest in establishing a monarchy and indicated a preference for the Duke of Orleans. Pueyrredón, to give substance to his proposal, assured the French agent Le Moyne that the inhabitants of the United Provinces would make every sacrifice to ensure the success of a foreign prince named to lead them. In Paris, General Jean Dessolle, president of the Council of State and minister of foreign relations, was sufficiently interested to inform Moscow of the negotiations and of France's disposition to favor an arrangement between Spain and its colonies, if a monarchy could be established under Spanish protection.[114] By the summer of 1819 France was zeroing in on the idea and was promoting the Prince of Lucca, with promises of aid while the new ruler was establishing his court. The strength of the local republican opposition in the Platean region to monarchy was not put to a test because French intrigues died aborning when Madrid refused to accept the concept of pacifying the Indies by erecting monarchical governments and France was not yet ready to break with its legitimist allies.

The Quai d'Orsai, nonetheless, kept alive the prospect of some way of installing monarchical governments in the New World. In 1825, for instance, leading Peruvian politicians were suspected of a clandestine attachment to the "French Party" whose existence in Peru appeared unquestionable. Captain Thomas Maling of the British Admiralty's Pacific Squadron reported to London that the French government had made overtures for establishing a monarchy in Peru with a French prince on the throne. At the same time Bolívar expressed a strong belief that France at different times had not only advocated establishing a monarchy in Peru, but in other new states, particularly

Mexico.[115] That French monarchical schemes were still alive as the decade drew to a close is indicated by developments in Chile and Argentina. On November 1829, Charles A. L. Le Forest, the French consul general at Santiago, wrote his government that the people of Chile wished for calm from civil strife and were outspoken in their aspiration. "They offer their aid and influence . . . in order to receive as the liberator of Chile a prince who would be sent them from Europe. No matter under what title he may present himself, they will all submit to his domination provided that he be the bearer of an act which will consecrate the recognition by Europe of Chile as an independent state."[116]

Meanwhile, the Polignac Cabinet in Paris and the French agent in Spain were reviving the prospect of creating a "European appanage" in the New World. Viscount Saint Priest, French ambassador to Madrid, in a letter to Minister Jules Polignac declared that the best solution for the problems of the Spanish Americans was to send an infante to rule over them. And under date of March 30, 1830, Polignac in a communication to Saint Priest remained attracted to the possibility of enthroning European princes in Argentina, Colombia, Central America, and Mexico. France, according to Polignac, would seize with alacrity an opportunity to promote such projects.[117]

Great Britain wished no less than did France that the former Spanish colonies would opt for monarchy. The Court of St. James shared with other European governments the belief that the Napoleonic Wars had vindicated hereditary monarchy as the surest guarantee of political and social stability. It also shared with continental governments the view that republicanism in the United States was a threat to European influence in Latin America. Throughout the years of intense insurgency His Majesty's Government's self-imposed rule not to intervene officially in the wars between Spain and its colonies prevented the Foreign Office, headed first by Viscount Castlereagh and then by George Canning, from offending Madrid by appearing to sponsor monarchical projects in the New World. A policy of neutrality notwithstanding, up to the moment for British recognition of the ex-colonies as sovereign states, Canning believed it possible that they would embrace the monarchical system. This conviction comes through clearly in his secret communication to Lionel Hervey, named commissioner to Mexico, to explore whether its status warranted recognition. Referring specifically to Mexico, but in terms equally applicable to all the former empire, Canning identified four conditions that in his view favored monarchism. They were (1) the constitution of Mexican society, (2) the great number of large landed proprietors, (3) the wealth and influence of the clergy, and (4) the long experience of viceregal administration invested with monarchical forms.[118] Woodbine Parish, British consul in the Plata region, added to Canning's list the profound ignorance of the native populations, which disqualified them from coping successfully with representative government.[119] Canning also determinedly defended monarchy where it already prevailed, as in Brazil.

Canning did not see his hopes for Spanish America realized. He fared better in Portuguese America. He missed no opportunity to entrench the monarchical system there, where it had taken root and where Great Britain enjoyed a special relationship by way of Lisbon, a relationship that historian Joseph B. Lockey characterized as one between "suzerain and subject." The relationship dated back at least to the Treaty of Metheun (1703). It had been reinforced in 1808 when the British navy conveyed the Portuguese royal household to Brazil when it fled before the armies of Napoleon. By 1810 British-Portuguese bonds gave London a place of trust in the empire. Despite British ties to Lisbon, Whitehall warmly approved the separation of Brazil from Portugal in 1822, thereby preempting the political arena for the Brazilian monarchist. Then in 1825 Great Britain enhanced its influence in Brazil by mediating a peaceful recognition by the King of Portugal, João VI, of his son Dom Pedro, as Emperor of Brazil. For Canning, keeping Brazil in the monarchist camp was a major victory. Savoring that success, he boasted that Brazil would cure the evils of universal democracy and assure that America would not become a republican domain.

Canning's predilection for monarchy was shared by many British agents assigned to Latin America. H. G. Ward, chargé d'affaires in Mexico, for example, reported that the political climate there was more favorably disposed to monarchy than when Emperor Augustín Iturbide was at the helm.[120] Lord Ponsonby in Buenos Aires wrote, "I do feel a peculiar desire to see the throne of the Emperor [Pedro I of Brazil] secure, to see the House of Braganza, ancient ally of our king flourish in prosperity and honor, and to see the Monarchical Principle take root, and pierce deep into the soil of America."[121] James Henderson, British consul general at Bogotá cherished the hope that Bolívar might eventually give approval to a monarchical government in some form or as a minimum join with Emperor Pedro I to bridle republicanism.[122] As late as 1829 Patrick Campbell, commissioner in Bogotá, wrote that 99 percent of Colombians would vote for monarchy, if a helping hand from London was extended, and that Colombia must be chaotic without monarchy.[123] Shortly thereafter, the death of Bolívar brought to an end any real expectation that any of the Spanish American states would voluntarily opt for a monarchical system.

The United States found itself the sole foreign government favoring republicanism in Latin America. Faced with the possibility of being ideologically isolated if Latin America were to adopt the monarchical system, Washington's immediate objective in the region was to keep it from falling under the tutelage of one or more European kingdoms and thereby threatening U.S. independence, security, or other vital interests. In pursuit of that objective, Washington evolved a threefold policy: (1) within a broader framework of neutrality, a warm sympathy for the insurgents in their struggle against Spain, (2) recognition of the new governments as soon as de facto control of their destinies was believed to be established, without reference to the system of government the new states might elect, and (3) both before and after recognition enjoin the leadership to opt for republicanism and to oppose the intrusion of monarchical Europe in this hemisphere—the Monroe Doctrine or two-sphere concept.

Washington's concern over the republican/monarchical issue is apparent in the instructions to special envoys and ministers assigned to Latin America. In one of the earliest instructions to an agent named to Latin America, Secretary of State James Monroe wrote Alexander Scott, "You will be sensible that the United States cannot fail to take a deep interest in the establishment of a Republican Government in those Provinces [Venezuela and Colombia] from a belief that the people will be happier under it, and the greater confidence which must exist, in consequence of it, between us."[124] The instructions that Joel R. Poinsett received on the occasion of his being named United States Minister to Mexico admonished him to show an unobtrusive readiness to explain the workings of the federal republican system.[125] Secretary of State Henry Clay sounded much the same theme in his instructions to William Miller, appointed United States chargé d'affaires to the United Provinces of Central America. "You will answer, in the most frank and full manner, all enquiries from that government having for their object information as to the practical operation of our own, or any of our Institutions."[126]

Official correspondence, meanwhile, left little doubt with respect to the incompatibility of monarchy with the objectives of the New World, as Washington conceived those objectives.

A hankering after Monarchy has infected the politics ... of Buenos Ayres, and being equally contrary to the true policy of the Country ... has produced its natural harvest of unappeasable dissentions, sanguinary civil Wars, and loathsome executions. .... The Independence of an American nation can never be completely secured from European sway, while it tampers for authority with the families of European Sovereigns. It is impossible that *any* great American interest should be served by importing a petty prince from Europe to make him a king in America. The special right that we have to object to them, is, that they are always connected with systems of subserviency to European interest: to projects of political and commercial preferences to that European nation from whose stock of Royalty the precious scion is to be engrafted.[127]

Despite the U.S. disapprobation of the monarchical form of government and although the two-sphere concept, as enunciated in the Monroe Doctrine, became, along with the "no transfer" principle, one of the cornerstones of the U.S. hemisphere policy, monarchy did not influence the recognition policy of the United States in the immediate postindependence era. Before and after Monroe's message, Washington steadfastly adhered to the principle that each nation "is exclusively the judge of the government best suited to itself, and that no other nation can justly interfere by force to impose a different government upon it."[128] It was in that spirit that the United States recognized Emperor Augustín Iturbide of Mexico in 1822.

Later when the question of recognizing the Brazilian Empire came before Monroe's cabinet, Secretary of War John C. Calhoun argued that to decline recognition of Brazil because it was monarchical would be a departure from policy hitherto observed and would introduce a new principle of interference in the internal government of a foreign nation. President Monroe, during the course of the same meeting, observed that to recognize the Brazilian Empire would affirm that the United States did not make a difference with regard to the form of government a nation might adopt. Secretary of State Adams agreed with the sense of the meeting and was commissioned to initiate the process leading to the recognition of Brazil. The recognition of Brazil in no sense signaled a decline in U.S. opposition to monarchy in America; that opposition may be considered to have reached new heights in the late 1820s when Henry Clay, as secretary of state, expressed his deep displeasure to Bolívar over reports reaching Washington that the Liberator was leaning in favor of a monarchical government for Colombia.[129] What the recognition of Pedro I did signal was that put to the test the United States had, at the time, no intention of permitting a particular form of government that it disapproved of in principle to stand in the way of regularizing political and commercial relations with an important new hemisphere nation.

Given that hereditary monarchy was the normal form of government in the Western world in the early nineteenth century, why did republicanism prevail in Latin America? Why did a region accustomed to monarchical form for three centuries suddenly embrace republican forms? Why did a strong European legitimist monarchy (France) and a powerful constitutional monarchy (Great Britain) accept, without armed struggle, republicanism throughout newly independent Latin America, Brazil excepted? The explanation is not so far to seek as might be anticipated. Much of the explanation can be extrapolated from the local scene. The disaster of Iturbide's short-lived monarchy in Mexico had confirmed what the European states, except Serbia, created in the early nineteenth century, had discovered, namely, that local jealousies, past history, and family and personal connections made it impossible for the citizens of a state to begin a new dynasty by accepting one of their own as monarch. Further, Latin America did not have a nobility with extensive possessions and influence to provide the courtly atmosphere that would set monarchs safely apart and above their subjects. Everywhere in the region were Creoles in positions of influence and power who had believed in and fought for the principles laid down by the French Revolution. For some of them censure of monarchy had dwindled amid the confused aftermath of war, but it was beyond their capacity to forgive Spain its brutal, senseless war against them and to forget the heavy burden bequeathed from three centuries of Spanish domination. Other Creoles, few in number and sometimes forgotten, would have opposed any prince committed to protecting the Catholic Church for ideological reasons and because they saw in its holdings the only accumulated wealth that could be readily appropriated and used to buy political support.

To the personal factors operating against the adoption of monarchical systems were two others of a very practical nature. First, even if the old colonial empire had been broken up into two or more parts, immense distances over extremely rugged terrain would have made ruling difficult, as proved to be the case under republican systems. Second, the new monarchs, wherever their capitals, would have inherited disrupted economies and depleted treasuries. Fiscal revenues would simply not have been adequate to establish a court and maintain military forces of the kind that royalty might reasonably expect, much less an excess for developmental purposes. That being the case, monarchs must have failed or alternatively they and their subjects must become beholden to outside forces.

In the final analysis, France, the most persistent monarchical plotter in the New World, in truth had little to offer the new states. Its history of meddling on the Peninsula had not won it friends among those who had fought successfully against Ferdinand. Its support of legitimacy had cost it much of the good will it had accumulated through its contribution to the Enlightenment and the principles associated with the Revolution of 1789. The princes it sponsored were generally of low quality and none of them had shown enthusiasm for trying their fortunes overseas. Even with an invitation from well-placed national elements, a monarchical regime anywhere in Spanish America would have had to be sustained by force, and France, after years of war on the continent, would have been hard pressed to justify over time such a strain on its resources, a strain that would have been maintained by pressures from the United States and Great Britain whose commitment in the region was far greater than France's. But to put a cap on early French monarchical schemes: the overriding concern of the Latin American leadership was obtaining commercial and financial succor. Aid in that form, were it to come, would be from industrialized Great Britain, not from strapped France. It did not take an abundance of philosophical reasoning or political acumen to recognize that it made little sense to expect Great Britain to bankroll a society under the political tutelage of France.

Great Britain throughout the 1820s would have, under the proper set of circumstances, welcomed the creation of monarchical governments in Spanish America, as it did in the case of Portuguese Brazil. From the onset of the Wars of Independence, however, His Majesty's Government's top objective in Latin America was basically economic not political. Under Canning the expansion of trade with the region became *the* British goal. Sitting in Commons for commercially minded Liverpool, Canning was ever mindful that England's future welfare did not rest alone on political foundations, much as he admired constitutional monarchy. Like Lord Liverpool before him, he was acutely aware that the United States, a republic, had proved to be a more profitable trading partner than had any monarchy. Based on a wealth of evidence, he had concluded that if Great Britain played its diplomatic cards right, it would be the chief economic beneficiary from the collapse of Spain's New World empire. When the time seemed right to extend recognition to the ex-colonies, the ones that held the greatest promise as importers and exporters and the first ultimately to be recognized—Colombia, Argentina, and Mexico—the first two from the beginning had been in the republican camp, and Mexico, after a brief flirtation with monarchy, had also opted for the republican system. Thus, three major indicators—Great Britain's objective in the region, the favorable experience of trading with republican United States, and the obvious political preferences of the Spanish Americans themselves—suggested that for the Foreign Office to have made recognition contingent on the new states adopting monarchical forms would have been contrary to Great Britain's interest. Canning interpreted the indicators in that light and, against the wishes of traditionalists, successfully directed the debates in Parliament so that it based recognition on economic rather than political principles.

The United States endorsed republicanism in Latin America no less enthusiastically than France and Great Britain championed monarchism. The extent to which its endorsement influenced the outcome of the issue, however, is problematical. The United States initially may have had some influence, as certain of the new states fashioned their constitutions after that of their northern neighbor. Countering any moral or modeling influences, however, were substantive considerations that under different circumstances actually could have led to a rejection of a system associated with the United States. The Liberator, Simón Bolívar, who figuratively speaking had Colombia in the palm of his hand for over a decade, had an abiding distrust of the United States because of what he saw as Washington's ill-concealed ambition to dominate Latin America while unilaterally determining what its relations with the region would be. Mexico, meanwhile, well before 1830 was cognizant of the danger to itself of U.S. expansionist tendencies. The U.S. ability to influence political thinking in Buenos Aires was so minimal as to be practically nonexistent. Given Colombia's and Mexico's concerns and Buenos Aires being beyond the U.S. sphere of influence it is difficult to give the United States much credit for Spanish America staying in the republican camp.

Moreover, at least until the recognition process was set in motion the United States considered Latin American independence more important than the system of government under which independence might be preserved. By the time the first of the new states was accepted into the community of nations, there is no doubt whatever that the United States had given its own security interests and trade with the new states higher priorities than it did the political systems the ex-colonies might adopt. Furthermore, as conditions in Latin America deteriorated in the late 1820s Washington might well ask: What had been the advantage to the United States of its encouraging Latin America to adopt republican forms that were foreign to their principles, manners, customs, and education?

As late as 1829 France continued doggedly to promote monarchy in the New World. That policy changed abruptly under Louis Philippe, Duke of Orléans, who became king in August 1830. Almost immediately on assuming control, the new regime set in motion a recognition process, without reference to the principles of government. Unlike Great Britain, France did not couple recognition with treaties of friendship and commerce, but just as surely had the thought of a "more brilliant" future for French foreign commerce in mind.[130] Although Great Britain favored monarchism over republicanism, its political preferences were not permitted to impede the advance of British economic interests in Latin America. The U.S. policy objectives were redirected during the late 1820s away from the promotion of republicanism and toward national security interest and commerce. The goals of the three major external contenders for influence in Latin America thus lead to the conclusions that (1) abstract political principles had minimal relevance as the three nations strove to achieve economic benefits in the ex-colonies, and (2) the decision of the new nations, Brazil excepted, to reject monarchism in favor of republicanism was made by their own leadership elements without respect to coercion from abroad.

This chapter examined four issue areas and their impact on early hemisphere relations. Rapid industrial and infrastructural development, and westward expansion, by putting heavy strains on the nation's limited human and financial assets, were instrumental in the federal government's decision to reduce its attention to Latin America once the region freed itself from the metropolitan powers. The Catholic and monarchical issues, on the other hand, were found to have had limited impact on the formulation and implementation of official policy positions. This observation was particularly apparent after 1825 by which time the United States, in recognizing the Brazilian Empire, had served notice that its commitment to republicanism in Latin America could be scuttled when national interests appeared to dictate a contrary course. Taken collectively the four issue areas provided grounds for the United States to reduce its attention to Latin America. They alone, however, would not have warranted the sharp turn in U.S. policy away from Latin America that actually occurred between 1823 and 1830.

2 DOMESTIC FACTORS II
Racial and Ethnic Influences

The United States "discovered" Latin America at an unpropitious moment in the evolution of the two regions. In Latin America storms of revolution that were freeing the colonies from external authority were also tearing them apart internally. The legacies of colonialism, geographic diversity, economic backwardness, social prejudices, plundering armies, and administrative ineptness denied the emerging states the wherewithal to fill the vacuum left by the expulsion of the metropolitan powers, to guarantee their borders, or to ensure domestic tranquillity. They were rudderless ships in a choppy sea.

The United States experience was quite different. It was modern at birth. It had no long-established church, no standing army to put strains on public treasuries, no peasantry bound to the soil. Its territorial limits were expanding. Much of its vast frontier was being peopled with small farmers who held title to their lands. The common man responded favorably to appeals to equality, an equality that excluded women, Indians, blacks, mulattoes, and aliens, and to democracy of a particular variety. Confidence born of political stability, belief in the universality of their version of republican institutions, the art of obeying without servility, economic prosperity, and secure borders were everywhere evident. Self-made individuals testified to the nation's essential vigor. The arts remained derivative, but Anglo-Saxon Americans were confident that they would soon achieve intellectual independence from Europe. Deeply conscious that they had established a government on a new basis, they did not doubt their own exceptionalism or their future.[1]

A few individuals, mainly from the middle and upper sectors, cast an objective eye on society and perceived that its golden dream had some base alloys in it. There was, however, little room on the printed page for skepticism or self-criticism. How could it be otherwise? As early as 1789 Congregational minister and successful textbook author Jedidiah Morse, after asserting that "it is well known that empire has been traveling from East to West," informed his readers that "probably her last and broadest seat will be America."[2] In 1816 Jefferson wrote John Adams, "We are destined to be a barrier against the return of ignorance and barbarism. Old Europe will have to lean on our shoulder, and to hobble along by our side, under the monkish trammels of priests and kings, as she can."[3] Elsewhere he declared that North America would be the nest from which the entire hemisphere would be peopled.[4]

In 1825 Charles Sprague, banker and poet of Boston, for example, assured his audience that "the achievement of American independence was not merely the separation of a few obscure colonies from their parent realm; it was the practical annunciation to created man that he was created free!"[5] That the United States would be the greatest, most powerful country in the world was an article of faith. Eulogies to the Constitution, cheers to the new nation, and the waving of the flag on festive occasions encapsulated the spirit of patriotism. The hoopla continued, "It is not too much to say that the future character and destiny of the human race depend more upon the conduct of twelve million Americans of the present generation than it does upon that of ten times this number in any other part of the world.[6] Not surprisingly perhaps, de Tocqueville found the patriotic prating of Americans irritating.[7]

To the temporal "proofs" of a brilliant future was added that longstanding conviction that the United States was "God's American Israel"; that "He had marked Anglo-Americans to lead the war between good and evil, between progress and reaction, between freedom and slavery." As the "chosen"[8] Americans would export virtue, selfgovernment, and equality, and ultimately go forth to convert the heathen world, install system where chaos was believed to reign, and become the trustee in bankruptcy for crumbling empires. Americans had not yet but were about to embrace that mystical doctrine "Manifest Destiny" whose postulates were that Anglo-Saxons were a superior race, that Protestant Christianity held the keys to heaven, that only republican forms of political organization were free, and that the future, even the predestined future, could be hurried along by human hands.[9]

The point that the Untied States was richly endowed and destined for greatness was too frequently made after 1815 for North Americans not to be conscious of their own importance. Their earthly fortunes confirmed that they were the elect. Those considerations did not, however, satisfy certain psychological needs. What Americans wanted to know was what made their culture unique. In the final analysis they did not go far afield in their search for answers. Their discoveries epitomized the concept we know today as ethnocentrism. They had become a super people, it turned out, because of historically derived behavior patterns, sets of values, beliefs, attitudes, laws, customs, and physical characteristics that they associated with Anglo-Saxonism. Their characterization of themselves, however, lacking in philosophical foundations, was understandable. It provided practical reinforcement in their daily lives. It was also understandable in the sense that most, if not all, societies are ethnocentric and celebrate their "virtues" at the expense of every other part of the human species. What is ethnocentricity but ego psychology at work?

By 1810 North Americans had formed mental pictures of societies circling the globe. Except for the British with whom they had an ongoing love/hate affair, the rubrication tended to be harsh, categorical, and left little room for the identification of socioeconomic groups or even intrepid individuals within a given society. There was nothing tentative or fitful about the labels once formed. Modifications occurred only when clearly dictated by self-interest. While Anglo-Americans were yet British subjects and before they established their military prowess and aggressive trading tactics the rubrics mattered little. Once they established their competitive position and were sallying forth around the world and seeing not what actually existed but what their antecedent experiences dictated, their beliefs mattered mightily.

By Yankee standards the three primary racial stocks in Latin America—Iberians, native Americans, and Africans, and the "mixed races" resulting from generations of their "crossings" in and out of wedlock—all received low rankings on the scale of human achievers. This chapter identifies the prevailing perceptions in the United States of the various components of the Latin American racial synthesis, defines the nature of their presumed inferiority, and shows how in specific instances those perceptions were manifested in hemispheric affairs in the years before 1830. Since, as mentioned earlier, by their very nature perceptions and images are ambiguous and their influence on societal beliefs and public policy is impossible accurately to measure, it hardly seems necessary to note that interpretations of how Anglo-Americans reacted to Iberians and the peoples of Latin America are matters of opinion or that today they are generally rejected by the liberal establishment.

The Spanish Character

Although many if not most Spanish bureaucrats and businessmen had fled or had been driven from the mainland by the 1820s, Spaniards continued under intense criticism from Anglo-Americans. For two centuries the British and British colonials had been finding endless flaws in Spaniards. The negative buildup began in the classroom, if not before.[10] Geography textbooks[11] with a minimum of elaboration informed children that Spaniards would undergo any sacrifice for the honor of their country, were honest in their business dealings, temperate, and that for "narrative invention" Spanish writers were not rivaled by any European nation. Spaniards were, however, haughty, self-righteous, cruel, revengeful, and indolent. They relished titles of nobility (an anathema in republican United States), were often indelicate in their conversations, and favored bullfighting over all other forms of entertainment. Furthermore, they were fanatical Roman Catholics, who tolerated huge numbers of bigoted, ignorant ecclesiastics. In America they had ruled arbitrarily and capriciously.[12]

Readily available adult literature amplified what schoolchildren were being taught. The *North American Review*, for example, informed its readers, "It was long a prevalent opinion among the Spaniards that God conversed with Moses on Mount Sinai in the Spanish language, and revealed to them long ago all the many secrets and hidden mysteries of nature."[13] Later the same review reported that "it is generally acknowledged that the Spanish grandees are intellectually and morally the most degraded and imbecile body of nobility in Europe."[14] Alexander H. Everett, a protégé of John Quincy Adams, while minister to Spain during the Adams administration, struck a similar, if undiplomatic note, in a volume in which he called attention to the "notorious decrepitude and wretched imbecility of Spain."[15]

Spanish political life was a disaster. The nation had neither force enough in its government nor virtue enough in its officials to give stability to its institutions or security in its people.[16] Unwilling to trust peers, the elites suffered feeble monarchs who ruled by divine right. Corruption was institutionalized in government. At home the voracious appetite of bureaucrats for wealth accounted for the rapacity of government and in the colonies for excesses, particularly against defenseless Indians. Adults were further informed that it was safer to assault the person of a living monarch than to deface the statue of a dead virgin.[17] The secular clergy, it was widely accepted, were immoral, consciously promoted superstition, and kept their flocks in ignorance.

In no civilized country of equal advantages and equal antiquity have the interests of learning been so feebly supported as in Spain. The moors . . . in the tenth century were learned for that period, but as a nation the Spaniards are at present a full century behind every other nation of Europe in the arts of life, the refinements of society, and enlightened views of civil polity; and almost a millennium, in the modes of education, and intellectual culture. It may be questioned whether they have taken a step in the right road of learning since the days of the Cid.[18]

George Ticknor, who became the first distinguished scholar of Spanish literature in the United States, in his account of his travels on the Peninsula during 1818, achieved a level of judiciousness that, to my knowledge, is not to be found among his contemporaries who recorded their thoughts on Spain and its culture. Although often critical of what he observed, he found the people uncommonly honest and possessed of a kind of instinctual uprightness that prevented them from being servile. The less privileged classes he believed to be the "finest material" he had met in Europe. Overall he found Spaniards to have more national character, more originality and poetry in the popular manners and feelings, and more force without barbarism than elsewhere in Europe.

The privileged classes—the section of society most often noticed in the foreign press—did not, however, live up to Ticknor's expectations. The government in Madrid was a confusion of abuses not equaled since society was organized. As for King Ferdinand, he was a vulgar blackguard. The political system provided for a degree of bureaucratic independence that gave officers the power of resistance. That independence, however, produced a train of abuses. There was nothing that could not be done by bribery. With the "middling classes" oppressed and ignorant, a nobility so gross and unworthy, and the high court worse than all below it, there was little that the general public could expect from government. The Inquisition, according to Ticknor, though much talked about, was more a bugbear than anything else, except for its influence on public instruction and freedom of the press. Still friends cautioned him about his conversations in public.[19]

Others found Spanish armies to be "popish legions." Catholic fanaticism closed Spain, and by extension the Crown's possessions in America, to the discoveries and novel ideas emanating in North Europe, the consequence of which was that the nation was in a state of decay and the colonies languished.[20]

Most devastating to Spain's image in the United States were the views disseminated about what has been known in the twentieth century as Black Legend literature.[21] The basic propositions of the Legend were that Spain was culpable for having protected the Inquisition, "that most hideous of religious institutions," for the barbarism in the conquest of America, and the subsequent mistreatment of the Indians. The legend embedded itself in Anglo-American thought from several directions. The earliest settlers had brought with them vivid accounts of Spain's "monstrous crimes" in the name of Roman Catholicism during the Counter-Reformation.

This initial enmity toward Spain was nourished throughout the colonial era by British publications that quickly found their way to America.[22] Of the early British writers no one contributed more to the defamatory literature than the late-sixteenth–early-seventeenth-century publicist Richard Hakluyt with his oft-repeated theme of Spanish barbarism and Spain's responsibility for snuffing out the lives of millions of Indians.[23] In the mid-seventeenth century Hakluyt's charges seemed to have been affirmed by Thomas Gage, an Englishman who spent a decade in the New World as a Dominican turned Protestant. The report of his travels, usually entitled *A New Survey of the West Indies*,[24] in addition to accusing Spain and the Catholic clergy of crimes against society, especially Indian society, and in calling attention to the wealth and defenseless condition of Spain's New World colonies, is said to have aroused the cupidity of the English and to have influenced Cromwell's "Western Design" and the seizure of the island of Jamaica in 1655.[25]

The tarnishing of Spain's reputation was not reserved to England. France was a full and enthusiastic participant in the act.[26] Montaigne's scathing castigation of the conquerors of Peru and Mexico for their treachery, covetousness, desolation, and inhumanity has seldom been equaled, and never by an author of Montaigne's stature.[27]

Great Britain and France had ill-concealed political motives for deprecating Spain. Throughout much of the sixteenth century they had spent their resources in domestic political and religious conflicts that left Spain and Portugal free to create and consolidate vast overseas empires. Now there was catching up to do. How better to arouse imperial ambitions than to focus attention on Spain, the most successful of all modern imperial powers and the one whose endeavors were to be blunted if others were to share the spoils of discovery, conquest, and colonization in the New World. More immediately important, New World riches permitted Spain to field great armies, which posed a continuing threat to all Europe and especially to Protestant Europe.

The British campaign to blacken Spain's image was undiminished as long as the thirteen colonies remained a part of the empire, and intentionally or not gave the impression that the period of the conquest and early colonization sufficiently represented Spanish deeds and Spanish character for all periods. And during the two decades after the Wars of Independence began, a period during which British-Spanish relations alternated between war and peace, the images of Spain transmitted across the Atlantic from England were unchanging.

North American negative perceptions of Spaniards and Spanish institutions, kept alive for two centuries by Black Legend literature, were sharpened during several decades of uneasy relations between Washington and Madrid. Spain had participated in the Revolutionary War, but as an ally of France, not of the United States. From the U.S. perspective, Spain's assistance had never been more than half-hearted. From the first the Madrid government was believed to have harbored unfriendly sentiments toward the new republic, initially having actually refused to recognize it. During the negotiations that led to the Treaty of Paris (1783), Madrid along with Paris had favored a weak United States confined to east of the Appalachians. Washington, furthermore, was fully aware that the highly regarded John Jay, on the basis of his personal experiences as minister to the Spanish court, profoundly distrusted Spanish diplomacy.[28] During and subsequent to the end of hostilities with Great Britain, the United States openly accused Spain of providing Indians of the Southwest with firearms to be used against American settlers. Furthermore, in 1784 Spain, in control of the mouth of the Mississippi River, had closed it to American traffic, an order that remained in effect until 1788 when the river was re-opened subject to payment of stipulated duties.

In the Pinckney Treaty (1795), Spain made further concessions in respect to navigation of the Mississippi, granted the right of deposit of goods in New Orleans for transshipment, agreed to restrain the Indians along the Southwest frontier, and recognized U.S. claims to territory down to the 31st parallel, but it only momentarily reduced tensions. By 1802 those tensions were such that Spain ceded Louisiana to France in the hope that the French government would provide a barrier to Yankee designs on highly prized Texas. That hope was short-lived. In 1803 cash-short Napoleon sold Louisiana to the United States with the result that the United States and Spain were once again confronting each other across uncertain boundaries.

A series of grievances during the late teens again raised emotions to near the boiling point. U.S. charges against Spain came about from a series of border incidents for which Madrid was held responsible. Spain, for its part, bitterly complained of Washington's failure to take adequate measures against Spanish colonial insurgents using U.S. ports to outfit privateers to prey upon Spanish shipping. The reaction of the *New Orleans Gazette* to the diplomatic exchanges was that "if [war] must take place, we know of no nation with which it would be more to our interest to go to war, and none more consistent with the feelings of the people, than with Spain."[29] The *Richmond Enquirer* asked: "Have we vanquished the Leviathan of the deep, to be insulted by a minnow?"[30]

A few months later the craggy, impetuous Tennessee general Andrew Jackson pursued Indians into Spanish-held Florida, apparently in violation of orders from Washington. He captured Spanish forts at Saint Marks and Pensacola, leaving Spain in possession of only one important fort, that at Saint Augustine.[31] In the Senate resolutions condemning the willful Jackson were voted down by comfortable margins, and the public for its part accorded him rousing ovations for his aggressiveness against Spain.

Jackson's invasion of Spanish Florida put a temporary halt to negotiations for Florida that had been in process for several years.[32] When negotiations resumed, Madrid, confronted with domestic issues and hoping for a freer hand in dealing with insurgent colonials, accepted the inevitable and surrendered the Floridas (1821) rather than chance a no-win war. Throughout the negotiations Washington had relentlessly charged Spain with procrastination, dilatoriness, and irresponsibility, charges that were embraced and elaborated upon by a vituperative press.

Differences between Madrid and Washington notwithstanding, Spain was an important U.S. trading partner and nearly all that commerce was carried in U.S. bottoms. Shippers, merchants, factors, and seamen taking part in the trade had opportunities to observe firsthand their counterparts and port officials in the performance of their duties. Cuba, still a Spanish colony, was, like Spain itself, a major market for U.S. exports as well as for foreign manufactures transshipped in U.S. vessels.[33] There, as in Spain, all major commercial transactions were carried on with or through Peninsulars, who almost without exception held key posts in the civilian administration and security forces. North American traders also maintained frequent contacts with Tampico (through which much of Mexico's gold and silver was shipped), Veracruz, and Alvarado on Mexico's Caribbean coast. Until 1822 each of those ports was officially under the control of Spanish bureaucrats and merchants. From the mid-1790s onward U.S. merchants, whalers, and sea otter hunters, who often were not adverse to illegal trading, made calls at Spanish ports on both the Atlantic and Pacific coasts of South America. They thus observed firsthand the cynicism and corruption that were associated in the Anglo-American mind with Spanish officialdom.[34] We have no sure knowledge of how the experiences of those Yankees who ventured to Spain and to Spain's New World possessions in search of profits helped to shape opinions, but that they influenced perceptions to some degree, particularly in the mid-Atlantic and New England states from which most of them sailed, seems undeniable. We know that travelers and armed forced personnel frequently return home from short stays abroad with fixed views of the host societies, views that interestingly enough are uncommonly close to the Anglo-American stereotypes of those societies.

Informed by Black Legend literature, desultory diplomatic relations, and the experiences of the private commercial sectors, North Americans were well prepared to accept at face value the anti-Spanish reports from Latin America that flooded the news media when insurgency broke out in Spain's New World colonies. A few examples of the news reporting must suffice. "The Indians of Mexico had been priest ridden and king ridden until they are neither fit for soldiers, sailors, or citizens."[35] The *Aurora* contributed the news that Spanish armies were waging barbarous war without quarter to man, woman, or child. In Lima bodies of patriots reportedly were left to turkey buzzards or burned by order of the Spanish officer in charge.[36] The *North American Review* left no doubt of its view of the conduct of Spain in the New World: "A tyranny so shameless in its aggression on the rights of man, so iniquitous and selfish in its motives, and so desolating in its action, as that whose iron arm was stretched over Spanish America, from the bloody era of the conquest down to the beginning of the present century, has never been known at any period of the world, whether civilised or barbarous."[37] As the wars drew to a close and Spain had been stripped of its mainland colonies, the *Daily National Intelligencer*, in reporting the fall of the Spanish fortress of Ulloa, off Veracruz, referred to it as "the last resting place for the iron hoof of tyranny.[38]

The tenor of the comments about Spain by U.S. officials at home and abroad closely paralleled those carried in the press. As early as January 4, 1816, Special Agent Robert K. Lowry wrote of U.S. sailors being cast into dungeons and of being chained to the decks of Spanish men-of-war.[39] Christopher Hughes, aboard the USS *Macedonian*, wrote, "From what I received at Carthagena and from what I saw at Santa Martha [Colombia], I feel no hesitation in saying that the cruelties inflicted upon officers and men belonging to American vessels seized by the Spanish authorities are unexampled among Christian nations."[40] Three days earlier Thomas L. Halsey, U.S. consul at Buenos Aires, had written Secretary of State James Monroe, "The cause of the people of this country to free itself from an odious tyranny is a just & sacred one."[41] Addressing Congress in support of Henry Clay's bill to vote funds to send a minister to La Plata, Representative George Tucker of Virginia spoke of "these unhappy people, who have long been struggling to throw off the most galling yoke, the most hateful slavery, that has ever tortured and degraded man."[42] In Washington Secretary Adams found it "impossible that such a system as Spain had established over her colonies should stand before the progressive improvement in this age, or that the light shed upon the whole earth by the results of our Revolution should leave in utter darkness the regions adjoining upon ourselves."[43]

The Portuguese

In the view of Anglo-Americans the Portuguese as individuals rated less well than did the lowly regarded Spaniards. The Portuguese, however, suffered less adverse criticism than did Spaniards as a consequence of their conquest of Brazil and the conditions under which their New World empire was dismantled. The Portuguese were recognized as having been leaders in astronomy, geography, and navigation during the fifteenth and sixteenth centuries, but by the eighteenth century had, it was contended, lost that spirit of adventure and enterprise that had made their forefathers so illustrious. Earlier successes had in fact made them effeminate.[44] Furthermore, the present generation was guilty of prolonging the African slave trade despite growing criticism of that practice.[45]

Fidalgos, who assumed their titles on the "basis of noble descent," were "petty tyrants." Most of them were "ignorant and intolerant wretches," who "grind the faces of the poor."[46] Portuguese peasants were friendly and hospitable, but dreadfully backward.[47] Beggars were to be seen everywhere, "not entreating charity, but demanding it."[48]

Portuguese were "bigotted Roman Catholics. . . . The established religion of Portugal was popery in the strictest sense."[49] "Friars were much too conspicuous . . . and rather more immaculate in their appearance than in their practice." The "lower classes" were reported to have few qualms about stealing, but with the most scrupulous exactitude conformed to all the external ceremonies of their religion, obtaining absolution for the one crime more rapidly than for the other.[50]

As in most other respects, the Portuguese were held to be more backward than Spaniards in education and literature. Nathaniel Dwight came near expressing the standard view when he wrote that Portugal paid less attention to education than "any other country almost in Europe."[51]

The *Encyclopaedia Britannica* summarized what appears to have been the generally accepted image of the Portuguese: "[They] are represented as inferior to the Spaniards both in person and genius and extremely haughty, treacherous and crafty in their dealings; much given to avarice and usury; and vindictive, malicious, and notwithstanding, it must be owned, that they have shown themselves on many occasions a brave and warlike people, famed for their skill in navigation and for their discoveries." The *Encyclopaedia* added, "Both men and women make great use of spectacles, often not so much to aid their sight as to denote their wisdom and gravity."[52]

For several reasons the Portuguese in America were not so severely criticized as were the Spanish. Portugal did not have contact with high and densely populated Indian civilizations such as the Aztecs, Mayas, Chibchas, Quechuas, and Aymaras around whom the Spanish colonies took form. Brazilian Indians proved unadaptable to hard, continuous work and found escape from arduous labor relatively easy, simply by fading into the "bush" and rejoining their migratory or semi-sedentary tribes. Because Indians in Brazil proved to be undependable agricultural laborers, the Portuguese turned to blacks, whose exploitation and treatment elicited relatively little concern in England and its colonies until the late eighteenth century. Also, Brazil did not in the second half of the eighteenth century produce mineral wealth near the scale that attracted avaricious Northern Europeans. The Inquisition, one of the most damning marks against Spain, did not reach the extremes in Portugal or Brazil that it did in Spain and its colonies. Lisbon, meanwhile, was an ally not an enemy of London; treaties of 1654, 1662, and 1703 authorized the English to send to Lisbon for transshipment all the goods they thought the Brazilians would buy, and English representatives were permitted to live in Brazilian ports to supervise the trade. The British, too, were the principal beneficiaries of the lucrative Portuguese smuggling activities in the Plata area and through there with other parts of the Spanish Empire. Great Britain, thus, had good cause to create favorable images of the European component of Brazilian society. Because of the Portuguese monarchy's flight to Brazil in 1808 under British convoy and the decision in 1815 to make Brazil into a kingdom united with the kingdoms of Portugal and Algarve into a single political body, Rio de Janeiro in effect became the capital of the empire. The colony remained tranquil until 1817. It thus did not attract the attention that the tumult in the Spanish colonies did.[53] Finally, Brazil did not figure in U.S. security concerns the way the Spanish-held Floridas and the Caribbean islands did.

However, when disturbances occurred in Pernambuco in 1817 and the decision of João VI to return to Portugal in 1821 led to widespread discontent and disorder, the Anglo-American image of the Portuguese in Brazil changed dramatically. The royal bureaucracy was almost immediately submitted to a barrage of charges. A relaxation of morals was found to be evident throughout the government. The Imperial Court favored corruption and extortion. Justice was badly administered. Trick and cunning passed for sagacity and wisdom. Government regulations and increased taxation were leading to a decline in industry and commerce. Rio was living in relative luxury at the expense of the remainder of the country. The monarchy was waging a foolish war in the Plata region. The Catholic Church was corrupt and dissolute.[54] What was missing in the communications on Brazil were the reports of the cruelties and barbarisms attendant to the independence struggle in Spanish America. There were no such cruelties and barbarisms in Brazil; it gained its independence from Portugal with a minimum loss of life, with few atrocities against the populace, and with almost no damage to personal or public properties.

Creoles

Until Spain and Portugal were expelled from the New World, information reaching the United States was clear enough about who were Creole patriots in Latin America. They were Spaniards and Portuguese born in America. After independence the term *Creole* began to give way to national identification—Argentines, Chileans, Brazilians, and so forth—and before 1830 foreigners commonly referred to the aristocracy or "elites," meaning Creoles associated with landholding, and the civilian, military, and religious bureaucracies. The more favored Creoles in effect did become a new aristocracy following the legal abolition of titles of nobility. But racially Creoles were not always as they seemed. Latin American society was highly fluid during and immediately after independence; it was not unusual for members of the "mixed races," most notably those in the armed forces, to demand and be granted a share in government and the security forces. This was especially true in Mexico, Peru, Bolivia, and Venezuela, where they penetrated the power structure even before separation from Spain was assured. Once the mixed races worked their way into influential positions they tended to think of themselves as Creoles, to claim the privileges accorded Creoles and to mesh their interests with those of the Creoles.[55] Thus, for purposes of establishing U.S. perceptions of Latin American Creoles, I assume that individuals referred to by commentators as "Creole" or "elite" or "white" were persons or groups accepted as "creoles" by their compatriots "without any inquiry"[56] but understanding that within the Creole category were individuals who in the United States would not have been acknowledged as "white."

Perceptions in the United States about independent Latin America and its peoples were frequently colored by the transference to that region of images initially formed about Spain and Portugal. Creoles, the group most closely associated with Peninsulars by birth and culture, were initially at once the major beneficiaries and primary victims of the transfer. The image of their being Europeans, albeit Spaniards and Portuguese, was crucially important during the independence movements. It gave Anglo-Saxons on both sides of the Atlantic confidence that, as leaders of the new nations, Creoles could be trusted to erect political and economic systems congruent with those of the North Atlantic community. The Creoles were victims of the transfer because they were the New World offspring of Iberians. Accordingly they were saddled with the more or less undesirable traits associated in the Anglo-Saxon mind with their progenitors. Many Anglo-Americans were, of course, impartially prejudiced against Spaniards and Spanish Americans alike. Consequently, Creole failures, and failures there were, often were attributed uncritically to Creole traits inherited from their metropolitan forebearers, with little allowance given for the political, economic, and social vacuums created by the sudden departures of those forebearers with which they had to contend.

Between 1810 and 1830 the United States received a mixed bag of reports on the Creoles. As long as the outcome of the struggles for independence remained uncertain the Creoles had the well wishes, but not the full confidence, of foreign observers. With the metropolitan powers defeated and Creoles in control of civil and military affairs doubt as to their personal and administrative qualifications for leadership quickly multiplied and by 1830 the foreign purveyors of doom for the new nations held a near monopoly on Latin American image making.

Ambivalence about the Creoles appeared regularly in the reports of U.S. agents posted to Latin America during and following the independence struggles. Agents in Buenos Aires were particularly friendly. Consul W. G. Miller at Buenos Aires found the Creole leadership there avoided excesses.[57] Thomas Lloyd Halsey reporting from the same post regretted that the freedom fighters in Argentina had not a single friend.[58] Special Agent W. G. D. Worthington in Buenos Aires made a point of Creole friendliness to the United States[59] and Special Commissioner Caesar A. Rodney, who went out of his way to be favorable to the Creole insurgents, believed that Argentina and Chile would find ways to create a close union and praised the *porteños* (residents of Buenos Aires) for taking measures to liberalize commerce, for relaxing censorship of the press, and for creating a spirit of improvement.[60]

For each word of praise and encouragement there were, however, several of doubt. Alexander Scott in 1812 found the inhabitants of Venezuela in general a mild, generous, friendly people, but timid, indolent, ignorant, superstitious, and incapable of enterprise or exertion. More to the point, he found them lacking in the moral and intellectual habits that fit individuals for the enjoyment of a free and rational government.[61] A decade later Robert K. Lowry concluded that the Venezuelan Creoles remained ill prepared for the "Rights of Civil Liberty" and that the leaven of Spanish despotism had infected their rulers as much as it ever did their former masters.[62] Poinsett while lauding the Creoles' pursuit of laws was profoundly concerned that military and ecclesiastical *fueros* (privileges) and the spirit of litigation, in all of which the Creoles had the major voice and stood to be the chief beneficiaries, threatened harmony and confidence. He further regretted that candor and dignity were in short supply, whereas corruption, cunning, tricks, and artifices were evident in abundance.[63] Consul Michael Hogan stationed in Valparaiso found a total want of character in the Chilean leadership.[64] From Guatemala came word that ignorance, superstition, and oppression had been engrafted on all of Central America's social institutions.[65] As minister to Mexico, Poinsett rated Mexicans "spoilt and wayward," the effects of pride, ignorance, and prejudice.[66]

In Washington, meanwhile, the heated debates in Congress over the issue of sending representatives to the Panama Congress of 1826 brought to public attention what were considered the faults of the inhabitants and institutions of the new republics. In particular, the Creole leaders were harshly attacked as Negrophiles for supporting the emancipation of Afro-Americans and for recognizing all racial groups as equal before the law, and the ecclesiastical hierarchy was attacked for promoting superstition by denying education to the popular elements.[67]

Nonofficial observers in general denied the Creoles even a brief honeymoon and by 1830 had found them to lack all manner of character. They were haughty, claimed rank on the basis of their "whiteness," and were contemptuous of those below them.[68] The *Christian Herald* assured its readers that Argentine Creoles suffered from indolence, with its legitimate offsprings, vice, bigotry, and ignorance, but added that since the revolution the vices were becoming less common.[69] J. A. B. Beaumont who spent considerable time in the Plata area recorded that Creoles were polite and attentive to strangers, but listless, unpunctual, and always trusting that "provoking word" *mañana*.[70] The Chileans "though they may be said to possess in no degree a single virtue have the credit of having fewer vices than other creoles."[71] Peruvian Creoles were endowed with more generosity than the Spaniards, but they were not "so constant in their pursuits," were "careless of to-morrow," and "dissipated."[72] According to the German scientist J. S. von Tschudi, Peruvian Creoles were effeminate and passionately fond of gambling.[73] R. W. H. Hardy, who spent many months in Mexico, found the political morality of the country below that of the Turks.[74] When at the end of the 1820s there was considerable talk in the United States of acquiring Texas, hopefully by purchase, the *Richmond Enquirer* advised its subscribers that "the Mexicans steeped to the lip in poverty . . . and threatened by an invasion by the mother country, will part with [Texas] or anything else for the sake of money."[75] In February 1830 the *Enquirer* charged that "there is no power known in all Mexico . . . but the army."[76] It could have been echoing the *Weekly Register* which in April 1829 advised its readers that "the new republics of America—if so some of them may yet be called . . . shew [sic] a generally unsettled and unhappy condition, and . . . military power is ascendant."[77] In an article concerned in part with the traffic in slaves, an author in reference to Brazil, noted, "Yet these importations are, in fact, not only useless, but injurious to the country and indeed, could only be tolerated by a race of men destitute of all energy, and wholly given up to the habits of sloth and indolence."[78]

Native Americans

Throughout their history Anglo-Americans were confirmed in their perceptions of Spaniards and Portuguese and before 1830 they had fixed perceptions of descendants of Iberians in the New World. North Americans were not so sure about their perceptions of Indians or where Indians fitted into the Latin American scene. Images of Iberians and Creoles had leaped out of the printed page, but Indians were a living reality in their midst, as they had been for two centuries. Perceptions of them developed erratically over time, and from region to region, with security, economic factors, and distance separating Indian from white being recurrent determinants.

In important respects Anglo-American images of the Indian did not reproduce sharply when projected onto the Latin American scene and some did not reproduce at all. This section explores only those perceptions of North American Indians that provided Anglo-Americans with a basis for comparing the status of North and South American natives in their respective white-dominant environments.

At the outset white-Indian relationships in North America were ones of tenuous friendship secured in common distrust. As white settlers, under the pressure of demographic expansion, renewed their beginnings on the then western frontiers and tribes were emboldened to resist white encroachment, they became the antithesis of the Puritans' way of life.[79] Nonetheless at the end of the seventeenth century the prevailing view among white settlers was that the Indians were rational beings, and qualified for eventual assimilation into white society. That view lost much of its following during the eighteenth century as the Indians' presumed warlike nature and their lack of loyalty to English settlers seemed confirmed during the several wars in which they chose to fight not with but against the colonials. In the Seven Years' War, for what were rational reasons, most Indian nations, especially those west of the Allegheny Mountains, allied with the French and Spaniards. Historically Frenchmen and Spaniards and Catholic clergy had related to the Indians more easily than had the English and Protestant missionaries. Furthermore, the French and Spaniards gave fewer indications than did the colonists of increasing demands on tribal territories. The French lost the war, and Anglo-Americans were embittered for what they viewed as Indian treachery and inhumane treatment of prisoners. Still, His Majesty's Government, contrary to the wishes of many colonials, did not seek retribution in the form of massive land seizures. When a few years later the Revolutionary War erupted the Indians chose to ally with the British rather than the colonials. Their reason was again a rational one; namely, that a foreign administration would be less interested in the wishes of colonial subjects than would a home government to its citizens. The Indians had chosen the losing side a second time, and this time the winning side demanded land as the price of peace. Then in the War of 1812 the Indians again allied with the British and for basically the same reason as they had in the Revolutionary War. A U.S. victory, if so it may be viewed, in the War of 1812 and the subsequent mopping up campaigns opened the way to huge land seizures, all of which were justified on the ground that the Indians either were defeated enemies, or were making inadequate use of the land, or simply could not survive indefinitely in contact with "civilized" whites.[80] During a cabinet meeting in December 1825, Secretary of State Henry Clay, who in his public statements often attacked the ruthlessness of expansion, however, candidly told Secretary of War James Barbour that "it was impossible to civilize Indians; that there never was a full-blooded Indian who took to civilization." As a race they were not "worth preserving." Barbour was shocked at Clay's remarks, but President Adams believed there was "much foundation" for them.[81]

Indians fared no better from their economic ties than they did from their military alliances. The decline of the fur trade cost them their most important economic role in a profit-conscious culture. With few important exceptions, for example, the Cherokee Nation, whose agricultural and educational accomplishments went largely unnoticed or, at least, ignored in government circles, Indians were portrayed as content to live by hunting, fishing, and gathering—thus failing to contribute to the economy either as producers or consumers. Their need for vast reaches of land to provide for themselves made them detrimental to agricultural development. As the white population expanded and the demands for agricultural land grew, the question was increasingly put: Was one of the fairest portions of the globe to remain the haunt of a few wretched savages, when it seems destined by the Creator to give support to a large civilization? The question asked, the answer was self-evident. The unappeasable hunger for land by whites must ultimately prove the downfall of the native peoples. It was a case of the concept of Indian rights collapsing in a world of conflicting ideologies. Whites had always found means to obtain Indian territories and after the War of 1812 two ways were popularized. The first was to encourage the tribes to incur debts that they could discharge only by ceding lands. The second was to seize tribal lands in reprisal for Indian attacks upon isolated families and small communities. The second way was an Anglo-Saxon version of Spain's "Just War" and it netted whites millions of acres; in fact, by such means nearly all Indian lands east of the Mississippi passed into public or private hands by 1830.

Since the Indians were unlikely military allies and now no longer an economic plus, tension between Indians and white settlers and the tendency, especially in official circles, to portray one tribe's society and culture as exemplary of all Indians extinguished any chance of their assimilation becoming a reality.[82] What was to be done with them? The official answer was to make them infantile. They would be cast as the unspoiled children of nature. President Jefferson spoke of them as "My Children." Explorers and military personnel on the frontiers told them of the "Great White Father" in Washington. Chief Justice John Marshall referred to them as being in a state of pupilage. Under such pretenses, by the 1820s the government had assumed control over the Indians' persons and property. In legal transactions they had become "wards" of the state. To think of Indians in familial terms was understandable since America was, at the time, organized around families, but a familial relationship was devastating to the integrity of Indian cultures. Furthermore, few in government assumed that treating the Indians as infants would prepare them for eventual assimilation into a vibrant Anglo-Saxon culture and still fewer conceded them as a people anything in the way of permanence.

Though government officials thought of Indians in tribal terms, the general public thought of them as individuals and particularly as male individuals. Textbooks, newspapers, journals, and captivity novels at times sought to project a sympathetic view. Indians, thus, were variously objects of rational benevolence and victims of the white man's greed.[83] In their totality, however, public images of the Indians left the impression that they were superstitious, anarchic, irresponsible, improvident, indolent, cruel, and addicted to alcoholic liquors. The conviction that Indians could not live in proximity to whites ultimately lent credence to the argument that to relocate eastern tribes west of the Mississippi was a favor to them as it would prolong their existence.[84] Congressmen, determined to expel the Indians from the East at any cost, played upon the survival argument throughout the debates on the future of the eastern tribes. The issue was put to vote on May 26, 1830, and the Senate by 28 to 20 and the House by 102 to 97 passed legislation that provided for the forced removal of the Indians to west of the Mississippi, legislation that was promptly signed by President Jackson, a longtime advocate of a policy of force. The Removal Act was not intended to guarantee native survival, but to allow natives to die a natural death. The fate of the Indian nations as manifested in the Removal Act had a parallel in contemporary art. An Indian princess, symbolic of American genius following Independence, was giving way by 1815 to a symbolic African-Indian boy and by 1830 to Uncle Sam and a Miss Columbia of neoclassic design.[85]

Indians figured only marginally in reports from Latin America during the insurgency and early republican years. The accounts, such as they were, at once invited Anglo-American sympathy and challenged their images of the Indian, without, however, shaking the conviction that as a people native Americans would not play an innovative or progressive role in the dominant societies of either North or South America.

Anglo-American compassion for the Indians of Latin America came from a number of directions. Reports reaching the United States from Latin America confirmed that for three centuries they had been one of the principal determinants of events in the region. The record also left no doubt that they had been the victims of harsh oppression. Once the bars against foreigners entering the colonies were relaxed or simply violated with impunity it became obvious that the mistreatment of Indians was in no sense limited to Spaniards and Portuguese. Rather, it turned out that the natives were abused by every other racial group—Creoles, black, mixed.[86] Three centuries of oppression had left them lamentably ignorant and submissive. Their indoctrination into Roman Catholicism was, for Anglo-Americans, another reason for being sympathetic toward them. Converted to Christianity by means of the sword, and kept in a permanent state of superstition by a bigoted clergy, they had been crushed spiritually and economically and thus could not be reproached for not having developed beyond their present state.

Compassion there was for the Indians of South America, but the Anglo-Americans' presumed knowledge of tribesmen on the frontiers of the United States did little to inform them about the Indians of those areas recently freed from Spanish rule. In very basic ways the Indians of Spanish America were found to bear little resemblance to those of North America other than in physical attributes, most notably a common tawny complexion. But unlike North American Indians whose numbers were declining and who, it was assumed, would ultimately become extinct, the numbers of Indians in Spanish America were increasing, as they had been for a century. The growth in their numbers, furthermore, was taking place in those areas where arable land available to them was diminishing because of soil erosion and exhaustion and the usurpations of stockmen. And far from being exiled from white civilization, as was inherent in the Removal Act of 1830, Indians in Latin America for the most part lived in close proximity to members of "white" society and served in a wide range of activities, for example, as artisans and as domestics, agriculturists, shepherds, and cowboys.

Also, unlike those of North America who had a reputation for being warlike, the tribes of Spanish America were reported to be peaceful by nature. To be sure, they had engaged in insurrectionary activities during the eighteenth century, particularly in Peru and Bolivia. In Central Mexico, too, they had, under the guidance of their Catholic priests, taken up arms in 1810 against their oppressors. In southern Chile, the Araucanians—the Comanches of South America—unconquered after nearly three centuries, fought on the side of the royalists against the patriots, in the belief that Spaniards posed a lesser long-range threat to Araucanian lands and culture than did the patriots. The rationale behind the Araucanian decision to side with the Spaniards recalls the basis of the Indian-British alliances during the Revolutionary War and the War of 1812. In nearly all other instances the major Indian societies, accepting that they had little to gain in allying with either royalists or patriots, made determined efforts to avoid involvement in the independence wars. Those who were forcibly pressed into service proved to be uninspired warriors, and desertions among them were inordinately high.[87]

The Anglo-American perception of Indians as unable or unwilling to engage in sustained manual labor was proved contrary to fact.

Members of the major tribes of Latin America—Aztecs of Mexico, Mayas of Central America and Mexico, Chibchas of Colombia, Quechuas of Ecuador and Peru, and Aymaras of Peru and Bolivia—were readily acknowledged to be the backbone of the mining industry and of highland agricultural economies, either as laborers or producers of foodstuffs and livestock. Anton Z. Helms, in 1817, credited the Indians with being the only industrious class he observed in traveling between Buenos Aires and Lima by way of Potosí; he added, "To the labour of these patient drudges we are indebted for all the gold and silver brought from every part of Spanish America."[88] A decade later J. A. B. Beaumont proclaimed the "descendants of . . . civilized Indians . . . the most orderly and industrious inhabitants of the country [Argentina]."[89]

However sincere Anglo-American sympathy and however much Anglo-Americans found Latin American Indians to possess positive qualities lacking in North American tribesmen, in the final analysis they were not of such a magnitude as to overcome the ingrained prejudices of most whites against native Americans. Ultimately the Indian societies of Spanish America were victimized by the more devastating of those prejudices. They continued to be thought of in terms of the barbarism of pre-Columbian Aztecs.[90] They were considered superstitious, addicted to spirituous liquors, irresponsible, and pusillanimous and improvident much as North American Indians were considered to be.[91] Furthermore they were guilty of wasting their meager resources on pagan and Catholic Church pageants. There were more basic charges. After two centuries of contact with Spaniards they remained outside the fold of white civilization.

Blacks

In the United States, Indians were found to lack the potential for amalgamation into the larger society only after long and sometimes heated debate. Afro-Americans, meanwhile, were not at any time during the eighteenth and early nineteenth centuries considered as politically, socially, or physically assimilable into white society. On the contrary, as their numbers increased in proportion to the whites in the total population[92] and as the number of manumitted slaves grew, Afro-Americans were in one way or another driven into an ever-shrinking corner of the American community.

It was precisely during the decades the "shrinking process" was shaping interracial relations in the United States that the general public learned not only that large areas of Latin America were populated by Afro-Americans, but that freed blacks enjoyed legal rights and a level of social acceptance that miscellaneous legislation in the United States meant to deny them.

During the half-century after 1776 nothing troubled the conscience of Anglo-Americans more than did the white–Afro-American problem. In not one of a wide range of topics debated did blacks, whether freed or enslaved, come out winners, as whites increasingly accepted the inconsistency of liberty and African slavery. Scientists, except for a few dissenters and religious philosophers, agreed on the unity of the races, but that blacks were in some way inferior to all other races, a view shared by a majority of white Anglo-Americans in both the South and North.[93] As early as 1800 the *Monthly Magazine and American Review* had noted, "We and our slaves are not different but opposite."[94] That was an extreme position. Though it was generally accepted that there were vast differences between whites and blacks, a debate over whether the differences were a consequence of environmental factors, cultural deprivation, or innate moral and intellectual degeneracy raged for the next several decades. As early as 1830, however, a mixed bag of pseudosciences, speculation, and observation was pointing in the direction of the unambiguous concept of black inferiority which gained widespread acceptance in the late nineteenth century.[95]

Leading statesmen had done little to abate the antiblack trend. Franklin, for example, had favored antislave legislation not out of concern for blacks but because he did not want more blacks in the country.[96] Jefferson, although denying infallibility and proclaiming that he was always eager to be shown otherwise, throughout his public life held fast to his opinion that blacks were inferior to whites.[97] As governor of Virginia, future President James Monroe had asked President Jefferson if there were not some place outside Virginia where persons (meaning blacks) obnoxious to the laws and dangerous to the peace of society might be moved.[98] As president, Madison opposed slavery not in defense of humanity and morality but in the interest of efficient government and a concern that slavery fostered an aristocracy that threatened democracy.[99]

Blacks fared no better with organized groups of white lay persons. Antislavery societies that proliferated following the Revolution would abolish slavery by degrees, but paid practically no attention to preparing newly freed blacks to meet the burdens of freedom.[100] The basic premise of colonization societies that sprang up in both the South and the North was that white society would be better off with blacks removed from its core.[101]

Except for Quakers and Moravians, the established churches generally endorsed slavery or at least tolerated it, from which it followed that they found spiritual inequality compatible with distinctions that contributed to the concept of superiority and inferiority. Among the consequences of that view among churchmen were the creation of black branches of worship, a definite negligence in their concern for the sanctity of the family, and the segregated education of blacks, limited as it was, in generally inferior institutions.[102] Segregation was in no sense limited to places of worship and classrooms. Before 1830 few voices, within or without the religious denominations, were raised against, for example, segregated housing, penitentiaries, hospitals, and cemeteries.

Most of all, blacks were victims of legislation written by elected representatives responsible only to the whims and prejudices of white electorates. Early federal legislation excluded Afro-Americans from certain rights and privileges and sanctioned a number of territorial and state restrictions. Thus, from the admission of Maine in 1819 until the end of the Civil War the original constitutions of each new state restricted suffrage to whites.[103] Local legislative bodies added further restrictions, for example, not permitting blacks to testify in courts against white persons or to possess lethal weapons. "You can never trust a black with a gun." In courts, particularly in the South and border states, presided over by ill-trained, provincial-minded judges responsive to strongly felt public opinion, Afro-Americans were commonly judged and sentenced by sets of standards different from those for whites. Where legislation and the courts did not manacle blacks, extralegal codes enforced by public opinion invariably subordinated them to a position of social inferiority.[104] If my sampling of the vast literature on the white-black problem correctly reflects contemporary and modern writing on the subject, no part of it has been more thoroughly covered than that of law and justice.[105]

White actions designed to separate the races stemmed in past from black responses to white mastery. Those responses, belying assertions that slaves were happily servile, ran from subtle sabotage in the fields and workshops, to running away, to establishing settlements of escaped slaves in protective swamplands, to arson and various forms of murder, to outright rebellion. The number of insurrections of groups in excess of a couple of dozen was small. They occurred often enough, however, to imprint the threat of uprisings in the slaveholders' minds and to confirm that rebellion would occur again. The concerns raised by the behavior of blacks provided some of the justification for regarding free blacks, who were widely believed to be guilty of encouraging slaves to radical actions, as at best nuisances and at worst dangerous. Probably the greatest fear, at least in the South, was that were a rebellion to succeed it would spread and that slaves would not be content with freedom, but would insist on mastery over whites, and that in victory they would avenge white sensual exploitation of black women over the centuries.[106] Slavery thus came to be regarded by most southern whites as necessary to their self-preservation in the midst of large numbers of blacks.[107] In such a climate of fear, the argument of slaveowners that slaves, as property, should not be set free by a government devoted to the protection of private property was specious.

While federal, state, and local laws and regulations were legally separating the races, the white public was simultaneously forcing an invidious group identity on blacks. According to the prevailing wisdom, blacks were emotionally unstable, superstitious, capricious, overly assertive, improvident, sensual, and criminally inclined. They were also deficient in the skills associated with the arts and sciences and were generally incapable of elevation and improvement. They were, however, conceded to have musical talent! In sum ethnocentrism had provided whites with the rationale for denying blacks those qualities required to survive in a free white society.[108] It was with such perceptions in mind that Anglo-Americans encountered blacks in Latin America.

Blacks were important actors in most Latin American societies of the early nineteenth century. They were especially prominent in those geographical regions devoted to tropical agriculture, the ones with which North Americans were best acquainted through personal contact and current literature. Whether major actors or not, they, unlike native Americans, attracted the attention and concern of U.S. citizens, both public and private, who visited Latin America during the independence era. Except for physical features and an association with enforced servitude blacks in Latin America, in fact, had little in common with blacks in the United States. They were, nonetheless, commonly perceived by North Americans as possessing the same traits and as posing the same threats to white society as Afro-Americans in the United States.

The eminent German scientist Alexander von Humboldt estimated that blacks constituted 19 percent of the total population of the Western Hemisphere at the end of the eighteenth century and that the mixed races (notably mestizos and mulattoes) an added 18 percent.[109] If one assumes Humboldt's figures to be within the ball park it is safe to conclude that given the prevailing logic in the United States that a drop of black blood made an individual black, at least one in four inhabitants of Latin America was black. In this section I limit my remarks to "blacks" as the term was generally used in Latin America, not as it was employed in the United States.[110] Moreover, the proportion of blacks in the Caribbean and the Atlantic and Pacific ports frequented by shippers, merchants, sailors, whalers, and adventurers was far greater than one in four. In the Caribbean, except in Cuba and Puerto Rico, the black population everywhere exceeded 80 percent. Haiti by 1825 was for all intents 100 percent black. Jamaica's population was at least 90 percent black as was Antigua's and Grenada's.[111] The major mainland ports, meanwhile, were demographically predominantly black and some, for example, Salvador da Bahia, Rio de Janeiro, Guayaquil, and Panama were overwhelmingly black by the mid-1820s. Of the major ports, only in Montevideo, Buenos Aires, Valparaiso, and possibly Callao/Lima did nonblacks outnumber blacks.[112] Thus for those whose economic interest directed them to Latin America, there were excellent reasons to view the region as demographically black.

Latin American blacks received a mixed press in the United States. They were generally acknowledged to have fine bodies. Haitians, for example, were portrayed as being a physically hardy race.[113] Blacks resident in La Guaira were known for their fine athletic bodies and muscular strength. An article in the *Atlantic Magazine* contrasted them with "the puny, wan appearance of the whites."[114] The Englishman John Mawe described blacks in Brazil as "a very excellent class of men, tractable and gentle in their disposition and by no means deficient in intellect."[115] Those in Lima were "a very large fine race of men and extremely strong."[116]

In societies where the basis of production rested on coercive labor and where nothing degraded a person so much as manual labor, few foreigners questioned the high quality of black slaves as laborers. Baptis Irvine, United States agent in Venezuela, for instance, judged that one black did the work of four Indians.[117] They were considered the most active and industrious class in Colombia.[118] Johann Baptist von Spix and C. F. P. von Martius noted matter-of-factly that blacks and mulattoes constituted the working class of Brazil.[119] John Fitzhugh, naval surgeon aboard the U.S. frigate *Congress*, in a sympathetic treatment of blacks in Rio de Janeiro, compared their work to that of mules.[120] Mawe found blacks in Brazil to be good workers who performed nearly all the manual tasks.[121]

If a group's fine physical attributes and its excelling at menial labor whites refused to do can be considered positive traits, as they both were meant to be by contemporaries, then the third and final area in which blacks in Latin America sometimes received positive marks was as soldiers. It is now generally recognized that blacks constituted a large and vital share of the patriot armies throughout South America, excepting Paraguay.[122] In northern South America, patriots, recognizing that their chances for victory over Spain without the support of their African slaves were minimal, made a virtue out of necessity by offering slaves their freedom in return for military service.[123] Jeremy Robinson wrote Secretary of State Adams from Lima, "I do not believe that the patriots can gain control of the country without emancipating the coloured population."[124] Blacks responded generously to the offer of emancipation in return for military service. According to Francis Hall they became the firmest supporters of independence in Colombia.[125] Bolívar's armies which were ultimately decisive in freeing present-day Venezuela, Colombia, Ecuador, Peru, and Bolivia were made up mainly of blacks,[126] and blacks continued to compose a major share of Colombia's armies after independence was guaranteed. Consul J. M. MacPherson unmistakably made that point. "There is," he wrote, "a curious feature in the formation of the army of Colombia. . . . It is that the whole body of privates and non-commissioned officers are negroes, mulatos [sic] and Indians and that the officers with very few exceptions are also of these different colours."[127]

In the Southern Cone blacks represented a smaller share of the total population than they did in the North and they may not have been so vital to final victory as they were in the North. They were, nonetheless, an important factor in bringing about victories in the region. There were approximately two thousand blacks who as in the North had been emancipated in return for military service in San Martín's armies which helped to free Chile and Peru.[128]

Favorable commentary on blacks in the Latin American labor force and patriot armies had little lasting impact on Anglo-American assessments of them. The written record leaves no doubt that North Americans took with them to Latin America the array of negative perceptions that they had formulated over decades if not centuries. For them Latin American blacks like blacks back home were assertive, untrustworthy, improvident, and carnally promiscuous. Important as were those perceptions to whites, they do not come across with the same intensity as do the possible consequences of the emancipation of the enslaved population and the potential threat of blacks to the white power structure.

The relation between master and slave in Latin America was a puzzle to foreigners. Thomas Lindley, for example, found it "astonishing to see how little subordination of ranks is known in this country [Brazil]: France, in its completest state of Revolution and citizenship, never excelled it in that respect."[129] Alexander Caldcleugh was impressed with how slaves in Brazil wrangled with their masters and how "in many cases they [slaves] appear to do as they please and completely rule their masters."[130]

In such a social environment and given the presumed tendency for blacks to be assertive, what might be expected of manumitted blacks? By the mid-1820s when in fact most of the republics had bestowed citizenship upon all classes irrespective of origin or complexion and thousands of needy blacks had been issued arms, what the answer to the question would be became one for whites to contemplate. The consequences of Haitian victory over the French were well known. Insurrections in the British West Indies, although on a lesser scale, were disturbing.[131] It was inevitable that black activities in the Caribbean would become known throughout the hemisphere. What if blacks from that area were to join ranks with mainland blacks elsewhere who might strike for freedom?

U.S. agents posted to Latin America were particularly alert to the potential of white-black conflict. Joel R. Poinsett, who had returned to the United States after a stint in Latin America, commenting on Peru as of 1818, noted that there had been no revolutionary movement there. He believed it was because proprietors of large estates were fearful that any attempt to change the form of government would be attended by the loss of their properties; and, "from the great number of blacks and mulattoes in this viceroyalty the contest would probably terminate in the same manner as the revolt in St. Domingo [Haiti]."[132] In a similar vein, John B. Prevost informed Washington that in his opinion it was only the common fear of blacks, "discontented and anxious to avail themselves of the moment," that kept Spaniards and Creoles from warring with one another.[133] Special Agent Jeremy Robinson on several occasions called attention to the possibility that blacks could become a threat to the emerging societies. Writing from Lima on August 12, 1818, he observed that the army of some five thousand troops were mostly blacks, mulattoes, and Indians.[134] About the same time he reported that a force of from five to seven thousand was necessary to prevent carnage by the "coloured population."[135] And from Valparaiso he observed that Lima had been saved from black pillaging by San Martín's forces.[136] P. Sartoris, ex-acting consul in Rio de Janeiro, sounded a like warning about Brazil. "We must not forget that ¾ if not ⅞ of the population of Brazil are blacks who must be both watched and kept in awe by an army."[137] A decade later four thousand troops in Pernambuco actually took control of the city and joined by a large number of blacks and persons of color sacked and robbed stores and residences until routed by forces assembled by the city fathers.[138] Finally, from Central America came word that the coastal area was under the control of ill-disciplined black troops, commanded by black officers with no sense of the large political issues threatening the interior.[139]

Mixed Races

Early generations of settlers in Anglo-America made a desperate effort to maintain their heritage and to retain the civilization they knew. Social and personal restraint was the hallmark of that civilization. Any mingling of settlers with Indians or blacks would be incontrovertible evidence that sheer animal sex was governing the society's destiny. Despite repeated strictures that the "crossing of stocks" would erode the character, corrupt the manners, and "have negative biological consequences," there was by 1700 abundant evidence that especially on the frontiers and on southern plantations the sexual impulses of individuals had not been bridled.

During the following century and beyond, many lay persons and an occasional public figure, for example, Jefferson, dared speak out in favor of integrating the white and red races as an alternative to the extinction of the latter. The current of public opinion, however, ran strongly against miscegenation in general and powerfully so against racial mingling that involved white-skinned and black-skinned peoples. Whether one favored or opposed the amalgamation of white and Indian stocks, it could be anticipated that as a group the offspring of such unions would die, either actually or symbolically, along with the Indians who, it was presumed, were on their way to extinction. Blacks, unlike Indians, were, as noted above, increasing in numbers, and it was widely assumed that any letting down of legal or social barriers, as appeared to be in the offing, would lead to an increase of mulattoes in the population.

Prevailing prejudices against racial crossing ill-prepared Anglo-Americans for the universal profligacy of interracial sex in Latin America, where the Iberians' casual attitude toward race mixing had made miscegenation the very basis of Spanish American and Brazilian society. Nowhere else in the Western world had interracial mixing taken place on such a scale. After three centuries of mixed marriages, concubinage, simple promiscuity, and outright violence against Indian and black women, miscegenation was everywhere visible. Racial classification had become vague. Before independence the Church had adopted more than a dozen terms to designate what its clergymen considered the degree of the different racial components an individual appeared to possess. Offspring from the same parents might be assigned to two or more different categories. As a general rule, skin coloration determined where a person fitted into society, although wealth commonly became a variable. Whiteness was preferred, if for no other reason than with whiteness went most of the benefits society had to offer. In such societies there could be no universals. The adage "You

are rich because you are white—you are white because you are rich"
overstates the situation, but not by much.

The Liberator Simón Bolívar certified to the degree of interracial
crossings when he lamented:

> It is impossible to point with propriety to what human family
> we belong—the greater part of the Aboriginals have been an-
> nihilated, the European has mixed also with the American and
> with the African, and the latter has mixed also with the Indian
> and the European. All children of the same mother, our fathers
> various in origin and in blood, are strangers, and differ all in
> figure and form from each other.[140]

On another occasion the Liberator in a moment of despondency declared, "We are the abominable product of those predatory tigers who
came to America to shed its blood and to interbreed with their victims before sacrificing them—afterward mixing the dubious fruit of
such unions with the offspring of slaves uprooted from Africa."[141] The
North American Review used views similar to those expressed by Bolívar in commenting on the Missouri question. In an 1820 issue in
which the question was discussed it called attention to the disorders
in Latin America that could be traced to the amalgamation of Europeans, Creoles, Indians, and blacks constituting the societies of the ex-
colonies. From what the author saw as the Latin American example,
he drew the conclusion that if harmony and strength were desirable
objectives, "reason and example" concurred in believing that they
must be formed by a "free and unmingled race of men."[142] That view
fitted well into the thought patterns of the Anglo-American majority.
Their faith in their own culture and their distrust of others were repeatedly affirmed in textbooks, periodicals, journals, travel accounts,
and, on occasion, given explicit expression in the course of Washington's relations with the new states.

To race-conscious Anglo-Americans, mestizos, who numbered in
the millions, were the embodiment of racial impurity. In sum they
were reputed to have all the faults of the Spaniards, but none of their
worthwhile virtues, which automatically placed them below the
lowly regarded Creoles.

It mattered little from what part of Latin America the reports on
mestizos came. As early as 1803 the distinguished North American
essayist, publicist, and federalist Fisher Ames, in reference to the mestizos of Mexico wrote, "As to principles, the otters would as soon obey
and give them effect as the *Gallo-Hispano-Indian omnium gatherum*
of savages and adventurers."[143] They suffered from the effects of pride,
ignorance, and prejudice, qualities that, along with a tendency for in-

trigue, unfit them for the privileges and responsibilities of citizenship.[144] According to the Englishman Mark Beaufoy Mexican mestizos were almost entirely destitute of the attributes of order and security[145] and were greedy for money and would put it above patriotism.[146] The *vaqueros* (cowboys) of Mexico were lively, brave, and good-tempered, but "profoundly ignorant."[147] Jedidiah Morse informed his readers that the gauchos of Argentina would "beg, steal, rob or murder rather than work."[148] The gaucho followers of the Uruguayan *caudillo*, José Gervasio Artigas, were "very little better than our Missouri Indians."[149] The *inquilinos* (rural laborers) of Chile possessed an evident independence, but they were universally illiterate and indolent, fawning, and deceitful. To cheat and go undiscovered was for them a major achievement.[150]

Had North American and British narrators felt the need, which obviously they did not, to support their evaluations of mestizos they could have turned to the findings of two young Spanish naval officers Jorge Juan and Antonio de Ulloa, who were in Peru and Ecuador in the mid-eighteenth century and whose reports, first published in 1806, scathingly attacked the mestizo element on the West Coast of South America. They wrote:

> If, for refusing to work and having a propensity towards laziness and sloth, one should be condemned to the mita [system of forced Indian service], no group deserves it more than the mestizos. They are useless, particularly when they have no official duties to perform. How much better it would be if they could do forced labor and make some contribution, since they are not burdened with tribute payments. For the mestizo however, it is dishonorable to cultivate the land or do lesser tasks. Thus, cities and villages are full of mestizos, living off what they steal or doing other unspeakably obscene things.[151]

Reporting from Brazil, United States Consul Henry Hill expressed much the same view of Brazilians as Bolívar had of the inhabitants of northern South America when he noted in 1821 that upon the "parent stock" there had been engrafted African and Indian stocks, "which had caused an admixture of blood and color in the Brazilians that defies all description, as it does all example."[152] Much as Juan and Ulloa had described the character of Peruvian and Ecuadorean mestizos, the Englishman John Luccock discovered in Brazil that the *caboclos* or *mamelucos* (persons of mixed racial origins) possessed an unusual preponderance of evil and found it unnecessary to maintain a shadow of virtue.[153]

Overall, foreigners gave mulattoes somewhat better marks than they did mestizos, probably because as a group mulattoes occupied a lower rung on the social-economic ladder and thus did not attract the adverse criticism directed against those nearer the sources of power.[154] As were blacks, mulattoes were acknowledged to be healthy and robust and to possess greater energy than other racial groups.[155] Humboldt believed that in Mexico, the mixture of Europeans and blacks produced a race of men more active and more assiduously industrious than the mixture of whites and Indians.[156] In Peru mulattoes were reported to show considerable aptitude as cobblers, tailors, carpenters, barbers, and some had acquired a knowledge of medicine.[157] The mulattoes' character, however, like that of the mestizos, was generally considered to be tainted rather than improved by the admixture of their parent stocks.[158] This degeneration was reflected in their consumption of alcohol and their inclination to work only enough to provide themselves with the minimum requirements of food, shelter, and clothing.[159] The Spaniard Antonio Alcedo in summarizing his feelings about mulattoes noted, "It is a certain fact that throughout the vast domains of the king of Spain there are no better soldiers than the mulattoes, nor more infamous men."[160] English-speaking observers almost uniformly saw mulattoes as quintessentially marginal people who engendered class relationships that contributed to social instability.

Conclusion

This chapter has identified certain Anglo-American perceptions of the major racial stocks and their mixed progeny in Latin America at independence. The perceptions are important in the context of the larger study only insofar as they may have influenced private and official decisions in the United States in respect to the emerging states of Latin America. With yet another reminder that today with the benefit of a highly developed mass media, scientific polling, and sophisticated methodologies available to the scholarly community, establishing the import of ethnic categorization in international relations is considered a venturesome intellectual undertaking, I offer by way of a conclusion the following observations on the role of perceptions in hemispheric affairs at the private and official levels over a century and a half ago.

First in the private sector, it is generally accepted that ethnic and cultural differences in and of themselves are not important inhibitors to private entrepreneurs engaged in international trade. I found no contrary evidence in regard to U.S. traders engaged in commerce with Latin America in the postindependence era. Ethnic perceptions historically have sometimes influenced the flow of investment capital, but U.S. citizens had such limited amounts of capital to send abroad that knowing precisely how much and where it was invested would explain next to nothing in terms of hemispheric relations.

The obvious area in which perceptions of the public could have directly influenced relations with Latin America was at the polling booths. As it turned out, the public's electoral effect on hemispheric relations was seriously restricted for two reasons. First, foreign policy was a quite marginal issue in the elections of 1824 and 1828. Clearly voters did not go to the polls to vote their pro– or anti–Latin American sentiments. Second, voter turnout in the two elections was small relative to the total public. In the 1824 elections, when the estimated total population of the nation was put at 10,924,000, only a total of 356,038 voters, or one in thirty of the population, cast ballots for the four leading candidates. In the 1828 election, by which time the estimated population had climbed to 12,237,000, the total popular vote for leading presidential candidates reached only 1,155,000 or approximately one vote for each 10.5 of the population.

Establishing ethnic categorization as a factor in early official relations between the United States and the Latin American governments is as risky as doing so on the private level. There are at least five reasons why this is true. First, reliable empirical data are in short supply and mostly left to us by nonprofessional observers or individuals who possibly had ulterior motives. Second, in the realm of international relations, irrespective of time or place, there are few occasions when one-to-one relationships linking race and culture and national policy can be detected, outspokenness to the contrary notwithstanding. Third, ethnic perceptions seldom, if ever, appear as the central or single most critical factor in international affairs. Perceptions must, in fact, at all times and places, as a minimum, compete with the security and economic concerns of policy makers. To insist on that point is not meant to diminish the importance of perceptions but simply to recall that all consequential historical developments are determined by more than one factor. Fourth, the consequences of negative perceptions of a people ordinarily are indirect, are sensed rather than articulated or documented. A legislative act or a newspaper editorial may show a definite predilection for or against a nation or people, without revealing the degree, if any, to which race or cultural perceptions influenced the ultimate position of the author(s).

Although the links between ethnic images and national policy generally must be established by the use of indirect evidence, there were, in fact, three occasions during the 1815–30 era when the relationship between perceptions and U.S. policy was explicit. The first occasion arose over the recognition of Haiti. After the thirteen mainland British colonies, Haiti was the first European possession in the New World to free itself from foreign administrative dominance and become an independent nation (1804), but it was not recognized by the United States until 1862, when the South was in revolt. Though not speaking directly to the question of recognition, President Monroe in 1823 in response to a resolution of the Senate noted that the Haitian constitution retained sovereignty in the hands of "the people of color" and placed citizenship and economic restrictions on "all white persons." Several years later President Adams in response to a House of Representatives resolution noted that Haiti was only nominally sovereign since it had granted special commercial privileges to France in return for recognition.[161] Over the next several decades Monroe's and Adams's remarks would be repeated, but not nearly so often as predictions of what might be expected from black insurrections of the kind that occurred in Haiti or the dangers of Haitian revolution catching fire and spreading throughout the Caribbean and even to the United States.[162] Thus, I find it reasonable to conclude that if blackness was not the sole ground on which the United States based its nonrecognition policy toward Haiti, while welcoming the breakaway Spanish and Portuguese colonies into the comity of nations, it was the vital and persistent one.

The second occasion came about over the proposed venture of Colombia and Mexico to liberate Cuba and Puerto Rico, which, used as naval bases by Spain, posed a threat to the sovereignty and commerce of the former colonies fronting on the Caribbean. How serious Mexico and Colombia were about the joint operation, given the fact that Mexico had nothing by way of a navy that could help to keep supply lines open or challenge Spanish squadrons on the high seas, is unclear. Washington, however, for several years viewed the project as a possibility. Only in the late 1820s, with Mexico and Colombia suffering serious internal dissensions, and Washington, by then having made it clear that it would look upon the venture as an unfriendly act, did the United States accept that the project would not materialize. Before that conclusion was reached Washington found several reasons to be concerned about its possible success, nearly all of which were in one way or another related to race. First, it was assumed that were Colombia and Mexico to launch an attack on Cuba or Puerto Rico their only hope of victory would be to gain the support of blacks on the island(s). Second, to obtain black support the invaders would have to, among other inducements, offer their black allies their freedom, as patriot leaders had done on the mainland. Third, the invaders, even were they so inclined, could not prevent blacks from taking revenge on their former masters. Fourth, a successful black revolt in Cuba might have dangerous repercussions in nearby slaveholding states in the United States.

The third instance in which race was an obvious consideration in U.S. relations with Latin America occurred in 1825–26 when Congress debated sending delegates to the Panama Congress of 1826. The Congress was called by Simón Bolívar with the goals of promoting the unification of Latin America, defense of the independence of the new states, the liberation of Cuba and Puerto Rico, the creation of a system of treaties of alliance, commerce, and friendship, and the adjudication of disputes arising out of the treaties. Late in 1825 an invitation to attend the Congress was extended to the United States. The Adams administration favored accepting the invitation, but opponents of the administration in Congress took the occasion to embarrass the president and his secretary of state, Henry Clay. Various objections to the mission were raised and debated, including those made by elements determined to prevent the United States from participating in an international conference in which it was believed that antislavery measures would be adopted and that some delegates would be of black descent. During the debate on that issue Latin America and its people, especially its black population, were repeatedly slurred. The remarks of Senator Thomas Benton (Mo.) in regard to Haiti may be taken as expressing the tenor of the racial remarks voiced during the debates.

Our policy towards Haiti, the old San Domingo, has been fixed for three and thirty years. We trade with her, but no diplomatic relations have been established between us. We purchase coffee from her, and pay her for it; but we interchange no consuls or ministers. We receive no mulatto consuls, or black ambassadors from her. And why? Because the peace of eleven States in this Union will not permit the fruits of a successful negro insurrection to be exhibited among them. It will not permit black consuls and ambassadors to establish themselves in our cities and to parade through our country, and give to their fellow blacks in the United States proof in hand of the honors which await them, for a like successful effort on their part. It will not permit the fact to be seen, and told, that for the murder of their masters and mistresses, they are to find *friends* among the white people of these United States. No, this is a question which has been *determined* here for three and thirty years, one which has never been open for discussion, at home or abroad, neither under the Presidency of Gen. Washington, of the first Mr. Adams, of Mr. Jefferson, Mr. Madison, or Mr. Monroe. It is one which cannot be discussed in *this* chamber on *this* day; and shall we go to Panama to discuss it? I take it in the mildest supposed character of this Congress—shall we go there to *advise* and *consult* in council about it? Who are to advise and sit in judgment upon it? Five nations who have already put the black man upon an equality with the white, not only in their constitutions but in real life: five nations who have at this moment (at least some of them) black generals in their armies and mulatto senators in their congresses![163]

After long and often acrimonious debate a mission to be made up of two members was finally approved. Approval, however, was given so tardily and opposed so strenuously that it had the effect of a rebuff to Adams's administration, and to the people and leadership of the new states.

Blacks were the principal targets in each of the three instances in which racial attitudes clearly impacted on U.S. policies toward Latin America during the 1820s. The case against mixed races and Indians, meanwhile, was being framed. That view found explicit official expression during the debates over the indemnity that would be demanded of Mexico following the U.S.-Mexican War. The "All Mexico" proponents who claimed a desire to save Mexicans from cruel and selfish rulers and to bestow on the nation the blessings of order, peace, and freedom lost their case; the opposition arguing, among other things, that the population of central and southern Mexico, being overwhelmingly of mixed and Indian races and speaking a foreign tongue, would be too difficult to make fit to enter the nation.[164] The United States finally settled for absorbing only a half of Mexico!

3 THE LATIN AMERICAN FACTOR

Between 1810 and 1830 U.S. views of Latin America ran the emotional gamut from idealistic enthusiasm to disillusionment. With the colonies ablaze in revolution most officials, editors, and the aware public threw their weight on the side of the insurgents, as they had supported French revolutionaries in the early 1790s and as they would Greek freedom fighters in the 1820s.[1] By 1818 when the question of recognizing the polities being created out of the collapsed empires was laid before Congress, the prevailing view, while still one of ardor for the revolutionaries, was not permitted to override what were seen as practical national interests. Caution was the watchword then and for the next half-decade, when recognition of the ex-colonials began despite certain skepticisms, often suppressed in the spirit of friendship, about the ability of the Latin Americans to enjoy the blessing of freedom.[2] Once Washington took the lead in welcoming the new entities into the community of Atlantic nations, misgivings about them quickly surfaced and enthusiasm for their cause began to give way to disenchantment. By 1830 the standard view in the United States was that Latin Americans, despite the rightful pride they took in their independence and in filling the administrative gaps left by departing imperial bureaucrats, were on a self-destruct course. Any remaining traces of sentimentalism, compassion, and hopes of bonds being forged from mutual concerns were overtaken by U.S. interest in the islands still in the possession of Spain that controlled Caribbean transit and in the borderlands of the Southwest that stood in the pathway to the Pacific.

This chapter reviews sketchily U.S.–Latin American relations up to the moment of recognition and concentrates on the institutions and economics of the new states in the post recognition period to 1830, when U.S. goals and developments in Latin America mandated a shift of interest away from the region. First should be noted those often overlooked positive achievements of the emerging nations and certain similarities between Latin America and the United States not factored into the mix that led the United States to recast its approach to hemisphere affairs. First, only occasionally was it acknowledged, and the thought was never seriously pursued, that unlike the experience of the Anglo-American colonies where the independence struggle was fought with the encouraging assistance of a foreign ally (France), the long and devastating wars against Spain were won without overt foreign aid. Second, while the contestants still remained locked in conflict, it was not unusual for the U.S. press to characterize the patriots as slaves seeking to emancipate themselves, but with emancipation a fact, commentators largely ignored the difficulties of accepting "slaves" as responsible freedmen.[3] Third, in like manner Latin Americans who had been castigated for being so long slaves of despots were now rebuffed, in important quarters, for granting freedom to their own slaves.[4] Fourth, not adequately acknowledged in the United States was the necessity for the emerging nations to contend with heterogeneous and only partially assimilated peoples. Fifth, when it became time to write constitutions and the Catholic Church was given a spiritual monopoly in country after country, critics in the United States censored the political leadership without understanding, or at least acknowledging, that without conciliating the people and their priests the revolution could never have been effected or Spain and Portugal expelled. For the new governments to have placed severe limits on the Church might have, probably would have, produced counterrevolutions or at a minimum risked alienating potential supporters. Sixth, Anglo-Saxons looked approvingly on Protestant behavior of the kind they condemned when associated with Catholicism. They, for example, largely disregarded Protestantism's long history of bigotry;[5] that many became ministers in the new and fast-growing Methodist and Baptist denominations as a result of being "called" rather than having any claim to intellectual training, theological or otherwise; that Protestant sects sponsored their own schools for the same reason that the Catholic Church did, namely, the better to preserve a kind of sectarianism that tended to strengthen approved ways of thinking;[6] that like the Catholic Church in Latin America, Protestant sects in the United States were subsidized by local, state, and federal authorities, most notably in the form of exemption from civil taxes; and that in the United States the constitutions of every state, except Rhode Island, contained articles discriminating against Catholics.[7] Seventh, also overlooked was the necessity for the United States to countenance an intolerant religious spirit to effect its own revolution and that a half-century after 1776 science remained to a degree a victim of religious dogmatism, although obviously not to the extent that it did in Latin America.[8] Eighth, most often the new states were faulted because of the disjunction between their beliefs as recorded in their constitutions and their political practices. There was much truth in the charge and it is equally true that the new leaders unquestionably made mistakes, but psychologically better for them and their people that they made the mistakes than to have cistlantic courts make mistakes for them. Ninth, U.S. officials and commentators leveled countless charges against the new governments for their treatment of foreigners among them. Those charges minimized that foreigners had overestimated the wealth of the region and that at independence Latin America became a happy hunting ground for not a few financiers, merchants, and foreign agents with shady reputations, who flooded the capitals in hopes of sharing in the imagined riches. There were, for instance, three thousand Britishers in Buenos Aires by 1824.[9] Many lesser foreigners duped, swindled, complained, and engaged in business practices not in accord with those at home;[10] and many of the greater ones collected commissions for arranging loans that at once freed despots from seeking public sanction for their economic decisions and burdened the new states with debts on which they invariably defaulted.[11]

Portugal and Spain had held sway in the New World for three centuries when in 1810 the flames of revolution engulfed their empires. Taking their cues from Anglo-Americans, French, and Haitian revolutionaries, colonials had gone to war intent on winning autonomy. Portuguese colonials accomplished their freedom almost without bloodshed; not so Spain's subjects. Only after long and devastating wars fraught with excesses on both sides did the insurgents strip Spain of its mainland empire and on the remains erect a dozen nations, each with its resources drained and social structure shattered, its people inured to war.

The Emergence of Washington's Policy toward the New States

When insurgency focused attention on the Iberian empires, they were basically *tierras incognitas* in North America. The mother countries had seen to that by nearly three centuries of commercial exclusion,[12] press censorship, and the threat of inquisitorial courts. The scattered bits of information that filtered out of the colonies did less to inform about traditions and customs than to encourage fantasizing about their economic promise once unencumbered by Iberia. Informed individuals, of course, had some literary acquaintance with the colonies; and commercial contacts had been increasing as Spain's monopoly weakened under European wars and British pressure, but the amount of authoritative information about the region was minimal.[13]

The immediate response in Washington to reports of fighting was, as has been noted, to anticipate an entire hemisphere peopled by republicans, their political systems and moral virtues modeled on the United States and, like the United States, aloof from Europe. With such prospects at hand sentiments in the United States strongly favored the revolutionaries. President Madison set the official tone when in his Annual Message to Congress on November 5, 1811, he referred to an obligation on the part of the United States to the Spanish colonies. A month later, on December 10, a committee of the House offered a resolution of sympathy for the insurgents. Public feelings for the patriots varied regionally; enthusiasm for them was greatest in the agricultural West, least in the commercial Northeast. Despite sympathy for the patriots in the executive and legislative branches, the United States, for reasons set forth below, officially followed a neutral (today the less precise nonalignment) policy that cautiously favored the revolutionaries. The instructions of Joel R. Poinsett, appointed "Special Agent of the United States to South America," dated June 1810, certified to Washington's decision to stay clear of the approaching storm while cherishing "the sincerest good will towards the people of South America."[14]

The better to comply with its responsibilities as a neutral, the United States passed the Act of March 3, 1817, Sections 2 and 3 of which went to considerable lengths to make illegal the outfitting in U.S. ports of vessels to be used against nations with which the United States was at peace.[15] Still further to fulfill its commitment to neutrality the United States on April 2, 1818, passed an Additional Act, Section 2 of which made illegal the enlistment of U.S. citizens as soldiers or seamen to serve on the vessels of war, or privateers, and made offenders guilty of high misdemeanor.[16]

Popular sympathy for the insurgents or greed or official corruption, however, made U.S. neutrality a farce before and after the enactment of legislation. Agents of patriot leaders had little difficulty identifying private individuals willing to embark on illegal enterprises favorable to the colonials and government officials to wink at violations of federal laws. From New Orleans and Atlantic ports, ships were sold, outfitted, and repaired, military stores augmented, and sailors recruited in plain sight of officials.[17] John Quincy Adams singled out Baltimore as filled with private citizens, judges, and government officers "fanatical" in the South American cause and enthusiastic to circumvent neutrality legislation.[18] President Monroe was close to the mark when in a lengthy justification for not acknowledging the independence of the colonies he noted that they were already receiving all the advantages the United States could grant them were they sovereign nations.[19]

The U.S. policy was too noncommittal to mollify those fighting for their freedom. Bolívar, as early as 1815, complained of Washington's empty professions of sympathy. Four years later Charles O. Handy, purser of the USS *John Adams*, wrote Secretary John Q. Adams, "The people of Venezuela think that the U.S. regard with an eye of indifference their struggle for independence, and that they have never enlisted our sympathies."[20] Henry Clay, once he became secretary of state under Adams, countered such contentions with the observation that "in the war which has been so long raging between Spain and her colonies the United States have taken no part, either to produce or to sustain it. . . . The best proof of the fidelity with which they have strictly fulfilled its obligations is furnished in the fact that, during the progress of the war, they have been unjustly accused, by both parties, of violating their declared neutrality."[21]

The first major test of how the United States stood officially on the independence struggles occurred in 1818. In the intervening years since 1811 the revolutionaries generally had fared poorly. By 1816 their armies everywhere except in La Plata (Argentina) had been defeated. Early in 1817, however, their fortunes took a turn for the better when José San Martín, with well-drilled forces, pushed over the Andes from Argentina and defeated the royalist army at Chacabuco in Chile and plans were set in motion for an attack upon the Crown's stronghold in Peru. The United States, meanwhile, had escaped defeat at the hands of Great Britain.

The time was, therefore, right for Washington to take a greater interest in its southern neighbors. With that in mind President Monroe, who earlier, as secretary of state, had gone on record in favor of the insurgents and who remained warmly supportive of them, determined in early 1817 to send a fact-finding mission to visit various regions along the Atlantic coast of South America. Three commissioners were named—C. A. Rodney, John Graham, and Theodorick Bland—and Henry M. Brackenridge was attached as secretary of the mission. All members of the mission were known adherents of the patriot cause. After several delays the mission weighed anchor at Norfolk on December 4, with instructions from Secretary of State, ad interim, Richard Rush and Secretary of State John Q. Adams[22] that underscored the importance of determining the durability of the existent governments, what might be expected of successor regimes, and the state of fortifications of the port cities, and of explaining and justifying U.S. neutrality as in the best interest of the patriots.[23] About the same time John B. Prevost was sent on a similar mission to Chile and Peru; Joel R. Poinsett had been sent on a fact-finding mission to Chile and Argentina as early as 1810.[24]

The Monroe administration had ample reasons to despatch the missions other than the update on the situation in South America that they were expected to provide. They would, it was believed, help to appease opposition groups in Congress that were pressuring the administration to end its policy of neutrality and take a positive stand in support of the revolutionaries. Also, the missions would signal to the insurgents U.S. good will and that they might in turn be induced to end their indiscriminate issue of privateering licenses, which were being used by unscrupulous skippers to prey on U.S. vessels.[25] Most of all, the missions would buy time while the administration reexamined its policy toward the contestants.

Henry Clay, who launched his national career as a representative from Kentucky, became the champion of those groups that would ally the United States more closely with the cause of Latin American independence. As Speaker of the House he had, as early as 1816, initiated a vigorous campaign in favor of the beleaguered patriots and the following year voted against the continued neutrality of the United States. Then, on March 24, 1818, he introduced an amendment to the appropriation bill for outfitting a minister to La Plata. In a speech lasting three days he defended the amendment, but to no avail, as it was voted down 115 to 45, with only the West giving the measure major support. Though defeated, the amendment set off a prolonged debate that ended with the adoption of a recognition policy in 1822.[26] The ultimate outcome of the debate was never seriously in doubt; the timing was. Those pressing for early recognition made their case on moral grounds; the United States as the stronghold of liberty had a special responsibility to the freedom fighters and recognition would inspirit them to sustain their battle. Monroe and his cabinet, however, refused to be stampeded. Sobered by the responsibilities of public office they resorted to delaying tactics as they pragmatically reviewed domestic issues, and the ever-changing Latin American and European scenes, with an eye to their possible consequences for the nation's security and economic interests. Secretary Adams, more than any other individual, was the restraining influence during this period. Although he would later soften his feelings toward the insurgents, as late as 1821 he had little faith in their ability to govern themselves, and most particularly he rejected the argument that the objectives of the Latin Americans were the same as those of the United States in its revolution.[27]

In justification of their cautious approach, Monroe and his advisers offered a wide range of arguments, important both because of their immediate relevance and because of their reassertion in the postrecognition era. At home, sectional differences over slavery, state's rights, tariffs, and the conflicting claims of agricultural and commercial elements on the federal government held the nation in a state of unease. Early recognition, moreover, carried the risk of postponing the resolution of outstanding international issues and the raising of new ones. Should recognition arouse the jealousy of Great Britain, it would, at the very least, mean the postponement of territorial issues carried over from the Treaty of Ghent, notably the boundary with Canada, fishing rights off Newfoundland, and all the touchy problems incidental to the ongoing controversy over the freedom of the seas. Also, Madrid would be alienated, and alienation would mean a halt in negotiations over Florida, as well as a great diminution of the valuable trade with Spain and possibly with its royal colony Cuba. Powerful commercial elements benefiting from that trade were little inclined to sacrifice profits from it to gratify the feelings of alien Latin Americans. The most obvious new issue was the prospect that recognition of the new states might involve the United States in the embroilments of Europe, and though it was not publicly advertised, the United States was ill prepared to wage land wars beyond its own borders. Finally there was a strong belief in Washington that European attempts to negotiate a settlement of the wars based on the principle of restoring the colonies to the subjugation of Spain were doomed to failure, and once the inevitable occurred the United States would be at liberty to recognize the new government without chancing a collision with legitimist elements in Russia and France sympathetic to Spain.

As for the fledgling states, the actions of their leaders in veering ever more from those that had produced success in the United States were disappointing. Buenos Aires' claims to sovereignty over the whole of the former Viceroyalty of La Plata was subject to challenge at any time from Paraguay, the Banda Oriental, and Portugal. Well-founded reports of monarchical tendencies in La Plata and Mexico[28] and strong predilections throughout the region for friendship and trade with Great Britain were disquieting. Also worrisome, leaders in Latin America seemed unable or unwilling to come to grips with critical social-economic issues. Not least of concerns in Washington was the questionable fitness of the political figures of the new nations to lead their people along democratic lines.

By 1820 positive developments had overtaken the ones that had argued against recognition. In February the Florida Treaty had been ratified. Insurgent victories, notably in Colombia and Mexico, heralded the final expulsion of Spain from the mainland. The Riego Revolt (1820) in Spain, by weakening the Crown's influence at home, gave promise of further successes in America. The continued stubborn refusal of Spain to come to terms with its colonies strengthened the hands of those in Washington favoring early recognition. It was in that still uncertain but improving climate that President Monroe and his cabinet concluded that Washington should manifest greater solicitude for the insurgent cause if the United States were to expect a fair share of their future favors. Accordingly, in a clear shift in his administration's policy of neutrality, Monroe, in his Annual Message to Congress in November 1820, broadly implied that it was time for the United States and the European powers to recognize the new governments. Within the next few months the intent of the message was given explicit confirmation. During February 1821 Clay, still the ardent champion of the insurgents, and his cohorts obtained the adoption by the House of Representatives of a resolution expressing the "deep interest" of the United States in the patriot cause and congressional support of the president whenever he deemed it expedient to recognize their governments.[29] Then, on March 8, 1822, confident of broad legislative backing, Monroe sent to Congress a message recommending that La Plata, Chile, Peru, Colombia, and Mexico be recognized, and requesting Congress to make an appropriation for that purpose. The appropriation bill was passed with little opposition, and on May 4, 1822, it received the president's signature. Colombia and Mexico were recognized during 1822, La Plata and Chile in 1823, the Confederation of Central America and Brazil in 1824, and Peru in 1826. The remainder of the republics were recognized only after 1830.[30] As will become clear below, the decision to recognize was taken from a purely United States point of view and was in keeping with the two-sphere thesis first enunciated in George Washington's farewell address.

Once recognition was underway the new states, except Mexico, attracted attention only occasionally during the remainder of the decade. One such occasion followed Monroe's Annual Message of 1823 to Congress. Two passages in the Message contained the substance of what became known as the Monroe Doctrine. In those passages Monroe laid down the basic principles of U.S. foreign policy. The New World henceforth should not be considered subject to future colonization by any European power and any attempt by a European power to extend its political system to any part of the Western Hemisphere would be viewed by the United States as a manifestation of an unfriendly disposition toward it and as dangerous to its peace and safety.

The Message, thus, was at once a challenge to Europe, a challenge, however, that Monroe correctly gauged would not be taken up in his time, and the self-proclaimed leadership of the United States in the Americas. The doctrine produced a brief flurry of speculation in the United States and Latin America over the practical implications of the warning and what it meant in reference to the hemisphere. It was not at all clear from the document itself, but the new governments soon learned that Washington was determined to interpret the passage's intent unilaterally in response to specific developments. A distinguished British historian, in a summary statement of the Monroe Doctrine that can be taken to represent the prevailing European view, at least throughout the 1820s, wrote that it was a vague statement of policy, a lecture, a doctrine, an ideal. It was not a rule of action that the government was prepared to enforce. It had no juridical value, and its statement of principles did not pledge the government to execute its menaces.[31] In no event were Monroe's words to be turned into a binding commitment to protect any of the new states. The United States stood pledged only to its own self-interest.

The debate over the naming of official delegates to the Panama Congress of 1826 provided a second occasion for Congress and the press to ventilate opinions about U.S. relations with the new states. The discussions made good copy for several weeks. The debates, as noted in chapter 2, are best remembered for the attacks upon the new states for granting minorities, especially blacks, legal equality and the concerns of important groups in Washington over the possibility that if delegates were sent to Panama they would be seated alongside blacks. Given widespread attention was the charge that the leaders of the new states were not duly appreciative of the contribution of the United States to the independence movement, including being the first power to acknowledge their separation from the metropolitan states. Joel R. Poinsett, who had spent considerable time in Argentina and Chile, was among the first to make the point. In a summary statement on developments in the area, written in 1818, he noted, "The governments of Buenos Ayres since their first establishment and in all their changes have invariably acted toward this country [the United States] as toward a secondary power."[32] Secretary Adams leveled a similar charge in an entry in his diary for July 1820: "There is something disheartening in all our correspondence and transactions relating to South America. We have done everything possible in their favor, and have received from them little less than injury in return. No satisfaction has been attained from them upon any complaint, and they have been constantly endeavoring to entangle us with them and their cause."[33] And just as the Panama debates were getting underway, John M. Forbes wrote from Buenos Aires, "These people are so servilely English that they wish to forget or deny any obligation to us."[34]

Unlike the momentary absorption in Latin American matters generated by the Monroe Doctrine and the Panama Congress, interest in Mexico ran at a moderately high level throughout the 1820s. Although Mexico had embraced republican forms after a brief experiment with monarchy, it had consistently shown a distinct preference for Great Britain as an economic partner and protector.[35] Mexico, however, was especially newsworthy because of its common, but unagreed upon, border with the United States. As is well known, U.S. citizens aspired to lands belonging to Mexico according to Mexican interpretations of where the border ran. Washington initially proposed to resolve the issue by outright purchase of the desired territory. When Mexico, by now deeply fearful of U.S. transgressions, refused to bargain, U.S. agents attempted to bribe officials, an undertaking that led to further diplomatic exchanges which in turn heightened public reaction toward Mexico.

Important sections of the U.S. press took up the issue and launched a full-scale propaganda barrage against all things Mexican. The barrage proved especially effective because travel accounts and a tradition of reporting on Mexico's political, economic, and military torments, social incoherence, religious affiliation, and ethnic composition had conditioned the North American public to expect the worst from its southern neighbor. The most telling charge during the 1820s was that Mexico was totally incapable of carrying out regulatory and civilizing missions in the disputed territory. In the context of U.S.– Latin American relations, the negative characteristics of Mexican society imprinted on the North American mind[36] were not unlike those associated with other parts of Latin America and were used to reinforce the view that the United States had little to lose from reducing its contacts with the new states. Limitation of ties with the new governments in fact became a dominant feature of U.S. policy by the late 1820s. The conditions in Latin America that Washington believed warranted such a policy are at the core of the following discussion.

Social Conditions of the New States

The new nations, underpopulated and deprived, had wrested the scepter from Spain and Portugal, but had kept much of their spirit. New patterns were present, but did not prevail. Nowhere had the newly independent societies found legitimate substitutes for a firm Crown and an unchallenged Church, the bonding elements during three centuries of colonial rule. Ethnically and socially hierarchical, society was divided horizontally by race—which was not so sharply defined as in the United States—and vertically by divergent loyalties to Church, regions, municipalities, and individuals. There were, in fact, no bonds of union, no community of interest, no environment in which loyalties might gestate.[37] There had been no rehearsals for dealing with freedom. While the wars had sputtered on, old habits of civil obedience and social deference had been lost. A relaxation of social controls had encouraged the less privileged of the urban center to adopt contumelious attitudes toward authority. In the absence of social-economic middle sectors, a small aristocracy of race and wealth—the traditional aristocracy had been abolished—dedicated to the principle that government should protect property at all costs, rested comfortably on a human foundation of ignorance, poverty, and servility.

Indians

Indians who at independence constituted approximately 40 percent of the total population of the area[38] formed the base of the social pyramid. With the Iberians discredited by the overthrow of imperial rule, the peak of the pyramid went by default to Creoles. In between Indian and Creole were layered upward from the Indian foundation Afro-Americans and the mixed races commonly referred to as *prados, ladinos, las castas.*

Indians had proved defenseless against the distempered will of their conquerors. Once defeated in battle, their families violated, their property usurped, demeaned as lazy, vicious, shiftless, and bestial, and systematically relegated to subject status, Indians quickly succumbed to social and economic exploitation. *Los naturales* and *los indios* were everywhere terms of derision. Oppression and grinding poverty drove them to the fatalistic acceptance of their condition. Resistance to their masters, usually silent and passive, but also stubborn and tenacious, became a mechanism for preserving their patrimony. A century after independence, the Peruvian poet José Santos Chocano wrote of them:

> Mysterious and ancient race
> Your hearts are wholly fathomless
> You witness joy without delight
> You witness pain without distress[39]

and the Mexican novelist Gregorio López Fuentes characterized them as a people who listened with indifference, making no sign of contradiction or approval.[40]

Isolated throughout the colonial era in villages that stood still in time or on sprawling haciendas, and ostracized when they ventured to enter Spanish and Portuguese centers other than as menial labor, Indians were coveted only as recruits to Catholicism, as laborers in field and mine, as household servants, and as bed partners.

When the wars of independence shattered the colonial calm, the Indians' condition changed dramatically, but only temporarily. Then their foodstuffs and their beasts of burden, without which their agricultural economies could not function, were permanently lost to military requisitions. Their males were torn from their communities and forced into insurgent and royalist armies and marched over pathless waste to fight battles in which they had neither interest nor stake. Unlike promises to the Afro-Americans, no attempt was made to strengthen native American loyalties or to give them rights. Rather they were ill fed, ill clothed, and buffeted about. To return to their families was their abiding ambition. With Spain expelled, Indian soldiers, along with millions of their kind, returned to the hermetic, stratified system of the past. Everywhere, without exception, the social order ordained that they live precarious existences, pay taxes, and be held responsible by the power elites for Latin America's slow development.

The Indians' primordial way of life and the viciousness of their environment invited occasional romantic sentiments. But Indians figured only negatively when at all in the realistic world of U.S.–Latin American relations. The leadership on both sides assumed that they lacked the competitive qualities required to survive in the kind of urbanized economies that foreigners foresaw for the new societies. Considered to be inept in dealing with abstractions and to be moved by passion rather than reason, they were believed to be equally poor political material. If they returned to their imagined passivity of the colonial era they would, it was believed, become the tools of irresponsible political aspirants. If, alternatively, they were to build on their increased awareness of their rights and the lessons in organization and discipline learned in emancipation armies, they would become a politically turbulent element with narrow parochial views. Not surprisingly, the future of the new states with large Indian populations was generally regarded as unpromising.

Blacks

Blacks, dishonored by servitude but cherished as laborers on tropical plantations and as domestics, occupied a rung on the social ladder only a notch above the Indians. When insurgency erupted in the Spanish Empire, black males who remained enslaved, and they were a majority, were promised their freedom in return for joining the patriot armies, an offer that royalists matched. Most blacks enlisted in the patriot cause, but in Venezuela and Colombia many enrolled in the

Spanish ranks. The patriots' promises of freedom had a humanitarian inspiration that came out of the French Revolution, mainly by way of Haiti, but they were also heavily tinged with political and military expedients. Protected in insurgent armies, blacks would be immune to royalists whose appeals to blacks focused on the fact that the typical slaveowner was a Creole.[41] More pressing for the moment, the revolutionary forces badly needed recruits. Good to their word, the victorious insurgents granted freedom to those who enlisted under the patriot banner (by war's end a large but undetermined number of blacks who initially enlisted in royalists' armies had switched sides), and the new governments, except in Brazil, made abolition of the slave trade and slavery an early order of business. By the 1850s they had, again excepting Brazil, abolished slavery as a legal institution.

Blacks, as has been noted, gave a highly creditable account of themselves on the battlefields of a half-dozen nations, but that counted for naught in terms of their social and economic improvement in peacetime. Disdain for them within the now dominant Creole element remained strong. To the traditional antipathy for enslaved Africans was added a fear of them and a concern that freed from the trammels of slavery they would not adjust readily to free labor status. As it turned out freed blacks as a rule were unwilling to compete with their enslaved brethren for jobs and consequently were frequently forced to live as vagabonds or engage in banditry.

Spirited black soldiers meanwhile had returned to civilian life with guns and a "long debt of vengeance for slavery to pay their masters." Creole humanitarianism had gone as far as granting them legal equality, but stopped there. Creole elites, at heart ambivalent about the new reform legislation, found ways to burden blacks without restraining themselves. Blacks were denied enfranchisement. Black men and women remained subject to economic and sexual exploitation. Jobs open to them were the ones they had had while in bondage. Their economic status denied them equal access to the courts of the land. In sum, much like the Indians, they witnessed the privileges of freedom not as beneficiaries, but as onlookers.[42]

Mixed Races

Unlike Indians, who sought obscurity, the mixed races were turbulent in their demands for greater participation in society. Without the security that family, extended family, and communal organization often gave the Indian, and discriminated against at the higher levels of the civil, religious, and military bureaucracies, the mixed races responded by making a virtue of unruliness and refusing certain kinds of employment. It was the asocial behavior of mestizos and mulattoes and the ramifications thereof that first caught the eye of foreign observers.

The mixed races responded in different ways to freedom from Spanish and Portuguese authoritarian control. Some chose to escape white and Indian societies entirely by flight, as was the case of mestizos to the pampas of Argentina and Uruguay, mulattoes to the remote interior of Brazil, and both mestizos and mulattoes to the *llanos* (plains) of Venezuela and Colombia. Freed from the restraints of "civilized" society they ordinarily chose hunting, herding, or brigandage. Others sought out Indian villages. In them they trampled on the debased Indian while contributing minimally, if at all, to the economic welfare of the community. Still others chose life in provincial municipalities. In them the entrepreneurially aggressive became economic brokers by monopolizing commerce, by lending funds for festive occasions, and by making loans to small farmers to "carry them" from spring planting to fall harvest. The Creole term for such individuals was "gutter aristocrats." But the gutter aristocrats also on occasion acquired agricultural and grazing lands (along with the Indian families attached to the land), thereby sharing with the traditional landed aristocrats political power at the provincial level. Finally there were those who opted for the cities. Most of them, if they worked at all, were customarily engaged in the crafts or as clerks, almost anything to avoid the appearance of being a member of the menial labor force. A few improved their social-economic status by replacing Spanish and Portuguese retailers. Fortunes to be made in commercial enterprises, however, were limited and most often went to Creoles with family or political connections or to foreigners with access to contacts and credit abroad.[43]

Because Creoles and foreigners largely controlled commerce, the armed forces proved to be the surest route to wealth and influence for those of mixed origins. Andrés de Santa Cruz (Bolivia and Peru), Agustín Gamarra (Peru), Vicente Guerrero (Mexico), and José Páez (Venezuela) are among the better known leaders of mixed racial origins who in the immediate postindependence era parlayed meritorious service into the highest civilian posts in their respective countries. There were, however, many others who settled for lesser but still politically and economically advantageous seats of influence in the provinces. Whether national presidents or provincial officials, those of mixed origin seldom challenged Creole values; rather they joined those privileged Creoles dedicated to the survival of old ideas and forms and the protection of wealth. Those of mixed parentage who adopted such values necessarily abandoned the groups from which they sprang. The general run of individuals of mixed racial descent, meanwhile, remained trapped in the mold into which they were born: depressed, bearing grudges, and periodically under the leadership of local or regional officials, resorting to arms to make known their frustrations and desires.

Creoles deeply disapproved of upstart mestizos and mulattoes who climbed with arms in hand. They had, however, no alternative but to accommodate to them if they held or shared political power. Creoles reached the necessary accommodations by using to advantage their prestige, superior wealth, education, control over Indian labor, administrative experience (limited as it was), and the preferences of foreigners for them over mestizos and mulattoes. Also, accommodation was less costly than might have been the case because, as adverted to above, successful mestizos and mulattoes nearly always willingly adopted the Creoles social code and economic values in return for being received into Creole society.

Mestizos were a major focus of attention in accounts flowing from Latin America in the immediate postindependence era. Irrespective of what Anglo-Americans thought the consequences of miscegenation to be,[44] it was readily apparent in Latin America that mestizos would play key roles at both the provincial and national levels. Occasionally they received high marks for their political and economic acumen; the consensus view, however, was distinctly negative.

They were numerous. They were restless and ambitious for power. They could be ruthless. Though they might voice the rhetoric of liberty their tendency was toward despotism. They were more antiforeign than were Creoles. That the progeny of mixed unions should exercise power in the new states was, in the view of foreigners, unfortunate enough; that they should do so before being tested in politics and administration was to court disaster. North Americans, like Creoles, nonetheless, of necessity had to accommodate to those untried, distrusted leaders of mixed descent in order to carry on relations with the fledgling governments. That, however, did not prevent Washington and most of the nation's media from early reaching the conclusion that those parts of Latin America that had surrendered themselves to the leadership of individuals of mixed origins were rushing blindly into a bleak future.

The Creole Elites

The evidence suggests that the Creoles, although a distinct demographic minority, took over from the departing imperial bureaucrats. Liberal intellectuals among them were imbued with Enlightenment ideology gained either from independent study, as students in colonial universities, notably the University of Chuquisaca in Bolivia, or occasionally from study and travel abroad. Articulating the philosophical and juridical justifications for rebellion against tyranny and authoritarianism, they had been at the cutting edge of the independence movements. Like Creoles generally, the liberals had been kept in a sort of permanent infancy in respect to public affairs. The result was that nearly all their thoughts and their understanding of politics and administration evolved from ideological convictions rather than from experience.

Their advocacy of rebellion against the metropolitan powers coincided with the heyday of Western constitutionalism and enthusiasm for constitutional government. A conviction that rationally conceived written codes of law could provide and guarantee liberty and progress was a significant element in their thinking. In quest of their ideal they called conventions. They elected representatives. They hammered out abstract systems of law that borrowed heavily from Europe and the United States without seriously questioning the suitability of the borrowings to local interests and traditions. They amended constitutions and discarded them. Chileans, for example, lived under five constitutions between 1818, when independence was won, and 1828. Popular revolts at the end of the colonial epoch and during the independence wars, though not successful, had been menacing enough to stiffen the landed elites in their opposition to a renovated society founded on restless peasantries and ambitious mestizos. They came to power convinced that only those who possessed property could be trusted to create and sustain the kind of society they had in mind.

The landed oligarchies knew the kind of society they wanted, but few were prepared to participate in politics in order to satisfy their wishes. The few who did so had internalized their pride and prejudices and were blinded to the possible evils their values might bring to societies suddenly left to their own resources after being held together for centuries by distant authorities.

Those of the elite membership—a large majority—who chose to avoid direct political responsibility were generally content to sit back and give their sanction to the armed forces. The armed forces, after having been nurtured to maturity during a decade and a half of brutal war against Spain, had turned on the liberals. Once they did so liberals were swiftly driven from power.

The Armed Forces

When military officers, who were to lead the attack on the liberals, first exchanged civilian clothes for army uniforms they were filled with idealism. During years of constant war against primitive forces and against primitive nature their loyalty to idealism had given way to frustration, self-pity, and egotism, and then to an exalted conviction of their providential role. Gradually at first, more rapidly later, officers directed their frustrations against stay-at-home merchants and bureaucrats who they believed were using the wars either to enrich themselves or to entrench themselves in power. The stage was set for the disintegration of the moral forces and convictions that undergirded the independence movements. Officers began to worry about their rights in peacetime society and to take a proprietary interest in the governance of the states their swords were carving out of the shattered empires. Faith in the destiny of America became confused with concern for the destiny of individuals.

Discontent within the armed forces was the prelude to insurrection. Armed forces officers were in a frame of mind to listen to those conservative groups ambitious to assert their hegemony over urban intellectual liberals. Assured of the sanction of the landed caste and its urban and religious adherents, officers used their raggle-taggle followers to affront violently and with impunity civilians and constitutions. Any thought of pounding swords into plowshares was forgotten. San Martín was one who remembered. "I am the instrument of order," he wrote Bolívar. He failed to instill his standards in his lieutenants, several of whom proved to be tyrants or near tyrants.

Once the liberators turned upon the liberated the trumpets of civil war reached a crescendo. Intelligence was subordinated to will. Violence became an accepted feature of the political process. Coercion by violence was rationalized for each new situation. Violence and force took on the force of habit. Terrorism was maintained at inordinately high levels. History is replete with examples of rape and pillage by soldiers loosed upon society after prolonged submission to the rigors of war; the liberating armies of Latin America were not content with such acts. Their regiments, like a deadly virus, spread throughout the bodies of the new nations. Armies marched and countermarched. Internecine conflicts without perceived national interest raged throughout the region. As it seemed at the time, and as future events were to confirm, a spark could produce an explosion of anarchy anywhere at any moment. Naked force became the ultimate form of power. Power was in the barrel of guns. Generals, usually with little professional competence and devoid of talent as civilian administrators, came to serve as surrogates for deficiencies in political party organization. They set up and pulled down governments as their and their elite adherents' interests or caprices dictated. They did not seek or need political consensus. They did not need to test their avowed political beliefs because power not doctrine was decisive. Their power could be ended only by uprisings. The coup virtually became the only method of transferring political power. It served the function of elections in the United States. The juridic concept of democracy was not repudiated, it was ignored. All that remained of representative government was its outward manifestations. Under such a state of affairs, armies, not surprisingly, took on a peculiarly domestic orientation. Their officers became more concerned with local matters than with planning their nations' defenses or seeking glory through foreign conquest. Hostility was internal rather than external. Their enemies were their own people, not foreigners.

Civilians were slow to react to generals bent on seizing political power. When and where they did react it was too late, if in fact the opportunity to resist military intrusion into politics ever existed in the emerging states. Civilian reticence is understandable on at least a half-dozen scores. (1) The cult of the successful military hero was as strong then as it is today in much of the world. (2) By Spanish tradition the military was a favored caste, enjoying the special privileges of the *fuero militar*, which, according to Lyle McAlister, in Mexico permitted officers to "make sport of justice, avoid payment of their debts, establish gambling houses, and lead a dissolute life under the protection of their epaulets."[45] Officers of the patriot armies claimed and were normally recognized as entitled to similar privileges and, it followed, being a special group within the wider society. (3) Insurgent armies had appeared spontaneously and with a clear and definite purpose: to fight for independence. They, thus, could wrap themselves in the mantle of liberty and with some justification claim to be the synthesis of nationalism. (4) Because the more privileged elements of society tended to disdain entrepreneurial activities, there was no group to view with contempt the idleness of the soldier, as did the hard-working, money-minded bourgeoisie of England and France, who had small thanks for the soldier who fought to preserve their way of life. (5) The armed forces were the only organized group in society, and that fact alone gave disorganized civilian groups reason to view the militaries with trepidation tempered with considerable caution. (6) Military successes were often the only achievements to which the new societies could point with pride. Poets, essayists, and editors, with good conscience eulogized the soldier and celebrated victories on the battlefields. Lawmakers generously acknowledged the public's indebtedness to liberating forces. Presidents, in their role as commanders-in-chief, felt compelled to promise officers and regulars pensions and other emoluments even when mindful of their lack of obedience to civilian authority.[46] Lavish praise and rewards, as it turned out, nourished only a slightly veiled egregious arrogance in the "heroes."

Once the armed forces established their ability to arbitrate Creole differences, they became such valued allies of the landed class that the one came to lean on the other too much to quarrel seriously. Their differences were of a nature that contending groups could fight for advantage without involving the great body of the population. Thus was formed the oligarchical-military alliances that allowed armies to exact a high financial and political price for the dubious services they rendered.

Irregular Armies

The elevated status that the institutionalized armies came to enjoy did not assure them a monopoly of force and violence. Their influence was at all times subject to challenge by provincial *caudillos*, those men on horseback who personified the virtues and vices of the rural population. Caudillos were usually large landholders with an elementary knowledge of politics and a strong awareness of their own and their class's economic interests. The servile masses were their built-in armed retainers. The forces of nature—rivers, swamps, jungles, deserts, and immense stretches of uninhabited territory—were their trusted allies. With but few exceptions each province had a single urban center upon which all local lines of travel—most of them mere cattle walks—converged. Thus isolated by vast distance from national capitals and cosmopolitan seaboards, where the idea of rebellion and reform had their roots and where customs were introduced, the residents of provincial centers were loyal to their town and their church. For all intents, they were devoid of national sentiment.

Physical isolation from civilizing capitals and even from neighboring provinces produced lasting jealousies and antipathies. Much like their Iberian ancestors, who considered local institutions more vital than central authority, provincial inhabitants were reflexively hostile to any encroachment on their *patria chica* (little fatherland) by contiguous provinces or a central government. This deeply ingrained desire for local autonomy played directly into the hands of caudillos ambitious to extend their fields of operation.

The men on horseback ordinarily were content to be territorial barons, but often enough their lust for power expanded to encompass an entire nation. When a caudillo determined to try his hand at extending his influence beyond his own locale he first cloaked himself in some legal authority such as might be granted by a municipal council he controlled. With his "legal" charter in hand he could seize public funds, levy taxes, make forced loans, and demand levies of soldiers. If ultimately victorious over regional and national opponents he became the *Jefe Supremo*. He ascended the presidential chair from which he imposed the will of the unlettered interior over the capital city.

In power, caudillos freely substituted government by decree for government by laws, but they were not revolutionaries. They viewed issues in very personal, class, or provincial terms. They were content to repress views contrary to their own; they, however, did not try to bridge the gap with ideology as do modern dictators. Neither did they challenge the Catholic Church to such a degree as to invite a show-down with that institution. Nor did they make more than feeble and short-lived attempts to restructure basic social and economic systems. Thus it was that caudillos and armed forces officers—there are numerous examples of officers of the regular armies becoming caudillos once driven from power—with little cost to themselves, without altering the basic values of society, and without threatening the "mansion people," kept the new nations in a state of turbulence that stifled their development by leaving the problems of political infancy unattended. Nonetheless, complete disintegration of some state or region seemed always just around the corner.

The basic conservatism and sense of self-preservation of those who bore arms meant that they were not innovative. Their innate propensity to live by established norms was encouraged by legislators and public functionaries. Legislative bodies were a paradox. Constitutions provided for them. Members were elected to them. In the real world, however, legislators, individually and collectively, most often were political eunuchs. They had the option of ratifying proposed legislation handed down from the executive branch (read the president or *Jefe Supremo*) or be prorogued. Because legislators were without power they had nothing of profound importance to discuss so they had plenty of time to discuss it. That being the case legislators tended to drown issues in a flood of flowery verbiage, and to invest trivial matters with undue significance. The republican members of the Mexican Congress of 1822 were a notable exception to the above characterization. Their public opposition to the emperor Iturbide was instrumental in bringing about his abdication.

Public functionaries, meanwhile, were with few exceptions biologically or maritally related to the rural oligarchs and dependent upon them for employment. These downwardly mobile individuals shared the rural elite's traditions, values, and manorial world view. Lacking training or practical experience in administration and finance, they were incapable of administering even the limited services the governments pretended to provide.[47]

This first generation of crucially placed mediocracy had an almost unblemished record of not tinkering with the values and practices inherited from the colonial epoch. They were content to carry out the wishes of superiors in return for receiving more or less regular salaries (supplemented by *mordidas* [bribes] for service they presumably were paid to provide), and the privilege of residing in the capital or a major port, where they might have early exposure to goods, customs, and news arriving from overseas. Rural areas were left unattended or surrendered to local leaders who were almost always less competent than the incompetent bureaucrats of the capital and more inclined to use public office for political climbing. Incompetence aside, governments based on patronage and personal loyalty were unqualified to serve as objective arbiters of social conflicts, much less to formulate and aggregate common interests.

The Courts

Along with their powerful grip on the executive branches, the legislatures, and the bureaucracies, and their working relationship with those who bore arms, the Creole elites had a hammer lock on the courts. Theoretically the judiciary occupied the same position as in the United States, an independent branch of government serving as the vital link between the government and the governed.[48] In practice the judiciary was hardly distinct from the executive in part because the constitutions that created the highest courts also gave the chief executive, alone or with the approval of one or both bodies of congress (which as noted above turned out to be mere rubber stamps), the privilege of naming judges. Judges, consequently, were almost always subject to manipulation and intimidation before taking the oath of office, and docile instruments of higher authority once on the bench. Judicial veto or even restrictions on presidential decrees were a novelty, and their occurrence meant little to a determined chief executive. Power struggles between the executive and judicial branches, such as occur in functioning democracies, understandably, were unknown. In practice, the role of judges of the highest courts turned out to be little more than putting judicial seals on presidential decrees, abrogating the constitutional rights of the public, censoring the press, certifying the results of fraudulent elections, and distributing the nation's resources as determined by the executive branch.

In dealing with the general public, judges of the lower courts were notorious for their lack of knowledge of the law and their susceptibility to corruption. Successful litigants were relatives or those with resources and determination to carry their cases to the highest courts and, on the way, prepared to buy off avaricious judges.[49] Consul Henry Hill perhaps capsulized the situation in the lower courts when he reported in reference to Brazil, "A poor man has no more chance in court than a cat in hell without claws."[50] And as others noted, "Justice is for friends, laws for enemies." The doctrine of Thrasymachus in Plato's *Republic* that "justice is in the interest of the stronger" was after two millennia alive and well throughout Latin America.

The venality of the courts and the capricious dispensation of justice were a constant against which U.S. businessmen railed to local officials and to agents from Washington. Their railing, however, brought minimal success except perchance they managed somehow to reach one of the individuals who named the judges and controlled the courts.

The Church

Creoles dominated the hierarchies of the ubiquitous Catholic Church, as they did the other areas of social control. For three centuries of imperial rule temporalities and spiritualities were coetaneous. The Crown ruled and the Church provided the adhesive that held colonial society together. The Church's standing became ambiguous during the insurgency when its hierarchies generally favored the Crown over the patriots. The Church, nonetheless, survived the breakup of the empires largely unimpaired. On occasion it was made to submit to forced loans, commonly by anticlerical regimes, and the Creole leadership insisted that Creoles replace Europeans in the Church's hierarchies, but through it all the institution's rating with the public remained high, most especially in nations with a large percentage of Indians.

Three basic forces operated in favor of the Church and largely explain its standing with the public. First, many of its regular and secular clergy, for example, Hidalgo and Morelos in Mexico and Creoles who had taken orders in Argentina, often fostered political and social protest. Second, the Church was the one institution that transcended all political and geographic barriers. Third, it was accepted that Catholicism best expressed the new societies' moral identity and therefore was of all institutions best positioned to promote social harmony. Bolívar was the first among major spokesmen to acknowledge that the Church was a greater social unifier than were the emergent and unstable secular governments, and would remain so for the foreseeable future. After a decade and a half of opposing the Church, he turned back to it as a political ally. In the late 1820s he asked the Archbishop of Bogotá to serve on his advisory council. He restored chaplains to military service. He annulled an 1821 law that abolished convents cloistering fewer than eight persons. He outlawed secret societies (most specifically the anticlerical Masonic Lodge), prohibited the use of Jeremy Bentham's text in higher education, and restored Dominican and Franciscan foundations in Mérida and Maracaibo.[51] To the south in

Chile, Diego Portales (the strongman of the Joaquín Prieto regime that
came to power in 1830), a rank conservative and skeptic but one who
esteemed the Church as an instrument to restrain the popular elements, restored it to the influence it had lost during the independence
struggles and gave it full partnership with the state.

The clinching evidence of the Church's power and influence is
found in the early constitutions of the new nations, nearly all of
which assured it a spiritual monopoly and by extension made it the
interpreter of the social value system.[52] The Mexican Constitution of
1824 was explicit on that subject as others would be. Title I. Article 3
of that charter read, "The religion of the Mexican nation is, and shall
be perpetually, the Catholic Apostolic Roman. The nation protects it
by just and wise laws, and prohibits the exercise of any other."[53]

The Colombian Charter of 1830 reflected the intent of most constituent congresses throughout the region during the half-decade after
their separation from the mother countries. It read: "Title II, The Religion of Colombia, Article 6: The Apostolic Roman Catholic Religion
is the religion of the Republic. Article 7: It is the duty of the Government, in exercising the patronage of the Colombian Church, to protect
it and not tolerate the public exercise of any other religion."[54] Catholic clergyman, meanwhile, were members of legislative bodies, were
frequently employed in the administration of public affairs, and were
the spokesmen for their parishioners on nearly all domestic issues.
Ecclesiastical *fueros* gave the Church rather than the civil courts control over the actions of its clergy in most instances of civil miscon-
duct. That Catholicism was the only recognized creed did not always
keep the Church from being a major target of liberal politicians, but
except for a few extremists no one wanted to destroy it as a religious
institution. Liberals knew, as did the Liberator Bolívar, that for all the
well-founded complaints against it, the Church provided the glue that
kept the disorganized societies from becoming completely unstuck.
The Church, for its part, well aware of its importance and knowing
that its future was more dependent on the devoutness of the rich and
the fanaticism of the poor than on legal statutes, bent only slightly, if
at all, to the will of anything as ephemeral as a civilian political regime.

Over time the Church customarily aligned with the politically
conservative landholders and their military allies. From the Church's
perspective its siding with the conservatives was at once partly a matter of conviction and partly of convenience. The Church approved or
at least condoned much of the less savory aspects of the conservative
agenda, for example, Creole exploitation of Indian labor, African slavery where it was still legal, as in Brazil, and the Creole dominance of

institutional hierarchies. The other flip of the coin was that the Church often needed conservative support in fending off the raids of anticlerical elements bent on confiscating its holdings (the only source of large amounts of wealth readily convertible to liquid capital) and restraining its traditional temporal responsibilities, such as operating schools, hospitals, and charities, the recording and guardianship of such demographic data as births, deaths, and marriages, and the control of cemeteries.

The Church's preferences in domestic politics was of minor concern to the United States in the course of its normal relations with the new states, for example, those involving trade and commerce. There were, however, situations in which churchmen added heat to hemispheric affairs. They connived with politicians engaged in monarchist plots with Catholic France, raising concerns in both the United States and Great Britain. Of a more continuing nature, clerics fueled official and public denunciations of the United States by adding the charge that it was a heathen country and its citizens in league with the devil. On such occasions the clergy had the capability to raise antiforeign hysteria to such a pitch as to endanger the lives and property of North Americans and, thus, to strain official relations.[55]

Economic Conditions

Early enthusiasm in the United States for the political independence of Latin America was only very briefly shared with respect to its economic future and as a trading partner. Information available in the United States by 1820 identified what Anglo-Americans viewed as grave flaws in the economies the colonials were about to inherit. Then, with independence assured, chronic political turbulences and a belief in the United States that American Spaniards lacked entrepreneurial skills seemed certain to make the region's development painfully slow. Within a decade the U.S. government and commercial elements had, in fact, drawn up an impressive list of what were viewed as obstacles to Latin America's economic welfare, and why for the foreseeable future Anglo-Americans had little to gain in aggressively seeking to create incentives for close economic ties.

Land was the most valued commodity in the fledgling states. Throughout the eighteenth century agricultural production had grown in relation to mining. At independence total income from agricultural enterprises, largely limited to supplying the major cities and mining communities, exceeded that from the mining industry. Even in Mexico where mining production expanded steadily during the late eighteenth century, the total income from agriculture, at the end of the colonial period, exceeded that from mining by 25 to 60 percent annually. Anglo-Americans, committed as they were to agriculture, had no problem in recognizing the merits of an economy based on agriculture over one dependent on mining. What they saw as particularly endangering the economic prospects of the region was not agriculture per se, but the terms under which Creoles held land and the purposes for which they valued it.

The United States viewed what confronted the new states' agricultural future and by extension their overall economic well-being as follows. The Crown had granted land to Indian villages to be held in common. It had also awarded land to religious orders, as well as to private individuals, including conquerors, court favorites, and military bureaucrats. Although the grants often entailed extensive plots, they were quite limited in number and, as the colonial period drew to a close, most land remained unallotted. The new governments fell heir to that valuable resource in the form of public domain, along with certain estates seized from loyalists. They promptly awarded much of their inheritance to favored individuals or disposed of it on highly attractive terms to the fortunate recipients. The Catholic Church at once the largest landholder (other than the central government) and lending agency in the colonies, meanwhile, not only finessed every effort to destroy its temporal power by divesting it of its properties, but during the decades following independence, actually added to its direct holdings as the beneficiary of wills, and informally from loans on rural estates that borrowers in lieu of redeeming paid the Church annual rents.[56]

According to contemporary economic thought in the North Atlantic community, to which the new states generally adhered, each of the three major landholding systems suffered at least one serious fault. The transfer of land in accordance with the tenets of capitalism was restricted by the communal practices of the Indian villages, although it is well known that those lands constantly changed hands as a result of encroachments by neighboring *hacendadoes* (large landholders). Ecclesiastical holdings, meanwhile, were held in mortmain and as such did not fit into the Western system which held that both capital and goods must be liquid and that farmers must own their own property as an inducement to produce maximally. The absence of direct taxes on privately held land strongly favored the continuation of the latifundia system. Carried over from the colonial era, latifundia encouraged extensive overintensive farming, for example, livestock raising rather than cultivated crops as a source of income. Furthermore, although privately owned estates changed hands from time to time, the exchanges were between individuals or families possessed of considerable wealth, wealth incidentally commonly acquired in urban enterprises. Each of the landholding systems effectively eliminated in Latin America the embattled small- to medium-sized yeoman farmer in whom Anglo-America had so much faith and was prepared to stake its future progress.

Problems, other than landholding systems, portended a dim future for the new states' agricultural economies. No state had the fiscal resources to overcome grossly inadequate means of transportation. Without improvement in surface transportation agricultural produce could not be exchanged on a national basis and coastal cities would turn their backs on the interiors. Because of the high rates for overland transportation, Buenos Aires, for example, found it cheaper to import foodstuffs from Europe and the United States than from its hinterlands. A ton of goods could be shipped from the port of Guayaquil in Ecuador through the Strait of Magellan to New York for less than over the mountains to Quito, two hundred miles distant. Above all, primitive means of transportation dictated that families with sprawling holdings distant from population centers emphasize the raising of livestock, which could be moved to market on the hoof, rather than bulk commodities such as cereals with potential for markets in industrializing Europe. Also because transportation costs were exorbitant and because armed bandits roamed the countrysides unmolested (law enforcement outside the capitals was usually in name only) large private and ecclesiastical estates tended to look inward and to create self-contained units, producing their own foodstuffs, textiles, pottery, alcoholic beverages, and leather goods.[57] Looking to the future one could assume that large agricultural estates would in only a quite limited way contribute to the development of well-rounded economic societies and domestic markets, much less to the growth of healthy international trade patterns.

Unquestionably, another major deterrent to land fulfilling its potential as an economic stimulant was its being commonly valued for other than its productive capacity. It was an attractive investment because it withstood the ravages of fratricidal wars better than did mines and urban real estate. Marauding armies might burn buildings, destroy irrigation systems, and trample crops, but they left no lasting scars on the land itself. Land also offered probably the safest available hedge against the cheap money policies that the new republics embarked on early in their careers. Most of all, because land had the mark of permanence it helped to make its owners appear to be symbols of stability. For the politically ambitious among them, land conferred social prestige that could be translated into political influence. Everywhere, as noted above, within a decade of independence landholders directly or through their military allies came to dominate governments that protected their well-defined interests. Those interests were, as will be recalled, carryovers from the primitive agricultural societies of the colonial era.

The United States viewed the condition of Latin American agriculture as a long-range problem. The immediate concern to Washington and the North American business community was that their hopes for a flourishing trade with the new societies had been dashed. Scattered reports and centuries of rumors had led Western Europe and the United States to believe that a New World freed of Iberian mercantile practices and embracing the principles of economic liberalism would prove an El Dorado or Garden of Eden. Its treasures of gold and silver, it was imagined, would provide the bullion for a buoyant consumerism,[58] for the rapidly expanding Far East trade, and, in the case of Great Britain, to pay its own armies and help to subsidize those of its allies on the Continent.[59]

On-site inspection quickly made clear that Latin America's mineral future was not nearly so promising as had been envisaged. The richest veins of gold and silver at Potosí, Guanajuato, and Zacatecas had long past been worked. The output of the gold and diamond mines of Brazil had peaked a century earlier. During the wars, mines in the former Spanish colonies had been neglected. Supporting timbers had not been replaced as needed. In some instances, tunnels had flooded. Skilled labor had been drafted into passing armies or had fled to avoid service. In short, the mining industry was in such a state of disrepair that little could be expected by way of increased production without large injections of capital and the introduction of advanced mining technology.[60] The report of United States Minister to Peru Samuel Larned on the economic state of Peru could have as well served as a summary of conditions in every mining society in the region.

> The resources of these countries . . . have been overestimated. The truth, they are poor; and their resources every day diminishing. As respect Peru, her almost entire dependence is upon her mines,—as well the government for its revenues, as individuals for their means of traffick [sic] and support. Her exports, independent of the precious metals, are not sufficient to pay for the bread she consumes! Nothing can be more uncertain and contingent than the profits of the mines. The adventurer in a lottery can count with nearly the same probability upon drawing the high prize. This dependence upon the mines, and the uncertainty attending this occupation, gives rise to frequent fluctuations and great unsteadiness in trade here. When the mines are

productive, money is abundant and trade brisk—introduction and consumption are augmented, the revenue of government increased, and its obligations as well individuals punctually met. The vital current flows circulating freely through the whole social body and produces a corresponding healthy action in all its members. When these [the mines] cease to yield their precious returns everything stagnates. Peru has little to give in payment for foreign goods, than silver and gold—when she has not these, she has nothing; and either she cannot purchase or if she does she cannot pay.[61]

With metallic currency and bullion in short supply and getting shorter, with agricultural production for export not expanding,[62] and with the demand for U.S. products in decline once liberty was won, the prospects for North America to carry on a profitable commerce with Latin America were bleak. Secretary Adams, as early as March 1821 had recorded in his *Memoirs* that he had little expectation of any beneficial result to the United States from future commerce with the area: "They want none of our production, and we could afford to purchase very few of theirs."[63]

It did not take long for Adams's prognostication to be validated. The war-induced pent-up demand for those products that the United States had for export—wheat flour, coarse cottons, forest products, candles, soap, and salted codfish—was quickly met and the market for them soon hinged on the level of political and social tranquillity, and the output of mines in the new states. The East Coast found it hard to believe how badly trade with Latin America had been overestimated. Newspapers, journals, and government officials anguished over the situation. Nowhere did markets evolve as anticipated. Buenos Aires had been thought to hold considerable commercial promise, but domestic disturbances repeatedly caused disappointment to traders. Overstocking and consequent low prices seemed the order of the day. "There never was a market in so deplorable a state."[64] Traders with Argentina in mind were warned that they were at the mercy of buyers whose reputations for business practices were questionable,[65] and must be prepared to sell at ruinous prices.[66] A merchant who came off "with a living profit" was in a distinct minority.[67] Vessels entering Valparaiso, Chile, during June 1825 could not sell their cargoes;[68] and by mid-1829 the Valparaiso market was in a slump due to political disorders.[69] Conditions for trade in Peru were generally unfavorable.[70] In the Lima area, Chilean wheat was driving U.S. wheat and flour from the market[71] and trade was threatened with complete annihilation because of excessive duties.[72] A frustrated U.S. minister reported from there that there was no prospect of retaliation because Peruvian vessels never visited U.S. ports. The choice, thus, became one of abandoning the trade or carrying on according to terms laid down by Lima.[73]

Reports from Brazil were abundant and nearly always overwhelmingly depressing. The Rio market was overstocked. Trade with its port was not considered to be worth pursuing and there was not the least chance of improvement as long as the war with Buenos Aires lasted.[74] The Bahia market was "dull" for all articles of U.S. produce,[75] and "bad" in La Guaira, Venezuela. In La Guaira flour was the only article wanted and demand for it was limited.[76] A year later only the necessaries of life would sell.[77] In neighboring Puerto Cabello, business of every kind was at a "stand" and collections could not be made from persons who had bought goods on credit.[78] From Cartagena, Colombia, came word that the price of flour could produce a profit, but it was "true" that a very small supply was apt to stock the market. That not a single U.S. vessel had entered Cartagena in three months was indicative of the size of demand for its produce.[79] The Santo Domingo market was completely oversupplied with all kinds of American produce.[80] Commerce in Cape Haytian, Haiti, was "deplorable," and there was growing apprehension for the future.[81] Mexico was originally believed to offer considerable trading possibilities but like Buenos Aires it, too, proved a disappointment because of chronic political instability.[82] As early as mid-1825 U.S. produce was "a mere drug" on the Mexican market.[83] Veracruz was "very sickly" and demand was quite "dull" as a consequence.[84] The next year Veracruz continued to be sickly, "money was scarce," and the state of commerce "deplorable." There were two years' stocks in the market and no money to pay for them.[85] To the obstacles to trade created by man was added the greatest hazard of all: the price of miscalculating the start and the end of the yellow fever season.

In September 1828 the *Newport Mercury* summarized the situation throughout Latin America with the single word *bad*.[86] Thus by 1829 all thought of a flourishing trade with the new polities had vanished, not to be revived for a half-century, by which time the United States was well on its way to becoming an industrial power seeking markets for its manufactures.[87] The emerging societies, despite having embraced the concept of commercial liberalism of the North Atlantic community, had failed to send out any signals that they were about to play a significant role in the international economy.

Several reasons other than political instability within an essentially static social order accounted for the unfavorable commercial climate. Furthermore the United States could do little to correct the situation. The most apparent explanation for its poor showing was the British successes in the region. Great Britain had begun to outstrip North American traders during the war years. By 1822 the volume and value of U.S. commerce with Latin America were less than half those of England's and U.S. emissaries were chafing under the swelling British preeminence in trade and influence with the new governments.[88] And there were no indications that Great Britain's advantage would soon be challenged. Secretary Adams had taken a realistic view of the situation in June 1822. He recorded in his diary, "Do what we can, the commerce with South America will be much more important and useful to Great Britain than to us, and Great Britain will be a power vastly more important to them [the new states] than we, for the simple reason that she has the power of supplying their want by her manufacture. We have few such supplies to furnish them."[89]

By 1825 it was abundantly evident within government circles in Washington and in the port cities of the Atlantic seaboard that Great Britain's ability to provide the Latin American elites with a wide variety of manufactures of better quality, at cheaper prices, and usually on better terms was but one edge it had over the United States. It had also endeared itself with the new political leadership by flooding the cash-short states with public loans and investing in mining ventures that seemed to portend future prosperity[90] and by maintaining a naval shield that guaranteed the new polities protection from European aggressions. The English hardly needed any additional advantage over the United States, but they had one in that, being aristocratic themselves, they were better able than North Americans to appreciate the historical experience that informed Latin America opinion.

The British were a problem for U.S. commercial interests, but not so great a problem as was Latin America itself. North American businessmen could readily understand British competition, but they had trouble with the Latin American values, many features of which were incongruent with what North Americans considered their social-economic priorities. According to North American conventional wisdom Latin Americans were improvident and inclined to expend their limited resources on nonessentials of the kind the United States was not as yet manufacturing. British Consul General in Peru Charles Ricketts took note of that trait when he informed the Home Office that "so great has been the avidity of the Peruvian females to acquire their [French] trifles that their merchants have latterly usurped the money which should have been paid to English creditors."[91] Especially disturbing was the degree to which personal relationships entered into business matters. Creole merchants used their personal and family connections to obtain legislative and judicial protection rather than compete openly with foreigners in the marketplace.

At least four domestic conditions had long-range negative consequences for international commerce. First, until 1850 and in most cases well beyond that decade, the governments of the various states failed to provide political protection beyond the immediate environs of the capital cities. Armed bands preyed on merchants using the major trade routes, for example, between Mexico City and Veracruz and between Buenos Aires and Tucumán, necessitating the hiring of private security forces. Second, the grossly unequal distribution of wealth and income guaranteed that for the future only a small segment of the total population made up of the mansion people, upper-level public and military bureaucrats, selected members of the clergy, a few professionals, and foreigners residing in scattered urban centers would have the wherewithal for more than the bare necessaries. Third, those with accumulated capital tended to shy away from investing in enterprises that would have created employment for individuals to earn sufficient wages to enter the domestic markets.[92] Fourth, Latin Americans could not be dependable trading partners as long as they relied on extractive industries for their purchasing power; those industries by their very nature enriched only a few and did practically nothing to expand the labor force.[93]

Finally, the U.S. government itself was, in a sense, guilty of laming the country's competitive position in Latin America. To a degree, admittedly unmeasurable, North American merchants were often victimized by the actions of official agents sent to protect their interests. The diplomatic and consular services were new and appointments to them were often treated as little more than "patronage plums."[94] London and the capitals of Western European countries were the most desired posts and as a rule went to qualified individuals, including such well-known statesmen as John Quincy Adams, Richard Rush, and Rufus King (London), Albert Gallatin and James Brown (Paris), and John Forsyth (Madrid). Latin America, outside regular channels of communication, backward by U.S. and Western European standards, politically unstable with limited security forces, plagued by epidemics, and with quite limited medical services, was considered a "dumping ground."[95] Inexperienced in diplomacy, and sharing their fellow citizens' ethnocentric view that all societies would benefit from adopting U.S. values and presumed standards of public service, ministers, chargé d'affaires, special agents, and consuls named to Latin American posts freely took sides in domestic politics. Among the better known cases during the early nineteenth century of agents acting irresponsibly were those of Joel R. Poinsett, who involved himself in the independence struggle in Chile and later participated openly in Mexican politics;[96] Baptis Irvine in Venezuela;[97] John B. Prevost, who was ordered to leave Buenos Aires; Condy Raguet, consul at Rio de Janeiro, whose hasty actions over a minor issue could, under different circumstances, have led to war;[98] William Henry Harrison, who was declared persona non grata after seeking to inform Liberator Simón Bolívar of the errors of his ways;[99] and Anthony Butler in Mexico.[100]

John M. Forbes and William Tudor were two agents who added some luster to this service. Forbes held various posts in Buenos Aires from 1820 until his death there in 1831. During a decade when Buenos Aires suffered tumult, bloodshed, and swift changes in the power structure, he blended force with dignity in ways that won him the acclaim of Argentines of different persuasions. William Tudor, consul in Lima beginning in 1820 and from 1827 to 1830 chargé d'affaires in Rio de Janeiro, where he died after a prolonged illness, was a major literary figure in Boston and the first editor of the *North American Review*. He won the respect of official Brazil by consistently acting in accordance with correct diplomatic practices, including respect for those with whom he was in constant negotiations over difficult commercial issues.

The conduct of U.S. agents, including their occasional vilifying of one another and siding with those who opposed their superiors in Washington had a chilling effect on the respect that Latin American statesmen had for the United States.[101] But it was the truly chilling words from Washington that put Latin America's respect to the full test. Politicians bent on expanding the nation's territorial limits at Latin America's and especially Mexico's expense were loudly vocalizing their demands. Official Washington, meanwhile, was warning Colombia and Mexico off Cuba. And the liberal racial views of the various Latin American nations were being brought under attack in Congress. Latin Americans had few ways to vent their displeasure with their northern neighbor. One avenue open to them was to take measures in the form of exclusionary legislation and discriminatory tariffs against North American traders. I have not a shred of evidence that the problems faced by U.S. merchants in Latin American during the 1820s were rooted in the too often unsavory behavior of U.S. agents assigned to the area or in the ethnocentric rhetoric of "Manifest Destiny" types in Washington. My guess is that they were and I do not find the thought at all fanciful. Be that as it may, by the late 1820s Latin Americas would have been less than human if they had not taken some retaliatory action, and the regulation of trade was the one most ready at hand.

The Implications of Instability

Thought and ideology were not to be motors of development in the former colonies. Those who had provided the philosophical content of the insurgent cause failed in peacetime to find the prescription for building a following without provoking opposition forces, and were quickly supplanted politically. Knowledge ceased to confer power. With their influence curtailed all thought of majoritarian consensus and of established constitutional government abruptly dissipated. They were succeeded by an exclusive circle of obscurantist property owners, allied with opportunistic military officers and bureaucrats or provincial caudillos, in command of servile followers.

Although these elites agreed on the preservation of Hispanic values, their desperate struggles with one another for political and economic advantage kept the new nations in a state of violent convulsions. Everything was unstable except the idea of instability. Everywhere there were cynical disavowals of integrity and good faith. Cruelty and terrorism were substituted for electoral campaigns. Winning factions, once installed in power, left no political space in which the opposition might maneuver within the government structure. Because there was no sharing of the political arena, popular sovereignty could not exist. Political competitions became a superficial phenomenon. Irrespective of political forms and nomenclature each regime seemed as socially repressive and economically repressive as the one before it. Societies remained highly stratified along racial and socialeconomic lines. Economic inequalities were legitimized by tradition and laws that mirrored the economic interests of the landholders. The rights of individuals were conspicuous by their absence. Any hope of the popular elements for judicial equality were squashed by corrupt courts.

By the close of the decade of the 1820s the popular elements had been quieted, but the elite power struggles had brought all of Latin America to the brink of political anarchy. In Mexico, in 1829 the old revolutionary become president, Vicente Guerrero, was overthrown and executed on February 14, 1831; and the unbalanced Antonio López de Santa Anna was masterminding revolt that would land him in the presidency in 1832. In Central America, José Arce, unable to weld together the five states of the Confederation, resigned the presidency. In 1821 Santo Domingo had proclaimed its independence from Spain and the next year fell victim to Haitian armies and remained under the ever-threatening control of Haiti until 1844. In South America, Peru and Colombia were, in 1828, locked in desultory combat. Colombia, the handiwork of Bolívar, was breaking up with Venezuela, splitting off in November 1829, and Ecuador in September 1830. Bolívar, the towering figure of the entire independence movement, resigned the presidency of Colombia and died in Santa Marta in June 1830 while on his way to self-imposed exile. Francisco de Paula Santander, vice president under Bolívar and the individual most responsible for keeping the Colombian armies under the Liberator in men and supplies through the war years, was saved from execution by being sentenced to exile in 1828. Antonio de Sucre, talented and respected lieutenant of Bolívar, victor of Ayacucho, and for a time president of Bolivia, was assassinated in June 1830. Civil wars between leaders who had achieved prominence during the war years had brought Peru to near political anarchy by 1830. In Chile, a series of civil wars ended only in April 1830 with the victory of conservative General Joaquín Prieto. In Argentina, President Manuel Dorrego was overthrown and executed in 1828 by Juan Lavalle, who in turn was defeated by the tyrant Juan Manuel Rosas, who ascended the presidency in December 1829. Uruguay, contended for by Argentina and Brazil for over a decade, was declared an independent nation in 1828 and almost immediately fell prey to local chieftains. In Brazil, Pedro I, having failed to uphold Brazil's claims to Uruguay and confronted by a series of local uprising, chose to abdicate in 1831.[102]

What were North Americans, with their limited forbearance of foreigners and by 1830 well on their way to their "Manifest Destiny," to make of Latin America's political tumult and economic stagnation? Their initial reaction toward the insurgents had been one of hope mingled with large doses of misgivings. Then, when the chasm separating the two cultures proved wider than foreseen, and worse, the prospect of it narrowing seemed remote, the impression grew that Latin America would remain in an arrested state of development. Furthermore, Great Britain would be the chief beneficiary of any economic good that might come out of the retarded region. The situation being what it was, and by 1830 assured that the new Spanish states would embrace republicanism and that lack of social harmony and their repeated political buffetings precluded their posing a threat to U.S. security interests, Washington confidently redefined its objectives and strategies in ways that reduced the new states, Mexico excepted, to a role of secondary importance.

4 THE BRITISH IMPACT ON UNITED STATES–LATIN AMERICAN RELATIONS

The Treaty of Ghent formally ended the War of 1812, but left unresolved several issues that had contributed to the outbreak of hostilities. From Washington's perspective, the most serious omission was the treaty's failure to deal with impressment and search as practiced on the high seas by Great Britain. From London's vantage point, the treaty had done nothing to check the advance of the United States, already the major challenger to Great Britain's commercial supremacy in the Atlantic community and, after the downfall of Napoleon, the remaining source of Jacobin infection. Differences over fishing rights on the Newfoundland banks, fortifications on the Great Lakes, relations with the Indian tribes of the Old Northwest, and the parceling of the Pacific Northwest wilderness, all unattended by the treaty, remained as potential sources of tension. Later, the British West Indian trade opened up yet another area of possible discord. Finally, an adversary relationship existing between Secretary of State, and later President, John Quincy Adams and Foreign Secretary, and later Prime Minister, George Canning, key decision makers during much of the period under review, negatively influenced relations between the two governments.

In the spirit of the age contemporaries were inclined to accept that major international issues must ultimately be decided in combat and, thus, that the Treaty of Ghent would at best postpone the day of another military confrontation between the two powers. In that vein politicians, propagandists, and editors on both sides of the Atlantic voiced charges which were amplified by a loud and effective *vox populi* of war persuasion and against which the appeals of peace advocates were drowned.[1] Ex-president John Adams wrote Jefferson, "Britain will never be our friend till we are her master."[2] Kentuckian Henry Clay in 1816 declared that "man must be blind to the indications of the future, who cannot see that we are destined to war after war with Great Britain until, if one of the two nations be not crushed, all grounds of collision shall have ceased between us."[3] In the same year the *Weekly Register* informed its readers that "if there be such things as a 'natural enemy' between nations . . . Great Britain must be such an enemy to this nation."[4] A month later the *Daily National Intelligencer*, organ of the Madison administration, reported: "It has been predicted by our most perspicacious statesmen, that future wars of a sanguinary character are to take place between Great-Britain and the U. States.— These are events which, though perhaps as certain as mortality to man, it is agreeable to be enabled to believe are placed at a remote distance from us."[5] In January 1820 the *Weekly Register* returned to the fray with a prediction that war would result from the United States acquiring Florida.[6] The British media was no less convinced that the clash of interests between the two powers would be continuous.[7]

That warfare had infected minds in the United States and Great Britain and that armed combat was viewed as the instrument for the resolution of differences between nations not only found expression among contemporaries but also in later generations of authors writing on U.S.–British relations with Latin America, during and subsequent to the collapse of the Iberian New World empires. I believe those authors mistaken who over time have held that competition for favor and commerce in Latin America carried with it a grave threat of armed conflict between the United States and Great Britain. They failed, I hold, to give sufficient weight to those fundamentals that favored cooperation, if not friendship, while basing their analysis too heavily on adversarial relationships, the suspicions of often poorly qualified diplomats, the fervid prose and slurs that wounded national sensitivities, and fears that one or the other power would engage in a preemptive strike to protect its interests in some commercially or strategically important land mass. This chapter makes a case for a closer look at the fundamentals in order better to understand why the United States and Great Britain, despite bickerings and occasional displays of bravado, not only averted war, but by 1830 had achieved sufficient agreement on all important issues relating to Latin America that each could go about exploiting the region as best it could without fear of the resort to force from the other.

This chapter surveys on two levels U.S.-British responses responses to developments arising out of insurgency and independence in Latin America between 1815 and 1830. It first reviews those developments upon which the two nations were in basic agreement and which favored mutual acceptance when not actual cooperation. It then discusses two issues—the Family Compact concept and the disposition of Cuba and its neighboring islands—which could have sparked a war at any time prior to their resolution.

Areas of Agreement

Realistically the immediate future of large areas within Spain's crumbling New World empire—for instance, Cuba, the Floridas, Texas, Central America, the Banda Oriental (Uraguay) and the island of Chiloé off the coast of Chile—rested primarily in the hands of Great Britain and the United States. That the two Anglo-Saxon powers would dominate economic relations with the new states was equally apparent. By 1819 Spain was hanging on by its fingernails. Portugal had been and remained a satellite of Great Britain. The new nations themselves, torn by dissension, with undisciplined armies and nonexistent navies, and jealous of one another, were in no condition to withstand a determined attack upon their territorial flanks by a major seafaring power.[8] Given their unchallenged statuses and divergent goals, London and Washington might well have escalated tensions over a number of developments. They chose not do do so; rather they sought grounds for conciliation on a number of matters and kept well within acceptable bounds strains over those differences with the potential for serious conflict.

The first in a sequence of developments in Latin America on which the United States and Great Britain were in essential accord in their responses actually antedated the War of 1812. The development was the unanticipated successes of the Haitian revolutionary, Toussaint L'Ouverture, against the French colonial government. The objective on which Washington and London collaborated was to prevent the Haitian revolution from spreading to neighboring islands and Louisiana. The objective was achieved and demonstrated the ability of the two Anglo-Saxon nations to cooperate when dealing with controversies.[9]

With the onset of insurgency in Spanish America developments that favored collaboration between the two nations multiplied. The first such occasion for keeping potential controversy from overheating occurred when Washington and London took opposed positions on the future of Spain's New World empire. From the outbreak of the independence struggles the United States favored full emancipation of the colonies. For its part, Great Britain, enmeshed in European diplomacy and still at war with Napoleon, assumed the role of mediator between Spain and its colonies, with the objectives of holding the empire together, but of the colonies being granted increased autonomy and Spain being stripped of its historical monopoly on legal trade with them.

Washington's and London's preferences did not become grounds for discord, because, once having established them, each side elected to pursue a policy of neutrality which in effect became neutrality in favor of the patriots. The United States, as noted in the preceding chapter, legislated neutrality laws which its citizens circumvented in their pursuit of keeping the insurgents provided with war material, ship supplies, and often with crews they needed to sustain their struggle. His Majesty's Government passed neutrality laws[10] that were as ineffective as those of the United States. While British mediators shuttled back and forth between London and the Peninsula and Whitehall stubbornly denied the beleaguered colonials belligerent status until 1819,[11] British subjects openly flaunted official neutrality.

Practically from day one, British naval officers and sailors were prominent in the insurgent navies. Then, with the Napoleonic Wars at an end and England's economy sagging, young British and Irish males turned to Latin America in search of employment for which they had been bred or simply in search of adventure. In 1818 alone, six British expeditionary forces were illegally dispatched to South America's North Coast. There they were formed into the "British Legion." Its ranks filled with seasoned and disciplined men, commanded by experienced officers, the Legion served brilliantly under Bolívar. The passage of the Foreign Enlistment Act in 1819 did not curb the enthusiasm for the insurgents. Agents for the patriots recruited openly in Ireland. British and Irish troops other than those in the Legion ultimately fought in every region of South America where war raged. British war materiél, meanwhile, arrived by the shipload. In a cynical way some British merchants were more respectful of their nation's neutrality than were soldiers and sailors. In Peru, for example, when the struggles were reaching a climax, British merchants reportedly supplied "with an impartial neutrality both parties with all the means of war they have . . . and even trust both parties still."[12] British support of the colonies, particularly in the form of fighting personnel, was for everyone to see, and their presence had the effect of helping to convince the insurgents that England, not the United States, was their true friend and ally.[13]

By 1819 Washington and London had concluded that Spain was doomed. That decision reached, the stage was set for recognition of the patriots, clearly an unneutral act. Soon after the United States began to recognize the new governments, it further revealed its partisanship in President Monroe's Annual Message of 1823 in which he laid down the two-sphere concept. Great Britain with the powerful Royal Navy at its command, moved more slowly and subtly, but no less determinedly. It removed all vestiges of neutrality when in a communication to the French ambassador in London, the Prince de Polignac, Foreign Minister George Canning informed France and the Holy Alliance that their interference in the New World in support of Madrid would not be tolerated.[14]

Neutrality again failed to become an issue when war erupted in 1825 between Brazil and Argentina over control of the Banda Oriental (Uruguay). In that crisis Washington and London played roles earlier rehearsed during the independence struggles. The United States declared its neutrality, but clearly favored Argentina. Great Britain again assumed the role of mediator, while also favoring the Argentines.

U.S. and British neutrality in the wars involving Spanish and Portuguese America ultimately led to friendly cooperation when the two powers moved to protect their merchantmen from pirates and privateers infesting the Caribbean and the waters off the East and West coasts of South America. The advantages of cooperation in the war against what Washington and London alleged to be illegal attacks upon neutral shipping arose when Spain failed to take adequate measures against pirates using the harbors and inlets of Cuba and Puerto Rico for refuge, refitting, and concealing captured ships and cargoes, and both Spain and the insurgent governments licensed privateers who commonly did not distinguish between enemy and neutral shipping. Later when Argentina and Brazil went to war over the Banda Oriental and resorted to widespread use of privateers, Washington and London again found grounds for cooperation.[15]

The use of private vessels (privateers) had peaked in the North Atlantic during the decades before the War of 1812, when western seafaring nations, including the United States and Great Britain, sanctioned the practice. When Spain and its insurgent colonies found themselves without meaningful navies, privateering was ready-made for them and they quickly adopted it. The simple issuance of letters of marque and reprisal licensed the recipients to engage in privateering, and they were in business. Blank commissions were meted out freely and many fell into the hands of nonnationals and individuals who had never so much as set foot in the country under whose flag they operated.

In the view of the United States and Great Britain, privateering, as sanctioned by Spain and the insurgents, was indistinguishable from outright piracy,[16] and they so argued in their correspondence and exchanges with the governments involved. Since the State Department and the Foreign Office ordinarily did not make discernible distinctions between pirates (piracy) and privateers (privateering) I will, in the interest of brevity, use the terms interchangeably below.

In principle the United States and Great Britain were in full agreement in their opposition to unregulated privateering. Because they were at once sympathetic to and seeking the favor of the revolutionaries, both foreign offices, however, initially assumed a wait-and-see attitude. President Monroe could have been speaking for both the State Department and the Foreign Office when he acknowledged the concerns of shippers and traders while he was actually pursuing a policy that (1) implicitly recognized that, for peoples without merchant marines, diplomatic wrangling over privateering was a small price to pay in return for the benefits derived and (2) avoided actions that might unduly embarrass the new states, and invite retaliation in the future.[17] National self-interest also figured in Monroe's stance. In particular, he feared that unrestrained privateering might lead to European intervention in the hemisphere.[18]

The depredations of privateers and pirates could not be indulged indefinitely, however. Trading communities in the United States and England simply carried too great a political clout. While Monroe hesitated, others, who considered any crew who committed acts unknown to "civilized warfare" as prima facie pirates, fueled the controversy. Less generous in his views of London than was Monroe, Secretary of State John Quincy Adams was a member of that group. In his instructions to the Rodney-Bland-Graham Commission, Adams called attention to "irregular, injurious, and . . . unwarranted use of their [the insurgents] flags and of commissions real or pretended derived from them" and instructed the commissioners to "remonstrate . . . in the most serious manner against the practice of issuing indiscriminate commissions to the abandoned and desperate characters of all other nations," whose objects in using their authority and flags were not to promote the cause of liberty and independence, but merely to amass plunder for themselves.[19]

Earlier in 1817 Washington had made clear its exasperation with the inability or unwillingness of the warring parties to control their privateers when U.S. gunboats participated in the capture of Amelia Island, a Caribbean paradise for privateers and smugglers, and "a receptacle for fugitive negroes,"[20] and the USS *Ontario* was dispatched to the Pacific to protect U.S. interests, especially the whaling fleet, endangered by Spanish privateers.[21] In 1819 the United States added to the pressure. It assigned the USS *Firebrand* to the Caribbean to watch for privateers and pirates; and Congress passed the Piracy Act. That piece of legislation empowered the president to order all commanders of the nation's publicly owned ships to take any armed vessel "which shall have attempted or committed any piratical aggression, search, restraint, depredation, or seizure upon any vessel of the United States, or of the citizens thereof, or upon any other vessel: and also, to retake any vessel of the United States, or its citizens which may have been unlawfully captured upon the high seas."[22] Privateers and pirates,

nonetheless, continued to operate; during the year following the enactment of the Piracy Act two Baltimore citizens were convicted of
piracy and executed and others followed them to the gallows.[23]

Privateering and piracy in the Caribbean and to the south commanded the attention of the United States throughout the 1820s. In
1822 Captain James Biddle of the frigate *Macedonian*, according to
British Consul H. T. Kilbee in Havana, requested of the Captain General of Cuba permission to land troops on the island in pursuit of pirates and was "highly offended" when his request was refused. Kilbee
continued, "It has long been a favorite doctrine of the Americans and
particularly of the officers of the American navy that the Spanish governments are unable to protect their own coast, they must consent to
allow foreigners who are the principal sufferers to assist them."[24]

The most notorious U.S. response to privateering and piracy in
the Caribbean is associated with Commodore David Porter. In 1823
Porter took command of the "Caribbean Squadron." He was known to
be an impetuous individual who firmly believed that "illegal privateers" and pirates should not be given quarter. When one of his lieutenants landed at Fajardo, Puerto Rico, in pursuit of "pirates" and was
"abused" by Spanish officials, Porter quickly concluded that his lieutenant had been prevented from doing his duty and that the United
States flag had been willfully insulted. With a landing party of seamen
and marines he marched into town and informed the alcalde that he
was there to demand satisfaction for outrages heaped upon a United
States officer and for aggravated insult to the national flag. The alcalde was allowed one hour for deliberation. The officials gave Porter a
public apology and promises they would thereafter respect United
States officers. Thereupon Porter returned to his boat and embarked.
He had intimidated Spanish officials but not his superiors. He was recalled to Washington and court-martialed for having taken hostile actions against a friendly power.[25]

President Monroe took notice of the problems raised by pirates
and privateers in his message to Congress on December 2, 1823. Although he would have preferred to be conciliatory toward the new
states, he felt obliged to devote more space in the message to the question of illegal seizure of U.S. vessels and the methods to control the
responsible parties than to the now famous doctrine itself. The number of prizes taken by privateers appears to have dropped temporarily
following Monroe's declaration, thanks in part to measures taken
against them by Argentina,[26] but rose sharply when Spanish naval
forces and privateers operating out of Cuban and Puerto Rican bases
stepped up the pressure on Mexico and Colombia, and Mexico City
and Bogotá responded by commissioning privateers. Also, as alluded

to above, when Argentina and Brazil renewed their struggle over the Banda Oriental, privateers quickly swarmed into the Caribbean and the waters off the coast of Brazil.[27] The problem had not abated, and Secretary of State Henry Clay, in his instruction to envoys to the Panama Congress, devoted considerable space to the need for the cooperation of the new states in the battle. The Latin American states, for their part, were not yet able or willing to join the battle, which was not finally won until the United States Navy obtained a sufficient number of sloops and schooners that drew little water and thus could enter inlets and attack the enemy in their secluded hideouts.[28]

The British Foreign Office and especially the English trading community applauded U.S. aggressiveness. The Foreign Office, however, despite its approval of U.S. measures, wavered between being firm and conciliatory, a policy that resulted in Great Britain failing consistently to act as strongly against the provocateurs as did the United States. The policy of the Foreign Office can be explained on several grounds. When privateers flying the flags of Spain and the insurgents began to range New World waters in large numbers, London was playing the role of mediator between Spain and the colonies. Also, far stronger than the United States and deferred to by most groups involved in the breakup of the empires and the creation of new societies, Great Britain, by cajoling and threat, was ordinarily more successful than the United States in obtaining satisfaction through diplomatic channels. Probably the overriding concern of British officialdom was that the right of visitation and search had proved invaluable to England, and to preserve it inviolate the Royal Navy dared not systematically deny the "right" to others. In an extended editorial on the subject of privateering during the war between Brazil and Argentina the *Times* reminded its readers that there was more than one side to the subject:

> ... that the conduct observed by England towards neutral powers, when she was herself a belligerent, has established a precedent capable of much abuse, and convertible to vexatious purposes against her commerce, now that she has ceased to be a belligerent, and that others who are engaged in war conceive themselves justified in applying to her the measures which she set the example of employing towards other neutrals.[29]

The British business community was deeply disturbed that its government was less attentive to their concerns than the U.S. government was to the problems of its citizens, and often took occasion to vent their feelings. For example, when the U.S. strike force in the Caribbean captured and restored to their rightful British owners ships that had been taken by pirates and privateers, the United States was praised in Parliament and newspapers and the Admiralty accused of supineness.[30] As late as 1828 the *Times* continued to level charges against the Admiralty for its failure to protect British merchant ships and their cargoes. In commenting on an incident involving the seizure by a Mexican privateer of a U.S. brig, the *Times*, apparently ignoring the attacks by pirates and privateers for over a decade on U.S. merchant ships, exalted, "Now that they have commenced plundering American vessels, there may be some chance of a stop being put to those shameful piracies."[31]

Blockades decreed from time to time by Spain and the former members of its empire provided another area for mutual understanding between Washington and London. They contended that their blockades were invalid and in violation of established practices of international law because the warring parties lacked the naval resources systematically to patrol the vast coastlines they decreed out of bounds to neutrals. A brief review of the U.S. and British responses to the problem of blockades must suffice. As early as 1819 a U.S. warship ran a blockade imposed by Chile on the Peruvian coast. Two years later, largely in response to Chile's "paper blockade," the United States established the Pacific Squadron with responsibilities extending from Chile all the way to Mexico and California.[32] In 1822 a West Indian Squadron was established, an in 1826 the Navy Department created a South Atlantic Squadron to patrol the East Coast of South America.[33] At that point, three of the four existing U.S. squadrons were in the Latin American zone, the fourth being in the Mediterranean. In each case the purpose was to curb privateering, piracy, and alleged blockades.[34] In 1823 Secretary Adams justified breaking a Chilean blockade on the grounds that "the principle is too important to be surrendered to any belligerent power, however favorably disposed one may be to his course; for we cannot concede it to him without yielding it alike to his enemy."[35] The following year Adams turned his attention to the Caribbean where Spain had proclaimed a blockade of the Venezuelan coast. He wrote to the United States minister posted to Madrid:

> The renewal of war in Venezuela has been signalized on the part of Spanish commanders by proclamations of blockade unwarranted by the laws of nations, and by decree regardless of those of humanity. With no other naval force than a single frigate, a brig, and a schooner . . . they have presumed to declare a blockade of more than twelve hundred miles of coast, an outrage to which the United States would not submit.[36]

United States Chargé d'Affaires in Buenos Aires John M. Forbes, reaffirmed Washington's stance in a communication to Vice Admiral Rodrigo José Ferreira Lobo in command of the Brazilian blockading fleet in Argentine waters. Forbes insisted that a blockade of an extensive coast, "not supported by the active presence of a naval power competent to enforce its simultaneous, constant, and effective operation on every point of such coast, is illegal throughout its whole extent, even for ports which may be in actual blockade." Since Brazil had declared 20 degrees latitude of the Argentine coast in blockade and had assigned a single corvette to enforce the decree, he continued, "If . . . there can exist anything like an imaginary blockade, this is, most unequivocally, one of that description and consequently wholly inadmissible on the part of the Government of the United States."[37]

The sheer lack of sufficient naval forces to effect blockades drew most of Washington's fire but by no means all of it. During the 1820s it registered almost every conceivable complaint against the blockading powers. After Bolívar declared the coast of Peru in a state of blockade it was reported to the State Department that his naval officers would allow ships to violate the decree in return for a fee, thereby making the purpose of the blockade to pillage neutrals rather than to distress the enemy.[38] During a debate in the United States Congress over Brazil's "paper blockade" or "alleged blockade" of the Argentine coast, with consequent "embarrassment" of U.S. commerce, a series of indictments were leveled against the court in Rio de Janeiro. It was charged with cupidity and rapacity, using the blockade as a justification for violating neutral rights, requiring ships sailing southward to be bonded against entering Argentine ports (an unnecessary burden on shipowners and striking evidence that the blockade was ineffective), sanctioning the practice of blockading ships and not distinguishing between vessels that may have been attempting to elude the blockade and those in distress and seeking a hospitable port, and holding United States citizens illegally. Such harassments of neutrals and the Brazilian government's unacceptable responses to official complaints against them had led the United States consul at Rio de Janeiro, Condy Raguet, to affront the Brazilian government by demanding his passport without prior approval of the State Department.[39]

London was as outraged as was Washington over the vexations caused neutrals by paper blockades proclaimed by Spain and the new governments. The language used in one official report left no doubt about the British view. Because it spells out in some detail the British position on blockades I quote at length from it. This particular communication was from Thomas Hardy, commander of the British fleet in South American waters, to Bernardo O'Higgins, supreme director of the Republic of Chile, and dated September 27, 1820.

> I beg . . . to point out to your Excellency, after the fullest consideration: the inadequacy of the force to be employed effectually to constitute the Blockade of even a very limited portion of this extensive coast—and the reason why the present Proclamation ought not to effect neutral commerce in those parts of the Coast said to be blockaded.
>
> The Government of His Britannic Majesty are well aware that a Blockade cannot be considered illegal merely on the grounds of its extent, yet this legality must eventually depend according to the law of nations upon the adequacy of the Blockading force to hold the Ports and coasts intended to be blockaded, in such a constant state of blockade that no vessel can enter or depart without eminent danger of detention—that if the force is inadequate to enforce the blockade generally, the whole in all its part is thereby null and void, nor can the blockading ships enforce it partially when they happen to be present. . . .
>
> Upon these grounds the alleged Blockade of the Coasts in question, must in the judgment of His Britannic Majesty be denied and taken to be wholly illegal—and consequently I find myself called upon to protest in the strongest manner for the reasons before stated, against the legality of the Blockade—and I trust that your excellency will be pleased to cause the Proclamation of Blockade to be so modified or altered and such further orders given to the Commander of the Blockading squadron as may prevent any restraint not warranted by the law of nations, being enforced against the ships and property of His Majesty's subjects under the pretext of blockade.[40]

Several years after Hardy lectured O'Higgins on the British interpretation of the Law of Nations regarding blockades a series of incidents occurred that gave London occasion to reaffirm its position. During late 1828 British naval forces recaptured the *Nestor*, which had been taken by Brazilian blockaders. Defending the decision to retake the *Nestor*, Lord Ponsonby, British minister assigned to Buenos Aires, informed the Foreign Office that he "was convinced that nothing but an act of force done by British marines would ever bring the Brazilian government to have the smallest regard even to decency of appearances in their system of plundering the British commerce, much less justice."[41] Shortly thereafter Ponsonby threatened Brazil with reprisals if he did not receive an acceptable reply to his communication regarding ships seized as the result of the Brazilian blockade of Argentina.[42]

Still dissatisfied with Brazilian conduct, Ponsonby wrote Lord Aberdeen, "I will venture to state my opinion again that force alone can make the [Brazilian] government act honestly."[43] An unsigned draft of a communication from the Foreign Office to Consul Woodbine Parish in Buenos Aires, dated February 27, 1829, confirms that as the decade drew to a close Great Britain continued to hold firmly to its opposition to what it considered paper blockades. The draft read in part, "With reference to the Decree of Blockade by the Peruvian government of the coast of Columbia [sic[on the Pacifick [sic] . . . I am instructed to acquaint you that H. M. Govt. have been informed that the naval force at the disposal of Peru is quite inadequate towards carrying the blockade into effect. Under these circumstances the blockade will not be recognized by this country."[44]

While Washington and London strove to protect vessels flying the Stars and Stripes and the Union Jack from pirates, privateers, and blockaders they were besieged with requests from nervous agents and private citizens resident in the new states for protection from periodic outbursts of antiforeignism and political and social disturbances. Michael Hogan could have been speaking for the diplomatic corps and merchants in general when he wrote that

> the course this Government [Chilean] has pursued for some months past appears calculated to annihilate commerce, they expect to obtain an acknowledgment of their Independence by coercion, commercial restitutions & seizures of property in all directions, their enmity to our Flag is obvious & were there no Naval force in this port I strongly suspect I would very soon be ordered to depart & leave out ships & property in eminent [sic] danger . . . . Difficulties in commercial intercourse with them are multiplying daily & their subordinate Officers knowing the temper of their Government emulate their superiors in Office.[45]

Showing the Stars and Stripes and the Union Jack usually sufficed to give assurances to official agents and private citizens of both countries. In fact, the United States was not obliged to land marines in Latin America to protect a diplomatic mission until 1835.[46] Great Britain, however, at the request of its agents, sent marines ashore or had them at the ready on several occasions during the 1820s. In August 1824 one hundred marines were landed from HMS *Cambridge* and quartered at the British consulate in Lima.[47] As it turned out they were not needed, but proved to be a "beneficial influence,"[48] and remained ashore for six weeks before returning to the *Cambridge*.[49] In 1827, with Argentina at war with Brazil and confronted at home with political unrest, Lord Ponsonby in Buenos Aires alerted Admiral R. W. Otway of the possible need for protection,[50] and stressed the importance of the appearance of a real force. HMS *Forte* was sent and appeared off Buenos Aires, but was not called on to act.[51] In 1829, however, marines were landed at Buenos Aires for the safety of British Chargé Woodbine Parish and his family, and remained ashore for two months.[52]

Several months after Chargé Parish in Buenos Aires turned to the Admiralty for protection one of the more significant incidents, underscoring the British government's determination to defend the interest of its subjects, occurred in Peru. The incident arose on land and then moved out to sea. According to British accounts, the Peruvian government forcibly seized from the Mexican vessel *Hidalgo* a reported $30,000 in bullion and coins belonging to British citizens. When the Peruvian officials refused to give satisfaction and began circulating the coins and melting down the bullion before the courts had handed down a decision Proconsul Thomas Willimott, after consulting with Captain H. Dundas of HMS *Sapphire*, informed the Peruvian minister of state, "We have considered it to be our duty . . . to detain and hold in deposit an equal amount of Peruvian government property, wherever it be met with."[53] Captain Dundas almost immediately took a Peruvian vessel belonging to the national government and removed $12,000. Before seizing the vessel Captain Dundas had written, "I . . . now intend to detain a Peruvian vessel whether of war or otherwise that might have government property on board. It is a disagreeable business but it must be done."[54]

Throughout the years that the United States and Great Britain had a common objective in containing piracy and privateering and limiting the effects of paper blockades they also shared the goal of restricting French designs in the New World. France, in fact, had to a considerable degree eliminated itself as a prime contender for influence in the emerging states by having fallen victim to Napoleon's ambitions, by suffering financial exhaustion as a consequence of years of war,[55] by playing a lead role in the pro-Spanish Holy Alliance, by invading the Peninsula in support of Ferdinand VII (the archenemy of Spain's former colonials), by diverting its attention to Algeria (where it need not compete with Great Britain or the United States in ways that might provoke war), by bowing to the Polignac memorandum, which forbade the use of arms or menace for the satisfaction of French demands on the new states, and by the Quai d'Orsai lagging behind the State Department and the Foreign Office in extending formal recognition to the embryonic polities.[56] Finally, after the loss of its claims to Canada by the Peace of Paris (1763), its defeat by Haitian revolutionaries, and the sale of Louisiana in 1803, France's base of operations in the New World was restricted to a few small islands and outcroppings in the Antilles (all encircled by British possessions) and French Guiana on the South American mainland. Still, its activities in the New World bore close watching. In Western Europe France was a power second only to Great Britain. It could be expected to make a determined effort to reclaim its pre-Napoleon role as a trading nation, and a profitable commerce with Latin America would be a step in that direction. It was suspected of having territorial ambitions in South America. It staunchly supported the monarchical system, which had adherents in places of influence in the new states. It was Catholic, as was the population of Latin America, and its contenders were Protestant. It had a formidable navy which could operate from bases in the French-held islands of the Caribbean.

As it turned out, France's encumbrances in conjunction with Latin Americans' opposition to its policies ordained that it follow in the wake of Great Britain and the United States. Of its three main objectives in the New World—commerce, the creation of monarchies ruled by Catholic princes, and territorial expansion in South America—the United States and Great Britain accepted in principle only the first, that of commerce. As advocates of free trade and the most-favored-nation concept in respect to trade, they acknowledged French competition, which, as it developed, did not seriously challenge Great Britain's industrial markets or the U.S. agricultural markets and strong position in the carrying trade.

France had stood most to gain from the Spanish colonies remaining under the strict control of the Spanish Crown. It was with that in mind that Paris used its diplomatic connection in unsuccessful endeavors to have the Holy Alliance assist Ferdinand to reestablish his control in the New World. That maneuver collapsed when Canning, in the above-mentioned memorandum to Prince Polignac, informed France that Great Britain would resist, with force if necessary, any effort on the part of the Alliance to rescue Ferdinand.[57] France could not afford another war with England and, as a consequence, was compelled to brake that objective.

As if in anticipation of Ferdinand's ultimate failure to retain his empire, France began to intrigue to create New World monarchies under Catholic princes whom Paris could dominate to its diplomatic and commercial advantage. Beginning in the late teens and continuing until the end of the twenties, France pursued that goal. Its schemes received their warmest responses in Buenos Aires where individuals in the highest quarters were receptive to the monarchical form of government.[58]

In each case, France's monarchical plots failed for at least three reasons. First, although important political figures in Latin America would have at various times welcomed the creation of monarchical governments, to have done so would have been to reestablish a system of rule against which the wars had been waged. Republicanism, on the other hand, while often accepted with less than enthusiasm, at once offered a tested alternative to legitimacy and ratified the break with Europe. Second, Ferdinand stubbornly opposed enthroning members of his house in any part of the former empire. Third, Great Britain, although it did not oppose the new nations selecting monarchs from their own inhabitants, refused to accept the enthroning of Catholic princes of European lineage, other than those belonging to the branch of the Bourbon dynasty headed by Ferdinand, on the grounds that members of other houses would be beholden to France. The United States was as opposed as was Great Britain to France's intrigues on behalf of monarchical regimes. Its opposition, however, stemmed primarily from political and security concerns. Monarchism once established in the New World might become infectious to the detriment of republicanism and in any event would serve to strengthen New World ties to the Old World and thereby pose a challenge to the two-sphere concept favored by Washington and as proclaimed in the Monroe Doctrine.

My evidence does not establish how seriously France aspired to expand its territorial holdings in South America. It does establish that Washington and London took seriously the possibility that France might try to gain one or more footholds in Latin America, especially after it monarchical intrigues came to naught.[59] One case in point: in the summer of 1825 London learned that a French fleet consisting of twenty-seven vessels had sailed from Martinique on June 30 and was believed destined for Cuba.[60] In the course of exchange of diplomatic notes over the incident, London discovered that Count François Donzelot, governor of the island of Martinique, had been authorized, if requested by the Cuban administrators, to provide a military force to assist in the repression of internal disturbances on the island.[61] Canning reacted sharply to the news and instructed Viscount Granville, British ambassador in Paris, "to state in the most explicit terms that any attempt by any power to gain a military footing on Cuba would constitute an imminent hazard to the peace of the world." He then added, "It is fit that the French government should understand that no plea whatever could justify in our eyes the introduction of a French military force into the Spanish islands."[62] Within a week Granville had received from Baron de Damas "unequivocal assurances" that no French troops would be sent to Cuba.[63]

The U.S. response to the incident was delayed, but heated. Henry Clay, now secretary of state, instructed Minister James Brown in Paris to inform the French government that hereafter the United States expected to be informed beforehand of the purpose of any similar movement. Uppermost on Clay's mind, however, were Cuba and Puerto Rico. Turning to them, Clay noted that France had earlier been informed that the United States could not see with indifference those islands passing from Spain to any other European power. Now, Minister Brown was to reaffirm that position and to add to it that the United States could not consent to the occupation of those islands by any European power other than Spain under any contingency whatever. He continued:

> If any sensibility should be manifested to what the French minister may choose to regard as suspicions entertained here of a disposition on the part of France to indulge a passion of aggrandisement, you may disavow any such suspicions, and say that the President cannot suppose a state of things in which either of the great maritime powers of Europe, with or without the consent of Spain, would feel itself justified to occupy or attempt the occupation of Cuba or Porto Rico without the concurrence, or, at least, the knowledge of the United States.[64]

In reply to Brown's inquiries, the French government explained that the fleet was composed of ships that had sailed from France at different periods and were destined to protect French commerce on the Atlantic and Pacific coasts and that they were collected in the West Indies with a view to making such a demonstration off Santo Domingo (Haiti) as might incline the Haitian government to accede to the terms and conditions of the royal ordinance for the recognition of its (Haiti's) independence.[65]

The fleet incident that led to a showdown with France had occurred at a time when the three powers were in the process of negotiating an accord that would guarantee that no one of the three would occupy Cuba. The United States and Great Britain had already tacitly agreed that neither should seek to occupy Cuba and the next year France joined the pact.[66] The accord was followed by a lull during which Washington and London did not find cause to believe that France might seriously be considering making a bid for territory in South America. In 1829, however, they were again put on the alert, this time in the South Pacific.

Because of domestic unrest and an upsurge of antiforeignism in Chile the French consul general, Le Forest, who it was believed had been assigned to Santiago for political rather than commercial purposes,[67] had been attacked and wounded by gunshot, his property destroyed, and he was obliged to flee with his family to the protection of foreign ships anchored off Valparaiso.[68]

Following the attack on Le Forest, French war vessels appeared off Chile in unusually large numbers. U.S. and British officials in Chile believed that the fleet was probably bent on retaliating for the mistreatment of Le Forest and that France had in mind the occupation of the island of Chiloé. Such a possibility did not take Washington or London by surprise. As early as 1823 the *Guardian* (Manchester) carried an item on the large number of French vessels in New World waters while the French "mercantile shipping was seen as next to nothing. *This mysterious force remaining unheeded by the stupid and listless governments of South America* [emphasis in the original], and we believe has been as little attended to by the bright cabinet of St. James."[69] Then, at the time that the French fleet in the Caribbean was creating a diplomatic stir, Captain James Maling of HMS *Cambridge* had expressed his conviction that the French fleet in the Pacific had interests other than the protection of commerce.[70] Several months before the attack on La Forest, United States Consul Michael Hogan had reported to Washington that France was seeking to work out a deal to cut timber on Chiloé, even though timber on the island was of little use for naval purposes. He then made clear his major concern: "The Archepelego of Chiloé is the master key to the whole west coast of the Pacific, in the hands of a great maritime nation Chile is at once in its power; And did France possess it, it would in a very few years become one of the most wealthy countries in the globe."[71]

British Vice Consul Thomas White also alerted his government to French activities in Chiloé. In early 1829, with information learned from Commander King, who had observed French naval personnel on the island, White reported to the Foreign Office that "the procuring of Naval Timber was not the only motive of the visit to it [Chiloé] of the French ship of war *Le Tarne*," and that its captain "had evinced great anxiety to sail from the island upon the appearance of HMS *Heron*— in order perhaps to avoid the real object of his visit being known."[72] Aberdeen was further apprised that White had put senior naval officers of H. M. Squadron in the Pacific on notice of the importance that H. M. Government attached to having closely watched all operations of such a nature as those carried on by the French on the island.[73]

Rear Admiral Thomas Baker lent support to Consul White's analysis in reporting that France had in the Pacific or on the way there six ships of war.[74] Three months later Baker commented on the "comparatively" large number of French warships "now accumulated" in the Pacific, and noted, "It has long been reported and believed that the

French have a design upon the valuable and interesting island of Chiloe belonging to the Chilian Republic; and I shall feel no surprize if, under the plea of demanding satisfaction for the indignities offered M. Le Forest, . . . they should seize upon Chiloe as a security for reparations." To add substance to his interpretation of what the French might be up to, Baker noted that Captains Bingham, Coghlan, and Waldegrave while senior officers in the Pacific all expressed their suspicions of the French, and "as negotiations were certainly at one time pending between the French and Chilean governments for granting the former the *exclusive* privilege of cutting Ship Timber on Chiloe, it is clear that the French are not unaware of the real value of such an acquisition."[75]

History records that no territorial transfers ultimately came from French interest in the island of Chiloé. It is, however, perhaps of more than passing interest to recall that soon after the British and U.S. uneasiness about the French possibly occupying the strategic archipelago, England occupied the Falkland Islands (Las Malvinas) off Argentina, important to the control of traffic through the Strait of Magellan. The British first claimed the Falklands in 1765. Between that time and 1832, when Great Britain reasserted its claim to them, the islands were claimed by Spain and then by Argentina; and Commander Silas Duncan of the U.S. sloop of war *Lexington*, following a diplomatic exchange between Buenos Aires and Washington over the seizure of fishing vessels of United States registry, landed and declared the islands free of all government. In late 1832 and early 1833 Great Britain, over the objections of Buenos Aires, claimed the islands as *terra nullius*.[76] Not only that the United States did not challenge the British occupation, which in the strictest sense was a violation of the Monroe Doctrine, but that British and U.S. agents at Buenos Aires acted in close understanding and made effective decisions relating to the occupation with little guidance from their respective governments,[77] may be viewed as a classic example of the degree of understanding Washington and London had of the limits of their freedom of operations in Latin America.

British Racial Attitudes

Prevailing North American and British views of private citizens and public figures in Latin America provided an added incentive for cooperation as the two powers confronted the perils of carrying on relations with the new states. As it turned out, with independence achieved there was indeed little that ethnocentric Anglo-Saxons found in Latin America to inspire confidence and faith. The obloquy in reports to the United States and England soon came to lack variety or novelty. The influence of early information about Latin America to image making in the United States is reviewed in chapter 2. What follows is meant to be no more than a large enough sampling of views extracted from numerous reports reaching England to warrant the conclusion that in nearly all respects Anglo-Americans and British saw eye to eye on Latin Americans and their institutions and that what they saw foreshadowed little promise for the region.

Indians

Much as did Anglo-Americans, the British took with them to Latin America negative views of Indians that were strongly influenced by two centuries of encounters with tribes in North America. For British Commissioner and Chargé H. G. Ward the natives of Mexico were a "useless race."[78] Elsewhere Indians were found to be guilty of squandering their meager resources on liquor and pageants. After more than two centuries of contact with Europeans they remained outside the fold of white civilization. Although the dominant population in several of the republics they had shown no interest in participatory government.[79]

Blacks

Since the British worked after 1800 to terminate African slavery as a legal institution, it might have been expected that the English view of blacks in Latin America would differ substantially from that of Anglo-Americans reared in a society that still accepted their enforced servitude. That was not the case. As observers of the Latin American scene, North Americans and Englishmen came to nearly identical conclusions regarding Latin American blacks. Both sides praised the initial accomplishments of blacks in Haiti.[80] They agreed, too, that blacks, when in a state of servitude, were better laborers than Indians and were in fact the indispensable component of the labor force in those sectors of the agricultural economy devoted to export commodities. In the words of British Consul Thomas Rowcroft, Brazil would be "nothing" without them and he found much the same situation in Peru from where he reported that blacks were the life of the country.[81] Blacks freed from the trammels of slavery, however, were undependable laborers.[82] Their "love of power . . . love of an inactive life . . . , desire for change and novelty, which over the negro mind hold uncontrollable dominion,"[83] and their jealousy of whites made them a menace to that element.[84]

Blacks, a conspicuous component of the patriot armies, were often described in such terms as the "dregs of society,"[85] "the refuse of the people," and "God knows what."[86] Under arms they tended to defect and to be unruly,[87] and could become monsters.[88] According to Ponsonby, the Brazilian infantry was composed largely of blacks and mulattoes and as a consequence was more numerous than serviceable, and Rowcroft found blacks in Peru to have unfavorable fighting qualities.[89]

The British and North Americans shared essentially the same views about racial miscegenation and the ultimate outcome thereof. Yet the attitudes of the English toward mixed races in their West Indian possessions were obviously more enlightened than were those held by many within the dominant elements in the United States, in which resided two sizable minorities. The *Encyclopaedia Britannica* summarized well the traditional thinking on miscegenation in both countries. Those who intermarried at once surrendered to "their hearts and their freedom ... their virtues and their religion" and "when a pure society mixes with a profane, the better principles of the one become soon tainted by the evil practices of the other; which verifies the old adage, evil communication corrupts good manners."[90]

Mixed Races

British agents reporting from Latin America left little doubt that mestizos and mulattoes epitomized what Anglo-Saxon societies viewed as the worst consequences of miscegenation. In Colombia, Creoles, blacks, and Indians had intermingled with one another to "form an amalgamated mass of population, without any marked national characteristic, but with the moral and physical properties of each race, tainted, rather than improved, by admixture."[91] The majority of Peruvian mestizos or "half castes" could neither write or read. Those among them who were informed possessed "in general" just that extent of knowledge that led to "the unfortunate vanity of supposing that they [had] nothing to learn." They looked upon the "poor Indian" with "haughty contempt." The "operation of contracted minds" was traceable in all their actions. "Pure principles of honesty, patriotism, and good faith" were unknown among them. The proud chivalrous feeling of the Spaniard had "degenerated into meanness, littleness, and stubbornness."[92] Argentine gauchos were "ferocious in the extreme and in appearance and habits not unlike gypsies of Europe."[93]

Britishers writing for publication supported the views of those serving the Foreign Office. According to John Luccock, among those of mixed origin was "a universal preponderance of the evil: and a much larger proportion than might be anticipated, appeared to be altogether depraved."[94] Luccock's contemporary Alexander Caldcleugh found mulattoes in Brazil to have a considerable degree of aptitude, "but it is well known that an increase of honesty and sobriety does not generally accompany . . . talent."[95]

Creoles

The interests of British citizens resident in Latin America brought them first of all into contact with the economically and politically dominant Creoles, who impressed them unfavorably. According to Consul Thomas H. Hood, stationed in Montevideo, Uruguayan Creoles were from infancy taught "fraud, deception, lying and flattery. Integrity, truth and punctual fulfillment of engagements do not form any part of their education." The "man who makes a sacrifice of his interest to his character and sense of moral obligation, they consider a very good sort of man, but a very great fool."[96] Peruvian Creoles were egotistical and ambitious,[97] but there was hope, for although they had imbibed the many vices of their Spanish ancestors they were beginning to feel that their pomposity and indolence were "sorry substitutes" for the industry and activity of their foreign competitors.[98] Colombian Creoles had inherited the vices of their ancestors to the degree that their own "may now be considered indigenous,"[99] and, furthermore, they were "in general mean and extremely fond of money."[100] Adherence to principle was not a Creole virtue and they were so capricious and changeable that it was "impossible to feel any confidence of their thinking tomorrow what they thought today."[101]

Creoles in their roles as public figures fared no better than they did as individuals at the hands of the British. The vanity of the Argentines in higher positions of government was so excessive and their ignorance so great that "they were as likely as not to mistake kindness for fear."[102] Colombian Creoles viewed government "solely as a palladium of their rights, while their duties to it have been studiously concealed."[103] Their "bombastic language" and their irresponsible verbal attacks and incompetence indicated future discord.[104] Although one could not be sure that Creoles predominated in the Mexican officialdom, the complaints against public officers in that country had the same ring as those leveled against Creoles elsewhere. They decided the most important issues not on real merit but by a tissue of intrigue,[105] and the slowness with which they transacted public business was distressing to the commercially minded English.[106] From Central America the Foreign Office learned that public "leaders on both sides look for nothing but ascendancy and the emoluments of office."[107] Peruvian officials were ignorant of politics.[108] The issues over which they were willing to sacrifice their honor could only "be rendered attractive by investing them with a fictitious character of importance."[109] Consul P. W. Kelly found General Antonio La Fuente, at the time supreme director of Peru, well versed in the intriguing character of his countrymen and added, "if I may be permitted to make use of an old adage that of setting a thief to catch a thief, which phrase I believe applicable to H. E. [La Fuente] as well as to most of these people, and it would be, as far as I can judge, doing the generality of the inhabitants of the other states of South America an injustice to exclude them from the same consideration."[110]

British and North American views regarding the court systems of Latin America were so similar that one could reasonably ask, Who was borrowing pejorative terms from whom?[111] Minister Ponsonby found that "venality" permeated the court system of Argentina.[112] It was "notorious" that in Colombia justice was bought and sold and "the laws perverted in favor of the highest bidder by the very authorities who ought the most vigilantly to watch over their rigid observance."[113] In Guatemala "the universal remark" was that "there is neither government, nor law, nor police, nor army, nor money, nor administration of justice."[114]

As in many other areas, the United States and Great Britain were free to pursue their objectives in the spiritual realm without fear of creating a conflictual environment. Figuratively speaking North Americans and British marched into Latin America hand in hand in their Protestantism. Left at home were the heated debates over the separation of church and state, as favored by the United States and opposed by Great Britain, and the endless philosophizing about Roman Catholic doctrines. There simply was no time or place for strong advocacy of Protestant doctrine by those seeking advantage in the secular sphere.

Until approximately 1825 North Americans and British had hopes, however glimmering, that the new states would embrace Protestantism or as a minimum would opt for Catholicism without "papism." That was not to be; and by 1830 the constitutions of the new nations uniformly made Roman Catholicism the only recognized creed.[115] Faced with a united front of an officially sanctioned Roman Catholic religious monopoly, British agents, restrained for political and economic reasons from publicly denouncing the Church, vented their anti-Catholicism in communications to the Foreign Office. They were unrelenting in their castigation of the Catholic clergy, and the malice in their attacks appear to have exceeded that of U.S. agents. Secular priests were portrayed as ignorant, immoral, idolatrous, superstitious, fanatical, violent, and inimical to the establishment of all liberal principles and forms of government. The regular clergy were dissolute and indolent and their educational institutions no more than nurseries of bigotry.[116]

Exposing the Church's flaws undoubtedly relieved certain frustrations in the correspondents; it did little in serving better the wishes of British Protestants living and dying in Latin America. They were more solicitous of the personal problems they faced as practicing Protestants than in exposing weaknesses in the Catholic Church and its clergy. Those problems ranged from freedom of worship, to the holding of funerals, to finding suitable burial grounds, and to the exchanging of marriage vows. The resolution of those issues ultimately devolved upon the home government in London, and it pursued that responsibility with determination and persistence. Its efforts paid off handsomely when commercial treaties with the new nations were ratified. In each case the religious prerogatives granted British Protestants in those treaties were broader and more explicit than those won by the United States on behalf of its citizens.[117]

The care with which the British government went about protecting the religious privileges of its citizens is apparent in Article XII of the commercial treaty of 1826 with Argentina:

> The subjects of His Britannick Majesty residing in The United Provinces of Rio de la Plata, shall not be disturbed, persecuted, or annoyed on account of their religion, but they shall have perfect liberty of conscience therein, and to celebrate Divine Service either within their own private houses, or in their own particular churches or chapels, which they shall be at liberty to build and maintain in convenient places, approved of by the Government of the said United Provinces:—liberty shall also be granted to bury the subjects of His Britannick Majesty who may die in the territories of the said United Provinces, in their own burial places, which, in the same manner, they may freely establish and maintain.
>
> In the like manner, the citizens of the said United Provinces shall enjoy, within all the dominions of His Britannick Majesty, a perfect and unrestrained liberty of conscience, and of exercising their religion publickly or privately, within their own dwelling houses, or in the chapels and places of worship appointed for that purpose, agreeably to the system of toleration established in the dominions of His said Majesty.[118]

Several explanations suggest why Great Britain wrested more liberal religious privileges than did the United States from officials in Latin America. First, His Majesty George IV as head of the Anglican

Church as well as of the state had a level of religious responsibility that the government in Washington was exempted from by the federal Constitution, which delegated the care and nurture of religion to the individual states. Second, in the treaty reached with Portugal in 1810 the British won important religious privileges and consequently had some sense of the limits to which religious issues could be pressed in dealing with strongly Catholic societies. Third, throughout the period of negotiations with the Latin American polities, the British government was struggling with the "Catholic question" at home and may have felt a special need to protect the religious rights of its citizens in the politically unstable states where the revival of vehement anti-Protestantism remained a possibility. Fourth, very likely the Foreign Office simply combined resolution on its part with the obvious dependence of the new governments on Great Britain and hinged commercial agreements on the granting of maximum religious concessions to British citizens. In other words, the Foreign Office assumed that in religious matters, as in other areas, the Latin Americans had little choice but to truckle to Great Britain, since the Battle of Trafalgar (October 21, 1805) made Britain the unquestioned mistress of the seas.

Areas of Disagreement

The United States, as has been noted, would have had the breakaway colonies join it to form a solid republican phalanx in the hemisphere. His Majesty's Government wished no less that the monarchical system be sustained as providing the surest link between the Old and New worlds. For a decade after insurgency engulfed the Spanish colonies the British government strove to hold the empire intact under the Spanish monarchy. Although it fell to Canning to accept the failure of that policy he continued to hope that the former colonies would ultimately embrace the monarchical system. He identified three conditions in the New World that in his view favored monarchism over republicanism. They were (1) the great number of large proprietors, (2) the wealth and influence of the clergy, and (3) the long experience of viceregal administration invested with monarchical forms.[119]

Canning's predilection for monarchism over republicanism was shared by most British agents posted in Latin America. Lord Ponsonby wrote from Buenos Aires, "I do feel a peculiar desire to see the throne of the Emperor [Pedro I of Brazil] secure, to see the House of Braganza, ancient ally of our king flourish in prosperity and honor, and to see the Monarchical Principle take root, and pierce deep into the soil of America."[120] Patrick Campbell, British commissioner in Bogotá, believed that Colombia would be ripe for monarchy for at least as long as Bolívar survived.[121]

However, not all British agents shared Canning's preference for monarchical systems in the shattered Spanish Empire. Especially after Great Britain began recognizing the former colonies as sovereign states, individuals holding important posts in the region came forward to express views unfavorable to the establishment of monarchical governments in the new nations. Consul Woodbine Parish wrote off monarchy in La Plata as incompatible with the sense of equality that existed in the population. If a monarchical government were imposed, he contended, it could be maintained only with an army of foreigners.[122] The same Lord Ponsonby who wished monarchy well in Brazil saw no chance of it succeeding in the Plata region.[123]

Admiral C. Fleeming of the Royal Navy, assigned to the North Coast of South America, was among the most outspoken British representatives against monarchy, and by extension in favor of republicanism, and he enumerated six reasons why he believed as he did. First, support for monarchy would come from *godos* (Spaniards) and two-thirds of the clergy, not in the interest of their country, but because the new republics would not listen to the pope as Spain had. Second, immense distances would make ruling from a single location extremely difficult. Third regional divisions would add to the problems of any monarch. Fourth, there was an absence of a nobility with extensive possessions and influence. Fifth, the military forces that a monarch would expect to have would take all available funds, and British bondholders would be left without a penny. Sixth, those who had gained by the revolution would protect their interests.[124] A report from United States Chargé d'Affaires Condy Raguet in Rio de Janeiro provides additional evidence that the British were not as one in favor of monarchy. In a communication to Washington in which Raguet commented on the conflict between imperial Brazil and republican Argentina over control of the Banda Oriental, he wrote, "There is not I believe, a single British subject scarcely, in this part of South America, whether he be a publick agent, naval Commander, or Merchant, who is not desirous to see Brazil dispossessed of Monte Video."[125]

When trade and commerce with the supposed El Dorado opened to competition for the first time the United States was approaching the point at which Great Britain had reason to be seriously concerned about retaining its preeminent role as a trading nation. The prospect of economic competition between the two nations over time led many officials, editors, and publicists to conclude that economic issues were the agent provocateur of early U.S.-British rivalry in Latin America. A close reading of the documents, I believe, leads to a different conclusion.

There is no question but that London made trade with the former Spanish and Portuguese colonies its prime objective or that by the mid-1820s the United States was well on its way to becoming a major commercial nation. Other things being equal, two major trading nations in competition for markets in an underdeveloped area could have led to heated rivalry. Other things were not equal, however, and I find that economic competition between the two nations produced considerably less friction than generally has been ascribed to it and that in fact it was carried on at no higher level of intensity than was, and is yet today, accepted as normal by capitalistic societies vying for advantage in materially less-developed states. This is not to say that flights of passion and national pride did not at times inflame the public mind. Nor is it to say that official agents posted to the area did not complain to their home offices that their counterparts were trying to steal a march on them. They did, and often. It is to say that mercurial oratory and the carping of minor officials are not the stuff to unleash the dogs of war.

Before pressing my argument I offer a word about an issue arising in 1825 from British restrictions on trade with its West Indian possessions. President Adams, in pursuit of his free ships, free goods, no impressment policies, attempted to impose on Great Britain terms that in effect would deny it the right to regulate trade with its own territories. The U.S. position was untenable, but Adams kept it alive. Andrew Jackson, upon assuming the presidency, quickly came to terms with London, and the incident and the irritants it produced passed into history. While the issue lived it had the potential for serious conflict, even naval warfare. The point, however, is that it had little to do with U.S.-British relations with Latin America. Thus, strictly speaking, to take note of the issue at all in the context of those relations rests on the weak reed of the British West Indies being situated amid waters and territories generally considered to be Latin American.[126]

As early as 1825, and in some cases before, Washington and London identified three realities of economic relations with Latin America that favored the view that each country could respect the commerce of the other without jeopardy to its own. The first was that, given their respective stages of industrial and commercial development and complementary activities, economic confrontation could only be detrimental to their interests. Great Britain was an industrial nation and a purveyor of manufactured articles, especially high quality textiles, iron products, armaments, and luxury items. Before the wars of independence terminated, the demands for its products were such that its exports to Latin America, Cuba excluded, were at least three times greater than those of the United States.[127] In the case of

Buenos Aires, British exports in 1822 were four times greater than those of the United States,[128] and the ratio remained approximately the same in 1830.[129] United States Consul John Forbes was acutely aware of the situation when he wrote despondently that the most valuable import trade was entirely in the hands of British merchants.[130] Heman Allen, United States minister to Chile, worriedly wrote Secretary Clay, "The preponderating influence of England, in the affairs of these countries is already seen and felt in almost every department; to the monopoly of their commerce and riches, she is already looking with a most steadfast eye."[131] The United States, meanwhile, despite its remarkable economic growth, still earned its foreign exchange from its farms, forests, fisheries, and shipping. Its primary interest in Latin American commerce was in the carrying and reexport trade, in which it competed successfully with Great Britain, and the sale of wheat flour. In 1822, for example, wheat flour constituted 50 percent of the U.S. market in Buenos Aires and in 1825 nearly 60 percent of U.S. products sold in Chile.[132] Course cottons, timber products, and salted fish, none of which faced stiff British competition, made up much of the remainder of U.S. exports to the new states.

The second reality recognized by both sides was that the British enjoyed a host of advantages other than their capacity to supply articles hungered for by the Creole elites. In the major ports, except Havana, the number of British merchants and merchant houses far outstripped their U.S. counterparts. In Buenos Aires, for instance, there were in 1824 thirty-nine British commercial houses with correspondents in Rio de Janeiro and Montevideo, compared to three from the United States.[133] Of untold advantage to British merchants in Latin America was their access to credit in England. This was a major item when the shortage of bullion became a continuing problem after the early 1820s, and other Latin American exports failed to take up the slack.[134] Furthermore, British subjects in general probably benefited from being represented by more experienced groups of diplomats and consuls than those representing U.S. citizens.[135] Communications with England by way of a line of packets established by the British government in 1824, with regular sailings between Liverpool and Buenos Aires, gave British merchants yet another advantage. Of major importance, and as alluded to earlier, British merchants benefited immeasurably from the deference shown their country because of its naval power. Finally, London was the only source of large amounts of capital required to sustain the new regimes and to rehabilitate the mining industry. As the saying goes, "Money talks and sometimes screams and yells." Following the Napoleonic Wars, the pace of economic expansion in England slowed and interest rates plummeted.

British investors were driven, or so they thought, to place their capital abroad, where theoretically returns would be greater than at home. The loans made to the new states—which incidentally freed their leadership from having to go to the public for funding—and investments in mines afforded Great Britain yet another valuable entry into Latin American markets.[136]

John Quincy Adams, encumbered though he was by a mountain of self-esteem and chauvinism and of intense dislikes and suspicions of Great Britain and especially of George Canning (who reciprocated in kind),[137] acknowledged British economic superiority in Latin America in his diary in June 1822: "Do what we can, the commerce with South America will be more important and useful to Great Britain than to us, and Great Britain will be a power vastly more important to them than we, for the simple reason that she has the power of supplying their wants by her manufactures. We have few such supplies to furnish them."[138]

The third potential obstacle to an amicable trading environment was eliminated when, in making treaties of friendship and commerce with the new governments, neither Great Britain nor the United States insisted on trading privileges in excess of those sought or accorded the other. From the outbreak of hostilities between Spain and its ultramarine provinces Great Britain had viewed the insurgent colonies as a market of vast potentialities. His Majesty's Government early determined that, irrespective of the outcome of the insurgency, Spain's antebellum control of the empire should not be restored. Such an occurrence, London assumed, would almost certainly mean a renewal of a policy of commercial exclusion and the consequent loss of markets, markets British merchants had sedulously fostered for at least two decades.[139] In 1822 the *Guardian* declared, "We are friends of unrestricted commercial intercourse,"[140] and at least by 1825 that had become the official view. In that year Canning instructed Viscount Granville to assure France's foreign minister, Baron de Damas, of his Britannic Majesty's determination not to seek any exclusive privileges in favor of English commerce.[141] London adhered to that policy in negotiating treaties of friendship and commerce with Spain's former colonies. The articles of those treaties, concerned specifically with commerce, protected the interest of British subjects, based on the most favored nation principle. In essence London demanded only a fair field and no favors,[142] an understandable and defensible position given the numerous industrial and commercial advantages Great Britain enjoyed.

The United States, for its part, throughout the insurgency and the negotiations leading to treaties of amity and commerce favored the principle of utility and perfect equality in its commercial relations with the new states. In the words of John Q. Adams, when still secretary of state, "Mutual advantage and reciprocity are all that we ought to ask, and all that we can be willing to grant. As to running a race with England to snatch from these new nations some special privilege or monopoly, I thought it neither a wise nor an honest policy."[143] In 1823, in his instructions to Richard C. Anderson, minister to Colombia, he picked up on Colombian Foreign Minister Pedro Gual's statement that it was the intention of the Colombian government "to treat all *foreign* nations upon the footing of equal favor and of perfect reciprocity," and reaffirmed his position: "This is all that the United States will require and this, so far as their interests are concerned, they have a right to exact."[144] Clay laid down the same principle in a communication to Poinsett, posted in Mexico, in which he asserted that the United States had never "claimed and do not now claim any peculiar favour or concession to their commerce or navigation," as a consideration for its liberal policy toward recognition of the new governments.[145] And in his instructions to envoys to the Panama Congress of 1826[146] Clay took the position that the new governments should reject all propositions founded on the principle of a concession and perpetual commercial privileges to any foreign government as incompatible with their actual and absolute independence.[147]

Having made similar treaties with the new states, the United States and Great Britain were free to compete as best they could in accordance with laissez-faire principles, and, I would recall, to commiserate over the vexations of dealing with the sensitive new governments and with bureaucrats, many of whom had reputations for being somewhat less than honest. It is also appropriate to recall that, although the treaties granted the new states reciprocal privileges, without industry, without financial institutions, and without merchant marines, they were placed at a disadvantage they have not as yet been able to overcome.

The Cuban Issue

As the wars on the mainland wound down Mexico and Colombia threatened to carry their struggle against Spain to its insular possessions, especially Cuba. That development had within it the ingredients of a potential crisis between the United States and Great Britain. The State Department was unalterably opposed to the invasion of Cuba by Mexico or Colombia either independently or jointly. Secretary Clay had made the U.S. position clear in communications to the concerned powers of Europe and the New World. The Foreign Office, fully informed, as it was, of the U.S. stance could have, had it chosen, provoked a serious international incident simply by encouraging an expedition against Cuba and almost certainly a war with the United States by providing naval support for such a venture. The Foreign Office, as it had on prior occasions, was careful not to take a position on the prospective invasion that might trigger a dangerous response from Washington. It became clear, however, that Canning was quite prepared to make what diplomatic hay he could out of Clay's démarche on the issue.

Mexico and Colombia had a multiplicity of justifiable reasons for invading the islands. As long as Ferdinand stubbornly refused to recognize the new states, the wars would be protracted and the islands would remain enemy territory. As Spain's possession they provided ideal bases from which a royal fleet might be assembled with the aim of attacking the mainland. Spain, in fact, did use Cuba as a base for attacking Mexico in July 1829. But whether or not the islands were used for such a purpose, the new states had to expend extraordinary amounts to defend themselves against such an eventuality. Short of actually attacking the mainland, Madrid could and did close its eyes to the use of the islands' harbors and inlets by privateers and pirates preying upon the shipping of the ex-colonies.

From the perspective of Mexico and Colombia an attack upon the islands either independently or as a joint venture would tend to quiet diverse groups that were destabilizing the two countries. An invasion of the islands was attractive militarily on three scores. First, as long as war with Spain continued the armies of liberation could not be disbanded and an attack on Cuba or Puerto Rico would contribute to their discipline. Second, carrying a war to the islands would forestall the unpleasant task of returning tens of thousands of conscripts to civilian life without adequate compensation for their services and with few prospects of worthwhile employment in the stagnating civilian sectors. Third, being able to launch an attack upon the islands would add immeasurably to Mexico's and Colombia's standing in military circles and should an attack prove successful would be a boost to their status in the international community. Then there was the added matter of mutual jealousy. Although they entertained the idea of a joint operation against the islands, both Mexico and Colombia were inclined to act independently, even hastily, to ensure that the other would not gain a leg up in the Caribbean by having underwritten a conquest of Cuba or Puerto Rico.[148]

The threat of the liberation or conquest of Cuba and Puerto Rico by one or more of the new republics alarmed Washington and presented a new question for U.S. foreign policy. John Q. Adams and his predecessors had laid down the dictum that the transfer of a colonial dominion in the New World from one European power to another could not be viewed with indifference. The no-transfer principle, however, did not provide for a policy in the event that a newly independent nation or an alliance of two or more of them should seek sovereignty over the islands or make them protectorates.[149] Rather than face the question head on, Adams, as president, and Clay, as secretary of state, initially tried to conjure it away. As early as May 27, 1823, Adams, while still secretary of state, probably had in mind the possibility of an attack on Cuba or Puerto Rico by one or more of the new governments when he wrote in his instructions to Richard C. Anderson, appointed minister to Colombia, of Colombia's central position upon the surface of the globe, its magnificent river systems, the fertility of its soils, and the richness of its minerals. After alluding to those advantages, Adams noted darkly, "If the natural advantages bestowed upon the Colombian territory were to be improved by its inhabitants only for the purposes of empire, that which nature has bestowed as a blessing upon them would, in its consequences prove a curse inflicted upon the rest of mankind. . . . Let her look to *commerce* and *navigation*, and not to empire as her means of communication with the rest of the world."[150]

Two years later, Secretary Clay, in a communication to Joel R. Poinsett in Mexico, was more explicit as to what might be expected from the new states. He wrote, "If the war be indefinitely protracted, to what object will the arms of the new governments be directed? It is not unlikely that they may be turned to the conquest of Cuba and Puerto Rico." With that possibility in mind the president "directs you . . . to keep a vigilant attention upon every movement towards Cuba, to ascertain the designs of Mexico in regard to it, and to put him, early, in full possession of every purpose of the Mexican Government relative to it."[151]

A month later Clay turned his attention to Spain. He informed Alexander H. Everett, United States minister in Madrid, that it was the belief of the Adams administration that, if the wars continued, Colombia and Mexico would attack Cuba and Puerto Rico. With that prospect and the cost in lives and property inherent in such an action in mind Everett was instructed, in the name of the president, to urge upon Spain the expediency of concluding the wars. As an added inducement, Everett could assure the Councils of Spain that the United States was satisfied with the present condition of the islands in the hands of Spain and with the ports open to U.S. commerce.[152]

In yet another effort to stop or at least stall a possible move by Mexico or Colombia against the islands, Clay appealed to Czar Alexander I. In a long communiqué to Minister Henry Middleton, the contents of which were to be made known to the Court of St. Petersburg, Clay first observed that as long as the wars continued on even a nominal basis the new republics could not disband their victorious armies without culpable neglect of all maxims of prudence and precaution. He next pointed out that it could not be doubted that the new states would direct their combined and umemployed forces to the reduction of the islands. He then made a pitch, through Middleton, to the czar to use his "great influence" in Spain to persuade the Court of Madrid that in Spain's own interest and that of humanity, it should come to terms with its ex-colonies and recognize their independence.[153]

Continuing his peace campaign, Clay on December 20, 1825, handed identical notes (copies of which were forwarded to Poinsett and Anderson in Mexico City and Bogotá) to the Mexican and Colombian ministers in Washington asking the suspension for a limited time of any projects that their respective governments might be formulating against the islands in order to give Russia time to act in response to the U.S. request that Alexander I use his influence to mediate differences between Madrid and its former colonies. Colombian Minister Salazar, without waiting instructions from Bogotá, expressed the view that the matter would be taken up at the forthcoming Congress at Panama.[154] Mexican Minister Obregón reported only that he would transmit Clay's communication to Mexico City. Mexico's reply, it turned out, was not heartening. President Guadaloupe Victoria, after asking and receiving a full explanation from Poinsett respecting the U.S. view of the Cuban situation, had declared that Mexico had no intention of conquering or possessing the island, but that his government was contemplating assisting Cuban revolutionaries to drive out the Spaniards and, in case they succeeded, to leave the people to govern themselves.[155] Guadaloupe Victoria had said nothing of suspending moves against Cuba, and it turned out he had something quite different in mind. In communications dated March 8 and March 18, Poinsett reported that Mexico favored an early attack on Cuba for two reasons; it wanted the advantages and glory of emancipating the island and it feared that if it did not move rapidly either independently or in alliance with Colombia, the latter would take matters into its own hands, and if successful in invading Cuba would annex it to Colombian territory.[156]

Despite U.S. efforts to cool the situation, evidence that the invasion was viewed as a genuine possibility occurred throughout 1823, 1824, and 1825. Consul Kilbee's reports from Havana to the Foreign Office corroborate that conclusion. In sequential order his communications called attention to the following developments: September 23,

1823, the chance of an invasion from the mainland was a matter of public discussion, and Cubans feared Colombians more than they did Mexicans;[157] October 20, there was an alarm on the island over the intention of the Colombian government which was said to be about to send a corps of two thousand *Samboes* (italics in the original) to invade the island;[158] February 8, 1824, a Colombian squadron consisting of a corvette, one or two brigs, and a schooner had "almost completely blockaded" Havana, and as Colombia and Mexico acquired stability and the means to fit out more formidable armaments "it is much feared" that, given the present state of the Spanish navy, they would be able effectively to blockade the port;[159] May 18, Colombian vessels reportedly were refitting in New Orleans and Pensacola, an expedition had been outfitted in Cartagena, communications with Mexico had been cut off, and a Colombian war vessel had captured a Spanish frigate;[160] November 30, Cubans were anticipating an attack by Colombia or Mexico, direct communications with Spain had been "almost completely" interrupted, it had been six months since any official letters had been received, and another Colombian landing was reported;[161] February 8, 1825, with victory in Peru, it was evident that the Colombian government would soon direct its view to this island, but for the present it lacked the necessary men, arms, or navy to effectuate an attack;[162] March 15, Cubans feared Colombia more than Mexico, there was "universal terror" of the Samboes of Colombia, and an expedition from Alvarado and Campeche (Mexico) had been suspended because reinforcements had reached Havana from Spain;[163] July 6, Mexico was believed responsible for a Negro uprising near Matanzas in which fourteen "whites" had been killed and "formidable dogs" had been used to suppress the outbreak.[164] Much the same kind of information was reaching the British Admiralty.[165]

Clay's efforts to bring peace between Spain and its former colonies, and thereby stymie any project designed to alter the political status of Cuba, received a cool reception in Europe, but they finally resonated in Latin America. On May 31, 1826, Poinsett informed Washington that President Guadaloupe Victoria in his message closing the session of Congress had stated the the Mexican expedition against Cuba had been dropped, at least temporarily, and that officials were anxious to know the course the United States would pursue in the event a decision to invade Cuba were to come out of the forthcoming Panama Congress.[166]

Whether or not favorable news from Mexico influenced Clay when he prepared his instructions for the envoys named to attend the Panama Congress, he took what might be considered an unequivocal stand on Cuba. He began by pointing out three possibilities into one of which Cuba must be expected to fall. They were: (1) become independent, (2) become independent with the guarantee of other powers whether European, American, or both, and (3) be conquered and attached to the dominion of Colombia or Mexico. He then set out to establish the impracticability and dangers connected with each. A "mere glance" at the island's limited extent and the moral and discordant character of its population must convince one and all of its incapacity to sustain itself as an independent nation, unaided by other powers. He continued, one portion of the inhabitants of the island as well as neighbors in the United States and "in some other directions" would employ all the means that vicinity, similarity of origin, and sympathy could supply to foment and stimulate revolution.

As to the island's independence guaranteed by one or more powers, the obstacles, he believed, were insuperable. Who should be the guaranteeing powers? Should they be exclusively American or mixed? What should be the amount of the respective guaranteeing powers' contribution to the protecting force, militarily or in other ways? Who should command the force? Would others not be jealous of the commanding power? In regard to the conquest of Cuba and its annexation to one of the new republics, the balance of power throughout the Caribbean would be affected. In that case the interests of other powers might be so influenced they would feel obliged to interpose themselves forcibly to arrest a trend to which they could not be indifferent. If a power or powers intervened only to prevent change "*the United States far from being under any pledge, at present, to oppose them, might find themselves, contrary to all inclinations, reluctantly drawn by a current of events to their side*" (emphasis added). Furthermore Mexico and Colombia were not destined to be first-rate naval powers. Clay then returned to what was his deepest concern: if an invasion were to result in a war that pitted one race against another, the United States to defend itself "against the contagion of such a near and dangerous example would act despite losing the friendship of Mexico and Colombia."[167]

By the time the delegates from Peru, Colombia, Central America, and Mexico convened in Panama City, on June 22, 1926, the position of the United States regarding Cuba could be anticipated. That knowledge, it is generally accepted, explains, in large part, why, although the issue of attacking Cuba was a frequent topic of conversation among the delegates, no decision on the issue came out of the open meetings nor did one appear in any known secret convention concluded by the delegates.

The Cuban issue, however, did not die in Panama City. Reports continued to reach the United States of Mexico and Colombian designs on the island. Rumors periodically made the rounds of Washington that Mexico might launch an invasion on the grounds that Spanish dominion over the island endangered Mexico's tranquillity and safety. The United States fretted most over the prospect of a Colombian attack. In Congress Representative William L. Brent of Louisiana did not mince words in stating his position. The independence of Cuba could not be effected without an attempt by "a certain part of its population attaining the ascendancy," and as a consequence his state would have the black populations of Mexico, Haiti, and Cuba for neighbors. That being the case, "What would be the condition of the Southern planters?" Minister Everett from Madrid reminded Washington, as if a reminder might be needed, that should Bolívar realize his project of invading Cuba he must do it almost wholly by the aid of the "coloured castes" who would, of course, under these circumstances form the dominant portion of the people. He went on to note that a military despot of talent and experience such as Bolívar at the head of a black army would not be "the sort of neighbor whom we should naturally wish, if we had the choice, to place upon our Southern frontier."[168]

Nothing ultimately came of Mexico's and Colombia's project to attack Cuba, because, other than the undisguised threats of Washington, the political and economic instability that soon overtook the two countries and the jealousy between them negated any chance of an independent or joint operation against the island. Cuba was saved for Spain.

London was in basic, if not total, agreement with Washington that Mexico and Colombia should be dissuaded from any action that seriously threatened the status quo in Cuba. That mutual interest in Cuba did not preclude diplomatic maneuvering became evident during the months immediately preceding the convening of Latin American delegates at Panama City. In a communication to Canning, dated December 21, 1825, British Minister Charles R. Vaughn, in Washington, noted that (1) he had suggested to Clay the advantages that might be derived from the United States exerting its influence to discourage Mexico and Colombia from any enterprise that would threaten to destabilize Cuba by its black population "being let loose upon the Whites," and (2) he had learned from Clay that he was drawing up instructions for United States ministers to Bogotá and Mexico City,

> directing them to endeavour to engage the Governments of those countries to suspend at least their intended operations for some months against Cuba; to point out also that, though this Government felt the difficulty of interfering to prevent a final attack, so long as Cuba should be made by Spain the point from

whence hostilities were to be carried on against the New States, yet that the United States would not see with indifference any proceedings which should tend to arm the black population against the white inhabitants, and the plenipotentiaries from this country would, therefore, be instructed to require the abandonment of any part of their scheme of conquest in which the aid of the Blacks was to enter as an essential part.[169]

Canning sharply rebuked Vaughn for his temerity in suggesting that Washington interfere to dissuade Mexico and Colombia from attacking Cuba and cautioned him that "the general maxim that our interests and those of the United States are essentially the same [in respect to Cuba] ... is one that cannot be too readily admitted."[170] More important, Vaughn's remarks re Clay's intention in respect to the issue of Mexico and Colombia attacking Cuba provided Canning with the material from which he fashioned a policy meant to win Great Britain diplomatic points, without surrendering the Foreign Office's policy favoring the status quo in Cuba. Knowing that the United States was determined to shield the island from invasion not only freed Great Britain from being a party to that obstructionist policy, but gave Canning an opportunity to cast Great Britain in a self-righteous role at the forthcoming Panama Congress.

London had been invited to send an observer to the Congress and had accepted. Edward J. Dawkins, an experienced diplomat, was named to fulfill that role. In the third of three separate instructions, all dated March 18, 1826, Canning first noted the well-known desire of France, the United States, and Great Britain that Cuba remain a colony of Spain. He then turned directly to the matter of putting the odium on the United States for preventing an expedition against Spain's insular possessions. Dawkins was to assure the Latin American delegates:

> The British Government ... are so far from denying the right of the New States of America to make a hostile attack upon Cuba, whether considered simply as a possession of a Power with whom they are at war, or as an arsenal from which expeditions are fitted out against them, that we have uniformly refused to join with the United States in remonstrating with Mexico and Columbia [sic] against the supposed intention, or in intimating that we should feel displeasure at the execution of it. We should indeed regret it, but we arrogate to ourselves no right to control the military operations of one belligerent against another.
>
> The Government of the United States, however, professes itself of a different opinion. It conceives that the interests of the

United States would be so directly affected by either the occupation of the Havannah [sic] by an invading force or by the consequences which an attack upon Cuba, even if unsuccessful, might produce in the interior of the Island, that the Cabinet of Washington hardly disguises its intention to interfere directly, and by force, to prevent or repress such an operation.[171]

Why Canning assumed that he needed to or could use the Cuban issue to manipulate the delegates of the Congress or those who might be manipulated could in turn influence national leaders is unclear. Great Britain already had a commanding lead throughout Latin America, Cuba excepted, and all indications were that it would retain a sizable advantage over all competitors for the foreseeable future. He was aware that Bolívar, who fathered the idea of a Panama Congress, had lost interest in it before the delegates convened and that without the Liberator's active support the Congress's impact must be limited. Canning knew, too, that Argentina never seriously entertained sending a delegate to a congress that was the handiwork of the Liberator and that monarchical Brazil, although it troubled to name a delegate, did not see to it that he reached Panama City. Canning must also have known that, except for Pedro Gual of Colombia, the delegates to the Congress were not of the caliber that might influence national leaders against the United States, who, though they rejected its leadership of a Western Hemisphere block, appreciated it as a trusted proponent of republicanism.

On the question of Cuba, Canning knew or should have known that Colombia and Mexico were more suspicious of each other than either was of the United States. Dawkins apparently was not instructed, and understandably did not attempt, to bring about a conciliation between the two because their jealously of each other reduced the chance of an invasion of Cuba, which, had it occurred, would have raised new and dangerous contingencies for his government. If Canning had been taken up on his neutrality offer and Mexico or Colombia had actually seized Cuba only to lose control of it to blacks (as the United States feared would happen), the British West Indies would have been surrounded by states under black leadership. Such a situation could not for long have gone unnoticed by the large servile element throughout England's Caribbean possessions. Finally, Canning's instructions on the Cuban issue were strictly negative. It is difficult to understand how he expected such a policy to enhance British ascendancy in the region where the most positive contribution that Great Britain could make was to promote peace and tranquillity, as it had claimed for fifteen years to be its purpose. In taking the position that

Great Britain would not arrogate to itself the right to control the military operations of one belligerent against the other, Canning, in fact, appeared to favor keeping alive a war that, as long as it dragged on, threatened to engulf neutral powers in the New World and Europe.

Overall, Canning appears to have missed his mark on the invasion issue. Whether or not that is an accurate assessment is not so important as U.S. and British agreeing by the date he wrote his instruction for Dawkins that nothing positive could possibly come out of an invasion of Cuba by one or more of the new states. The issue, thus, could not conceivably be raised to a level at Panama at which it could become any more than a bleb in U.S.-British understanding of their respective roles in Latin America. Canning knew well that playing a diplomatic game was one thing and that playing a war game was quite another.

On each occasion Washington and London found rational grounds for mutual understanding, if not active cooperation, on issues thus far discussed. Agreement in so many areas unquestionably eased the way for North American and British penetration of Latin America. I turn now to two issues that required early resolution if the two powers were to avoid a possible military confrontation. The issues were the "American Family" concept and, with Mexico and Colombia effectively eliminated for Cuba, how the United States and Great Britain would resolve the status of the "Pearl of the Indies" and its neighboring islands and banks.

The American Family Concept

The American Family idea, also sometimes referred to as the Western Hemisphere idea,[172] the American System, and in the words of then Spanish minister to the United States, Luis Onís, a project for a "Universal Republic of the Americas," envisaged a New World league or confederation, with the United States as its natural head, as a counterpoise to Europe. The concept dated back at least to the Jefferson presidency. Later, Henry Clay, still in the incendiary stage of his public career, cherished such a league and other public figures in the United States subsequently embraced the idea. Not only was it floated about without prior consultation with leaders in Latin America, but after it had been set forth as a national objective in 1823, Washington did not take the initiative in exchanging views with the league's presumed members. To the contrary, attempts some new states undertook in that direction were rebuffed in language that made clear that the meaning of the concept and how and when it would be implemented were matters to be determined unilaterally in Washington.

The rebuff did indeed have a chilling effect. There were, however, earlier indications and there would be later ones that an American system along the lines seen by Washington had little chance of getting off the ground. Bolívar's predilection for Great Britain and his distrust of U.S. ambitions suggested that the concept would not have smooth sailing. Sharply divergent policies over institutionalized slavery and related issues resulting from racial and cultural attitudes raised questions about identifying grounds for cooperation. Had ways been found to overcome those obstacles others would still have remained. The refusal of Washington to pledge not to add to its territorial frontiers at the expense of one of the new states did not bode well for a partnership arrangement. It was general knowledge that Jefferson, as president, after purchasing the Louisiana Territory, did not foreclose further expansion to the south and west, or even into the Caribbean.[173] His successors went on to wrest the Floridas from Spain and to view the borderlands with growing interest. Under the circumstances, as would be expected, leaders from various parts of the region shared Mexico's President Guadaloupe Victoria's concern, expressed as early as 1823, over the growing stream of emigrants from the United States flowing across the Texas border.[174] North American proposals for a road to Santa Fe, which Mexican authorities, on the basis of past experiences, saw as opening up for future occupation, by North Americans, of land claimed by Mexico as an heir of Spain, only added to the distrust.

Obviously Washington's policies were working at cross purposes with its avowed ambition to lead a hemisphere bloc. Its opposition to Colombia's and Mexico's plans to challenge Spain in Cuba and Puerto Rico[175] kept alive Latin America's uncertainties about Washington's intentions toward them. That Washington made no effort to counter those concerns by as much as suggesting that it would be content simply to be *primus inter pares* in a hemisphere confederation heightened the new states' sensitivities. But though it is true that U.S. policies did not hold promise for hemispheric cooperation, neither did developments in Latin America. Everywhere throughout the region centrifugal forces—provincialism, emergent nationalism, jealousies—were destroying the ties that had made possible victory over Spain. Colombia, for example, had treaties with Peru, Guatemala, Mexico, and Chile, but none involving two or more of those polities. By 1830 no two countries in the region stretching from the Canadian border to the Strait of Magellan could be trusted to maintain a sustained diplomatic front in the face of a serious challenge from a third party.

As it turned out the American Family idea was never formally presented to the Latin American governments. Enthusiasm for it was clearly on the wane by the mid-1820s. Henry Clay's ardor for hemispheric solidarity had cooled under the weight of his responsibilities as President Adams's secretary of state, beginning in March 1825. He and other members of the official family and the president himself had concluded that the Latin American nations, without navies, without an armaments industry, and without disciplined armies would be poor allies should the formation of a league produce a military challenge from Europe. Also, by 1825 the United States Congress was leaning heavily toward an isolationist position, soon endorsed by the Jacksonians. By the time that the Latin American delegates convened in Panama City, the lack of interest in the United States and the dubious prospects for lasting alliances in Latin America had put the concept on hold. There is no firm evidence that had the U.S. envoys to the Congress reached Panama they would have made a case for the compact; and without some pressure from the United States, the Latin American delegates preferred to lay the issue to rest. But Foreign Secretary Canning in London was not about to take chances.

Great Britain had been a keen observer of the evolution of the American Family concept. While London observed, the ex-colonies, except Brazil, entered the republican camp; London could not stand by and see the new polities become satellites of the United States as well. Great Britain's stake in the New World was too great not to take a firm stance against such a possibility. Republican political systems were one thing; an American league dominated by a republic and meant to restrict European activities in the hemisphere was quite another. If its progenitor's goals were reached they would amount to a mortal blow to Great Britain's economic aspirations throughout Latin America.

How far Great Britain was prepared to go to prevent the creation of a Western Hemisphere bloc under the aegis of the United States is, of course, a matter of speculation. Except for the actual occupation of Cuba by the United States, no other Latin American issue had as great a potential for military conflict between the two powers. The British government doubted that the United States had the necessary internal unity to lead a joint effort with Latin America to exclude Europe from the hemisphere. Much less did it believe that the United States could marshal a naval force strong enough to implement such a policy. Still, the issue was too important for London to chance being wrong in its estimates. It took the occasion of the Panama Congress to let the world know that it intended to exact a price if the Latin American delegates to the Congress were to be so ungrateful of London's past services as to recommend joining an alliance with the United States.

Canning's instructions to Dawkins certify to the Foreign Office's dim view of a league of American states that included the United States. Canning instructed Dawkins to lose no opportunity of transmitting to his Office whatever information he might be enabled to collect on the views and policy of the American governments, their feelings toward one another, and the degree of influence in their concerns they appeared inclined to allow to the United States of North America. The instructions continued:

> You will understand that to a league among the States lately Colonies of Spain, limited to objects growing out of their common relation to Spain, His Majesty's Government would not object. But any project for putting the United States of North America at the head of an American confederacy as against Europe would be highly displeasing to your Government. It would be felt as an ill return for the service which has been rendered to those States and the dangers which have been averted from them by the countenance and friendship and publick declarations of Great Britain, and *it would too probably at no very distant period endanger the peace both of America and of Europe.*[176] (Emphasis added.)

Dawkins was also to raise the question of what was meant by the statement that one of the objects of the Congress was "to confirm and establish intimate relations between the whole and each of the American States." On that point Dawkins was to seek opportunities to let it be known that if by "American States" was intended "only the States heretofore Colonies of Spain" the British government would not be disposed to question the propriety of such mutual and common engagement:

> But you must endeavor as soon as may be to arrive at a distinct understanding upon this point, and to let it be known that an association in such mutual engagements of any State not partaking of the Spanish character, would be viewed by your Government with great jealousy as approaching to that species of League of the Americas against Europe, which you are already apprized *His Majesty could neither acknowledge nor approve.*[177] (Emphasis added.)

Soon after his arrival in Panama City, Dawkins satisfied himself, and so informed Canning, that Great Britain need not be concerned that the Latin American delegates would seriously entertain associating their governments with a hemisphere body headed by the United States. They firmly believed that such an arrangement would not be in the best interest of their nations and, furthermore, that the racist overtones in the prolonged congressional debates in Washington over sending a delegation to the Congress raised questions about Washington's intent of cooperating with the new states.[178] Those assurances along with the Foreign Office's own analysis of the prospects for the league and its informed knowledge of the political climate in the United States, satisfied His Majesty's Government that an "American Family" under Washington's tutelage did not loom on the horizon. That conclusion reached, one of the two most threatening issues involving U.S.-British interests in Latin America was put in deep freeze.

Cuba and United States-British Relations

Historically Cuba has been at or near the heart of U.S. concerns about the state of Latin America. One need only recall the role the island plays in contemporary Central America and played in the Spanish American War, U.S. policies under the Platt Amendment and the Roosevelt Corollary to the Monroe Doctrine, the Cuban missile crisis, the creation of the Alliance for Progress, and the decision to invade Grenada, to appreciate Cuba's impact on hemispheric affairs. Perhaps only on two occasions, the Spanish American War and the Cuban missile crisis, were Cuba's impact on hemispheric affairs more decisive than in the 1815–30 era when Washington and London both considered the island so vital to their nations' welfare that any change in its status as a colony of Spain would unquestionably have sparked an international conflict. This section examines why in this early period they viewed Cuba as an issue of the first magnitude and how the future of Cuba and its island neighbors was resolved to the mutual satisfaction of Washington and London.

The sobriquets attached to Cuba in the early nineteenth century speak eloquently to its importance to the United States and Great Britain. In 1820 the *Weekly Register* referred to Havana as "the real key of the vast Gulf of Mexico" and "the darling object of [Great Britain's] amibiton."[179] Secretary of State Adams likened Cuba to an apple which when detached from the parent tree would be drawn by the laws of gravitation to the United States.[180] During debates over sending envoys to the Panama Congress (1826) Representative James Hamilton (S.C.) referred to the island as the "Gibralter of the Gulf of Mexico."[181] Four days later during the debates, Daniel Webster (Mass.) called the island "the most important point of our foreign relations and the hinge on which interesting events may possibly turn."[182] From Great Britain came the oft-repeated expression of "Cuba, the pampered child of the Spanish Empire" in reference to its special trading privileges, representation in the Spanish legislature, and the inconsistency of its top officials of respecting or not instructions from Spain,[183] and the description of it as "the Turkey of trans-Atlantic politics, tottering to her fall, and kept from falling by those who contend for the right of catching her in her descent."[184]

Cuba appeared on the horizon of U.S. policy when a series of developments during the first quarter of the century alerted Washington to the island's importance to the future of the nation. The acquisition of New Orleans guaranteed that the produce of the rapidly expanding trans-Appalachian region would have easy access to East Coast and world markets only if passage through the Florida Channel were assured. It was the need to guarantee midwestern farmers entry to major markets that first aroused interest in the Floridas as the site of naval bases from which possible challenges from Cuba could better be countered. About the same time, Spain, in support of France, entered the war between Great Britain and France, and was forced to open its colonial ports to neutral shipping in order that its colonies might be supplied with foodstuffs and other essentials. The United States was the primary beneficiary of free access to the Havana market, which proved to be highly lucrative. By 1809 the United States had become sufficiently aware of Cuba's importance to its economic welfare that Jefferson, who was opposed to the United States accepting any territory that would require a navy to defend, would have been willing to incorporate Cuba into the Union on the ground that it could "be defended by us without a navy."[185]

Interest in Cuba, thus, was at a high pitch, when Napoleon deposed Charles IV and some well-placed Cubans sent a delegation to Washington to suggest that the United States annex the island. The delegates were not given open encouragement, but the cabinet discussed their proposal. On the Peninsula, meanwhile, the remnants of the Spanish legitimate government welcomed the proffered aid of Great Britain. The full importance of the new British-Spanish relationship became evident when Spain's colonies rose in revolt and Great Britain was in place to assume the role of mediator between them and the metropolis. With three commercial and military powers possibly poised to seize Cuba, by force in the case of France, by Great Britain as a trade-off for services rendered, and by the United States in recognition of the island's military and commercial importance, Cuba was indeed about to become the Turkey of trans-Atlantic politics. Its future was out of its and Spain's hands.

Aware that Cuba was potentially the hottest spot in the hemisphere, President Madison as early as 1810 staked out a claim to a say in its future by going on record that the United States could not be a satisfied spectator at its [Cuba's] falling under any European government.[186] He sustained that position as did his successors. From 1810 forward there could be no peaceful disposition of the island without the consent of Washington; and if there were war the enemy must be prepared to confront the fastest growing economic and military power in the Western world, with the added advantage of proximity to the island. It was that simple.

With the United States standing tall and firm, the chances of France attempting a military takeover were more apparent than real. The United States and Great Britain were aligned against any territorial designs the Quai d'Orsai might have had on the crumbling Spanish Empire. In searching for a chance to scratch out some advantage France did engage in intrigue, but in the final analysis it had no reasonable choice but to accede to any decision acceptable alike to the State Department and Whitehall.[187]

Great Britain was another matter. It was a trading nation with a huge merchant fleet, backed up by the world's most formidable navy. Mexico, Central America, and Colombia, freed from the Spanish colonial system, were believed to promise ever-expanding markets for British manufactures. In the meantime, Mexico was the major source of bullion needed to grease the wheels of British industry and commerce. More immediately, His Majesty's Government had a responsibility to the planters of the sugar- and rum-rich British West Indies. Their produce, like that of Mexico, Central America, and Colombia could reach overseas markets safely and profitably only through the Florida Channel.

Once it became apparent—say by 1817—that Spain must ultimately lose strategically placed East Florida to the United States, London and Washington focused their attention on Cuba. The British press would have had the Admiralty occupy Cuba by whatever means, to which the United States press retorted that the United States must prevent the occupation of the island by any European power other than Spain, by war if that became the only alternative.[188] Cooler heads among those in positions of power in Washington and London prevailed, and the transfer of Florida to the United States took place without incident.

Even before East Florida was ceded to the United States, external forces had pretty well determined Cuba's fate. There remained only the working out of formal understandings. U.S. policy hinged on two principles: the maintenance of the status quo and no transfer. Maintenance of the status quo meant that Cuba should continue its political connection with Spain. No transfer meant in this case that the United States denied Spain the right peacefully to transfer the island to a European power.[189] By the 1820s the basics of the two policies were spelled out explicitly in numerous contemporary documents, only a sample of which follows. Secretary of War John C. Calhoun wrote General Andrew Jackson on January 23, 1820, "It [Cuba] is in my opinion, not only the first commercial and political position in the world, but is the key stone of our Union. No American statesman ought ever to withdraw his eye from it; and the greatest calamity ought to be endured by us, rather than it should pass into the hands of England."[190] For Jackson's part, "Cuba should not be permitted to fall into the hands of any European power. our [sic] aid can prevent it, and we ought not to hesitate on this subject it is too closely allied to our own safety and prosperity as a nation."[191] In April 1823, Secretary Adams instructed Thomas Randall, special agent of the United States to Cuba, to reply to inquiries with regard to the views of the U.S. government concerning the state of Cuba as follows: "You will say, ... the first wish of the Government was for the continuance in its political connection with Spain; and that it would be altogether averse to the transfer of the Island to any other Power."[192] Henry Clay, on becoming secretary of state, in a communication to Minister James Brown in Paris, the immediate subject of which was the appearance of a large French fleet in the Caribbean,[193] dotted the i's and crossed the t's in regard to the U.S. policy on both Cuba and Puerto Rico:

> The views of the Executive of the United States, in regard to them, have been already disclosed to France by you, on the occasion of inviting its cooperation to bring about peace between Spain and her former Colonies, in a spirit of great frankness. It was stated to the French Government that the United States could not see, with indifference, these Islands passing from Spain to any other European Power; and that, for ourselves, no change was desired in the present political and commercial condition, nor in the possession which Spain has of them. In the same spirit, and with the hope of guarding, beforehand, against any possible difficulties on that subject, that might arise, you will now add that we could not consent to the occupation of those Islands by any other European Power than Spain, under any contingency whatever. Cherishing no designs on them ourselves, we have a fair claim to an unreserved knowledge of the views of other great maritime Powers in respect to them.[194]

Great Britain had cause to take seriously the U.S. claim to a large voice in Cuba's future. It was not secret that by 1825 North Americans for a quarter century had been indoctrinated to believe that at the appropriate moment Cuba would be added to the Union. Jefferson had foreseen such a development.[195] The then popular doctrine of geographic porpinquity ordained that the island, only a few miles off shore, was but a detached segment of the North American continent. Secretary Adams, among many others, employed the propinquity argument in a communication to Hugh Nelson, United States minister to Spain, when he referred to Cuba and Puerto Rico as "natural appendages to the North American continent."[196] To the propinquity argument statesmen and the media repeatedly recalled, in terms that Europeans could not misinterpret, why for strategic and economic reasons Cuba, if not in neutral hands, must be under U.S. control. For example, Representative Brent (La.) warned that Cuba in the hands of a strong power such as England would be a disaster to the developing West.[197] That Cuba by the early 1820s had become a major, if not indispensable, trading partner was widely known. The United States had, in fact, far outstripped Great Britain in the bid for the Havana market and carrying trade.[198] In 1825 Cuban records showed that two-thirds of the vessels entering Havana flew the Stars and Stripes.[199] Representative Webster (Mass.) had such information at hand when he informed his colleagues that U.S. commerce with Havana was greater than "our whole commercial intercourse with France and all of her dependencies."[200]

London, though not unaware of the U.S. economic stake in Cuba, nonetheless received a sharp reminder to that effect in mid-1823. Under date of June 7, Consul Kilbee in Havana reported, "The Americans are in a fair way to monopolising the carrying trade of this Port. In the months of April and May of seventy one vessels which sailed for different ports of Europe, exclusive of the Peninsula, forty one were American."[201]

The Foreign Office had to anticipate four additional situations that might induce the United States to assume suzerainty over Cuba. They were (1) the landing of marines on the island to suppress piracy followed by an attempted permanent occupation, (2) insurgency movements accompanied by appeals for U.S. assistance or incorporation into the Union, (3) the possibility that the United States would occupy the island in lieu of permitting Colombia or Mexico from invading it, and (4) the likelihood that, were Cuba neutralized, Washington would seek control over islands or banks north of Cuba, thereby giving the United States bases on either side of the Florida Channel.

His Majesty's Government's agitation over the prospect of the United States violating Cuban territory while in pursuit of pirates peaked in early 1823. At the time the Navy Department was in the final stages of outfitting, at Norfolk, Virginia, an unusually large expedition under Commander David Porter to cruise the Caribbean in pursuit of pirates.[202] Washington made public the objective of the expedition, but the British suspected that the navy may have had in mind other than the announced goal—specifically that Porter would request permission to land marines in Cuba. His request would be denied out of hand at which point, the reasoning went, Porter would create a quarrel with the Cuban officials that could be used to justify a landing. Minister Stratford Canning in Washington, Consul William Gray in Norfolk, and Rear Admiral Charles Rowley with the Caribbean squadron were all alerted. Stratford Canning and Gray found no evidence to indicate that the United States had any other than the announced intention in mind and Rowley reached the same conclusion after sending Captain Bourchier in command of HMS *Athol* to cruise Florida waters in an effort to learn what he could of Porter's plans regarding the fortifying of Thompson Island (Key West).[203] Before the reassuring news reached London, George Canning had addressed an urgent memorandum to the cabinet, dated November 15, 1822, which began by declaring the necessity of a British fleet in the West Indian seas because of the danger of a U.S. attack on Cuba.[204]

With revolution abroad in the hemisphere rumors about plans for insurrectionary movements in Cuba circulated freely. Not open to speculation was recognition that the United States would play a key role in determining the outcome of any uprising aimed at changing Cuba's political relationship with Spain. From the first, evidence was heavily weighted in that direction. In 1809 influential persons in Cuba requesting the United States either to annex the island or make it a protectorate served early notice that despite the privileged position Cuba enjoyed within the empire all was not well on the island and that the discontented were inclined to look to the United States.[205] For the next decade and more rumors were rife of Cuban insurgents, urged on by revolutionaries from northern South America and Santo Domingo.[206] It was also rumored and equally plausible that privileged elements would seek the protection of either the United States or Great Britain in order to prevent a movement by the popular sectors from succeeding.

And as it turned out, in 1822, the "principal inhabitants" of Cuba, with the intent of guarding against a "revolution from below," drew up a proposal that would declare the island independent of Spain if the United States would welcome Cuba into the Union. The proposal was presented to officials in Washington and was discussed in cabinet on two separate occasions, at the conclusion of which the decision was to demur. At the same time officials took the opportunity to express friendly sentiments toward the people of the island.[207] The decision on that occasion conformed to the position of every president from Washington to Monroe: namely, that irrespective of what occurred on the mainland, the colonial structure in the Caribbean should obtain for the present.[208] In line with official policy, Adams had instructed Thomas Randall, special agent of the United States in Cuba, that should he learn of any group entertaining thoughts of striking for independence, he should make known that the wish of the United States was for the continuance of Cuba in its political connection with Spain. "You will cautiously avoid committing yourself upon any proposal which may be suggested to you of co-operation in any *change* of political control of its [Cuba's] people."[209] Later, Secretary Clay's instructions to Daniel Cook, assigned to Cuba as a confidential agent, were in a similar vein. They read, in part, "It does not enter into the policy views of the government of the United States, to give any stimulus or countenance to insurrection movements, if such be contemplated by any portion of its inhabitants."[210] Late in 1827 Alexander Everett, in Madrid, sharply rebuked a person who appeared to be an agent of Cuban insurgents, informing him that in the event Cubans initiated an uprising in favor of independence, the United States would side with Spain.[211] During the early decades of the century Washington never lost sight of Cuban annexation to the United States, but that act should be reserved for the future and the timing determined by Washington. For the present Spain should be assured that the United States had "no designs on Cuba whatsoever."[212]

Great Britain, between 1810 and 1830, was never a prime prospect for promoting an independence movement in Cuba or to be a beneficiary of such a movement, irrespective of its sponsorship. Its alliance with Spain during the war years precluded London exploiting politically Spain's weakened position in the New World. Later any encouragement to an independence movement would have been contrary to Whitehall's goal, which was assured by 1825, to ensure Cuba's neutrality under Spain. More to the point, at no time was it likely that any island group agitating for independence would have, if successful, solicited British protection. From his listening post in Havana, Consul Kilbee on one occasion did speculate, but with little conviction, that should "respected groups" on the island strike for freedom out of alarm over the gathering strength of the popular sectors, they would turn to Great Britain.[213]

His Majesty's Government, nonetheless, watched with intense interest the unraveling of events in Cuba that might lead to insurrection. Its interest was sustained not from any expectation of benefiting from such an action, rather from Whitehall's near morbid fear that the United States either as a sponsor or beneficiary of a successful revolutionary movement would gain an impregnable foothold on the island.

As early as 1820, Kilbee expressed the view that North Americans and persons connected with the United States were the most intelligent and active element on the island and were possessed of greater property both as merchants and landed proprietors than the British and in event of change would favor Cuba becoming a part of the "American Union."[214] In a later communication Kilbee judged that if, as a result of developments in Spain, the islanders should strike for independence, the "proprietors" would look to the United States. He went on to observe that Washington was well aware of the state of public sentiment and there could be little doubt that they look upon the accession of the island to the Union as an object of first importance. Having stirred emotions, Kilbee sought to calm them by offering the opinion that Washington would not, under present circumstances, venture to employ open force, not out of fear of Spain, but of Great Britain.

From Washington, Minister H. U. Addington sent additional reassuring words. He wrote that in reply to his question regarding the intentions of the United States with respect to Cuba, Adams had replied "without hesitation" that the United States "desired not the possession of Cuba or Porto Rico for themselves, but neither could they see them with indifference in the hands of any other power."[215] Great Britain did not drop its guard, but took comfort in the knowledge that the occupation of Cuba was not in the U.S. immediate plans.

By the late 1820s the concerns of the interested parties over movements aimed at Cuban independence or its becoming a protectorate of a major power had all but vanished. Exploring the circumstances that had so greatly reduced tensions over an issue of such vital importance can best be done by reviewing how each of the three principal actors—North Americans, British, Cubans—reckoned the consequences of the island being separated from Spain. Turning first to the United States: official Washington, as had been alluded to, for at least two decades had assumed that Cuba would one day be incorporated into the Union. That assumption had gained acceptance as the nation's growth added credence to the belief that it was fast on the way to dealing with Great Britain on equal terms, *but there was no wish in Washington at the time to put that belief to a test of arms.* Its proximity to the island, its naval presence off Florida and in the Caribbean, and its strong and growing following on the island added substance to the conviction that Cuba would ultimately gravitate to the United States, as Adams had predicted.

Other considerations, however, argued against the United States rushing to annex the island. At home an early occupation of Cuba would have carried with it the threat of reopening the heated slavery question only recently somewhat cooled by the Missouri Compromise. The incorporation of Cuba into the Union also would have heightened the ongoing debate over the anomaly of a republic possessing colonies.[216] Of greater moment than the impact on internal developments of annexing Cuba was the fear of the consequences on the island itself. The reasoning was that an insurrectionary movement there could succeed only if one or more of the contending parties brought black auxiliaries into the movement by granting them freedom and arming them. Furthermore, the reasoning went, the group most successful in appealing to the servile elements would be victorious. The thought of another black-led nation a few miles off shore was, as noted, anathema to Southerners, as well as to other elements of the nation, including large numbers of elected and appointed officials in Washington. Collectively the elements opposed to a change in Cuba's political status were numerous enough to cause Washington to have second thoughts about any ideas it may have had about altering the status quo on the island. Surpassing all other developments, however, and the one most certain to occur if the United States were to annex the island was that England's response would be an outright declaration of war, which it would probably win and in the process would seize Cuba. Once entrenched there (1) it probably could not soon be dislodged, and (2) from Havana it could at will apply a tourniquet on all Caribbean traffic.[217]

London had no more wish for insurrectionary movements aimed at Cuban independence than did Washington. Great Britain had no interest in gaining a permanent foothold in Cuba at the time or in the foreseeable future. In a fit of empire building it had over two centuries accumulated colonies around the globe, including dozens of kingdoms in Asia and Africa, a whole continent and major islands in the South Seas, Caribbean, and Canada. Now the blessings of colonies had come into question. The Western world was in rapid transition to free or open trade. The maintenance of monopolies over colonial markets was becoming more costly and less rewarding. As the price of imperial control rose and the advantages of free trade were acknowledged, formal empire became less necessary and the winning of trading partners became the name of the game. Great Britain responded to the new commercial mentality by adopting a policy of no more colonies. With that policy in place the Foreign Office sent signals in all directions that it was uninterested in adding to the territory it already held in the Caribbean and South America. Throughout the teens it declined to consider the acquisition of new territories in return for mediating between Spain and its colonies or in payment for its contribution on Spain's behalf in the Peninsula War. When in early 1816 John Q. Adams, then minister in London, asked Castlereagh about rumors that Spain had ceded the Floridas to England, he received a caustic reply from the usually genial Castlereagh, "You shall find nothing little or shabby in our policy. We have no desire to add an inch of ground to our territories in any part of the world. We have as much as we know how to manage. There is not a spot of ground upon the globe that I would annex to our territories if it were offered to us to-morrow."[218]

Castlereagh's immediate successors in the Foreign Office adhered to the no-more-territory policy. Early in 1823 Lord Liverpool informed Richard Rush in London that Great Britain "would not dream of seizing the island [Cuba] for herself."[219] A few months later it was known that Canning's instructions to commissioners being sent to certain of the new states to report on the advisability of extending them recognition specifically stated that the new governments should be assured that Great Britain desired no part of the Spanish colonies in America and that no engagement that might be construed as bringing the new states under His Majesty's dominion should be entertained.[220] Opposition to the acquisition of new territories was also voiced in the House of Lords.[221] Looking to the good will of Spain, Minister Frederick Lamb in Madrid was instructed to "disclaim in the most solemn manner" the "remotest design or desire on our [Great Britain's] part to occupy Cuba, or to appropriate that or any other of the Spanish possessions to ourselves. This disavowal has been made before, not only to Spain but other powers."[222]

The imperial no-growth policy aside, there were highly important considerations that the Foreign Office would have had to factor into any change in policy involving either the occupation of Cuba or its independence. Heading the list was an almost certain costly war with the United States, in which Canada would be held hostage. An invasion, furthermore, would have distracted attention from the Continent of Europe where Canning was playing a deadly diplomatic game of supporting insurgents with the objective of holding off Russia from domination of Western Europe. The occupation of Cuba would also have disrupted commerce with the United States, already Great Britain's major trading partner, inviting heated protests from the industrial and commercial sectors, and putting in jeopardy approximately $75 million in British loans owed by Washington and several states. The West Indian colonies would have raised a special set of problems. London still had the responsibility of seeing that their produce reached their accustomed markets. Then, too, there was the prospect that Cuba, larger than the other islands, replete with excellent harbors, bordering on major sea lanes, and overall better able than its island neighbors to absorb overseas capital, would under British control probably have drained capital from the West Indies to its more luxuriant soils. And worst of all worlds for British Caribbean planters would have been for the Home Government to make Cuba a colony, while honoring the longstanding privileges it enjoyed under Spain.

As British subjects the Cubans would have raised a set of knotty problems for London. The population would surely have chafed under stern British colonial rule after several years of relative freedom under Madrid. More immediately, British occupying forces would have been confronted with widespread local hostility. The British had not made themselves popular on the island. Still remembered was the loss of trade suffered at the hands of the British during the War of 1812. More recently the English had lost favor with the island's element loyal to Spain, when the Foreign Office openly disavowed Great Britain's neutrality by recognizing the new states that arose from the conflagrations on the mainland. Plantation owners also were embittered toward England both for its aggressive actions against slave ships and for having forced Spain to commit itself to the abolition of the slave trade, which some believed was meant to check the island's prosperity in the interest of benefiting West Indian planters.

What of the Cubans themselves? There were groups on the island that would have opposed annexation to or being made a protectorate of the United States, but neither of those possibilities would have created uncontrollable unrest within the general population. Much the same situation would have obtained had Great Britain become the overseer, although the elite, as noted above, would have chafed from being enmeshed in Britain's restrictive colonial system. Spaniards, Creole planters, and foreigners would have accepted Mexican or Colombian suzerainty only after having lost a costly racial war.

Indeed the islanders could have hoped to gain little from outright independence. The administration of justice on the island, although often perverted, was not so capricious as in Spain itself.[223] The future of the island's economy was promising. Its ports were open to world commerce. Its exports, mainly sugar and tobacco, were in demand in international markets. It did not suffer oppressive taxation. Productive capital was being augmented by royalists fleeing the mainland and from the United States whose limited funds entered the island in the form of land purchases, machinery for sugar production, and loans to Creole planters. On the negative side the population would have faced an uncertain future; among other reasons no leadership class had appeared to fill the political vacuum that the exit of Spanish administrators would have created. Weighing all the advantages and the disadvantages, those entrenched in power economically could see no sense in chancing the possible consequences of expelling a weak colonial overlord.

It might have been anticipated that once stalemated in Cuba, the United States would seek to entrench itself across the channel from Florida by gaining a foothold on one or more of the small islands or outcroppings north of Cuba. The United States House of Representatives made an early move in that direction on December 23, 1823, when it passed a resolution calling upon the president to negotiate with the British government for a cession of a part of Abaca Island, near a place called the Hole-in-the-Wall, on which the United States proposed to erect a lighthouse.[224] Richard Rush, in London, presented the contents of the resolution to the Foreign Office, which promptly rejected it.[225] Representative Edward Livingston (La.) feigned shock at the British rejection since the United States had "in the interst of . . . commerce," and "the greater good of humanity," requested but a "few square yards of barren rock . . . on which nothing but a sea bird can at present rest."[226] Commander David Porter, meanwhile, was entrusted to treat with the governor of the Bahama Territory, Lewis Grant, on the same matter. On what grounds Porter was expected to negotiate is unclear, because it must have been apparent that a governor of a territory lacked authority to alienate lands recognized as belonging to the Crown or property whose ownership was in question. Grant made that clear to Porter; all of substance Porter could report back to Washington was that an important consideration in any negotiation would be that the source of the Bahamian government's principal revenue was the cargoes of grounded vessels.[227]

The bones of vessels and their victims piled up on the beaches of the islands and coasts flanking the channel testified to the salvaging of shipwrecks as a lucrative source of income. A report from Secretary of the Navy Smith Thompson to President Monroe dated December 28, 1822, provided additional testimony to the importance of salvaging in the channel area. His report noted, "We are at this time in great measure dependent on wreckers of New Providence [Bahamas] for the protection of our properties in case of shipwreck. This not only gives employment to a great number of foreign seamen and vessels, but it subjects our merchants to heavy expenses."[228]

Washington's interest in territory across the channel from Florida became a matter of concern to the Admiralty at least as early as 1827. A communication from Governor Grant to Vice Admiral Charles Fleeming mentioned exchanges between Grant and Vice Admiral L. W. Halsted on the matter.[229] With the entry of the Admiralty into the matter the plot thickened. Under date of July 16, 1827, Governor

Grant informed Fleeming of the terms of the resolution passed by the House of Representatives. In strongly opposing the U.S. request, Grant raised the question of the ownership of the area at issue; he noted, "This [British possession] had been virtually acknowledged by the Government of Cuba, by the acceptance of our acquiescence that the inhabitants of that Island should not be molested in making salt in return for permission of Bahama small craft to wreck and turtle on the coasts of Cuba."[230] As if to establish a stronger claim to the banks, Grant favored building a battery or other lookout on Key Sal. Of more immediate concern to him, Great Britain should not suffer the commision of any act or deed whereby the vessels of any government, "particularly the Americans," as a matter of usage or in some other shape might later be put forth in support of a claim.[231]

Fleeming took it from there. In a communication to John Wilson Croker, the vice admiral found grounds for believing that U.S. interest in the island went beyond the erecting of lighthouses or other devices to warn off ships. It had been reported to him that vessels flying the Stars and Stripes had driven off a British vessel in the area of Key Sal, Double-Headed-Shot Key, and Anguilla[232] and had carried a ship in distress to Key West. Fleeming continued, "I have reason to believe that some American subjects have lately frequented those Islands and have views of making settlements thereon." Further to establish his distrust of U.S. motives, Fleeming noted that many North Americans were settled in Cuba and that it was not improbable that they, "under the pretense of being Spanish subjects will endeavor to form an establishment on the Islands in question which may at a future period afford them groundwork for raising claim to those possessions on the part of their original country."[233] Fleeming also took the trouble to order Commander Edward Holland to cruise the Key Sal waters in search of intruders. Holland found no "unlicensed" foreigners making salt "or otherwise invading the territorial right of His Britannic Majesty."[234]

Fleeming nonetheless persisted in his search for clues to U.S. interests in the banks. Within a few months he had learned "from sources which may be depended on" that a person by the name of Keene, a native of New York, earlier implicated in the "Affair of General Burr," had arrived in Havana from Madrid with royal orders for the payment of a considerable sum, said to be due him by the Spanish government, the said sum to be paid either in coin or land. The Cuban treasury had refused to provide money, except a small amount to cover certain of Keene's out-of-pocket expenses. Turned down in Havana, Keene next traveled about the island and returned to Havana, having selected some Crown lands on the North Coast and including

Anguilla Island. The captain general, intendant, and Commodore La Borde all rejected Keene's proposal that he be granted the land he had indentified, either on the grounds that such an isolated area would invite smuggling or weaken the island's defense system. The Spanish official had gone on to say Anguilla Island had always been considered as belonging to the English and that if any foreigners were to occupy Anguilla it was better that it be the English rather than the Americans "who would fill it, as they had done the Floridas, with pirates and smugglers." Having by then made his peace with the United States, Keene returned to Madrid and was reported to have been authorized to offer a hundred thousand dollars for the keys on Key Sal Bank.[235] The Spanish government, it was believed, had accepted the offer, but Cuban officials were stalling to gain time. Their stalling encouraged Fleeming to hope that, despite Spain's need of funds, the deal would fall through.[236]

In a communication of August 26, 1828, in which the above information from a dependable source was presumably an enclosure, Fleeming identified what he conceived to be yet another threat to the banks from the United States:

> The United States of America have had their eyes fixed on the territory [the Key Sal Bank], clearly seeing the great advantage which would accrue to them by getting possession thereof, or even by the Spaniards holding it; by which means not only the Gulph of Florida, but the Santarem passage, would be completely closed to the homeward bound Jamaica trade, and that of the Gulph of Mexico, which, when that country has a solid government must become of great importance to Great Britain.
>
> The giving it [the Key Sal Bank] up to the Spaniards would be tantamount to giving it over to the Americans, who would very soon wheedle them out of it, under pretense of erecting Lighthouses etc; for which purpose they have now an Agent employed.
>
> In expectation of His Royal Highness's Instruction on this important point; I beg to acquaint you, that I have agreed with Major General Grant, Governor of the Bahamas, not to permit any settlements to be made and if necessary to resist such an attempt by force.[237]

The Admiralty disapproved of Fleeming's proposed move and also of his proposal that he occupy Key Sal in the name of Great Britain, and so informed him in a communication from Croker:

I am commanded by My Lords . . . of the Admiralty to transmit
to you a copy of a letter from Mr. Backhouse stating the concur-
rence of the Earl of Aberdeen in the opinion of Secretary Sir
George Murray, that it will be expedient, until further evidence
is procured, to abstain from insisting on the right of occupying
or appropriating Key Sal Bank; at the same time that the intention is announced of resisting its occupation by Spain or any
other Power, and I am to signify to you their Lordships' direction
that you govern yourself accordingly.[238]

Washington chose not to make an issue of the Admiralty's position on Key Sal Bank. With that decision the future status of the islands and banks immediately north of Cuba and east of the Florida
Channel was put on hold. The U.S. failure to challenge the Admiralty
might have been anticipated. For two decades Washington and London
had shown a healthy respect for each other. Neither side had been
willing to become embroiled in a confrontation whose probable cost
appeared to outweigh possible benefits.

If in 1820 there had been cause for mutual understanding between
the two powers, there were better ones by 1830. After the czar's Ukase
of 1821 that would close broad stretches of coastal waters above Van-
couver Island to all foreigners, Washington and London had an outside
enemy who drew off some of their suspicion of each other. British influence in Europe, already on the decline, was threatened by further
diplomatic setbacks. On the Continent the political right which had
gained ascendancy by the peace of 1814–15 had provided a few years
of stability favorable to England. As the 1820s drew to a close, however, the right reeled under pressure from an emerging urban bour-
geois liberal left. Its discontent with the old order finally erupted in
violence in Paris in July 1830, quickly spread to Belgium, Poland, and
parts of Germany and Austria, and sent shock waves across the Channel. The Foreign Office had watched the gathering storm and foresaw
the possibility of a situation in which Britain would have a reduced
voice in European affairs. The Foreign Office was also acutely aware
that should such a development actually materialize His Majesty's
Government best have in the United States a friend rather than an
enemy. At home the Catholic and Irish questions, the shrill demands
for liberal reform, the Duke of Wellington's immoderate defense of
Tory reaction, meanwhile, created a political climate that demanded
official attention which might otherwise have been directed to Latin
America. Continental and domestic problems aside, a military confrontation with the United States would have been unpopular. The

British army and navy had shown no wish to fight the United States. Industrial elements would have rankled at losing their highly prized U.S. markets at a time when the economy was already depressed. The general public, meanwhile, exhausted from years of costly wars on land and sea against Napoleon, wanted peace and were prepared to pay a price for it.

In the United States another war with England was simply not in the cards. A military confrontation with the Mistress of the Seas would have directed human and material resources away from industry, infrastructural projects, and development of the West, and would have exacerbated sectional issues such as slavery and state's rights which were smoldering just below a surface calm. Had a war occurred, despite the strong preferences of both sides for peace, the United States probably would have annexed Canada, but Great Britain would almost surely have put a lock on Cuba, strengthened its influence in Mexico, and collapsed U.S. trade throughout the Caribbean area. At the time that would hardly have been considered a good trade-off. The decisive factor, however, in Washington's determination not to let differences with Great Britain come to a boil was a strongly shared confidence that on matters relating to Latin America, and especially to the Caribbean basin, time was clearly on the side of the United States. Sanguine of its destiny, once it became apparent that Cuba would be sanitized, the United States could safely leave all differences with London over Latin American issues to the future, when the United States would be better positioned to deal with them.

The state of the new Latin American nations supplied additional grounds for Washington and London not to permit their interests in the area to get out of hand. They had learned well before 1830 that the region was not the bonanza it was imagined to be while still in its colonial status. British investors had taken a hit there not soon to be forgotten. Every new state had become financially beggared and politically tumultuous. For the foreseeable future the new states offered little promise as reliable partners, of assuring stable markets, or the ability to protect foreign investments.

With their future far from bright, with France's influence in the region declining, with the expansionary dreams of Mexico and Colombia stymied, and with the thought of a united front of hemisphere nations shattered, the United States and Great Britain could, and simultaneously did, turn their attention to more promising regions of the globe. The United States directed its major efforts westward and encroached on Mexican territory with little danger of retaliation; Great Britain turned to the Mediterranean and the Far East. England did not begin reasserting its power and influence in Latin America until the 1850s. The United States, except in Mexico and Cuba, waited until the 1880s. By then there were numerous indications that the confidence Washington had shown in the 1820s that time was on its side in Latin America had been warranted.

5 WEIGHTING THE DETERMINANTS OF POLICY

I have observed, perhaps too often, that between 1815 and 1830 the United States' views of Latin America ranged from friendly solicitude to disappointment or even contempt. I have examined those issues that may have been, in varying degrees, instrumental in bringing about the changing images. The issues in order discussed were (1) the economic development and territorial expansion of the United States, (2) Roman Catholicism, (3) Monarchism, (4) racial views in the United States and Latin America, (5) developments within Latin America, and (6) United States–British relations with respect to Latin America. I propose now not so much to summarize what has been noted in the text (although a certain amount of substantive recall is in order) as to review the issues according to their ascending order of impact on hemispheric relations. I will at times venture beyond the realm of history and into that of intellectual speculation. Since no formula can be taken as good for all time, the relative influence on United States–Latin American relations of any one of the issues might be of greater or lesser importance in another era. My analysis will not lay to rest the question of the importance of the forces believed to have influenced the United States' relations with Latin America during the years immediately following the War of 1812; I hope it will cast light on the subject.

The Republican-Monarchical Issue

Of the issues considered, I conclude that the republican-monarchical one had the least influence in determining how the United States responded to Latin America in the period prior to 1830. The explanation of why the issue generated little heat is found in a complex of domestic and international circumstances.

In narrow definitional terms when Spanish America freed itself from Madrid's overlordship the only realistic political systems available in the Western world were republicanism and monarchism. During their prolonged struggle against a stubborn monarchical regime the ex-colonials embraced republican principles which they ultimately wrote into their constitutions. Certain of those principles were "unnatural" to their society generally and were especially incongruent with values of powerful elements whose aristocratic roots and monarchical propensities could not be ignored. The outcome was a compromise, an unusual achievement at the time. Republican constitutions were ratified, but to make them palatable to those with aristocratic-monarchical leanings, power, as it had been under Spain, was highly centralized either by legislation or by the edicts of strong-minded president/dictators. Thus, out of necessity was created a political hybrid that persisted despite its oft-proved inability to guarantee either social tranquillity or economic well-being. British monarchs, their powers increasingly encroached upon by Commons, might well envy the unrestrained power of an entrenched republican president of one or another of the new states. As early as March 30, 1827, the *Richmond Enquirer* had foreseen such a development when it observed that the political systems of the new states might "indeed be considered monarchies under the name republics."

At the abstract level, Portuguese Brazil, in adopting the monarchical system, differentiated itself politically from Spanish America. At the practical level, however, the difference was not so great as it seemed. Brazil, like Spanish America, had a landed aristocracy whose affinity for monarchical rule was strong and whose influence prevailed when the time came for the colony to cut the umbilical cord that reached three thousand miles across the Atlantic. And, as in Spanish America, the leadership element did not constitute a solid phalanx of like-thinking, politicized individuals. The voice of the opposition could not go unheeded. The result was that Prince Pedro, a scion of the royal house of Portugal, the Braganzas, was acknowledged as Emperor Pedro I, but his mandate was compromised by the restraints he accepted and to which, in broad outline if not in detail, a constituent assembly held him throughout his rule (1822–31). Pedro was indulged certain royal appurtenances, but his imperial title, not his ability to enforce his will upon the state, distinguished him from the average authoritarian president of republican Spanish America.

Latin American leaders had found a way, however unsatisfactorily, to reconcile the conflicting principles of republicanism and monarchism. Neither the leaders nor the new sovereign states, however, were free agents and the survival of the political arrangements they underwrote were in some degree dependent on their serving the interests of the United States, but largely, even determinatively, those of Great Britain.

Throughout the 1815–30 era the United States adhered to two sets of political principles in respect to Spanish America. During the struggles themselves, independence was the essential point of its policy. Once the flames of war had flickered out and Spain had been expelled from the mainland, self-government rather than the form of government became the core of U.S. policy. Jefferson had declared that each government should do its choosing and, to paraphrase John Q. Adams, each state was exclusively the judge of the government best suited to itself and no other nation(s) could justly interfere by force to impose a different government.[1] Adams and most other public figures in the United States were essentially pragmatists. They realized that the chief influence of the United States in Latin America was moral and that it offered a political alternative to the system against which the insurgents had fought.

Although in theory its policy precluded interference, there is no doubting that Washington, and even more the North American public, heavily indoctrinated as it was by the press, abjured monarchy (a Brazilian envoy found the United States so antimonarchist as to make him suspicious of its intentions in Latin America) and greatly preferred that the new states adopt the republican system. Without doubt the United States did what it could, short of force, to ban monarchy, at least European monarchy, from the New World; that comes through clearly in the Monroe Doctrine. The U.S. opposition to monarchy was founded not on theoretical or abstract grounds, but on the view that monarchies under European sponsorship on its doorsteps would endanger the nation. In sum the U.S. interest in the disruption of Spain's empire was to make sure, to the extent that its power permitted, that monarchies with strong European links not intrude in the former colonies in such a way as to threaten U.S. independence, security, or other vital interests. There was nothing devious or hypocritical about the policy.

Portuguese Brazil's opting for the monarchical system put the U.S. policy of freedom of choice to the test. The challenge was met with equanimity in Washington. The question posed, it became immediately clear to insiders that the answer would be in the affirmative. The United States rejoiced at the complete separation of Brazil from Portugal. The clean break encouraged the belief that, although an empire, Brazil would not become a focus of European influence. To officials in Washington the recognition of Brazil would be simultaneously to affirm that the United States was not opposed to monarchy on theoretical grounds and to signal that from Washington's perspective there was a distinction to be made between home-grown monarchy and monarchy in America under European tutelage.

Great Britain would have preferred that the newly independent nations embrace the monarchical system. As early as 1807 Castlereagh had considered sending European princes to the New World. A decade and a half later, Canning enthusiastically welcomed Brazil's decision to erect a monarchy, as assuring a link between Europe and America. London, however, was not disposed to carry its encouragement of monarchies beyond the limits proscribed by its policies with respect to Spain and the Holy Alliance. Its role as mediator between Madrid and its New World colonials precluded it supporting the enthronement in America of European princes of the Catholic faith, other than those of the Spanish branch of the Bourbons. That avenue was blocked when Ferdinand VII adamantly and repeatedly refused to entertain such a prospect. Meanwhile, to have intervened to impose a European prince, whether Catholic or Protestant, in America would have been for Great Britain to assume an interventionist role in Latin America it steadfastly denied to the Holy Alliance. Important as were the above considerations, the key to explaining the British position on monarchy in the New World is to be found in its policy that from first to last London had no wish to make Latin America a political appendage so long as access to its raw materials and markets remained open to British traders. Latin America was in no position to deny that wish. With the most admired non–Latin American nation content to countenance republics as long as British merchants enjoyed freedom of trade with them, the leaders of the new states were free to make their political choices without fear of being caught up in a U.S.-British power struggle.

Attitudes toward Roman Catholicism

Of the issues discussed, I conclude that next to the republican-monarchical issue, attitudes toward Roman Catholicism were the least important in determining how the United States would react to developments in the Latin American nations. Anglo-America, to be sure, was firmly Protestant. Membership in Protestant sects was on the rise, thanks mainly to the emergence of two new denominations, Methodists and Baptists. Determined attacks on the divine origins of the universe and a providential world view, however, were putting a stamp on society. Science, although still under religious wraps, had reached a stage of development that permitted the emphasis in theology to shift from scripture to nature as a source of revelation. That was but one indication that North Americans were ceasing to define their civilization soley in religious terms, and were, in fact, moving in the direction of greater freedoms offered by a secular society.

Between the War of Independence and the War of 1812 there had emerged a mentality in tune with materialism. The new view made it not only safe for those engaged in business to work for profit, but honorable to do so. Political and social connections rather than religious motivation became the source of success. The wider society subscribed to the view that businesses operate according to secular rather than religious standards of morality. In the West, Protestant and Catholic families found common ground in providing education for their offspring. Quite often the only education available was provided by members of the Catholic orders. In Washington, elected and appointed officials, though nearly always members of established Protestant churches, seldom took occasion explicitly to anchor their discourses on denominational foundations.

The shedding of spiritual restraints and the spawning of new social attitudes and values took place within the context of nationalism raised to the level of a civil religion. The United States, by 1815, had displaced institutionalized religion as the hub of life. As the new secular religion grew in strength and confidence, the fear of any religious sect subverting public institutions subsided. This new-found confidence trickled down to the state and local governments which abolished spiritual monopolies and struck religious tests for citizenship from their codes.

The Catholic Church was a major beneficiary of the new mood. To be sure, Protestants twinged as Irish Catholics became the major immigrant group by 1828, but they continued not only to come but to arrive in increasing numbers. There were, of course, individuals who would muddy social waters with anti-Catholic declaimers, but they marched against a swelling current of popular opinion. Anti-Catholicism, by 1830, had in fact been driven from the core of cultivated society. Within years, as nativism swept over the land, anti-Catholics would point the finger and claim to have been omniscient, but for the moment society was in religious balance.

With religious differences ameliorating at home, those in the United States who would inject religion into hemispheric relations were on their own, and alone they had no prospect of carrying the day. The federal Constitution in separating state and church denied would-be Protestant propagandists any claim to the time or influence of public agents or official sanction of any of their proposed endeavors. East Coast business personnel, meanwhile, had learned that commerce and religious doctrines or prejudices did not blend well. With that lesson in mind, those merchants who ventured to Latin America in search of profit left at home whatever religious convictions they may have had or, at least, seldom made a public case of expunging Catholicism from Latin American society. Protestants could expect no succor from the leadership of the new nations. Of those among them who sought relief from the Catholic Church's invasion of the secular world, few conceived of Protestantism as a viable alternative. With Washington legally restrained and the nation's business community unwilling openly to take an adversarial position on religious issues, there was no way that religion could intrude, other than incidentally, into the relations between the United States and the nations of the hemisphere. The United States would remain confident in its Protestantism, Latin America content in its Catholicism.

The Role of the New States

By 1830 the United States had settled on a relationship with the emerging Latin American nations that relegated them (Mexico excepted) to a quite limited role in its plans for the future. It had indulged the hope that an independent Latin America would add to the sum of human felicity. That hope soon vanished. The ex-colonials had proved powerful enough to cast off their foreign yokes, but too weak to erect viable structures on the foundations of Spain's and Portugal's crumbled institutional edifices. Emulation of the United States proved to have its limits. An unbroken succession of failures launched them in the direction of anarchy. To foreign observers the new polities appeared bent on destroying themselves in civil wars.

The new states, far from resolving the problems of political infancy, faced new ones. The agitated struggles of opposing power seekers replaced the stultifying calm of monarchical despotism. Undisciplined armies born of the liberation movements and led by audacious, unprincipled officers turned upon the liberated. Civil liberty disappeared as did funds from national, provincial, and municipal treasuries. Time and again men in uniform lent credence to the axiom that the ability to overthrow bad government is no proof of the ability to create a better one. The general publics, for their part, offered little promise of change for the better. Civilian leaders idolized the mechanics of free institutions without seeking their spirit. Few within the mass population possessed the habits of good citizens. Most were fettered by established habits. Everywhere was lacking a free and virtuous peasantry. Except as leaders might exploit their irrational passions, the publics played no part in either prompting or blocking the will of the determined few. Democratic republics envisioned by the United States clearly were not on the horizon.

Discord, unmistakably traceable to a system that fell short of the East Indian caste system but too rigid to induce the coalescing of classes, kept societies in disarray. Geography and parochialism inflated the realities of social dissension. Aversion and jealousy kept alive vivid memories of the response of the underprivileged in Haiti and Mexico once loosed upon their oppressors. Chary of changes in the traditional social structures, the elites chose to maintain social control by exploiting the animosities of Indians, blacks, and the mixed races. Informed nationals and foreigners predicted that such social structures guaranteed continued stagnation and the containment of energies that might otherwise have galvanized society into action.

On the surface culture appeared integrally Western. Below the surface was abundant evidence to the contrary. Wherever contested, Western enlightened intellectual ideologies fell victim to will. In such an environment there was good reason to doubt that independent philosophical and scientific inquiry would soon flourish.

The new states, beggared as they were in finances, held meager promise for the United States. Though they had accepted in principle the tenets of commercial liberalism, and treaties guaranteed the United States the same legal opportunities as England, Latin Americans had in fact staked their economic well-being on Great Britain. They were also so obsessed with the precious metals of their mines that they closed their eyes to the curse that New World bullion had on Spain. Their cities were little more than nodes through which minerals were funneled to Europe and the United States and European manufactures and United States foodstuffs were channeled to the new nations. The cities' occupational structures reflected their commercial function and their absence of industry. With cheap labor and limited markets there was little inducement to modernize agriculture or livestock raising. Mental lethargy and pent-up demand for foreign goods combined to negate the prospects for economic expansion on the part of national investors. Better for the time being that a few share among themselves the limited fruits of exploitive economies than chance investing in an uncertain future. Foreigners did not originate that view; they surely promoted it.

Fresh, vigorous, naive, aspiring, and supremely confident of the adaptability of its values and achievements to other societies, the United States viewed the ineptness of the new states in coping with critical issues as disqualifying them from having a constructive voice in how hemispheric relations should evolve. The United States accordingly set those relations on their course (a course that was generally followed for the next half-century) without prior consultation with the leaders of the new nations. It was the exclusion of Latin America from a positive role in fixing the limits of hemispheric ties that has led me to conclude that of the six variables discussed in the text, only monarchism and Catholicism played lesser roles than did Latin America itself in the decision of the United States to direct its interests elsewhere.

Racial Perceptions

With its institutions in shambles, even those North Americans who depicted Latin America in favorable terms equivocated when its future was measured against the destiny of the United States. In truth, the disequilibrium in the power of the United States, on the one hand, and the weakness of the new states, on the other, already was proving a major hurdle to cooperation. The hurdle was heightened as the United States expanded territorially and industrially and became preoccupied with its own internal progress, and domestic issues added heat to partisan politics. The most disconcerting issue was African slavery. Expansion raised the question in the white mind as never before of the place of the enslaved race and other minorities. The slavery issue called attention to the limited forbearance of Anglo-Americans for aliens. It was on the front burner during the debate over sending delegates to the Panama Congress of 1826 when the Adams administration was warned that liberal tendencies toward race and racial mixing in Latin America stood in the path of hemispheric cooperation. Racial perceptions and images invoked during the prolonged debate are at the core of the factor I have assigned the fourth spot on the continuum of six variables that most likely determined the drift of U.S.–Latin American affairs between 1815 and 1830.

At least three historical experiences support the assertion that ethnic prejudice dictated that race should be a fault line between the two cultures. The first was the miscellaneous assumptions, brought together over time, which encouraged North Americans to consider themselves God's chosen children. The second was that, after two centuries of fighting Native Americans and observing their habits, the white governing elite in Washington concluded that the Indian was wholly subject to animal impulses, had been untrustworthy, and was a hindrance to development; that uncompromising conclusion was reached at precisely the time the United States was assessing its relations with Latin America. It did not bode well for any sustained effort on the part of the United States to promote mutually beneficial ties with those extensive areas of Latin America populated by Indians and economically dependent on their labor.

African slavery was the third historical experience to invite a racial response to hemispheric matters. By 1820 the future of the institution had become a national issue. Whites who opposed African slavery often were more concerned to reduce the number of blacks in the total population than in their welfare once they were released from enslavement. Proslavery elements, meanwhile, loaded their verbal canons with charges against individual blacks as being perverse and incapable of handling the responsibilities of adulthood in a free society and, as a group, both dangerously rebellious and harboring burning desires to avenge centuries of servility.

Knowledge that large areas of Latin America were demographically black-dominated, and that elites, under compulsion, had adopted the principle that "all men are equal" did not rest well with North Americans who looked to benefit from Latin American independence. In the United States slaveholders and the public (except for a few suffering from post-Haitian neurosis) residing in areas with large concentrations of blacks were generally confident that, though slaves would sporadically rebel, any uprising of blacks would not get out of hand for long. Word from the Venezuelan and Colombian llanos and northern Brazil, however, was not encouraging on that score. That tens of thousands of blacks in those regions and thousands more in neighboring areas lived beyond the arm of the law was common knowledge and strongly suggested that only white regimes capable and willing to maintain strict social controls could hold large numbers of discontented blacks in rein.

There was an added consideration to ponder. Would freed blacks in Latin America contribute to economic production on the scale that they had as slaves? That question was being discussed, with an as yet unclear answer, when word reached the North Atlantic trading community that it was uncertain whether ex-slaves remaining in the countryside would produce more than enough for local consumption. Without assurances that blacks would remain in the fields, foreign capital would be chary of investing in tropical agriculture (the mainstay along with minerals of the various economies). Cuba, in possession of Spain until 1898, was the only exception. There slavery as a legal institution continued long after being abolished in the new nations and in the British and French Caribbean. There was, moreover, little chance that blacks who opted for the urban centers would contribute to production. By the very nature of the urban economies if freed blacks found employment at all it would nearly always be in the service sector.

The view that individuals of mixed descent inherited the least desirable attributes of both parents was widely accepted among Anglo-Americans after they learned that in Latin America mixed races nearly everywhere outnumbered the white population. The anticipated demands of only partially assimilated mixed elements gave North Americans additional doubts that the new nations would be able to cope with their multiplicity of problems. In fact it is fair to say that no group was held more accountable than the mixed races for the low regard that North Americans held for the peoples of Latin America generally. Anglo-Americans might consider Indians to be economically retarded, blacks to be socially unassimilable, Creoles to be social and economic parasites, but they held the mixed races to be at once biological degenerates, social outcasts, political troublemakers, and lacking in all the virtues associated with Western liberal capitalism.

If further evidence be needed that racial preconceptions found their way into U.S.–Latin American policies during the 1820s, the following two thoughts are probably worth considering. First, it seems reasonable to ask how linkages between ethnic views and policy could have been avoided in that era when Anglo-Americans so strongly preferred "whiteness". Second, Barbara Tuchman, in a rather stronger statement than some scholars would be inclined to accept, wrote, "In the first place policy is formed by preconceptions, by long implanted biases. When information is relayed to policy-makers, they respond in terms of what is already inside their heads and consequently make policy less to fit the facts than to fit the notions and intentions formed out of the mental baggage that has accumulated in their heads since childhood."[2] If Tuchman's analysis of how prior experience influences policy makers is essentially correct, as I have found it to be, the political coteries in Washington during the 1820s, given their exposure to Latin America from family gatherings, classrooms, pulpits, and the printed page, could not have failed to be unfavorably impressed with the region's racial composition, or to view the new states as unlikely political, economic, or military partners.

Domestic Developments in the United States

By the late 1820s concerns over political systems, religious preferences, the state of the new Latin American nations themselves, and conflicting views over ethnic and racial matters paled in comparison with domestic developments in the United States as influences upon the course that hemispheric relations were taking. National aggrandizement in the form of technological achievements and territorial expansion, on the one hand, and the preservation of national harmony, which was in jeopardy of succumbing to sectionalism, on the other, sharply focused the nation's attention on domestic objectives and disconcerting issues. A rash of canal building, turnpike construction, and the launching of sternwheelers capable of plying shallow river waters, all financed by a surge in demand for cotton and public borrowing from British banking interests, gave the nations a renewed sense of coherence. Simultaneously, factories that sprang up along the Fall Line produced goods that added variety to and expanded domestic markets and gave impetus to the specialization of labor. Shipping interests depended less on the reexport of European manufactures and more on the transport of domestic produce in which Spanish-held Cuba, Great Britain, and the Continent figured far more prominently than did the new, struggling states of Latin America.

Important as were infrastructural development, industrial growth, and a competitive merchant marine to the nation's well-being, the opening of the trans-Appalachian territories was of greater weight. The occupation of the Tennessee and Ohio valleys and the invasion of the great Mississippi basin became the most massive of all U.S. agricultural migrations. The movement was so in harmony with the popular vision of a Republic stretching from sea to sea, of subduing nature, and of peopling a virtually empty wilderness that expansion across the continent quickly became a national ideology and the central fact of Washington politics.

Had human and financial resources been the only price involved in taking possession of the West, the cost could have been met without so much as temporarily aborting the nation's remarkable growth record. Farm families and adventurers, with rifles in hand, and cotton planters with their gangs of African slaves were prepared to meet all initial costs other than getting their produce to market and maintaining military posts to protect against outlaws and marauding tribal bands. But western expansion involved more than possessing virgin lands. Most serious, expansion sharpened the differences among East, West, and South. The East viewed protected industry and the augmenting of foreign trade as vital to the nation's interest. The South, at once dependent upon slavery and resentful that the East would use foreign exchange earnings from cotton to tighten its grip on the Republic's economy, became increasingly alienated from the remainder of the country. The West, meanwhile, opposed southern slavery and charged the East with seeking to promote overseas trade at the expense of western agriculture. The central government's inability to moderate partisan differences during the 1820s signaled the social disorganization of the next several decades.

Still the positive aspects of the 1820s pointed to a remarkable future for the Republic. Involvement with foreign nations and alien peoples appeared only remotely relevant to a national constituency little versed in foreign affairs and to politicians who had already learned that payoffs in terms of votes, power, and influence were not so visibly rewarding in foreign affairs as in domestic policies. Geographic insularity, a fortuitous balance of power across the Atlantic, a view of Latin America that verged on contempt, and, at home, a well-developed sense of having created a unique culture that owed little to Europe, reinforced that opinion. President Jackson, in coming to terms with Great Britain on such lingering issues as trade with the British West Indies and the future of strategically placed Cuba made national policy consistent with public sentiment. For much of the remainder of the nineteenth century the people of the United States were preoccupied with their own internal progress and paid little heed to external affairs. In the words of Gabriel A. Almond, the main interest in foreign policy was negative.[3]

From one perspective—the commonly accepted one in the United States—President Jackson's foreign policy, in reaffirming Monroe's message that the Union was determined to go it alone, was isolationist. It was also isolationist (1) in asserting that the United States was a continental nation rather than a member with Europe of an Atlantic community and (2) in making apparent that the United States did not have in mind providing a protective shield for the new states. From another perspective, that of Latin America and especially Mexico, Jackson's policies, as had been Adams's before him, were, in their emphasis on territorial expansion, dangerously imperialistic. Both presidents viewed Mexico's northern territories as barriers to western farmers and southern planters (who had been infiltrating Texas in the early 1820s) and in the path of a Union envisaged by enthusiasts as reaching to the Pacific.

Great Britain's Influence

By the process of elimination His Majesty's Government becomes the dominant influence in determining how the United States would respond to developments in Latin America during the fifteen-year span after 1815. It could hardly have been otherwise. Great Britain's naval, industrial, and financial might gave it a strong voice in all matters relating to Western Europe and a powerful one in the affairs of those regions formerly claimed by Spain and Portugal. During the early years of the nineteenth century, when Great Britain's sway throughout the Western world was at its peak, the United States, although it claimed a continuing say on the course of Latin America's evolution, nonetheless resolutely turned its attention away from the area. It did so in the sure sense that its interests in Latin America would not suffer irreparably. Its confidence stemmed from the concurring views that Washington and London had reached (1) on all major current issues involving the new states[4] and (2) on Latin America's place in the future of the North Atlantic community.

That the two Anglo-Saxon societies, which during the preceding four decades had waged two bitterly fought wars against each other, found common ground in opening up a mineral-rich sixth of the earth's land surface was not so remarkable as it might appear. In fact, for either of them to have let Latin America become a sphere of sustained conflict would have been, on all scores, contrary to its interests. Latin America was ripe for picking. Great Britain and the United States were the best positioned to do the picking. Cooperation and, when not cooperation, mutual respect kept down the price of the picking. This is not to suggest that the tropics induced a heated Anglo-Saxon love affair or even that the two powers strode hand in hand in Latin America. They did not. There were points of stress. It is simply to say that by 1830 Great Britain and other powers acknowledged U.S. interest in Latin America and accordingly the United States could safely direct its human, technological, and financial resources to domestic development.

It is worthwhile to review the evidence. We can quickly dispense with four areas in which Great Britain might have but did not press its advantage, either because it was in basic agreement with the U.S. position on them or it did not choose to provoke Washington. First, the matter of religion. Both countries were Protestant and would have preferred that the new states opt for Protestantism and, if not that, then that they erect national churches independent of Rome. The emergent states failed to cooperate. Faced with the reality of having to deal with societies committed to Roman Catholicism, His British Majesty, as at once head of state and church, took a firmer stand in safeguarding the religious concerns of his subjects than did the United States, where religion was not a responsibility of the federal government. The insistence of the Crown was rewarded in Great Britain's treaties of friendship and commerce with the new nations. In them Britishers were granted more religious rights and privileges than those awarded Anglo-Americans in similar treaties. The added guarantees that the Crown won were not, however, of such a magnitude as to put North Americans at a disadvantage in nonspiritual matters, on which Washington did have a duty to represent the interests of its citizens. More important, neither London nor Washington had shown any intent to use religion as a possible way to win a point over the other. The United States in reviewing its goals in Latin America, thus was free to write off religion as a subject likely to be exploited by Great Britain.

Second, although one side favored republicanism and the other monarchism, neither was prepared to stake its future in Latin America on attempting to win the new states to its side. Free from external pressures, all, except Brazil, chose to be republics. Seemingly their decision favored the United States, but Great Britain did not see the advantage, if any, to the United States as cause for discord. Despite its pervasive influence it did not seek to reverse the decision of the new polities to go the republican route. Of critical importance in explaining London's acceptance of republicanism, however, was that Great Britain was a trading nation. In that role it had learned from its successes in developing profitable economic ties in India and the Far East and especially with republican United States that a thriving trade between the two countries was not dependent on their having compatible political systems. Secure in that knowledge, Great Britain was quite prepared to take its chances in the existing atmosphere of open competition.

Third, the two powers were essentially agreed on what turned out to be a decidedly negative evaluation of the principal racial groups making up the Latin American demographic scene. That being the case, there was little chance that race per se would give either side an exploitable issue, although there was a related matter that, under different circumstances, might have. Great Britain and the United States were in opposing camps on institutionalized slavery, with the former leading a campaign to abolish the institution and the latter, at least at the policy level, defending it as a price to be paid for national unity. If His Majesty's Government had used its influence to induce the new polities into making the abolition of slavery a formal requirement for the normalization of relations with the United States an international incident may well have been unavoidable. The benefits to Great Britain resulting from a confrontation over slavery, however, were so uncertain and the potential price so high that it was improbable that London would make it an issue, and Washington never officially took note of the possibility in calculating the limits of its relations with the new states.

Fourth, contemporary publicists and politicians on both sides of the Atlantic wrote and spoke of economic rivalry in Latin America as a major, if not the major, basis for differences between the two Anglo-Saxon countries. Over time many authors have written as if determined not to let the thesis die. From this distance in time it nonetheless appears clear that the heat supposedly generated resulted either from (1) misinformation provided by poorly informed travelers, official agents, and disgruntled businessmen, (2) the misreading of the scanty data available in the public domain, or (3) for no reason other than to mislead the public with the intent of keeping alive animosities stemming from differences wholly unrelated to Latin America. Whatever the reason, an objective reading of a variety of evidence confirms that trade and commerce with the newly developed nations led seldom to controversy (and then on only a local level) and often to cooperation, mutual understanding, or consent by silence.

The reasons are unmistakenly clear. In the 1820s the two countries were simply not competing for the same clientele, nor would they until several decades later. At the time, Great Britain was a supplier of finished goods, the United States of raw materials and foodstuffs. The exports of either country earned returns only if vessels carrying them avoided capture by privateers and pirates, who infested the seas, and home governments were constantly alert and prepared to use force to protect the interests of their citizens against paper blockades, irrational changes in commercial regulations, and corrupt port officials and judges, whose actions were often condoned by those charged with protecting the public interest. Keeping open sea lanes and providing a common front ashore were constant reminders of the benefits of cooperation.

If in the early years of the 1820s there had in fact been reasons to believe that competition for Latin American markets would endanger peace, they had, for all intents, disappeared by 1830. A decade of doing business in the area had demonstrated that the kinds of imports Latin Americans would buy had been established, as had the relative market share of the United States and Great Britain. Furthermore, and more important, few signals came out of the region to suggest that total trade would significantly expand. In response to the unfavorable outlook the British government was by 1830 in the process of closing down a number of its consulates in the area.[5]

Great Britain could not have accepted peacefully the implementation of the "Family Compact" or "League of New World Nations" that Washington for a time entertained as a way of limiting Europe's influence in the Western Hemisphere. As it developed London was not obliged to make the concept a matter of controversy. The idea, under the sponsorship of Henry Clay, had enjoyed popularity during the years that opinion in the United States was strongly on the side of the patriots. Its popularity waned rapidly as Clay, in his role as secretary of state, and others lost enthusiasm for it and official Washington generally recognized that none of Latin America's institutions, under Creole leadership, had the wherewithal to cohere society sufficiently to overcome its colonial heritage. It was the new nations themselves, however, that drove the final nail into the concept's coffin. They early concluded that the United States, far from seeing itself as a working partner, would thoroughly dominate any league of which it was a member, and further, that their northern neighbor intended to extend its borders at their expense. Great Britain came away from the Panama Congress convinced that the Latin Americans had no intention of letting themselves be yoked to Washington. With that knowledge and aware, too, that the United States was increasingly less inclined to look upon the new states as likely allies, London removed the concept from its file of diplomatically active issues. The United States, for its part, was more than willing to let the concept gather dust as Washington matured other plans to assure its leadership in the Western Hemisphere.

The potential for conflict between the United States and Great Britain over issues related to the newly independent Latin American nations amounted to little compared to the potential had Washington and London failed to agree on the status of Spanish-held Cuba. The island, commanding as it did the southern approach to the heavily traveled Florida Channel, was the most strategically important land mass in the New World. Either as a possession or a satellite, the island would give the United States control of both the north and south sides of the channel. As a possession or protectorate of Great Britain, Cuba would serve as a base from which to oversee Caribbean commerce and, in event of war, the movement of enemy naval forces. The island's importance, thus, was such that neither Washington nor London could live with Cuba in the hands or control of the other. The best and most reasonable solution, both sides agreed, was for the island to remain under Spain, which offered no threat whatever to U.S. and British activities in the Caribbean. There were, however, two serious hitches. First, Spain's tenuous hold on the island and unrest and rivalry among a number of socioeconomic groups there made it vulnerable to sudden changes in its status. Second, Washington and London had to be convinced that the other was sincere in its disclaimers about ambitions toward the island.

As long as Adams and Canning (who had an abiding dislike of each other) directed the foreign policies of their respective countries, there were repeated assurances from the State Department and the Foreign Office that their governments preferred that Cuba remain under Spain; but there was full trust on only one point, namely, that under no circumstance should France be permitted to occupy the island. When the Wellington ministry with Lord Aberdeen as foreign secretary replaced Canning's brief ministry with Lord Dudley as foreign secretary (1828) and when Jackson and Van Buren succeeded Adams and Clay (March 1829), distrust largely vanished and the diplomatic impasse over Cuba was broken. The United States and Great Britain implicitly agreed that they would guarantee Cuba to Spain, irrespective of the wishes of the island's inhabitants.

With Cuba (and by extension the entire Caribbean) neutralized, Washington was free to deal with or ignore Latin America on a no-risk basis. In the final analysis the "Pearl of the Antilles" had proved by 1830 to hold the key to the U.S. hemisphere policies. The island would play a similar role in the late nineteenth century as U.S. investments there skyrocketed and as the island figured in the War with Spain. And Cuba would continue to play a key role in determining U.S. policies in regard to Latin America during the twentieth century as a consequence of the Platt Amendment, its political and economic turbulence, and especially during the late twentieth century as Fidel Castro, bankrolled by the Soviet Union, made his ideology felt throughout the Caribbean and Central America as well as parts of South America and Africa.

In the Introduction to this study I indicated that my intent was to treat a discrete era and that my conclusions and speculations would not necessarily be applicable to other periods. I believe that I have held sufficiently well to that goal so that I can at this point claim the privilege of overstepping the restraints that I placed on myself in order to express a view I hold strongly. As far as Latin America is concerned, Cuba as a diplomatic bridge player has over time more often than not held the cards that have determined how the United States has had to bid its hands, and consequently the island's historical role in the formulation of hemispheric relations is deserving of far more scholarly, nonideological attention than it has received to date.

EPILOGUE

This volume has established that as of 1830 national security was the primary objective of U.S. hemispheric policies and that the policies derived from a set of identifiable assumptions, perceptions, and fears. The major assumptions were that French-sustained monarchies in the New World would pose an unacceptable threat to republican institutions, that Protestantism held the keys to heaven, and that Roman Catholicism was a retrogressive force in the world. The predominant perceptions were that Iberians, Indians, blacks, and the mixed races that made up the populations of the newly independent Latin American nations were inferior, that the nations themselves, given their state of development, would be neither dependable allies nor, for the present, valuable trading partners, and that the future of the United States rested on pushing the western frontier all the way to the shores of the Pacific, thereby assuring space for the nation to fulfill its destiny. The most persistent fears were that southern blacks in conjunction with their brethren in the Caribbean would become a menace to their masters and the nation's welfare, and that Great Britain might at any time threaten the Republic's security. Pivotal to restraining the Mistress of the Seas was the neutralization of the island of Cuba until such time that it could be annexed to the Union without upsetting the delicate balance of power among the East, West, and South. Over a time span of more than 150 years national security understandably has ever remained the number one objective of policy makers as well as the public. What has changed has been the relative importance of the other early determinants of policy.

The concern in Washington that part or all of Spanish America might adopt monarchical systems, never a major one before or after 1830, nonetheless lingered on for several decades. Although by 1830 the entire region, Brazil excepted, had opted for republicanism, there were everywhere coteries of well-placed individuals who by choice would discard republican forms in favor of monarchical systems guaranteed from Europe, France ordinarily being considered the most likely source of such a relationship. The views of New World monarchists were shared by elements in Europe who held that the inheritances and environments of the new nations and the turbulent character of the "Latin races" required that the emerging societies receive infusions of fresh European blood and that they be stabilized by leaders from established European royal lines. Those views were finally put to the supreme test and found wanting when in the early 1860s Napoleon III sent French armies into Mexico and godfathered the enthronement of the Hapsburg Prince Maximilian. The resolve of the Mexican people that brought a costly collapse to that adventure in interventionism ended the dreams of monarchy and the fears of republicans that foreign monarchs might take root and flourish in Spanish America.

United States–British Relations

Though Great Britain in 1830 was perceived as posing the major military and economic threat to the United States, in the course of time it, along with Canada, became the United States' staunchest ally. The transition from enemy to ally did not always proceed smoothly. Before the move toward the new relationship became unmistakable, the British Foreign Office had realized its primary goals in both Portuguese and Spanish America. It had shielded the area from non-Iberian powers. It had obtained advantageous trading rights from the fledgling states and had underwritten the Brazilian monarchy as a New World outpost against republicanism. The fulfillment of its early objectives did not prevent England from later intriguing in Central America, the West, and Texas, from carrying on trade with the Confederate states during the Civil War, and becoming involved in the Brazilian naval insurrection in 1893. Each of these occasions aroused resentment in the United States where the public seemed always ready to assert its "rights" and to twist the lion's tail.

The era of misunderstanding ended in the late 1890s when a British-Venezuelan boundary controversy coincided with a surge of jingoistic nationalism in the United States. The Cleveland administration made political capital of the nationalist fervor by demanding that Great Britain resolve the dispute on terms acceptable to Washington. In diplomatic terms what was most significant about the British decision of 1896 was Whitehall's explicit recognition that the United States had a special interest in questions involving Latin America. In acknowledging that special interest Britain became the first European country openly to accept the principles of the Monroe Doctrine. The occasion marked the beginning of a new era between the two Anglo-Saxon nations soon to be solemnized by the Hay-Paunceforte treaties of 1900 and 1901 by whose terms Britain bowed out of the Isthmus and gave the United States clearance to build and control the proposed canal. Over the next few years London took advantage of the new diplomatic climate to reduce its West Indian fleet and garrisons and inferentially to leave to the United States the role of watchdog of the Caribbean. The positions taken by the Reagan administration in support of Britain during the War of the South Atlantic (1982) stands witness to the value that Washington places on the friendship of its one-time nemesis.

Westward expansion proved to be the paramount reason for the United States turning its back on the new nations of Latin America during the late 1820s. Well before then the superiority of the farm, the wilderness, and the frontier over the city had been deeply engraved in the emotions of Anglo-Americans. Jefferson's purchase of the Louisiana Territory and his funding of Lewis and Clark that they might, as they in fact did, blaze a path to the Pacific, and, shortly thereafter, the acquisition of the Floridas and the peopling of the Ohio and Mississippi valleys revealed the depths of the nation's commitment to territorial expansion. The urge for land and more land took on new life beginning with the Jacksonian era. The Americanization of Texas, the recognition of the Lone Star State and its admission into the Union, the Treaty of Guadalupe Hidalgo (1848) by which Mexico surrendered New Mexico and California outright to the United States and confirmed its title to Texas as far as the Rio Grande, and the Gadsden Purchase which ceded to the United States what became the southern parts of New Mexico and Arizona rounded out a nation of continental proportions before the Civil War.

Well before 1890, by which time conventional wisdom held that the inexhaustible lands of the West were in fact exhausted, the nature of expansion had commenced to change. Following the Civil War a burgeoning factory system and mechanized farming began to turn out manufactures and foodstuffs beyond the capacity of the nation to consume. The answer to the industrial and agricultural outpouring was overseas markets. By the end of the century faith in commercial expansion not only to fuel the nation's economy but to relieve the tensions created by the intractable problems of industrialization and urbanization excited emotions much as had faith in the acquisition of new territories during the quarter-century after 1830. With such promising rewards in mind and concerns over the possible penetration of the Caribbean by an imperialistically minded Germany, the nation abandoned its historical policy of isolationism. The national government and private entrepreneurs launched a determined and often ruthless drive for overseas industrial, financial, and agricultural outlets and strategic maritime bases to protect them. Spain was forced into a war that it had no chance of winning. The Platt Amendment made Cuba a protectorate and along with Puerto Rico it became the anchor of a defense system designed to secure the approaches of any canal that might be constructed across the Isthmus or Central America.

With the search for foreign consumers in full swing Uncle Sam energetically courted the Latin American states, which the United States had deserted in the late 1820s, and declined to accept rejections of his advances. Overnight the Caribbean, Central America, and Mexico willy-nilly found themselves within his embraces as would the northern and western nations of South America immediately following World War I.

The Catholic Church

Catholicism played only a minor role in determining the bent of U.S. relations with Latin America during the early decades of the nineteenth century. In the United States Catholics were few in number, their political and economic weight decidedly limited, although growing. Although Protestant values still governed the lives of most individuals, more immediately relevant, the nation was secularist; in contests between moral certainties and the desirability of change and progress decision makers gave the edge to the latter. Washington, thus, pursued the nation's security, economic, and expansionist goals unrestrained by prescribed religious guidelines.

In Latin America, meanwhile, the Catholic Church, for all intents, enjoyed a spiritual monopoly, although there always existed an important strain of anticlericalism that occasionally achieved ascendancy, as for example in Mexico in the 1830s, 1850s, and again after 1910. The Church's grip on the emotions of the popular elements was unchallenged as religious folklore pervaded farming traditions, health, education, and social mores. The Church, however, surrendered any direct influence it might have had on hemispheric affairs by collaborating with and giving legitimacy to power-wielding political and military elites in return for their checkmating anticlericals from denying the Church its traditional temporal roles.

Theoretically abjuring politics, by allying with the elites the Church approved social arrangements that were very much political in nature. For instance, it was obliged to endorse the sanctity of private property and systems that welded Latin America to the world economy, positions that its criticism of the materialistic, exploitive character of western liberal capitalism could not conceal.

The Church-elite arrangement remained essentially intact until the late 1950s. At that time it came under severe strain as economies set in place between 1920 and 1940 began to falter, and loose coalitions of middle-sector reformers, progressive clerics, unionists, enlightened elites, and militant peasants heightened their demands for social benefits and a redistribution of national incomes, which in real terms were declining.[1]

By the early 1960s a Christian school of democratic thought known as the "theology of liberation" emerged from the activities of those who would hasten the rate of reform.[2] Liberationists opposed the separation of theology from contemporary political and social movements, held that change is ultimately rooted in social conflict, and viewed poverty as a structural rather than as an individual problem. The principles of liberation theology received theoretical legitimation and much publicity at the Second General Conference of Latin American Bishops held in Medellín, Colombia, in 1968.

The demands of the liberationists soon made Latin American Catholicism a focal point of religious and political activism. The Church hierarchies responded in different ways to the deteriorating economic environment and the demands of reformist groups. In Colombia and Mexico the hierarchies resisted actions that smacked of Marxist ideology. In Brazil and Chile bishops embraced reformism and set out a radical nonviolent Christian agenda for social change which drew on Marxist principles. Elsewhere the hierarchies basically strove to maintain the unity of the Church.

By the early 1970s liberation theology had won many adherents from among clerics and middle-sector civilians who had turned to "dependency" theories for orientation. The activities of radical elements of the Church impressed the media more favorably than did those of the conservative Societies for the Defense of Tradition, Family, and Property or the passivity of the millions who did not identify with either the left or the right, but who were essentially committed to conservative approaches to Latin America's social problems. That the media had overestimated the influence of the Liberationists became apparent with the fall of the socialist Salvador Allende in Chile in 1973; the strategies of the radical groups there and elsewhere failed to create disciplined coalitions with sufficient political sagacity to confront successfully the dominant orders.

The liberationists lost control of the Third General Conference of Latin American Bishops meeting in Puebla, Mexico, in 1978. On that occasion the bishops were nearly unanimous in voicing their support for social justice and in denouncing political authoritarianism. The majority, however, also committed themselves to nonviolent reform, a position that had the blessings of Pope John Paul II and signaled opposition to liberation theology.

The liberationists were driven into an ever-shrinking political corner when democratizing regimes in Argentina, Peru, and Brazil were added to those of Venezuela, Colombia, and Costa Rica which had withstood the authoritarian trends of the early 1960s and the 1970s; and the mainstream Church simultaneously chose to take a cautious, pragmatic approach to politics. It held that (1) effective exercise of evangelical leadership required an unromanticized assessment of political realities, (2) Marxist principles had lost their cogency as had dependency propositions which had argued economics from a world view at the expense of a sensitivity to the complexity of Latin America's social structures and political movements, and (3) a socially concerned, democratically political stance was in keeping with Catholic doctrine.[3]

Throughout this century the U.S. public and government have been on relatively good terms with mainstream Latin American Catholics, especially in Mexico, Chile, and El Salvador. In the case of Mexico the violently anti-Catholic Constitution of 1917 was received with indifference by a majority of North Americans. By the late 1920s, however, President Plutarco Calles's bitter attacks upon the Church and its clergy had definite repercussions in the United States. Under pressure from the Knights of Columbus and other Catholic groups Washington officially took note of the Church's plight. Later Ambassador Dwight Morrow played an unofficial role in bringing about an uneasy peace between Church and public authorities. In the early 1930s another Church-state controversy over the teaching of social doctrines and sex education in the primary schools of Mexico produced loud complaints in the United States; but Washington maintained a low diplomatic profile while expressing sympathy for the Catholic position. It is important, however, to recall that throughout the Church's struggles between 1917 and the mid-1930s Washington was far more up front in protesting threats to the lives of U.S. citizens resident in Mexico, in representing the interests of U.S. investors in Mexican petroleum and mining ventures, and attacking what Washington viewed as efforts on the part of the Calles regime to promote communism in Nicaragua than it was in taking sides on religious issues.

In Chile after leftist parties, dating from the 1930s, made impressive showings in the presidential election of 1958 and subsequent provincial and municipal contests, the United States strongly backed, including extending financial assistance, the Church-linked Christian Democrat Party and its presidential candidate Eduardo Frei, who won handily in the 1964 election. Following Frei's victory Church-related parties in Venezuela, El Salvador, Guatemala, and Panama made impressive electoral showings.

Since the failure of the Alliance for Progress (1961) the United States in search of allies has courted the mainstream Catholic Church. The two found grounds for cooperation in (1) their opposition to liberationist theologians and others well to the left on the political spectrum and (2) their congruent ideologies and programs that favor pluralist democracy as an alternative to collectivist state socialism. The success of the United States courting the Church was most apparent in the close cooperation in El Salvador where during the 1980s Washington and the Church both gave the Christian Democrat José Napoleon Duarte massive political, diplomatic, and financial support in his unsuccessful campaign against a tenacious leftist guerrilla movement.

Whether or not the awakened Catholic Church and the United States maintain a friendly relationship remains to be seen. There is, however, no disputing that irrespective of its relations with the United States, the Latin American Catholic Church is today and will be for the foreseeable future a major force in hemispheric affairs. It has shed its historical tendency to think in municipal and universal terms and has become a national actor. Furthermore, over the past three decades it has amassed a large body of data on political involvement, protecting its interests in evolving societies, and determining the likely limits of accomplishing church goals through political partisanship.

Race

The shibboleths of Anglo-Saxon superiority and the perceived innate inferiority of dark-skinned people have been major pollutants in the relations of the United States with its southern neighbors. As early as 1830, although racial tensions were at a low key compared with later periods, the juxtapositions of perceived Anglo-American virtues against what were conceived to be the negative qualities of Latin American racial stocks ushered in a lasting climate of misgivings in the North and distrust and fear in the South. The identification in Anglo-American folk wisdom of Latin America as black, mulatto, Indian, and mestizo augured badly for the peoples of the region. At home whether or not blacks possessed the elementary social techniques to survive in white society was being openly debated. Native Americans, moved to lands west of the Mississippi, their attacks on white communities subsiding, ceased to be considered a threat to whites. The mixed races it was assumed inherited the worst character traits of both parents.

The race question heated up in the United States in the aftermath of the Civil War, and Darwinian biology was popularized and was used as a rationale for racial attitudes. Under Darwinism white supremacy became a comprehensive philosophy of life and remained so for the next three decades.

After 1910 racist demagogy declined in intensity, but it would not go away. The tenets of racism were used to restrict immigration from various parts of the globe. Labor unions used racist ideology to justify excluding certain workers from membership. The Masonic Order had separate lodges for whites and blacks. Churches and cemeteries remained segregated. Many social issues at the local, state, and national levels continued to be viewed in black-white terms. Political cartoonists freely employed the cultural and verbal stereotypes associated with southern blacks in communicating their views of the peoples of Latin America.

The liberal establishment had largely rejected racism by 1940. Under liberal pressure the explicit use of negative stereotypes of nonwhites in the media and classroom textbooks declined significantly. Prejudices, however, clearly persisted, as a brief survey of public polls makes clear. The sociologist Emory S. Bogardus in 1928, using what would now be considered primitive public polling techniques, found among whites a strong bias against social intimacy with Mexicans. On December 10, 1940, the Office of Public Opinion Research conducted a nationwide poll in which respondents were given a card with nineteen descriptive words and were asked to indicate all the ones that seemed to describe the people of Central and South America. The result was as follows:

Dark-skinned	80%	Imaginative	23%
Quick-tempered	49%	Shrewd	16%
Emotional	47%	Intelligent	15%
Religious	45%	Honest	13%
Backward	44%	Brave	12%
Lazy	41%	Generous	12%
Ignorant	34%	Progressive	11%
Suspicious	32%	Efficient	5%
Friendly	30%	No Answer	4%
Dirty	28%	No Opinion	0%
Proud	26%		

Since respondents were asked to pick as many descriptive terms as they wished, percentages add to considerably more than 100 percent.[4] A Gallup poll taken in 1968 revealed attitudes much like those of previous years.[5]

The degree, if any, to which North American attitudes toward the peoples of Latin America have changed since the 1960s is open to question. There is no doubt but that the outward manifestations of hostility to Latin Americans have all but disappeared from scholarly studies. Historians have accepted that hostility toward aliens, especially those of African ancestry, has been greatest among unskilled and semiskilled laborers. Although that assessment seems reasonable, I know of no empirical data that measure the current attitudes of workers toward cheap migrant labor. Neither do I know of statistical measurements that establish whether members of the informed public have actually become more tolerant of aliens from the South or simply have learned to mask their innermost feelings. If one assumes that in their totality North Americans have become more racially tolerant, it bears recalling that in the United States tolerance has never meant equality.

The historical record is replete with evidence that race has often weighed heavily, although probably never decisively, in the outcome of official debates relating to Latin America. The debates have received so much scholarly attention that here my interest is to suggest how racial perceptions have served the ends of politicians of quite different stripes and how, perhaps paradoxically, they have at times helped to preserve the identity of weaker peoples.

First the case of next-door neighbor Mexico, which has been a constant source of concern for the United States. Until recently each time a problem surfaced Mexico's racial makeup was featured. Whether its was Mexico's inability to resist U.S. intrusions in Texas, to establish and maintain responsible governments, protect itself from British and French designs on its territory, fulfill agreements regarding the movement of Indians and laborers across the common border, or protect U.S. citizens and investors, the public could expect from Washington a barrage of anti-Mexican rhetoric rich in racial slurs. Examples of the "virtues" of Anglo-Saxonism contrasted with the "evils" of a people of mixed origins could be established from the debates arising from any one of a number of conflicts between the United States and Mexico. No example serves better than the debates by interested parties in Washington over what the price to Mexico of losing the United States–Mexican War.[6] Most of the denunciations of Mexico were echoes of those first voiced as a result of contacts between expansionist-minded North Americans and Mexicans resident

Republic and Haiti, followers of Sandino in Nicaragua, and student rioters in Cuba represented an emerging nationalism and should be taken seriously.

The Good Neighbor Policy (1933) finally addressed the race issue as well as the issue raised by an emerging nationalism. Under its auspices all U.S. troops were called home from the Caribbean and Central America, except those stationed in U.S. military bases. Bilateral reciprocity treaties, meant to promote trade, were signed with most of the republics. The United States created and funded the Export-Import Bank as a further effort to increase trade and to aid the republics to escape the lingering effects of the Great Depression. These steps by the United States reduced tensions throughout most of the hemisphere. The more favorable international climate, cooperation during World War II, the Cold War, and the Rio Security Pact (1947), however, had failed to heal Latin America's mental wounds, and they were reopened when the United States chose to devote its resources to rehabilitating its Western European allies and defeated Germany and Japan (the Marshall Plan) instead of making a concerted effort to assist its neighbors to modernize their backward economies. Washington's preferences were yet another reminder to Latin Americans that from the U.S. perspective the republics, as they historically had been, were second- or third-class economic and military partners. By 1960 bitterness toward the U.S. government was so profound and pervasive that when Fidel Castro came to power he inherited an overflowing reservoir of ill will that he deftly exploited to put Washington on the diplomatic defensive in the hemisphere, where it has remained.

The U.S. response to Castro's offensive was two programs with contradictory goals—the Alliance for Progress (1961) and a stepped-up anti-insurgency operation. At the core of the Alliance was a conviction that if the republics adopted U.S. democratic practices social and economic reform beneficial to the popular elements would follow. There were three catches. First, the United States would set the guidelines. Second, it was almost immediately apparent that the United States was unwilling to underwrite rewards commensurate with the sacrifices status quo-oriented bureaucrats and entrenched interests would have to make if the Alliance's political and social goals were to be met. Third, within months the hemisphere was awash with examples that showed the gulf between U.S. official behavior and U.S. ideals. The Alliance was doomed.

Before the Alliance was, for all intents, written off, the United States had an anti-insurgency operation in full swing. At the heart of that operation was a belief in the United States (and within elite elements in Latin America) that the more radical groups committed to improving the lot of the underprivileged were intent on destroying established economic and political structures and force would be required to combat them. Exit the Alliance for Progress. Enter the military. The armed forces of the republics had been deemed unfit allies in the event of a war against an extra-hemispheric foe. Ordinarily, however, they had an acceptable level of institutional organization and a commitment to force on which to build counterinsurgency units. They needed only specialized training and equipment. Thousands received the necessary training, and equipment was forthcoming. Some units used their training successfully to suppress guerrilla movements, for example, in Uruguay and Argentina. Others fared badly, as, for instance, those in El Salvador and Peru and the Nicaraguan Contras. With the Alliance for Progress in shambles and the outcome of anti-insurgency still in question, the United States invaded the Dominican Republic (1965) to turn back armed elements set on overthrowing the national administration. The three developments of the 1960s are instructive. The Alliance for Progress was the last occasion to date in which the United States operated on the assumption that Anglo-American administrative skills were so superior that they could be effective in quite a different culture. The counterinsurgency program served the ends of the Latin American elites, not the dark-skinned peoples the Alliance was meant to aid. That the invasion of the Dominican Republic was carried out without previously informing, to say nothing of consulting, members of the Organization of American States (created 1948; formerly Pan American Union, 1890) is a striking example of how Washington historically has judged the ability of the republics to respond to "crisis" situations.

Since the 1970s and particularly during the 1980s there were indications that the influence of the race factor in hemispheric affairs was declining. Ideological differences rather than racial preferences determined that the United States should support the Nicaraguan Contras in their effort to unseat the Nicaraguan Sandinistas. Ideological differences also determined the U.S. role in El Salvador. Editorial comment and newspaper art dealing with the debt crisis of the 1980s were remarkable for their absence of Latin American stereotypes so popular a generation ago. This is not to say that the public was not subjected to an abundance of reporting on Latin American "administrative inefficiency" and corruption. What was being said behind closed doors in Washington is unknown to me, but with Latin America's escalating role in world affairs and especially the growing importance of Mexico's relations with the United States, officials in the national capital responsible for news releases had learned not to parade any racial biases that may have been a part of their cultural baggage.

Economic and Political Forces

In 1830 the United States was an inward-looking society consumed with infrastructural development, industrial growth, westward expansion, its own cultural superiority, and the possible threat to its security by Great Britain. Today the United States is a global player of the first rank, but with less freedom to act independently in the hemisphere than at any time in this century. In the earlier epoch Latin America was a backwater suffering from chronic instability and economic lethargy. Central governments had little control over their own people outside the capital cities and almost none over how they and their people were perceived by the United States. Now a hundred and sixty years later in a vastly more internationally complex and ideologically competitive world their voices must be heeded in Inter-American affairs and international agencies.

The republics have followed a tortuous path in becoming the diplomatic power players that several of them are today. Everywhere as late as 1850 and in most instances considerably later, they continued to endure the heavy burden of prejudices and customs of a colonial mentality, latent social disorganization, and a belief that by political means alone they could somehow resolve their problems. Only after 1870 did strong administrations usher in a period of order favorable to the propertied elements who profited from what became known as export-import economies. Foreign investors were invited to put their funds into financial institutions, railroads, port facilities, mines, and meat-packing plants. Virtually no restrictions were placed on the entry and exit of foreign capital. In short order guano, nitrate, industrial and precious metals, beef, coffee, and sugar by the boatload were sent abroad to earn foreign exchange. A torrent of immigrants from Southern Europe and Germany poured into Argentina and Brazil and smaller streams into Uruguay and Chile. They provided much-needed labor in agriculture, transportation, and public works projects, but aroused cultural nationalists who fretted that the immigrants threatened the bases on which their societies rested.

Earnings from exports and profits from underpaid laborers were badly allocated. Earnings were plowed back into the export sector rather than into new products or processes. Absentee landlordism became commonplace. Luxury imports mounted. Corruption increased. Politics and the military remained favored routes to wealth. Fortunes sought refuge abroad at the first signs of political unrest. Only in Argentina, Uruguay, and Chile did a worthwhile portion of the new wealth find its way into human capital formation. Although undisciplined armies continued to frighten the publics more than they did enemies and force and fraud remained institutionalized at least in the more advanced polities, other inheritances from Spain and Portugal were diluted and on the surface the societies appeared to be proceeding in relatively orderly fashion toward their goals of becoming modern states. What they lacked were informed dedicated political leaders and an adequate body of evidence with which to gauge the advantages and disadvantages of heavy foreign economic and technological involvement in basically immature and insecure societies.

In the aftermath of a war fought in Europe in the name of democracy, political space in several of the republics was expanded to accommodate enlarged electorates. Simultaneously political parties proliferated, mostly notably in Chile. The effectiveness of their platforms, however, depended upon their acceptability to the propertied and powerful. Party competition, as a consequence, proved an insufficient condition for social progress. The republics' economies were slow to recover from the disruptions to international trade caused by the war. This condition provided economic nationalists, whose influence had overtaken that of the cultural nationalists, an opening to attack export-import economics as warping national development. The battle was joined when the Great Depression struck and the republics felt the full consequences of being victims of economic forces beyond their control.

The Depression brought economic catastrophe and a rash of unscheduled changes in government. Most of the new regimes were "populist," as for instance in Chile, Uruguay, Brazil, and Mexico. Some were conservative and propped up by the military, as was the case in Argentina until the early 1940s when Argentina, too, joined the populist camp. The populist regimes were quick to enfranchise the popular elements and expand bureaucracies as a means of bonding their relations with the workers without however unalterably severing their ties with the elites or transforming basic economic structures. Both traditional leaders and populists in the more materially advanced nations rejected the export-import model in favor of an import substitution model, the major economic features of which were state capitalism and high tariffs to protect local industry. The latter practice led to grossly inefficient industry and an indirect tax on consumers of nondurable and semidurable goods. Import substitution was also import sensitive and since the republics were unable to find new niches in foreign markets they persisted in relying for foreign exchange on their raw materials and primary products.

Once the effects of the Depression waned, import substitution generated relatively dynamic economies. By the late 1950s, however, its limits had become apparent. Growth rates slowed. The economies could no longer produce the surpluses that property owners and their allies had used to grant tactical concessions to reformist groups as a way of protecting their own fundamental privileges. Income gaps widened. Monetary reserves dwindled. Discontent among rural and urban workers mounted. The middle sectors became disillusioned as their economic status deteriorated. There were rumbles in the armed forces, as always distrustful of the intentions of leftist groups. With nods from the middle sectors the armed forces moved to center stage in one country after another. Before the middle sectors recognized their error they had been party to laying the foundations of a two-decade-long authoritarian rule. With little thought of the long-term social costs military juntas interdicted political parties, strong-armed unions and peasant leagues, and ruthlessly suppressed guerrilla movements in Argentina, Uruguay, and Brazil. In an atmosphere rampant with extrajudicial violence the mere suspicion that an individual might be collaborating with the "enemy" could mean torture, murder, or "disappearance." With the toppling of the Allende regime in 1974 military authoritarianism seemed fully consolidated throughout Latin America, but that soon proved an illusion.

The authoritarian, one-party governments dismantled what remained of reforms initiated by their predecessors. Economies were restructured by domestic and foreign interests connected with world markets and new investments centered on capital intensive industry. As was the case during the middle stages of import substitution the more economically advanced states, especially Brazil and Mexico, achieved "miracle" growth rates that masked a heavy cost to an estimated 80 percent or more of the populations unable to mobilize effectively. The global depression of the 1970s not only aborted miracle growth but sent the republics into economic tailspins which loans totaling billions of recycled OPEC dollars failed to stem.

Confronted with ever-declining buying power and ever-more firsthand experiences with state terrorism, the middle sectors, service sectors, and peasants finally organized protest movements (reminiscent of the populist movements dating from the 1930s minus charismatic leaders) which had the support of the Catholic Church and the cautious approval of Western European powers and the United States. Whether it was the political capability of those movements or that authoritarian regimes welcomed turning over to civilians the economic chaos they had created (never underestimate the survival instincts of the armed forces) or some of both, by the early 1980s the trend was toward the restoration of republican institutions. Of the larger countries only Mexico remained under a one-party system. The newly elected regimes, in debt to a variety of client groups and their actions monitored by the armed forces and foreign creditors, were unable to follow their own political and economic preferences. As of 1990 all the more developed countries had elected regimes, each struggling to moderate domestic dissension, redefine relations with foreign creditors, and find better ways to penetrate foreign markets other than by drug trafficking. To their credit the new administrations quickly established that widespread state terrorism could be stopped.

Latin American Initiative

There is indeed little in the above scenario to suggest that Latin Americans currently have more control over their destiny than at any time since the mid-1820s. Neither do the republics' relations with the United States between 1900 and the 1960s cast much light in that direction. The century began with the United States establishing an economic strangle hold over the Caribbean and Central American polities while it simultaneously increased its economic stake in Mexico.

Washington's objectives in the region were threefold: to eliminate extracontinental influences, to maintain order, and to promote democracy. It was remarkably successful in achieving its first objective, only moderately successful in the second, and failed badly in the third. Its efforts to promote democracy miscarried for several reasons. Its interventions in the politics of the region tended to be heavy-handed. It was more concerned about sanitized elections than democratic conduct. It was ordinarily too involved with affairs of the republics to be a neutral arbiter. Its concern for democracy periodically succumbed to a greater interest in political and public order. Finally, the United States seldom had as allies even the majority elements in the intervened country. Washington dared overlook its failed democratic initiatives because parties repeatedly sought to embroil it in their domestic rivalries. Its recognition remained crucial to the survival of most governments, and the republics, including those on the West Coast of South America, preferred North American over European economic advisers because they found themselves increasingly entangled in international markets dominated by the United States.[10]

Despite repeated appeals for it to take sides in domestic matters and its economic clout, by the mid-1920s the United States welcome in the region had worn very thin. Although the Pan-Hispanic movement of the 1890s had fizzled, other forces were at work to undermine the U.S. standing. Theodore Roosevelt's detachment of Panama from Colombia stamped the "colossus" as an aggressor and set off a wave of anti-Yankeeism that provided an emotional outlet for a latent broadly based nationalism. Once nationalism surfaced it fed on hated U.S. interventions. Nationalism had become a pervasive ideology by the time it received international attention at the Inter-American Conference held in Havana in 1928. The United States fended off the initial challenge; but five years later the Good Neighbor Policy marked its retreat from the use of armed force to intervene in the republics.

The Good Neighbor Policy turned out to be only a small victory for the republics. They still had no real alternative to depending on the United States to absorb their surplus raw materials and foodstuffs or to looking to Wall Street for investment capital. Not surprisingly when Washington turned to Europe after World War II Latin Americans were unsure whether to dislike the United States more for its dominance or for its ignorance and neglect of them. Their dismay notwithstanding, only in unusual cases during the 1950s did the republics fail to follow diplomatically the United States in its campaign to contain the Communist bloc countries.

Though Washington looked to the republics for diplomatic support it had little confidence in their willingness or ability to combat home-grown or foreign ideologies the United States viewed as endangering its own security and progress in the hemisphere. Thus, with small regard for how the republics might react, the CIA sponsored the exile invasion that toppled the left-leaning Jacobo Arbenz regime in Guatemala in 1954. A decade later delegates to the Organization of American States learned of the U.S. invasion of the Dominican Republic only after the fact. The snub marked the public burial of the OAS as an effective agency for debating hemispheric matters.

Paradoxically, when Latin America's respect in the hemisphere appeared to have hit a new low with the U.S. invasion of the Dominican Republic, the republics' autonomy in handling their own affairs had actually been on the increase and they continued on that trajectory. The explanation for the paradox lies in a complex set of circumstances with their origins going back to the 1940s. After war's end and particularly after the establishment of NATO in 1949 the United States moved away from its traditional policy of aloofness and nonentanglement to become a leader of a large number of coalitions of nations meant to combat the spread of communism. Once the United States began thinking seriously in global terms, Latin America, which during the interwar years had been a high priority area in U.S. foreign policy, ceased to be considered as a region of paramount interest. Spokesmen for U.S. policy tended to reflect that view. They perceived hemispheric concerns as remote and seemed either insensitive to or unaware of the possible consequences of their decisions to Latin America. In an era of heightened international tensions the new global role of the United States left the shunned republics freer than they had ever been to take advantage of many diplomatic, economic, and political options that were appearing.

Although most Latin American governments enlisted in the United States anti-Communist campaign they had done so against the wishes of many of their citizens. Some of those in the opposition were congenitally opposed to the United States; some seriously questioned the ability of the United States to distinguish between the Soviet variety of communism and native-born principles to leverage their bargaining position with capitalist and public employers; some had intellectually embraced Marxist/Leninist ideology; and still others believed that Latin America had little to gain from a polarized world. Committed Communist activists, meanwhile, awaited an economic turnaround and scientific breakthroughs in the U.S.S.R. so that Communism could be offered as an economically viable model for the future. That stage appeared to many to have arrived when in September 1949 the U.S.S.R. exploded an atomic bomb and launched Sputnik 1 during September and Sputnik 2 in October 1957, a few months before the United States put its first satellite in orbit (January 31, 1958).

The U.S.S.R.'s prestige among left-of-center elements received an added boost when it quickly responded to Castro's appeals for military, economic, and diplomatic aid in fending off the United States. His survival despite intense pressures from Washington was the first of a series of developments that over the past three decades greatly reduced the U.S. weight in decision making in Latin America. With nationalism on the rise Mexico refused to break relations with Cuba. Chile, Peru, and Ecuador during the 1960s defied the United States by extending to 200 miles their claims to control over Pacific Ocean waters and the regulation of commercial fishing in those waters. The Third World Movement begun by Yugoslavia, India, and Egypt offered an alternative to association with either the United States or the U.S.S.R. Brazil, especially, associated itself with that movement. In the United Nations the republics, beginning in the late 1960s, showed an increasing tendency to vote with the nonaligned nations on issues considered important by the United States. International economic agencies, notably the World Bank and the Inter-American Development Bank, gave the republics somewhat greater freedom in economic and social planning, as did investment capital from and trade with Japan, Germany, the U.S.S.R. and the East European bloc. A number of middle-range powers—Brazil, Venezuela, Argentina, Mexico—began to exercise limited influence beyond their own borders. Venezuela, for instance, took the lead in the creation of OPEC.

When Latin America moved dramatically from military authoritarism to democratically elected administrations in the early 1980s, the United States was faced with yet other challenges to its influence in the region. Washington lauded the move toward democracy, but because elected governments were less dependent than military regimes on the United States to retain the power the new governments were freer to initiate actions. That they would tend to be more assertive, particularly regarding regional problems, became evident after Washington's controversy with the Sandinista government dragged on into its third year. In January 1983 Venezuela, Colombia, Panama,[11] and Mexico formed the Contadora Group, with the objective of designing a regional approach to the dispute. Later in the year the Central American governments—minus Nicaragua—joined the Group. After several meetings the coalition came up with a plan—the Arias Plan—which was presented to the United States in January 1987. The plan, an offer to broker the United States–Nicaragua controversy was unacceptable to Washington as being unduly favorable to the Sandinistas, but being the work of a number of democratizing governments it could not be rejected out of hand as it could have been if set forth by nondemocratic governments. The Group, thus, was left to pursue its mediating efforts and to draw the United States into periodic negotiation in which it had no prospect of taking over the initiative. Finally, the United States in signing a missile treaty with the U.S.S.R. and working with it in search of other ways to reduce East-West tensions accepted that it could not work its will in the world. In acknowledging the changed diplomatic climate in Europe the United States further limited its ability to call the shots in the hemisphere, the point being that if East-West issues were in fact negotiable then the cold war, which for four decades had held much of Latin America together in the only hemispheric grouping in which the United States was the unquestioned hegemon, lost much of its effectiveness as a diplomatic issue.[12]

Conclusion

Monarchism, which by 1830 was the least important of the determinants influencing U.S. relations with Latin America, ceased to be in any way a determinant by the late 1860s when Mexico brought to an end the French-backed Maximilian monarchy. Great Britain, which was found to have had the major impact on how the United States related to Latin America in 1830, gradually surrendered that role and by the turn of the century had conceded to the United States hegemonic status in the Caribbean, Panama, and Central America and by

1910, although economically competitive in Mexico and South America, had become the United States' most trusted ally. Westward expansion, which had become a national obsession by 1830 and a major factor in the U.S. decision to turn its back on independent Latin America (but not Cuba, still a colony of Spain), by 1880 no longer played a significant part in determining what should be U.S. policy toward Latin America, its role being taken over by industrial development and overseas commerce as major determinants. Those objectives prompted the United States to look to rather than away from the republics. If this account ended in 1960, race, which was an important determinant prior to 1830 would have remained so, but during the last three decades, though skin coloration obviously has continued to warp the thinking of many individuals, it has largely disappeared as a major obstacle to understanding between the United States and the republics and has certainly been superseded by other factors.

There is indeed much evidence that U.S. influence in the hemisphere is on the wane, but there is no better evidence than that in the security area. As of 1989 only in Central America was the United States as involved with the Latin American armed forces as it was a quarter century ago. No more than three instances need be recalled to point up that fact. In 1965 only the military regime in Brazil felt obliged to respond in any significant way to the belated call from Washington for the republics to join in averting a "Castro-like coup" by participating in the second phase of the Dominican invasion. Then in June 1979 the OAS refused to go along with the U.S. proposal of peace-keeping force to put down insurrection directed against the dictator Anatasio Somoza in Nicaragua, and instead used the occasion to call for Somoza's resignation. By 1983 the U.S. influence in the Argentine armed forces had declined to the point that Washington simply had no control over the decision of the Argentine military to invade the Falkland/Malvinas Islands. Meanwhile, domestically produced arms, supplemented by those readily available from France, Israel, China, and the U.S.S.R. have greatly reduced the militaries' dependence on the United States as an arms supplier.

The role of the Catholic Church has been quite the opposite. Until about 1960 it remained, for the most part, aligned with the elites which were in turn closely allied with and beholden to the United States. The Church, thus, in effect gave its proxy in hemispheric affairs to the rich and powerful. However, since about 1960 when import substitution economics failed to build a bridge to a more promising economic future radical wings of the Church forced the mainstream to become politically involved in its own right. The result has been that today politicians of the center-right often must rely on the Church to swing votes and the Church in turn has a voice in domestic and international matters, especially in the social area and when Communism is an issue.

During the 1820s the emerging states of Spanish and Portuguese America, suffering chronic political instability and economic retardation, were largely ignored as the United States looked to its future. More because of worldwide ideological, economic, and military competition and Washington's attention being riveted on global issues than any political, economic, or social progress they themselves had made, the republics today have an important say in hemispheric affairs, and have shown a considerable capacity to restrict the United States "intermeddling" into their domestic and regional undertakings. In short, extracontinental issues had laid the foundations of a new era in hemispheric relations, an era in which, to all appearances, the major republics will be better positioned than heretofore to confront the United States. This development is critically important because the issues of concern to the United States—drugs, immigration, debts, the environment—are of such a nature that they can be resolved, if at all, only on a bilateral basis.

NOTES

Introduction

1. *Weekly Register*, March–September 1816.
2. Douglas T. Miller, *The Birth of Modern America,1820–1850* (New York, 1970), pp. ix–xvi.
3. Chester W. Wright, *Economic History of the United States* (New York, 1941), p. 304.
4. Allen Guttmann, *The Conservative Tradition* (New York, 1967), p. 3.
5. *North American Review* (Boston) 13 (1821): 60.
6. Perry Miller, *The Life of the Mind in America, from the Revolution to the Civil War* (New York, 1965), p. 109.
7. Lillian B. Miller, "Paintings, Sculpture, and National Character, 1815–1860," *Journal of American History* 53 (March 1967): 696–707.
8. Howard Mumford Jones, *O Strange New World: American Culture; The Formative Years* (New York, 1964), pp. 295–304.
9. On this point see K. E. Boulding, "National Images and International Systems," *Conflict Resolution* 3, no. 2 (1959): 122.
10. Gabriel Almond, *The American People and Foreign Policy* (New York, 1950), p. 142.
11. Alfred Jay Morrow, *Changing Patterns of Prejudice* (Philadelphia, 1962), pp. 38–40.
12. *New York Observer*, May 17, 1823.
13. James Cowles Prichard, *Researches into the Physical History of Man*, ed. George W. Stocking (Chicago, 1973), pp. xxxiv–xxxv.
14. *American Quarterly Review* 16 (December 1830): 32.
15. For a discussion of the problems involved in the use of travel accounts as historical evidence see Philip D. Curtin, *The Image of Africa: British Ideas and Action, 1780–1850* (Madison, Wis., 1964), p. 23.
16. Henry C. Allen, *Great Britain and the United States* (New York, 1955), pp. 144–47, contains a quite useful statement on the interest in British publications in the United States during the early nineteenth century. Hezekiah Niles in his popular *Weekly Register* was repeatedly enraged by British criticism of the United States, but his feelings did not prevent him or numerous other U.S. printers from publishing a host of British and Scottish books and reviews that were often critical of the United States. See Norval Neil Luxon, *Niles' Weekly Register: News Magazine of the Nineteenth Century* (Baton Rouge, La., 1947). Also see the Preface to Basil Hall, *Extracts from*

a Journal Written on the Coasts of Chili, Peru, and Mexico in the Years 1820, 1821, 1822, 2 vols., 3d ed. (Edinburgh, 1824), with respect to the popularity of travel accounts in the early nineteenth century, and Thomas Dilworth, *A New Guide to the English Language: A Facsimile Reproduction with an Introduction by Charlotte Downey, R.S.M.* (New York, 1978), as an example of an English textbook, written from the English point of view and used in the United States without adaptation.

17. Charles C. Griffin, *The United States and the Disruption of the Spanish Empire, 1810–1822* (New York, 1968), p. 43, n. 3, on the public's lack of information about Latin America.

18. H. Stuart Hughes, *Consciousness and Society: The Reorientation of European Thought, 1890–1930* (New York, 1958), p. 10.

Chapter 1: Domestic Factors I

1. W. B. Cairns, "On the Development of American Literature from 1815 to 1833," *Bulletin of the University of Wisconsin*, Philology and Literature Series 1, no. 1 (Madison, Wis., 1898): 1–87.

2. Frederick Jackson Turner, *Rise of the New West* (New York, 1906), p. 3.

3. Martha L. Edwards, "Religious Forces in the United States, 1815–1830," *Mississippi Valley Historical Review* 5 (March 1919): 434–49.

4. Russel Blaine Nye, *The Cultural Life of the New Nation, 1770–1830* (New York, 1960), p. 265.

5. Jones, *O Strange New World*, p. 265.

6. Joyce O. Appleby, *Materialism and Morality in the American Past: Themes and Sources, 1600–1860* (Reading, Mass., 1974), p. 282.

7. D. Miller, *The Birth*, p. 172.

8. Arthur P. Whitaker, *The United States and the Independence of Latin America, 1800–1830* (New York, 1964), p. vii.

9. Stow Persons, *American Mind: A History of Ideas* (New York, 1958), p. 83; Henry Nash Smith, *Virgin Land: The American West as Symbol and Myth* (Cambridge, Mass., 1950), p. 128.

10. Stuart Bruchey, *The Roots of American Economic Growth, 1607–1861: An Essay in Social Causation* (New York, 1965), p. 195.

11. Marcus Cunliffe, *The Nation Takes Shape, 1789–1837* (Chicago, 1959), p. 188.

12. Lewis Mumford, *The Golden Day: A Study in American Literature and Culture* (New York, 1957), p. 14.

13. Cairns, "On the Development of American Literature," p. 4.

14. Samuel Miller, as quoted in Perry Miller, *Life of the Mind*, p. 273.

15. D. Miller, *The Birth*, p. 25.

16. Ibid.

17. Persons, *American Mind*, p. 82.

18. P. Miller, *Life of the Mind*, p. 296.

19. Samuel Rezneck, "The Rise and Early Development of Industrial Consciousness in the United States, 1750–1830" *Journal of Economic and Business History* 4 (August 1932): 784–811.

20. For the petitions to Congress see U.S. Congress, *Annals of the Congress of the United States*, 16th Cong., 1st sess., December 6, 1819–May 15,

1820, pp. 38, 75, 119, 537, 778, 791, 800, 1821, 2286–96, 2307–23, 2411–24. For petitions to clothe the army in locally manufactured textiles see ibid., pp. 79, 490, 608–11, 613, 626, 674, 850.

21. Edmund Morgan, "The Puritan Ethic and the American Revolution," *William and Mary Quarterly*, 3d. ser., 24 (October 1967): 35–36; Bruchey, *The Roots*, p. 199.

22. D. Miller, *The Birth*, pp. 25–29.

23. Ibid., p. 32.

24. James Kirke Paulding, as quoted in ibid.

25. Ibid.

26. Ibid., p. 30.

27. For investment in canals by region see H. Jerome Cranmer, "Canal Investment, 1815–1860," Conference on Research in Income and Wealth, *Trends in the American Economy in the Nineteenth Century* (Princeton, N.J.) 24 (1960): 555 and for certain states, including New York and Pennsylvania, p. 563.

28. The first steam locomotive was imported into the United States in 1828. A rash of railroads was chartered in the next few years, but their feasibility was not established until the late 1830s and 1840s and thus beyond the terminal date of this study.

29. Douglass C. North, "The United States Balance of Payments, 1790–1860," Conference in Research in Income and Wealth, *Trends in the American Economy in the Nineteenth Century*, p. 577.

30. Ibid., p. 620.

31. Douglass C. North, *The Economic Growth of the United States, 1790–1860* (Englewood Cliffs, N.J., 1961), p. 64.

32. *Quarterly Review* (London) 31 (December 1824 and March 1825): 25–26.

33. Mary E. Young, "Indian Removal and Land Allotment: The Civilized Tribes and Jacksonian Justice," *American Historical Review* 54, no. 1 (October 1958): 31–45.

34. Persons, *American Mind*, p. 153.

35. Cranmer, "Canal Investment," esp. p. 563.

36. Ralph W. Hidy, *The House of Baring in American Trade and Finance: English Merchant Bankers at Work, 1763–1861* (Cambridge, Mass., 1949), p. 93.

37. North, "The United States Balance of Payments, 1790–1860," p. 581.

38. Hidy, *The House of Baring*, p. 92.

39. Figures vary, but see North, "The United States Balance of Payments, 1790–1860," p. 581, and Cleona Lewis, *America's Stake in International Investments* (Washington, D.C., 1938), pp. 13–24.

40. George Dangerfield, *The Era of Good Feelings* (London, 1953), p. 283; Lewis, *America's Stake*, pp. 12–13.

41. Hidy, *The House of Baring*, p. 65. Also see J. Fred Rippy, *British Investments in Latin America, 1822–1949: A Case Study in the Operations of Private Enterprise in Retarded Regions* (Minneapolis, 1959), passim.

42. Calvin Paul Jones, "Spanish-America in Selected British Periodicals, 1800–1830," (Ph.D. diss., University of Kentucky, 1966), p. 238.

43. Leland Hamilton Jenks, *The Migration of British Capital to 1875* (London, 1963), pp. 47–49; Harriet Martineau, *A History of the Thirty Years'*

War, 4 vols. (London, 1877–78), 2:1–23; J. Fred Rippy, "Latin America and the Investment Boom of the 1820s," *Journal of Modern History* 19 (1947): 122–29.

44. John J. Johnson, "Foreign Factors in Dictatorship in Latin America," *Pacific Historical Review* 20 (May 1951): 129–31.

45. Charles C. Cole, *The Social Ideas of the Northern Evangelists, 1826–1860* (New York, 1954), p. 12.

46. John R. Bodo, *The Protestant Clergy and Public Issues, 1812–1848* (Princeton, 1954), pp. 62–63.

47. Henry F. May, *The Enlightenment in America* (New York, 1976), p. 160; Ray Allen Billington, *The Protestant Crusade, 1800–1860: A Study of the Origins of American Nativism* (New York, 1938), pp. 16–17; John Gilmary Shea, *History of the Catholic Church*, 4 vols. (New York, 1886–92), 2:142.

48. Billington, *The Protestant Crusade*, p. 18.

49. Sister Mary Augustina Ray, *American Opinion of Roman Catholicism in the Eighteenth Century* (New York, 1936), passim; Shea, *History of the Catholic Church*, 2:160–61. For a discussion of how textbooks handled the Protestant-Catholic issue see Monica Kiefer, *American Children through Their Books, 1799–1835* (Philadelphia, 1948), pp. 29 ff.

50. The Catholic population rose from 35,000 in 1790 to an estimated 70,000 in 1799 and to an estimated 243,000 in 1820, of whom 75,000 were in the newly acquired territories of Louisiana and Florida, and 70,000 were added by way of immigration. For the 1790s' figures see Sidney E. Ahlstrom, *A Religious History of the American People* (New Haven, Conn., 1972), p. 535, and for the 1800–1820 period, J. F. Regis, "Loss and Gain in the Catholic Church in the United States (1800–1916)," *Catholic Historical Review* 2 (January 1917): 377–85.

51. Billington, *The Protestant Crusade*, p. 24.

52. See *Encyclopaedia Britannica; or A Dictionary of Arts, Sciences, and Miscellaneous Literature* (Philadelphia, 1798), s.v. "Inquisition"; *Weekly Register*, November 23, 1821; *New York Observer*, August 2, 14, 1824.

53. U.S. Department of Commerce, Bureau of Census, *Historical Statistics of the United States, Colonial Times to 1970* (Washington, 1975), "Immigration."

54. Ibid., "Population"; *New York Observer*, July 17, 1830; *Missionary Herald* 26 (1830): 127–29.

55. John Higham, *Strangers in the Land: Patterns of American Nativism, 1860–1925*, 2d ed. (New York, 1968), p. 181. According to Higham few adherents of the Catholic faith resided in rural areas where perhaps 90 percent of the population lived.

56. *Quarterly Register and Journal of the American Education Society* (Andover, Mass.), vols. 2 and 3 (1829–30), carried a number of articles on the growing status of the Catholic Church in the United States.

57. For the concern over the role Jesuits were said to be playing in France see, for example, the *Times* (London), May 18, 1825; *New England Galaxy* (Boston), April 3, 1829, p. 12; James Brown, United States Minister to Henry Clay, Paris, August 23, 1826, in *The Papers of Henry Clay*, ed. James F. Hopkins and Mary W. M. Hargreaves, 8 vols. (Lexington, 1973), 5:638–40.

58. Alice Felt Tyler, *Freedom's Ferment: Phases of American Social History to 1860* (Minneapolis, 1944), p. 364.

59. Ibid., pp. 364–65.

60. *Connecticut Observer,* January 11, 1830, as cited in Ralph Henry Gabriel, *The Course of American Democratic Thought: An Intellectual History since 1815* (New York, 1940), pp. 52–53.

61. Ahlstrom, *A Religious History,* p. 559. For a discussion of the Emancipation Act see G. I. T. Machin, *The Catholic Question in English Politics, 1820 to 1830* (Oxford, 1964), chaps. 8–9.

62. David Brian Davis, "Some Themes of Counter-Subversion: An Analysis of Anti-Masonic Literature," *Mississippi Valley Historical Review* 47 (1960–61): 205–24. See especially the extract from Francis Grund, "The Americans in Their Moral, Social, and Political Relations" (1837), in Henry Steele Commager, *America in Perspective: The United States through Foreign Eyes* (New York, 1947), pp. 85–96.

63. Jefferson to Alexander Von Humboldt, Montpelier, December 6, 1813, *The Writings of Thomas Jefferson,* ed. A. A. Liscomb and A. E. Bergh, 20 vols., Library Edition (Washington, D.C., 1903–4), 14:20–25. Also see Jefferson to Horatio G. Stafford, Monticello, March 17, 1814, ibid., 14:118–20.

64. Christopher M. Beam, "Millennialism and American Nationalism, 1740–1830," *Journal of Presbyterian History* 54, no. 1 (Spring 1976): 192 ff.; *New York Observer,* January 16, 1830.

65. Bodo, *The Protestant Clergy,* pp. 70–71.

66. *Christian Intelligencer and Eastern Chronicle* (Gardiner, Maine), April 1832, p. 54.

67. *Quarterly Register and Journal of the American Education Society* (Andover, Mass.) 3, no. 22 (1830): 89.

68. May, *Enlightenment,* pp. 276–77.

69. *New York Observer,* January 30, 1830.

70. Morgan, "The Puritan Ethic," p. 4.

71. Mumford, *Golden Day,* p. 15.

72. Joel R. Poinsett, Special Agent of the United States in South America, to James Monroe, Secretary of State, Santiago, February 20, 1813, in William Ray Manning, *Diplomatic Correspondence of the United States Concerning the Independence of the Latin-American Nations* (hereafter Manning, *Dip. Cor.*), 3 vols. (New York, 1925), 2:896–98.

73. Great Britain, Public Record Office, Foreign Office, 6/39, Woodbine Parish, British Chargé to the Earl of Dudley, Buenos Aires, September 25, 1830. Hereafter citations from the Public Record Office, Foreign Office will be identified according to the following form: PRO FO followed by the number assigned by the Public Record Office to each country or agency, volume number, and, as available, from whom to whom, place, and date.

74. *Weekly Register,* May 3, 1825, p. 141; December 24, 1825, p. 260; *New York Observer,* June 18, 1825; Robert Southey, *History of Brazil,* 3 vols. (London, 1819), 2:681, 878; Hall, *Extracts of a Journal,* 2:314–15.

75. George F. Lyon, *Journal of a Residence and Tour in the Republic of Mexico in the Year 1826 . . . ,* 2 vols. (London, 1828), 2:245.

76. *North American Review* 4 (April 1822): 430.

77. Joel R. Poinsett, United States Minister to Mexico, to Martin Van Buren, Sec. of State, Mexico, March 10, 1829, Manning, *Dip.Cor.,* 3:1674; Stephen F. Austin, "The Prison Journal of Stephen F. Austin," *Texas Historical Association Quarterly* 2 (January 1899): passim; William Bennet Stevenson, *A Historical and Descriptive Narrative of Twenty Years' Residence in South America,* 3 vols. (London, 1825), 1:252.

78. Lyon, *Journal of a Residence*, 2:244–45.

79. *New York Observer*, September 23, 1826; Stevenson, *A Historical and Descriptive Narrative*, 1:253.

80. United States National Archives, State Dept., Despatches, Special Agents, Roll 5, Jeremy Robinson to Sec. of State John Quincy Adams, Valparaiso, February 20, 1823. Hereafter, USNA, State, followed by title, from whom to whom, place, and date.

81. USNA, State, Despatches, Special Agents, Roll 4, Alexander Scott to Sec. of State, James Monroe?, Caracas, November 7, 1812. Also see John Miers, *Travels in Chile and La Plata; Including Accounts Respecting the Geography, Geology, Statistics, Government, Finances, Agriculture, Manners and Customs, and the Mining Operations in Chile*, 2 vols. (London, 1826), 2:223 ff.

82. *Baptist Missionary Magazine* (Boston) 10 (1830): 28.

83. William T. W. Ruschenberger, *Three Years in the Pacific: Including Notices of Brazil, Chile, Bolivia, and Peru* (Philadelphia, 1834), chap. 12; Southey, *History of Brazil*, 2:681.

84. Ruschenberger, *Three Years in the Pacific*, p. 321.

85. Adams to the United States Senate, December 26, 1825, and to the House of Representatives, March 15, 1826, in James D. Richardson, *A Compilation of the Messages and Papers of the Presidents, 1789–1908*, 11 vols. (New York, 1908), 2:318, 336.

86. Charles A. Barker, *American Convictions: Cycles of Public Thought, 1600–1850* (Philadelphia, 1970), p. 333.

87. Emerson as quoted in Bernard E. Meland, *The Secularization of Modern Cultures* (New York, 1966), p. 28.

88. William E. Nelson, "Emerging Notions of Modern Criminal Law in the Revolutionary Era: An Historical Perspective," *New York University Law Review* 42 (September–October 1967): 450–82.

89. The business community was reinforced in their thoughts and actions by recent arrivals from Europe who came to America to participate in commercial activities. See James Thomson, *Letters on the Moral and Religious State of South America . . .* (London, 1827), p. 109.

90. Persons, *American Mind*, pp. 89, 181 ff.

91. U.S. Congress, *Register of Debates of Congress*, 20th Cong., 1st sess., Appendix; *Quarterly Register and Journal of the American Education Society* 21 (1829–30): 221.

92. Edwards, "Religious Forces," p. 447.

93. Ibid.

94. Gilbert J. Garraghan, *The Jesuits of the Middle United States*, 3 vols. (New York, 1938), 2:196; Robert F. Berkhofer, Jr., *The White Man's Indian: Images of the American Indian from Columbus to the Present* (New York, 1978), pp. 149–53. U.S. Congress, 28th Cong., 1st sess., Executive Docs., Doc. 247, Serial 443, *Indian School Funding, Letter from the Secretary of War*, May 4, 1844, provides the annual breakdown of the "civilization" fund for the 1820s. Similar data appear in U.S. Congress, 27th Cong., 3d sess., House Docs. 1842–43, Doc. 203, Serial Set 423. Also see the voluminous correspondence of the Jesuits William DuBourg and C. F. Van Quickenborne with the secretaries of war during the 1820s in "Letters Received by the Office of Indian Affairs, 1824–1881—Schools," in USNA, War, Roll 4, pp. 772–74, which provides interesting data on the number of priests and students involved, as well as on construction and maintenance costs.

95. John Q. Adams to Richard C. Anderson, appointed U.S. Minister to Colombia, Washington, May 27, 1823, Manning, *Dip.Cor.*, 1:201–2.

96. Wilkens B. Winn, "The Issue of Religious Liberty in the United States Commercial Treaty with Colombia, 1824," *The Americas* 26, no. 3 (1970): 294–96.

97. Ibid.

98. On missionary societies see the *Quarterly Register and Journal of the American Education Society* 1 (1827): 133; John L. Thomas, "Romantic Reform in America, 1815–1865," *American Quarterly* 17 (Winter 1965): 657; Bodo, *The Protestant Clergy*, p. 89.

99. Henry Onderdonk, "A Sermon Delivered before the New York Protestant Episcopal Missionary Society," as quoted in William Gribben, "A Matter of Faith: North America's Religion and South America's Independence," *The Americas* 31, no. 4 (1975): 480.

100. New Hampshire Bible Society, *Sixth Report* (Concord), September 17, 1817.

101. See the *New York Observer*, May 24, 1823; *Missionary Herald* (Boston) 19 (June 1823): 188; 20 (January 1824): 22; 22 (1826): 6; 23 (1827): 10.

102. See the *Missionary Herald* 23 (October 1827): 321.

103. *Christian Herald* 11, no. 6 (March 20, 1824): 179–80.

104. *New York Observer*, April 18, November 25, 1826.

105. *Christian Herald* 11, no. 6 (March 20, 1824): 179–80.

106. *New York Observer*, November 25, 1826.

107. *Daily National Intelligencer*, August 20, 1828. Also see the *New York Observer*, November 25, 1826.

108. *New York Observer*, October 23, 1830.

109. Ibid., November 13, 1824.

110. Ibid.

111. See chapter 3.

112. Dexter Perkins, *Hands Off: A History of the Monroe Doctrine* (Boston, 1946), p. 109.

113. For a more detailed discussion of the Bolivian Constitution of 1826 see John J. Johnson, *Simón Bolívar and Spanish American Independence, 1783–1830* (Princeton, 1968), pp. 94–97, 200–214.

114. William Spence Robertson, *France and Latin-American Independence* (New York, 1939), pp. 160–65.

115. PRO FO 185/100, "Extract of a letter from Mr. Williams to Mr. Planta, Lima, February 17, 1825; PRO FO 50/14, H. G. Ward to George Canning (Secret and Confidential), Mexico, September 22, 1825, in C. K. Webster, *Britain and the Independence of Latin America, 1812–1830*, 2 vols. (London, 1938), 1:480–85.

116. Robertson, *France and Latin-American Independence*, p. 517.

117. Ibid., pp. 518–29. Also see PRO FO 6/3, Woodbine Parish to Earl of Aberdeen, Buenos Aires, September 26, 1829, in which the British consul, recalling the scheme to place Prince Lucca on a Platean throne, viewed the renewed interest of France in the La Plata as a matter of concern to London.

118. PRO FO 50/3, George Canning to Lionel Hervey (Secret), October 10, 1823, Webster, *Britain and Independence*, 1:436–38. Also see Canning to Sir William à Court, ibid., 2:390–93, and Frederick Lamb to Canning, Aranjuez, June 20, 1825, ibid., 2:442–47.

119. PRO FO 6/4, Parish to Canning, Buenos Aires, June 25, 1824.

120. PRO FO 204/Box 7, H. G. Ward to ?, Mexico, October 26, 1826.

121. PRO FO 6/16, Lord Ponsonby to Robert Gordon, Buenos Aires, January 4, 1827.

122. PRO FO 18/56, J. P. Henderson to John Bidwell, Bogotá, September 14, 1828.

123. PRO FO 18/74, P. Campbell to Aberdeen, Bogotá, March 6, 1830.

124. Sec. of State James Monroe to Alexander Scott, United States Agent to Caracas, Washington, May 14, 1812, Manning, Dip.Cor., 1:14–16.

125. Sec. of State Henry Clay to Joel R. Poinsett, Washington, March 26, 1825, Manning, Dip.Cor., 1:229–33.

126. Henry Clay to William Miller, Washington, April 22, 1825, Manning, Dip.Cor., 1:239–41.

127. John Q. Adams to Caesar A. Rodney, appointed United States Minister to Buenos Aires, Washington, May 17, 1823, Manning, Dip.Cor., 1:186–92.

128. For the no-transfer principle see John A. Logan, Jr., No Transfer: An American Security Principle (New Haven, Conn., 1961). John Q. Adams as quoted in Dexter Perkins, The Monroe Doctrine, 1823–1826 (Cambridge, Mass., 1927), p. 86.

129. Clay to Simón Bolívar, Washington, October 27, 1828, in Henry Clay, The Works of Henry Clay Comprising His Life, Correspondence, and Speeches, ed. Calvin Colton, 10 vols. (New York, 1904), 1:266–67. William Henry Harrison, at the time United States minister to Colombia, showed Colonel J. P. Henderson, British consul general to Colombia, "the official copy" of Clay's communication to Bolívar. See PRO FO 18/68, Henderson to John Bidwell, Bogotá, August 3, 1829. Also see William Henry Harrison, Remarks of General Harrison of the United States to the Republic of Colombia to General Bolívar on the Affairs of Colombia (Washington, 1830).

130. The importance of the economic factor on France's decision to rush recognition of the new states once Louis Philippe became king is discussed in Robertson, France and Latin-American Independence, pp. 526–35.

Chapter 2: Domestic Factors II

1. Frank Tannenbaum, The American Tradition in Foreign Policy (Norman, Okla., 1956), p. 10 and passim.

2. Jedidiah Morse, The American Geography or a View of the Present Situation in the United States of America (Elizabeth Town, 1789), pp. 468–69.

3. Jefferson to John Adams, Monticello, August 1, 1816, in Thomas Jefferson, Writings, 15:56–59; Arthur A. Ekirch, Ideas and Ideals and American Diplomacy: A History of Their Growth and Interaction (New York, 1966), p. 30.

4. See Walter LaFeber, The New Empire: An Interpretation of American Expansion, 1860–1898 (Ithaca, N.Y., 1967), p. 3.

5. Jones, O Strange New World, p. 303.

6. Oscar Handlin, This Was America: True Accounts of People and Places, Manners and Customs, as Recorded by European Travelers to the Western Shore in the Eighteenth, Nineteenth, and Twentieth Centuries (Cambridge, Mass., 1949), p. 173; Reinhold Niebuhr, The Irony of American History (New York, 1952), p. 28.

7. New York Observer, November 20, 1830.

8. William Haller, *Foxe's Book of Martyrs and the Elect Nation* (London, 1963), see chap. 7, "The Elect Nation."

9. Fredrick Merk, *Manifest Destiny and Mission in American History: An Interpretation* (New York, 1963), p. 265. For an example of the retention of the basic beliefs of the doctrine by important sectors of the American public see Albert Beveridge's turn-of-the-century remarks before the United States Senate on the United States as a redeemer nation in Ernest Lee Tuveson, *Redeemer Nation: The Idea of America's Millennial Role* (Chicago, 1968), Preface.

10. Kiefer, *American Children*; Ruth Miller Elson, *Guardians of Tradition: American Schoolbooks of the Nineteenth Century* (Lincoln, Nebr., 1965); Marie Léonore Fell, *The Foundation of Nativism in American Textbooks, 1783–1860* (Washington, D.C., 1941); Michael V. Belok, *Forming the American Minds: Early School-books and Their Compilers, 1783–1837* (Agra, India, 1973); Ruth S. Freeman, *Yesterday's School Books* (New York, 1960); and Alice W. Spieseke, *The First Textbooks in American History and Their Compiler, John M'Culloch* (New York, 1938), all discuss the treatment of foreign peoples and cultures found in early U.S. textbooks.

11. Geography textbooks rather than history textbooks were in the early nineteenth century the primary classroom source of information about foreign peoples. See Charles R. Carpenter, *History of American Schoolbooks* (Philadelphia, 1963), p. 196.

12. This summary statement is based primarily on Jedidiah Morse, *The American Universal Geography; or a View of the Present State of All the Kingdoms, States, and Colonies in the Known World*, 7th ed., 2 vols. (Boston, 1819). By the publication of the 7th edition Morse's was the most widely used geography textbook in the United States. See Ralph H. Brown, "The American Geographies of Jedidiah Morse," *Annals of the Association of American Geographers* 31 (September 1941): 145–217, and Belok, *Forming the American Minds*, chaps. 2, 8. Also see William Guthrie, *A Geographical, Historical, and Commercial Grammar: Exhibiting the Present States of the World*, 24th ed. (London, 1827), U.S. editions 1794–95 and 1820; Nathaniel Dwight, *A Short but Comprehensive System of Geography of the World*, 7th ed. (Northampton, Mass. 1814); John Hubbard, *The Rudiments of Geography*, 6th ed. (Barnard, Vt., 1814); Elijah Parish, *A Compendious System of Universal Geography, Designed for Schools* (Newburyport, Mass., 1807); William C. Woodbridge, *Rudiments of Geography on a New Plan, Designed to Assist the Memory by Comparison and Classification*, 18th ed. (Hartford, Conn., 1835); J. E. Worcester, *A Geographical Dictionary or Universal Gazetteer, Ancient and Modern*, 2 vols. (Andover, Mass., 1817).

13. "Traits of the Spanish Character," *North American Review* 5 (May 1817): 30–31. Also see 19 (July 1824): 158–208.

14. "De Stael's Letters from England," *North American Review* 26 (January 1828): 172.

15. Alexander H. Everett, *America: Or a General Survey of the Political Situation of the Several Powers of the Western Continent* (Philadelphia, 1827), p. 172.

16. See the discussion in the *Christian Herald* (New York), August 3, 1822.

17. *Aurora* (Philadelphia), October 30, 1819.

18. "Traits of the Spanish Character," *North American Review* 5 (May 1817): 30–31.

19. George Ticknor, *Life, Letters, and Journal of George Ticknor*, 7th ed., 2 vols. (Boston, 1877), vol. 1, chap. 10.

20. David Levin, *History as Romantic Art: Bancroft, Prescott, Motley, and Parkman* (Stanford, 1959), and Raymond A. Paredes, "The Origins of Anti-Mexican Sentiment in the United States," *New Scholar* (San Diego) 6 (1977): 139–65, contain numerous examples of anti-Spanish statements by early nineteenth-century travelers, authors, and newspaper accounts, as do David J. Weber, "Scarce More Than Apes, Historical Roots of Anglo-American Stereotypes of Mexicans," in *New Spain's Far Northern Frontier*, ed. David J. Weber (Albuquerque, 1979), and Arnoldo de León, *They Called Them Greasers: Anglo Attitudes toward Mexicans in Texas, 1821–1900* (Austin, 1987).

21. The term *Black Legend* was coined and circulated by scholars and publicists who held that historically Spain had been maligned by its enemies, usually for political purposes. This is not the place nor am I sufficiently well versed in the field to discuss the merits and demerits of the opposing views on the subject. Charles Gibson, *The Black Legend* (New York, 1971), pp. 2–27; Benjamin Keen, "The Black Legend Revisited: Assumptions and Realities," *Hispanic American Historical Review* (hereafter *HAHR*) 49 (1969): 703–19; and Keen, *The Aztec Image in Western Thought* (New Brunswick, N.J., 1971), provide useful abbreviated accounts of the issues involved. Keen in *The Aztec Image* has an especially useful discussion of the literary sources of the Legend. There is also a White Legend meant to promote Hispanism. It argues that the Spaniards brought Christianity to the Indians, eliminated human sacrifice and cannibalism from Indian society, and offered Indians draft animals, plows, and other material benefits; see Gibson, *The Spanish Tradition in America* (New York, 1971). But as Keen has pointed out, White Legend publications had little influence outside Spain; see Keen, *The Aztec Image*, pp. 257–59. That Black Legend literature is today generally recognized as an assemblage of myths and facts is not of concern here; what is important is that in the early nineteenth century the dominant Anglo-Saxon culture in the United States endorsed as gospel what later became Black Legend themes.

22. The cornerstone of the Legend genre was translations in whole or in part of treatises by Bishop Bartolomé de Las Casas and the Italian traveler Girolamo Benzoni which were highly critical of Spain's conduct in the New World. See Keen, *Aztec Image*, p. 143.

23. Ibid., p. 172.

24. *A New Survey of the West Indies* (London, 1628) appeared in five English editions by 1722. See the Introduction to the 1929 edition.

25. *Dictionary of National Biography*, s.v. "Gage, Thomas."

26. French translations of Las Casas and Benzoni appeared as early as did translations in English, and three French translations of Gage's *Survey* appeared between 1663 and 1677. See p. xxi of the 1929 English edition.

27. "Of Coaches" appeared in 1588 and was available in English translation by 1603.

28. Frank Monaghan, *John Jay, Defender of Liberty against Kings & Peoples . . .* (New York, 1935), pp. 125–83.

29. *New Orleans Gazette*, September 20, 1819, as quoted in Maury Baker, "The Spanish War Scare of 1816," *Mid-America* 45 (1963): 74.

30. *Richmond Enquirer*, October 12, 1816.

31. For disturbances on the Southwest frontier leading to Jackson's invasion of Florida see Baker, "The Spanish War Scare of 1816."

32. For a concise review of the negotiations over Florida, see Logan, *No Transfer*, chap. 4.

33. On the importance of the trade with Cuba see chapter 4.

34. Eugenio Pereira Salas, *Los primeros contactos entre Chile y Los Estados Unidos, 1778–1809* (Santiago, 1971), provides the most complete account of the early contacts between Anglo-Americans and civilian and public officials in South America. Also see Harry Bernstein, *Origins of Inter-American Interest, 1790–1812* (Philadelphia, 1945), and John J. Johnson, "Early Relations between the United States and Chile," *Pacific Historical Review* 13 (September 1944): 260–70.

35. "Extract of a Letter from a Gentleman in Mexico," *Richmond Enquirer*, May 24, 1822.

36. *Aurora*, January 6, 1825. Also see the anonymous report noting the extreme cruelty of Spanish General Pablo Morillo in command of royalist forces in northern South America, as reported in the *Weekly Register* 25 (November 1823): 155.

37. *North American Review*, "Travels in Colombia" 45 (July 1825): 154. For an imaginary dialogue between Hernán Cortés and William Penn meant to depict the cruelty of the former and the humanity of the latter see Caleb Bingham, *The American Preceptor: Being a New Selection of Lessons for Reading and Spelling*, 9th ed. (Boston, 1801), pp. 52–53.

38. *Daily National Intelligencer*, January 30, 1826.

39. Robert K. Lowry, United States Consul at La Guayra, to Sec. of State Monroe, Philadelphia, January 22, 1816, Manning, *Dip.Cor.*, 2:1169.

40. USNA, State, Special Agents, Roll 4, Hughes, aboard the USS *Macedonian* in Chesapeake Bay, to Sec. of State (no name given), July 6, 1816.

41. Manning, *Dip.Cor.*, 1:343–44.

42. U.S. Congress, *Annals of Congress* 15th Cong., 1st sess., March 27, 1818, 2:1585. Also see the anti-Spanish remarks of Nelson of Virginia, ibid., p. 1601, and especially those of Holmes of Massachusetts, ibid., p. 1579.

43. Adams to Anderson, May 27, 1823, Manning, *Dip.Cor.*, 1:193.

44. See for example the treatment of Portugal and the Portuguese people in Susanna Rowson, *An Abridgment of Universal Geography, Together with Sketches of History* (Boston, 1806), pp. 83–84, and Guthrie, *A Geographical, Historical, and Commercial Grammar*, p. 434.

45. *Analectic Magazine* (Philadelphia) 16 (July–December 1820): 263.

46. Morse, *American Universal Geography*, 5th ed., 2 vols. (1805), 1:311.

47. William C. Woodbridge, *Universal Geography* (Hartford, Conn., 1824), p. 303.

48. "The Sketch of the Manners of the Portuguese, from Murphy's General View of Portugal," *Monthly Magazine and American Review* (New York) 1 (1800): 143–45.

49. See note 43. Also see Guthrie, p. 495.

50. "Letters from Portugal," *Port Folio* (Philadelphia), 3d ser. 1 (1813): 268–69.

51. Nathaniel Dwight, *A Short but Comprehensive System of Geography of the World*, 7th ed. (Northampton, Mass. 1814), p. 79.

52. *Encyclopaedia Britannica*, 1798 ed., s.v. "Portugal."

53. See Henry Hill, United States Consul at Rio de Janeiro, to John Q. Adams, Rio de Janeiro, December 21, 1818, Manning, *Dip.Cor.*, 2:705; Wood-

ridge Odlin, United States Consul at San Salvador, to John Q. Adams, San Salvador (Bahia), February 18, 1821, Manning, *Dip.Cor.*, 2:709.

54. Consul Hill to Adams, Colombiana, Brazil, May 1821, Manning, *Dip. Cor.*, 2:713–21; John J. Appleton, United States Chargé d'Affaires, Rio de Janeiro, to John Q. Adams, Rio de Janeiro, July 21, 1821, ibid., pp. 721–22.

55. See, for example, "Notes on a Voyage to Caraccas [sic]," *Atlantic Magazine* 1 (May 1824): 57.

56. François R. J. de Pons, *Travels in South America, during the Years 1801, 1802, 1803*, and *1804*, trans. from the French, 2 vols. (London, 1807), 1:182.

57. W. G. Miller, United States Consul at Buenos Aires, to James Monroe, Sec. of State, Buenos Aires, July 16, 1812, Manning, *Dip.Cor.*, 1:326–30.

58. Thomas L. Halsey to Sec. of State James Monroe, Buenos Aires, January 30, 1817, Manning, *Dip.Cor.*, 1:348.

59. Special Agent W. G. D. Worthington to John Q. Adams, Buenos Aires, October 1, 1817, Manning, *Dip.Cor.*, 1:354.

60. Special Commissioner Caesar A. Rodney to John Q. Adams, Washington, November 5, 1818, Manning, *Dip.Cor.*, 1:510.

61. Alexander Scott to Sec. of State James Monroe, Caracas, November 16, 1812, Manning, *Dip.Cor.*, 2:1163.

62. Lowry to John Q. Adams, La Guayra, September 22, 1822, Manning, *Dip.Cor.*, 2:1223.

63. Poinsett to John Q. Adams, Columbia, S.C., November 4, 1818, Manning, *Dip.Cor.*, 1:439–43.

64. Michael Hogan, U.S. Consul, Valparaiso, to Sec. of State Adams, Valparaiso, August 28, 1823, Manning, *Dip.Cor.*, 2:1087; Heman Allen, United States Minister to Chile, to Sec. of State Henry Clay, Valparaiso, February 4, 1826, March 20, 1826, Manning, *Dip.Cor.*, 2:1109–10, 1111–12.

65. USNA, State, Despatches of United States Ministers to Central America, Roll 2, John Williams, United States Chargé, to Henry Clay, August 3, 1826.

66. Poinsett to John Q. Adams, July 18, 1827, "Poinsett Papers," vol. 4, as quoted in J. Fred Rippy, *Joel R. Poinsett, Versatile American* (Durham, N.C., 1935), p. 125.

67. Joseph Byrne Lockey, *Pan-Americanism: Its Beginnings* (New York, 1920), provides good coverage of the debates. The flavor of the attacks come through best in the debates themselves. See U.S. Congress, *Register of Debates of Congress*, 19th Cong., 1st sess., vol 1. The substance of the debates was carried in some detail in the *Daily National Intelligencer* and in an abbreviated form in the *American and Commercial Advertiser* (Baltimore), especially during the month of March 1826.

68. See the *Quarterly Review* (London) 30 (1824): 157–58; *Atlantic Magazine* 1 (July 1824); Lyon, *Journal of a Residence* 2:231–32. Anton Z. Helms in his *Travels from Buenos Ayres by Way of Potosí, to Lima* (London, 1806), p. 16, noted that because of the Creole's "inordinate love of pleasure" he is "enslaved by his mulatto and black females."

69. *Christian Herald* 2 (March 20, 1824): 179–80.

70. J. A. B. Beaumont, *Travels in Buenos Ayres and Adjacent Provinces of the Rio de la Plata* (London, 1828), p. 59.

71. Miers, *Travels*, 2:223.

72. Stevenson, *A Historical and Descriptive Narrative*, 1:28.

73. J. J. von Tschudi, *Travels in Peru during the Years 1838–1842* (New York, 1849), pp. 65–66.

74. R. W. H. Hardy, *Travels in the Interior of Mexico in 1825, 1826, 1827, and 1828* (London, 1829), p. 528.

75. *Richmond Enquirer*, September 8, 1828.

76. Ibid., February 9, 1830.

77. *Weekly Register*, April 25, 1829, p. 132.

78. *Quarterly Review* 32 (June–October 1825): 129.

79. Roy Harvey Pearce, *The Savages of America: A Study of the Indian and the Idea of Civilization*, rev. ed. (Baltimore, 1965), p. 4; Richard Slotkin, *Regeneration through Violence: The Mythology of the American Frontier, 1600–1860* (Middletown, Conn., 1973), p. 125.

80. For a useful, though not particularly objective, contemporary account of Indian alliances with the French, Spanish, and British see David Ramsey, *The History of the American Revolution*, 2 vols. (Lexington, Ky., 1815), 2:103–19. Writing in the heat of battle President Madison was merciless in his attack upon Indian nations of the Michigan Territory and the Ohio Valley, "that wretched portion of the human race," for their "savage" warfare under British influence. See his "Fourth Annual Message," November 4, 1812, in Richardson, *Messages and Papers of the Presidents*, 1:514–21.

81. As quoted in Reginald Horsman, *Race and Manifest Destiny* (Cambridge, Mass., 1981), p. 198.

82. Ibid., p. 198; Berkhofer, *The White Man's Image*, esp. pp. 15–31.

83. Clive Bush, *The Dream of Reason: American Consciousness and Cultural Achievement from Independence to the Civil War* (New York, 1977), p. 245; Michael Rogin, "Liberal Society and the Indian Question," *Politics and Society* (Los Altos, Calif.) 1 (May 1971): 269–312.

84. See, for example, *Richmond Enquirer*, February 18, 1830.

85. E. McClung Fleming, "From Indian Princess to Greek Goddess: The American Image, 1783–1815," *Winterthur Portfolio* (Chicago) 3 (1967): 37–65.

86. For a contemporary view on this point see the *Columbia Magazine* (Hudson, N.Y.) 1 (August 1787): 604.

87. Condy Raguet, U.S. Consul at Rio de Janeiro, to Henry Clay, Rio de Janeiro, March 11, 1825, Manning, *Dip.Cor.*, 2:811.

88. Helms, *Travels*, p. 17.

89. Beaumont, *Travels*. Helms's and Beaumont's assessments may be considered standard for the period 1815–30.

90. *Encyclopaedia Britannica*, 1798 ed., s.v. "Mexico."

91. Ibid., s.v. "America," subsection "California."

92. Thomas Jefferson, *Notes on the State of Virginia* (Philadelphia, 1825), pp. 188–89. The *Notes* was first published in Paris, 1784–85. Philip D. Curtin, *The Atlantic Slave Trade: A Census* (Madison, Wis., 1969), p. 28.

93. See David B. Davis, *The Problem of Slavery in Western Culture* (Ithaca, 1966), p. 46.

94. *Monthly Magazine and American Review* 2, no. 2 (February 1800): 81–84.

95. Scientific and philosophical thought about blacks has received lavish treatment. There is little point in listing even a representative sampling of the works on the subject. I found, however, several studies especially useful: Samuel Stanhope Smith, *An Essay on the Causes of the Variety of Complexion and Figure in the Human Species* (New Brunswick, N.J., 1810), and Jefferson,

Notes on the State of Virginia, were presumably the two most widely debated essays on the subject to be written by North Americans to the time of their publication. William Stanton, *The Leopard's Spots: Scientific Attitudes toward Race in America, 1815–1850* (Chicago, 1960), is both informative and highly readable. As with nearly every aspect of the white-black "problem," Winthrop Jordan's *White over Black: American Attitudes toward the Negro, 1550–1812* (Chapel Hill, N.C., 1968) and *The White Man's Burden: Historical Origins of Racism in the United States* (New York, 1974) are indispensable, as are the works of George Fredrickson, especially his *The Black Image in the White Mind* (New York, 1971) and "Towards a Social Interpretation of the Development of American Racism," in *Key Issues in the Afro-American Experience*, ed. Nathan L. Huggins, Martin Kilson, and Daniel M. Fox, 2 vols. (New York, 1971), 1:240–54. George W. Stocking, Jr., Introduction to *James Cowles Prichard: Researches into the Physical History of Man*, ed. George W. Stocking (Chicago, 1973), provides a first-rate synthesis of early anthropological studies.

96. Dwight W. Hoover, *The Red and the Black* (Chicago, 1975), p. 49.

97. See the *Columbia Magazine* 2 (1787): 141–44; Jordan, *White over Black*, chap. 12; F. M. Binder, *The Color Problem in Early National America as Viewed by John Adams, Jefferson, and Jackson* (The Hague, 1968), chap. 3.

98. Ira Berlin, *Slaves without Masters: The Free Negro in the Antebellum South* (New York, 1974), p. 106.

99. Binder, *The Color Problem*, p. 77.

100. Jordan, *White over Black*, pp. 352–53.

101. Fredrickson, *The Black Image in the White Mind*, p. 9.

102. Bodo, *The Protestant Clergy*, pp. 112–14; Leon F. Litwack, *North of Slavery: The Negro in the Free States, 1790–1860* (Chicago, 1961), pp. 114, 132, 134; Jordan, *White over Black*, pp. 133–35.

103. Litwack, *North of Slavery*, p. 79.

104. *Ibid.*, pp. 14–15.

105. The *Aurora* for 1819, the *Daily National Intelligencer* for the years 1826–29 and the *Weekly Register* for the years 1825–30 are particularly rich and almost always sympathetic to freed blacks who sought protection under the law in the border states. Jordan handles legislation, court decisions, and reporting of issues concerning blacks, both free and slave, unusually well. See especially *White over Black*, chap. 2; Litwack, *North of Slavery*, is outstanding on legislation in the North; see especially his chapter entitled "The Political Repression." Berlin's *Slaves without Masters* is a highly perceptive analysis of the restraints on free blacks in both the South and the North. Gary B. Nash, ed., *Red, White, and Black: The Peoples of Early America* (New York, 1974), and "The Origins of Racism in Colonial America," in *The Great Fear*, ed. Gary B. Nash and Richard Weiss (New York, 1970), are particularly useful for material that compares the advantages Indians had over blacks. Horsman, *Race and Manifest Destiny*, is concerned primarily with white-Indian relations, but chapters 5–9 contain relevant, clearly presented data on blacks. Studies by Richard Wade, "The Negro in Cincinnati, 1800–1830," *Journal of Negro History* 39, no. 1 (1954): 43–57; J. B. Brackett, *The Negro in Maryland: A Study of the Institution of Slavery* (Baltimore, 1889); and Daniel J. Flanigan, "Criminal Procedure in Slave Trials in the Antebellum South," *Journal of Southern History* 40, no. 4 (1974): 537–64, provide a useful analysis of the black experience in specific areas of the country.

106. James Hugo Johnston, *Race Relations in Virginia and Miscegenation in the South, 1776–1860* (Amherst, Mass., 1970), esp. chap. 2; Nash, "The Origins of Racism in Colonial America," p. 20.

107. For similar concerns of whites in Upper Canada see the "Resolution Passed by the House Assembly of Upper Canada," *Banner of the Constitution* (Philadelphia) 3 (April 3, 1830): 24.

108. Frederickson, *Black Image in the White Mind*, pp. 164–70; Jordan, *White Man's Burden*, pp. 170, 181. Also see *Youth's Companion* (Boston), January 31, 1828; *Daily National Intelligencer*, May 9, 1825, April 17, 1829; and the *Encyclopaedia Americana: A Popular Dictionary of Arts, Sciences, Literature, History, Politics, and Biography*, 13 vols. (Philadelphia, 1829–33), s.v. "Negro," which contains many of the commonly accepted negative stereotypes of blacks.

109. Alexander von Humboldt, *Ensayo político sobre el Reino de la Nueva España*, 6th ed. castellana . . . con una introducción por Vito Alessio Robles, 5 vols. (Mexico, 1941), 2:29.

110. For a discussion of the mixed races see below.

111. Jamaica, Antigua, and Grenada were British colonies, not Spanish or Portuguese, but it is generally accepted that in the early nineteenth century the North American public ordinarily did not distinguish between the two when dealing with the "black problem."

112. For the demographic composition of the Caribbean islands and the mainland ports see John J. Johnson, "The Racial Composition of Latin American Port Cities at Independence as Seen by Foreign Travelers," *Jahrbuch fur Geschichte . . . Lateinamerikas* (Koln) 23 (1986): 247–66.

113. "Haiti," *North American Review* 5 (January 1821): 112–34.

114. *Atlantic Magazine* 1 (May 1824): 53.

115. John Mawe in *Port Folio*, 5th ser. 1 (1816): 432–37.

116. Robert Proctor, *Narrative of a Journey across the Cordillera of the Andes and of a Residence in Lima and Other Parts of Peru, in the Years 1823 and 1824* (London, 1825), p. 287.

117. USNA, State, Special Agents, Roll 8, September 25, 1819. This comment by United States Agent Baptis Irvine appears in a document entitled "Notes on Venezuela" that runs from leaf 272 to leaf 515. The specific reference appears on leaf 320.

118. Manuel Torres, Chargé d'Affaires of Colombia at Washington, to John Q. Adams, Washington, May 20, 1820, Manning, *Dip.Cor.*, 2:1189–90.

119. Johann Baptist von Spix, *Travels in Brazil, in the Years 1817–1820: Undertaken by Command of His Majesty the King of Bavaria*, trans. H. E. Lloyd, 2 vols. (London, 1824), 1:134.

120. John Fitzhugh, "Diary," Rio de Janeiro, July 14, 1819, Library of Congress, Ms. Division.

121. John Mawe, *Travels in the Interior of Brazil . . . Including a Voyage to the Rio de la Plata, and an Historical Sketch of the Revolution of Buenos Aires* (Boston, 1816).

122. Leslie B. Rout, *The African Experience in Spanish America, 1502 to the Present Day* (Cambridge, Eng., 1976). See esp. chap. 6. Blacks also served the royalists. Their best known participation in the service of Spain was as soldiers in the army of José Tomás Boves whose forces, "The Legion of Hell," were infamous for their atrocities against civilians. Baptis Irvine reported to Washington that Boves's army of 8,000, recruited in the New World, was com-

posed almost exclusively of blacks. USNA, State, Special Agents, Roll 8, Baptis Irvine to John Q. Adams, Angostura, August 11, 1818. In fact black soldiers from Cuba and Puerto Rico as well as from Venezuela were in his ranks. Most of his recruits, however, are believed to have been llaneros, a segment of the Venezuelan population that, then and today, are generally considered to be in varying degrees of white, Indian, and black descent.

123. USNA, State, Special Agents, Roll 8, Baptis Irvine to John Q. Adams, Angostura, August 11, 1818.

124. USNA, State, Special Agents, Roll 6, Robinson to Adams, Lima, August 12, 1818.

125. *Colombia: Its Present State, in Respect of Climate, Soil, Productions, Population . . . and Inducements to Emigration* (Philadelphia, 1825), p. 19.

126. Rout, *The African Experience*, chap. 6.

127. USNA, State, Consular Despatches, Roll 7, Cartagena, MacPherson to Clay, March 30, 1827.

128. It was accepted in Washington at the time that blacks in the Plata region had been drafted and sent to Chile with the intent of finally being rid of them by "wasting" them in wars or of leaving them to be returned to civilian life in either Chile or Peru. See "Report of Theodorick Bland on the Condition of South America," U.S. Congress, *American State Papers; Foreign Relations*, 18th Cong., 2d sess., 1818, 4:298. This document also appears in Manning, *Dip.Cor.*, 1:382–439; see esp. p. 438. As it turned out most of the black troops from La Plata were killed in action or were disbanded in Peru, where they ordinarily remained. For a sampling of unfavorable views of black troops see chapter 3.

129. Thomas Lindley, *Authentic Narrative of a Voyage from the Cape of Good Hope to Brazil, 1802, 1803* (London, 1808), pp. 68–69.

130. Alexander Caldcleugh, *Travels in South America, during the Years 1819, 1820, 1821 . . .*, 2 vols. (London, 1825), 1:82.

131. *Guardian* (Manchester), May 7, 1831, p. 2.

132. Poinsett to J. Q. Adams, Columbia, S.C., November 4, 1818, Manning, *Dip.Cor.*, 1:446.

133. Prevost, Special Agent to Chile, Peru, and Buenos Aires, to J. Q. Adams, Santiago, Chile, June 10, 1818, Manning, *Dip.Cor.*, 2:929.

134. USNA, State, Special Agents, Roll 5, Robinson to Adams.

135. Ibid., Robinson to ?, no date, received Washington August 31, 1818.

136. Ibid., Valparaiso, August 21, 1821.

137. Sartoris to Adams, Rio de Janeiro, September 23, 1822, Manning, *Dip.Cor.*, 1:746.

138. USNA, State, Despatches, U.S. Consuls, Pernambuco, Roll 1, John T. Mansfield to Sec. to State, October 2, 1831.

139. USNA, State, Ministers to Central America, Roll 2, Rochester to Clay, Trujillo, May 14, 1828. For British views of blacks in Latin America see chapter 4.

140. USNA, State, Special Agents, Roll 5. The address in printed form follows Irvine to Adams, February 16, 1819.

141. Simón Bolívar quoted in Simon Collier, "Nationality, Nationalism, and Supernationalism in the Writings of Simón Bolívar," *HAHR* 63 (February 1983): 44.

142. *North American Review*, 10 (January 1820): 158.

143. Fisher Ames to Thomas Dwight, October 31, 1803, in Fisher Ames, *Works of Fisher Ames*, 2 vols. (Boston, 1854), 1:329. Merk, *Manifest Destiny*, p. 11. Weber, "Scarce More Than Apes."

144. Rippy, *Joel R. Poinsett*, p. 12; Hardy, *Travels*, p. 509.

145. Mark Beaufoy, *Mexican Illustrations, Founded upon Facts* . . . (London, 1828), p. 236.

146. *Richmond Enquirer*, September 8, 1828.

147. Lyon, *Journal of a Residence*, 2:233.

148. Morse, *The American Universal Geography*, 4th ed. (Boston, 1802), p. 755.

149. Henry M. Brackenridge, *Voyage to South America Performed by Order of the American Government in the Years 1817–1818*, 2 vols. (Baltimore, 1819), 1:176–88.

150. Caldcleugh, *Travels in South America*, 1:370. Theodorick Bland to John Q. Adams on the Condition of South America, November 2, 1818, Manning, *Dip.Cor.*, 2:991–92.

151. Jorge Juan and Antonio de Ulloa, *Discourse and Political Reflections on the Kingdom of Peru* . . . , ed. John J. TePaske (Norman, Okla., 1978), p. 145.

152. USNA, Despatches, U.S. Consulate, Rio de Janeiro, Roll 1, Henry Hill to Adams, Colombiana, Brazil, May 1821.

153. John Luccock, *Notes on Rio de Janeiro, and the Southern Parts of Brazil; Taken during a Residence of Ten Years in That Country, from 1808 to 1818* (London, 1820), p. 135.

154. See, for example, USNA, State, Special Agents, Roll 8, Irvine to Adams, Angostura, November 2, 1818.

155. Adrian R. Terry, *Travels in the Equatorial Regions of South America in 1832* (Hartford, Conn., 1834), pp. 80–81; James Henderson, *A History of Brazil; Comprising Its Geography, Commerce, Aboriginal Inhabitants* (London, 1821), p. 72; Proctor, *Narrative*, p. 237.

156. Alexander von Humboldt, *Political Essay on the Kingdom of New Spain*, 4 vols. (London, 1814), 1:235.

157. Caldcleugh, *Travels*, 1:85.

158. USNA, State, Despatches, U.S. Consulate, Rio de Janeiro, Roll 1, Hill to Adams, Colombiana, Brazil, May 1821. Parts of the communication appear in Manning, *Dip.Cor.*, 2:713–21. As noted on pages 716 and 719 the editor chose not to include 74 pages of Hill's communication in which he deals unusually offensively with the characteristics of various groups within Brazil.

159. Proctor, *Narrative*, p. 237.

160. Antonio Alcedo, *The Geographical and Historical Dictionary of America and the West Indies*, trans. G. A. Thompson, 5 vols. (London 1812–15), 3, s.v. "mulatos" [sic].

161. Monroe to Senate, February 25, 1823; Adams to House, March 15, 1826, Richardson, *Messages and Papers*, 2:205, 335–36.

162. See chapter 4.

163. Thomas Hart Benton, *Thirty Years' View; or, A History of the Working of the American Government for Thirty Years, from 1820 to 1850*, 2 vols. (New York, 1854–56), 1:69. Also see U.S. Congress, *Register of Debates of Congress*, especially for the month of March 1826, 19th Cong., 1st sess. Thomas O. Ott, *The Haitian Revolution, 1789–1804* (Knoxville, 1973), contains the best account available of the Haitians' struggle for freedom.

164. Merk, *Manifest Destiny*, chap. 3.

Chapter 3: The Latin American Factor

1. For an early official expression of concern for and good will toward the colonies see Madison's "Third Annual Message," Richardson, *Messages and Papers*, 1:494. On the enthusiasm for the Greeks see Ernest R. May, *The Making of the Monroe Doctrine* (Cambridge, Mass., 1975), pp. 9, 238.

2. See the *North American Review* 10 (January 1820): 157–59; Edward Everett, "South America," *North American Review* 12 (April 1821): 433–34; John M. Forbes, Special Agent to Buenos Aires, to Adams, Buenos Aires, March 10, 1821, Manning, *Dip.Cor.*, 1:369.

3. *Daily National Intelligencer*, August 22, November 2, 1826.

4. An article in the *Weekly Register*, March 18, 1826, pp. 33–35, in praise of the republics for their actions against African slavery was an exception in reporting on reform in Latin America.

5. Gustavus Myers, *History of Bigotry in the United States* (New York, 1943), p. 140.

6. Merle E. Curti, *The Growth of American Thought*, 3d ed. (New York, 1964), p. 140.

7. William G. McLoughlin, "The Role of Religion in the Revolution: Liberty of Conscience and Cultural Cohesion in the New Nation," in *Essays on the American Revolution*, ed. Stephen G. Kurtz and James H. Hutson (Williamsburg, Va., 1973), pp. 247–48.

8. See chapter 1.

9. PRO FO 6/3 Woodbine Parish to George Canning, Buenos Aires, April 1824; Federico A. Pezet, "Contrast in the Development of Nationality in Anglo and Latin America," in *Latin America*, ed. George Blaklee (New York, 1914), pp. 14–15.

10. See, for example, James Wilkinson to Henry Clay, Mexico City, August 20, 1825, Clay, *Papers of Henry Clay*, 4:581–84.

11. This point was made numerous times. See, for example, the London *Times*, December 21, 1827, in which it was reported that, if La Plata (Argentina) did not meet its dividend payment due on January 12, 1828, the failure of public credit would have made the rounds of all those American states that were formerly colonies of Spain. Also see the *Times*, February 22, 1825, and March 25, 1828.

12. Michael P. Costeloe, "Spain and the Latin American Wars of Independence: The Free Trade Controversy, 1810–1820," *HAHR* 61 (May 1981): 209–34.

13. *Daily National Intelligencer*, November 2, 1826.

14. Robert Smith, Sec. of State, to Joel R. Poinsett, Washington, June 28, 1810, Manning, *Dip.Cor.*, 1:6–7.

15. Francis Deák and Philip C. Jessup, *A Collection of Neutrality Laws, Regulations, and Treaties of Various Countries*, 2 vols. (Washington, 1939), 2:1084.

16. Ibid., pp. 1085–86.

17. *Weekly Register*, January 31, 1818; Lockey, *Pan-Americanism*, pp. 172–75.

18. John Quincy Adams, *Memoirs of John Quincy Adams, Comprising Portions of His Diary from 1795 to 1848*, ed. Charles Francis Adams, 12 vols. (Philadelphia, 1875), 4:318, 5:159; May, *The Making of the Monroe Doctrine*, p. 63. For alleged violations of U.S. neutrality laws by agents of the Buenos

Aires governments see Adams to John M. Forbes, July 5, 1820, in U.S. Congress, *American State Papers, Foreign Relations*, 4:820.

19. James Monroe, "Sketch of Instructions for Agents for South America—Notes for Department of State," in *The Writings of James Monroe, Including a Collection of His Public and Private Papers . . .* , ed. J. M. Hamilton, 7 vols. (New York, 1898–1903), 6:92–102.

20. Manning, *Dip.Cor.*, 2:1181. Handy had been assigned to the expedition to Venezuela under the command of Commodore Perry, who died in Venezuelan waters.

21. Clay to Henry Middleton, Minister to Russia, Washington, May 10, 1825, Manning, *Dip.Cor.*, 1:245.

22. Richard Bush, Sec. of State ad interim, to Caesar A. Rodney and John Graham, Special Commissioners to South America, Washington, July 18, 1817, Manning, *Dip.Cor.*, 1:42–45; Adams to Rodney, Graham and Theodorick Bland, Washington, November 21, 1817, Manning, *Dip.Cor.*, 1:47–49.

23. For reports of the commissioners see Manning, and Henry M. Brackenridge, *Voyage to South America Performed by Order of the American Government in the Years 1817–1818*, 2 vols. (Baltimore, 1819).

24. Manning, *Dip.Cor.*, 1:6–7.

25. See chapter 4.

26. For a contemporary review of Clay's activities in support of the insurgents see *North American Review* 25 (1823): 446–47.

27. *Memoirs*, 5:325.

28. For the U.S. views on monarchism see chapter 1.

29. U.S. Congress, *Annals of Congress*, 16th Cong., 2d sess., February 1821, pp. 1042–55, 1081–92.

30. On the matter of recognition of the new nations I have followed closely Whitaker's account in his *The United States and the Independence of Latin America*, but also see Monroe, *Writings*, 6:284–91; Lockey, *Pan-Americanism*; and Samuel F. Bemis, *John Quincy Adams and the Foundations of American Foreign Policy* (New York, 1956) (esp. chap. 17); they also provide detailed accounts of what transpired.

31. Harold Temperley, "The Latin American Foreign Policy of Canning," *American Historical Review* 11 (July 1906): 779–97. Also see Temperley, *The Foreign Policy of Canning, 1822–1827* (London, 1925), pp. 126–29.

32. Poinsett to Adams, Columbia, S.C., November 4, 1818, Manning, *Dip.Cor.*, 1:440.

33. *Memoirs*, 5:164.

34. Forbes to Clay, July 1, 1825, Clay, *Papers*, 4:495–96.

35. William R. Manning, "Poinsett's Mission to Mexico," *American Journal of International Law* (New York) 7 (1913): 781–822; W. J. Hammond, "The History of British Commerce Activity in Mexico, 1820–1830" (Ph.D. diss., University of California, 1929).

36. See Weber, "Scarce More Than Apes."

37. Frances M. Foland, "The Impact of Liberalism on *Nueva España*," *Journal of the History of Ideas* (New York) 19 (1958): 164.

38. Alexander von Humboldt, *Personal Narrative of Travels in Equatorial Regions of the New Continent during the Years 1799–1804*, trans. Helen Maria Williams, 7 vols. in 4 (Amsterdam, 1971), 4:127; C. Esteva Fabregat, "Poblacíon y mestizage en las ciudades de Iberoamérica: siglo XVII," in F. de Solano, *Estudios sobre la ciudad iberoamericana* (Madrid, 1975).

39. Mildred E. Johnson, ed and trans., *Swans, Cygnets, and Owls* . . . (Columbia, Mo., 1956), pp. 100–111.

40. Gregorio López Fuentes, *El indio* (Mexico, 1945), p. 207.

41. Magnus Mörner, *Race Mixture in the History of Latin America* (Boston, 1967), pp. 80–81.

42. For reports reaching the United States on the personal characteristics, economic importance, and military qualities of Latin American blacks see chapter 2.

43. Charles M. Ricketts to George Canning, Lima, December 27, 1826, in R. A. Humphreys, *British Consular Reports on the Trade and Politics of Latin America, 1824–1826* (London, 1940), pp. 126–27.

44. For a more detailed discussion of this topic see chapter 2.

45. See Lyle McAlister, *The "Fuero Militar" in New Spain, 1764–1800* (Gainesville, 1957), pp. 6–7.

46. See, for example, Great Britain, *British and Foreign State Papers, 1824–1825* (London, 1846), pp. 964, 1005–6; John J. Johnson, *The Military and Society in Latin America* (Stanford, 1964), pp. 26–29; Alain Rouguié, *The Military and the State in Latin America*, trans. Paul E. Sigmund (Berkeley and Los Angeles, 1987), pp. 44–61, contains a detailed account of *caudillismo*.

47. See for instance USNA, State, Despatches, Ministers to Colombia, Roll 4, Beaufort Watts, U.S. Chargé, to Sec. of State Clay, Bogotá, November 14, 1825.

48. See Helen L. Clagett, *The Administration of Justice in Latin America* (New York, 1952).

49. *Daily National Intelligencer*, August 22, 1826; Robert Southey, *History of Brazil*, 3 vols. (London, 1819), 3:871; Pons, *Travels*, 1:141; Hardy, *Travels*, p. 528; Humphreys, *British Consular Reports*, pp. 131–32; Poinsett to Sec. Adams, Columbia, S.C., November 4, 1818, Manning, *Dip.Cor.*, 1:445, USNA, State, Despatches, U.S. Consuls, Rio de Janeiro, Roll 2, Condy Raguet to Adams, June 4, 1823; USNA, State, Despatches, U.S. Ministers to Brazil, Roll 8, William Tudor to Clay, Rio de Janeiro, December 8, 1828.

50. USNA, State, Consular Despatches, Rio de Janeiro, Roll 1, Hill to Adams, May 1, 1821.

51. David Bushnell, "The Last Dictatorship: Betrayal or Consummation?" *HAHR* 63 (February 1983): 85–90.

52. See the *North American Review* 15 (April 1822): 429–501.

53. John M. Niles, *History of South America and Mexico* . . . , 2 vols. (Hartford, Conn., 1837), 1:127. Felipe Tena Ramírez, *Leyes fundamentales de México, 1808–1964*, 2d ed. (Mexico, 1964), p. 168.

54. William M. Gibson, *The Constitutions of Colombia* (Durham, N.C., 1948), p. 81; *Weekly Register* 38 (May 15, 1830): 217.

55. USNA, State, Despatches, Special Agents, Roll 4, Alexander Scott to Sec. of State Monroe, Caracas, November 7, 1812; Miers, *Travels*, 2:223. Robert Lowry, U.S. Consul, La Guayra, to Sec. of State Monroe, June 5, 1812, Manning, *Dip.Cor.*, 2:1158. For a discussion of U.S. views of the Catholic Church see chapter 2.

56. Special Commissioner Theodorick Bland asserted that Catholic religious institutions either in direct proprietorship or through mortgages held nearly all the landed property of Chile. William T. W. Rushchenberger recorded that according to a 1791 census nearly one-third of the properties in

Lima belonged to the Catholic Church or to charitable institutions, nearly all of which were directly associated with the Church. (*Three Years in the Pacific*, p. 209.)

57. It may be recalled that at the time Latin America could rightly be considered as living in an age of leather.

58. John B. Prevost, Special Agent to Chile, to Sec. of State Adams, Santiago, March 10, 1821, Manning, *Dip.Cor.*, 2:1049.

59. Costeloe, "Spain and the Latin American Wars of Independence," pp. 208–11; Webster, *Britain and Independence*, 1:13.

60. USNA, State, Consular Despatches, Vera Cruz, Roll 1, William Taylor to Sec. of State Clay, Veracruz, January 10, 1827; USNA, State, Consular Despatches, La Guayra, Roll 2, John G. A. Williamson to Sec. of State, January 1, 1828; USNA, State, Consular Despatches, Valparaiso, Roll 2, Michael Hogan to Sec. of State Van Buren, Valparaiso, June 27, 1829. PRO FO 61/8 Ricketts to Canning, Lima, December 27, 1826. This document may also be found in Humphreys, *British Consular Reports*, pp. 107–206.

61. USNA, State, Despatches, U.S. Ministers to Peru, Roll 1, Samuel Larned to Sec. of State Van Buren, Lima, March 5, 1830.

62. Argentina exported some hides and salted beef; Chile, wheat and wine; Venezuela and Central America, indigo, cochineal, and cocoa; Ecuador, cocoa; and Mexico, sugar. None of those exports earned significant amounts of hard currency. Brazilian coffee, which was enjoying an upsurge in demand in the United States and Western Europe, was the only agricultural commodity important as an earner of hard currency.

63. *Memoirs*, 5:325.

64. *Daily National Intelligencer*, August 1, 1829.

65. Samuel Haigh, *Sketches of Buenos Ayres and Chile* (London, 1829), pp. 182–85.

66. *Aurora*, June 7, 1828; *Daily National Intelligencer*, May 12, June 25, August 1, 1829.

67. *Richmond Enquirer*, October 24, 1826.

68. *Daily National Examiner*, October 10, 1825.

69. See note 60.

70. *Aurora*, May 18, December 1, 1828.

71. *Richmond Enquirer*, October 24, 1826.

72. *Newport* (R.I.) *Mercury*, July 26, 1828.

73. USNA, State, Despatches, U.S. Ministers, Peru, Roll 1, Samuel Larned to Sec. of State Van Buren, March 5, 1830.

74. *Richmond Enquirer*, March 17, 1826.

75. *Daily National Intelligencer*, October 8, 1825.

76. *Richmond Enquirer*, April 4, 1825; *Daily National Intelligencer*, October 10, 1825.

77. *Richmond Enquirer*, August 26, 1826.

78. Ibid., June 12, 1826.

79. *Daily National Intelligencer*, November 28, 1825.

80. *Aurora*, July 16, 1825.

81. *Guardian*, November 18, 1826.

82. *Aurora*, September 27, 1825.

83. *Richmond Enquirer*, May 31, 1825.

84. *Aurora*, July 29, 1825.

85. Ibid., September 23, 1826.

86. September 6, 1828.

87. For the general scope of U.S. commerce with Latin America in the immediate postindependence era see Whitaker, *The United States and the Independence of Latin America;* C. L. Chandler, "United States Commerce with Latin America at the Promulgation of the Monroe Doctrine," *Quarterly Journal of Economics* (Boston) 38 (1924): 466–86; North, *The Economic Growth of the United States, 1790–1860.*

88. Peggy K. Liss, *Atlantic Empires: The Network of Trade and Revolution, 1713–1826* (Baltimore, 1983), pp. 212–13.

89. Adams, *Memoirs,* 6:25.

90. See chapter 1.

91. PRO FO 61/8, Charles M. Ricketts to Canning, Lima, December 27, 1826. This document may also be found in Humphreys, *British Consular Reports;* see esp. p. 134.

92. Charles R. Middleton, *The Administration of British Foreign Policy, 1782–1846* (Durham, N.C., 1977), p. 39, treats Latin America's economic backwardness in general terms and refers to a growing lack of interest in the area on the part of Great Britain.

93. See, for example, Stephen F. Austin, "The Prison Journal of Stephen F. Austin," p. 199, in which Austin asserts that Mexico's economy would not prosper as long as the country depended on the export of gold and silver.

94. Adams, *Memoirs,* 5:153.

95. See Joseph Smith, *Illusions of Conflict: Anglo-American Diplomacy toward Latin America, 1865–1896* (Pittsburgh, 1979), pp. 13–14, and Smith's chap. 1, n. 49, which contains references to British and German views of the diplomatic and consular services.

96. Rippy, *Joel R. Poinsett,* passim; Manning, "Poinsett's Mission to Mexico," pp. 795–97.

97. Adams, *Memoirs,* 5:57.

98. Ibid., 7:270, 272–73, 288, 401; Whitaker, *The United States and the Independence of Latin America,* pp. 152–53; PRO FO 13/37, Robert Gordon, British Minister to Brazil, to Canning, Rio de Janeiro, April 3, 1827.

99. Dorothy B. Goebel, *William Henry Harrison* (Indianapolis, 1926), pp. 256 ff.; Perkins, *The Monroe Doctrine, 1826–1867,* pp. 34–35.

100. William R. Manning, *Early Diplomatic Relations between the United States and Mexico* (Baltimore, 1916), p. 343, n. 93; Gene M. Brack, *Mexico Views Manifest Destiny, 1821–1846* (Albuquerque, 1975), pp. 67–68.

101. Webster, *Britain and Independence,* 1:41.

102. Official documents, journals, and newspapers are rich in accounts of the political anarchy that plagued Latin America during the 1820s. Many official communiqués that document the tribulations of the new polities appear in Manning, *Dip.Cor.,* but numerous others, especially those from consuls, remain in manuscript form in the USNA. John M. Forbes, Chargé d'Affaires to Sec. of State Clay, Buenos Aires, September 25, 1826, which appears in USNA, State, Despatches from U.S. Ministers in Buenos Aires, Roll 4, contains a useful account of the gathering storms in southern South America. The *New York Commercial Advertiser,* February 19, 1826, and the *Banner of the Constitution* (Philadelphia), June 30, 1830, contain especially good accounts of the range and depth of instability throughout the region.

Chapter 4: British Impact on United States–
Latin American Relations

1. See, for example, President Monroe's Message to the House of Representatives, January 30, 1824, in which he wrote that "at least one-half of every century, in ancient as well as modern times, has been consumed in wars." Richardson, *Messages and Papers*, 2:222. On the tendency for warmongering see Merle E. Curti, *The American Peace Crusade, 1815–1850* (Durham, N.C., 1919), pp. 18, 22–25, 40, 41, 227. But in the midst of all the talk of possible war the "Annual Reports" of the secretary of the navy during the 1820s suggest that the navy was not giving undue attention to preparing for a possible war on the seas. Throughout the decade the tenor of the "Reports," the marked emphasis on the construction of smaller, lightly armed vessels, and the assigning of vessels and crews to various theaters, as, for example, the West Indies and the Mediterranean, indicate that the navy saw its primary responsibility, not to prepare for a maritime war, but to protect U.S. merchant ships from pirates and privateers. The "Annual Reports" for 1822 through 1828 may be found in U.S. Treasury Department, Sec. of the Treasury, *Reports of Finances, 1815–1828*, vol. 2, pp. 276, 313, 354, 393, 448, 464–65; for 1829, U.S. Congress, 21st Cong., 2d sess., Senate Doc. 1830–31, Doc. 6, pp. 30–31; and for 1831, U.S. Congress, 22d Cong., 1st sess., House Docs. 1831–32, Doc. 3, vol. 1, pp. 40–42.

2. Jefferson, *Writings*, 15:91.

3. Bradford Perkins, *Castlereagh and Adams: England and the United States, 1812–1823* (Berkeley and Los Angeles, 1964), p. 158. Perkins documents similar statements by prominent public figures, including Jefferson, John Q. Adams, and Richard Rush, pp. 158–60.

4. *Daily National Intelligencer*, 10 (March 2, 1816): 3.

5. Ibid., April 27, 1818. U.S. newspapers throughout the remainder of the decade and into the early 1820s freely predicted war. See especially the *Aurora* for the year 1819.

6. *Weekly Register* 17 (January 8, 1820): 306.

7. See, for example, "South America," in *Blackwoods Magazine* (Edinburgh) 15 (February 1824): 133–40, and the *Times* throughout the decade after 1815. Also see J. Freeman Rattenbury, "Remarks on the Cession of the Floridas to the United States of America, and the Necessity of Acquiring the Island of Cuba by Great Britain," *The Pamphleteer* (London) 25, no. 29 (1819): 261–80.

8. For the role of France see later in the chapter.

9. Bradford Perkins, *The First Rapprochement: England and the United States, 1795–1805* (Philadelphia, 1955), pp. 110–11; Lester Langley, *Struggle for the American Mediterranean: United States–European Rivalry in the Gulf–Caribbean, 1776–1904* (Athens, Ga., 1976), pp. 31–36, 50.

10. Herbert A. Smith, *Great Britain and the Law of Nations*, 2 vols. (London, 1932), 1:117–19, 123.

11. Edward H. Tatum, Jr., *The United States and Europe, 1815–1823: A Study in the Background of the Monroe Doctrine* (Berkeley and Los Angeles, 1936), pp. 151–53. Tatum's summary is based on diplomatic correspondence, congressional debates, and major journals.

12. PRO FO 61/2, Enclosure, Rowcroft to Canning, Lima, July 15, 1824. For additional evidence of British violations of neutrality laws see Richard

Rush, U.S. Minister to Great Britain, to Sec. of State Adams, London, August 24, 1819, and October 5, 1819, Manning, *Dip.Cor.*, 3:1456–57, 1458–59.

13. H. W. V. Temperley, "The Foreign Policy of Canning, 1820–1827," *Cambridge History of British Foreign Policy, 1783–1919*, ed. A. W. Ward and C. P. Gooch, 4 vols. (New York, 1923), 2:76; Charles O'Handy, Purser of the US *John Adams*, to John Q. Adams, Washington, September 29, 1819, Manning, *Dip.Cor.*, 2:1178–82, made a special point of Great Britain's popularity because of the visibility of British officers and men associated with the patriot cause.

14. PRO FO 146/56, Memorandum of a Conference between Prince Polignac and Mr. Canning, Webster, *Britain and Independence*, 2:115–20. Also see William W. Kaufmann, *British Policy and the Independence of Latin America* (New Haven, Conn., 1951), pp. 167–71.

15. On U.S.-British cooperation in the war against piracy see Monroe's "Seventh Annual Message" in Richardson, *Messages and Papers*, 2:214, and his "Eighth Annual Message" in which he submitted to the consideration of Congress "whether those robbers should be pursued on the land [meaning Cuba], the local authorities be made responsible for these atrocities, or any other measure be resorted to to suppress them." Richardson, *Messages and Papers*, 2:258.

16. For U.S. complaints about irresponsible actions by privateers see, for example, John Q. Adams to Caesar Rodney, John Graham, and Theodorick Bland, Special Commissioners to South America, Washington, November 21, 1817, Manning, *Dip.Cor.*, 1:47–49; Adams to John B. Prevost, Special Agent . . . Buenos Aires, Chile, and Peru, Washington, July 10, 1820, Manning, *Dip.Cor.*, 1:134–37; Lewis Winkler Bealer, *The Privateers of Buenos Aires, 1815–1821* (Berkeley and Los Angeles, 1935). Also see President James Monroe's "Fifth Annual Message" which stressed the need to have a fleet capable of combating pirates. Richardson, *Messages and Papers*, 2:108. Throughout the 1820s the Navy regularly received appropriations for carrying on the war against pirates and privateers and for the purpose of constructing and arming sloops of war, which had proved the most successful and cost-efficient naval vessels for pursuing pirates and privateers in the West Indian islands, especially Cuba and Puerto Rico. See U.S. Treasury Department, *Annual Reports of the Secretary*, "Reports of the State of the Finances." Webster, *Britain and Independence*, contains more than 30 manuscripts by British agents and officials in the Foreign Office that deal with privateering and piracy. See his index under privateering and piracy.

17. Monroe, *Writings*, 6:92–102; James F. Vivian, "The Paloma Claim in United States and Venezuelan-Colombian Relations," *Caribbean Studies* 14, no. 4:72. Richardson, *Messages and Papers*, 1:186.

18. Bealer, *The Privateers*, chap. 8.

19. Manning, *Dip.Cor.*, 1:47–49.

20. Ibid.; Griffin, *The United States and the Disruption*, pp. 103, 148–49.

21. Griffin, *The United States and the Disruption*, p. 99.

22. Charles G. Fenwick, *The Neutrality Laws of the United States* (Washington, 1913), pp. 35–41.

23. Adams to President Monroe, Washington, June 15, 1820, in John Quincy Adams, *Writings of John Quincy Adams* ed. W. C. Ford, 7 vols. (New York, 1913–17), 7:43–45; Adams to Hugh Nelson, Washington, April 28, 1823, Manning, *Dip.Cor.*, 1:166–85; Griffin, *The United States and the Disruptions*, pp. 99–105.

24. PRO FO 72/261, H. T. Kilbee to William Hamilton, Havannah, May 11, 1822. Also see PRO FO 72/304, Kilbee to Joseph La Planta, Havannah, November 30, 1824, which contains an extended discussion of piracy and the U.S. concerns over the failure of Cuban authorities to take adequate measures to control it.

25. Archibald D. Turnbull, *Commodore David Porter, 1780–1843* (New York, 1929), chap. 13.

26. James Monroe, "Message to the Senate," December 9, 1822, called for vessels capable of pursuing pirates into shallow waters. Richardson, *Messages and Papers*, 2:196. For Argentine moves against privateers see "Minutes of a Conference," Buenos Aires, September 17, 1821, Manning, *Dip.Cor.*, 1:585–87, and for the text of the decree, ibid., 1:590–91.

27. *Times*, May 27, August 14, September 10, 1828.

28. On Clay's appeal for cooperation from the new nations in the war against piracy see U.S. Congress, *Register of Debates of Congress*, 20th Cong., 2d sess., (Washington, 1830), Appendix, p. 42. Piracy in the Caribbean and especially in Cuban waters was a constant problem throughout the 1815–30 era. During the 1820s the United States Navy was geared increasingly to warfare against pirates, while at the same time directing less attention to the prospect of war with a maritime power. As it turned out, more U.S. naval vessels were assigned to the West Indies than to any other theater. In 1825, for instance, 9 of 19 vessels in commission were assigned to the West Indies. See U.S. Congress, *American State Papers, Naval Affairs*, 18th/19th Cong., 1824–27, 24:103. As late as 1830 the secretary of the navy was recommending against reducing the size of the forces in the West Indies because to do so would subject commerce to casualties there. See U.S. Congress, 21st Cong., 2d sess., 1830–31, Senate Docs. 1–40.

29. *Times*, July 28, 1826.

30. Great Britain, Parliament, *Parliamentary Debates* (Commons), New Ser. 7 (1822): 1725–29, 1858–66; *Guardian* (Manchester), November 9, December 7, 1822.

31. *Times*, August 14, 1828.

32. Charles Oscar Paullin, *Diplomatic Negotiations of American Naval Officers, 1778–1883* (Baltimore, 1912), p. 332; Harold Sprout and Margaret Sprout, *The Rise of American Naval Power, 1776–1918* (Princeton, 1944).

33. Sprout and Sprout, *The Rise of American Naval Power*, p. 95.

34. Whitaker, *The United States and Independence*, p. 299.

35. Adams to J. B. Prevost, December 16, 1823, as quoted in Whitaker, *The United States and Independence*, pp. 287–88.

36. Adams to Nelson, Washington, April 28, 1823, Manning, *Dip.Cor.*, 1:166–85. For an equally unequivocal position on blockades but worded somewhat more tactfully see "Documents Relating to the Panama Mission," U.S. Congress, *Register of Debates of Congress*, 20th Cong., 2d sess., Appendix, 2:42–43.

37. USNA, State, Despatches, U.S. Ministers to Argentina, Forbes to Vice Admiral Rodrigo José Ferreira Lobo, Buenos Aires, February 13, 1826. Given the conviction in important quarters in England that the Admiralty was not taking firm enough steps to protect British commerce from seizure as a result of blockades, it is significant that the full text of Forbes's communication appeared in the *Times*, June 7, 1826.

38. William Tudor, U.S. Consul, to Adams, Lima, May 3, 1824. Manning, *Dip.Cor.*, 3:1749–52.

39. U.S. Congress, *Register of Debates of Congress*, 20th Cong., 1st sess., 1827–28, 4:2509–14. For the effects of blockades upon the interests of the United States see USNA, State, Despatches, U.S. Consuls, Montevideo, Roll 1, Joshua Bond to Sec. of State Clay, June 20, October 28, October 29, 1826.

40. Great Britain, Public Record Office, Admiralty Office, 1/25, Thomas Hardy to His Excellency Bernardo O'Higgins, Supreme Director of the Republic of Chile, *Augusta Schooner* off Buenos Aires, September 27, 1820. Hereafter citations from this source will be identified as PRO ADM, followed by the number assigned by the Public Record Office, and as available from whom to whom, place, and date.

41. PRO FO 13/50, Ponsonby to Aberdeen, Rio de Janeiro, December 10, 1828.

42. PRO FO 13/60, Ponsonby to Aberdeen, Rio de Janeiro, February 24, 1829.

43. PRO FO 13/61, June 10, 1829. Also see the news item from Rio de Janeiro in the *Times*, June 22, 1829, in which it was anticipated that British forces would be obliged to retake "some" vessels before the Brazilian government would respond to British claims amounting to £442,000 for vessels taken or retained.

44. PRO FO 6/29, Foreign Office to Woodbine Parish, Buenos Aires, February 27, 1829. U.S. Chargé Samuel Larned in a communication to Sec. of State Clay, dated February 3, 1829, also found the naval force available to Peru inadequate to carry out the proposed blockade, USNA, State, U.S. Ministers to Chile, Roll 3.

45. See Michael Hogan, U.S. Commercial Agent, Valparaiso, to Adams, Valparaiso, May 6, 1822, Manning, *Dip.Cor.*, 2:1062–63.

46. David Trask, *A Short History of the United States Department of State, 1781–1981*, Dept. of State Pub. 9166 (Washington, January 1981), p. 12.

47. PRO FO 61/3, Thomas Rowcroft to J. La Planta, Lima, September 5, 1824.

48. Ibid., September 29, 1824.

49. Ibid., October 15, 1824. For public accounts of the incident see the *Times*, November 14, 1824; January 19, 1825; *Scots Magazine* (Edinburgh) 95 (January 1825): 114.

50. PRO FO 6/17, Ponsonby to Lord Dudley, Buenos Aires, March 9, 1827.

51. PRO FO 118/16, Draft, Ponsonby to Canning, July 15, 1827.

52. PRO FO 118/20, Draft, Parish to Aberdeen, June 9, 1829.

53. PRO FO 61/17, Proconsul Thomas Willimott to J. M. Pando, Minister of Foreign Relations, Lima, May 13, 1830. For justification of the decision after the fact see PRO FO 61/17, Thomas Willimott and P. W. Kelly to Lord Aberdeen, Valparaiso, June 21, 1830.

54. PRO FO 61/17, "Copies of Private Notes from Captain Dundas," enclosure in Thomas Willimott and P. W. Kelly to Lord Aberdeen, Valparaiso, June 21, 1830. For a detailed statement of the incident, including the amounts involved, as reported to Washington, see USNA, State, Despatches of United States Ministers to Peru, Roll 1, Samuel Larned to Martin Van Buren, Lima, May 29, 1830. United States Consul W. H. C. D. Wright in Rio de Janeiro considered the British action of such a nature that Willimott would be held to strict account by the Foreign Office, USNA, State, Despatches of U.S. Consuls, Rio de Janeiro, Roll 4, Wright to Van Buren, Rio de Janeiro, August 13, 1830.

55. Webster, *Britain and Independence*, 1:21–23.

56. See Perkins, *Monroe Doctrine, 1823–1826*, pp. 105, 242; Nancy N. Barker, *The French Experience in Mexico, 1821–1861: A History of Constant*

Misunderstanding (Chapel Hill, N.C., 1979), chap. 1; William Spence Robertson, *France and Latin American Independence,* esp. chap. 7. For a brief discussion of the Latin American view of France's activities see Edward J. Dawkins to Canning, Panama, June 10, 1826, Webster, *Britain and Independence,* 1:410–11. France recognized its former colony Haiti in 1825 and monarchical Brazil in 1826. It began recognizing the Spanish American republics only in 1831.

57. Webster, *Britain and Independence,* 1:10, 2:114, 115, 139, 152; Great Britain, *Parliamentary Debates* (Commons), 10 (March 4, 1824): 708–9; Algernon Cecil, *British Foreign Secretaries, 1807–1916 . . .* (London, 1927), p. 71; Temperley, "The Latin American Policy of Canning," *American Historical Review* 11 (1906): 779–97; Condy Raguet, U.S. Consul, Rio de Janeiro, to Adams, Rio de Janeiro, January 20, 1824, Manning, *Dip.Cor.,* 2:775.

58. See chapter 1. Also see "Translation of a letter from the Baron de Renoval, Minister of Foreign Relations, France, to Valentine Gómez, Deputy from Buenos Aires to the Courts of Europe," PRO ADM 1/25, undated, but the covering date of all papers in the box is 1820; Harold Temperley, "French Designs on Spanish America, 1820–5," *English Historical Review* (London) 40 (January 1925): 36. Whitaker, *United States and Independence* p. 323, n. 9; Robertson, *France and Latin American Independence,* pp. 162–75. On France's efforts to promote monarchy in Peru see PRO FO 185/100, "Extract of a Letter from Willimott to La Planta," dated Lima, February 17, 1825. For French intrigues in Colombia see Robertson, pp. 495–505, in which he discusses the clumsy diplomacy of Charles Bresson. For French efforts in Mexico, PRO FO 50/14, H. C. Ward to Canning, Mexico City, September 22, 1825, and Barker, *French Experience in Mexico,* pp. 26–27; PRO FO 27/333, Granville to Canning, Paris, December 15, 1825.

59. PRO FO 185/102, Frederick Lamb, British Minister to Spain, to Canning, December 25, 1825; Condy Raguet to Sec. of State Clay, Rio de Janeiro, September 23, 1826, Manning, *Dip.Cor.,* 2:861; B. Perkins, *Castlereagh and Adams,* pp. 324–25.

60. PRO ADM 1/277, Commander J. Wigston to Vice Admiral L. W. Halsted, HMS *Scout,* Port Royal, Jamaica, July 11, 1825; PRO ADM 1/277, L. W. Halsted to John Wilson Croker, Port Royal, July 12, 1825.

61. Granville to Canning, Paris, June 6, 1825, Webster, *Britain and Independence,* 2:182–83.

62. Canning to Granville, July 12, 1825, Webster, *Britain and Independence,* 2:184–85.

63. Granville to Canning, Paris, July 18, 1825, Webster, *Britain and Independence,* 2:185–86; Canning to Granville, August 1, 1825, ibid., 2:187–88.

64. Clay to James Brown, U.S. Minister to France, Washington, October 25, 1825, Manning, *Dip.Cor.,* 1:260–61. This document may also be found in U.S. Congress, *American State Papers, Foreign Relations,* 5:855–56.

65. James Brown to Clay, Paris, December 23, 1825, Manning, *Dip.Cor.,* 2:1416–17; Granville to Canning, January 26, 1826, Webster, *Britain and Independence,* 2:206–7; PRO FO 185/105, Kilbee to La Planta, Havanah, July 23, 1825; Kaufmann, *British Diplomacy,* pp. 206–7, provides a succinct account of the incident.

66. See Canning to Granville, August 23, 1825, and Canning to Granville, January 20, 1826, Webster, *Britain and Independence,* 2:194–95, 206–7.

67. PRO FO 118/20, Woodbine Parish to Aberdeen, Buenos Aires, September 27, 1828.

68. For an account of the incident see USNA, State, Despatches, U.S. Consuls, Valparaiso, Roll 2, Michael Hogan to Sec. of State Van Buren, Valparaiso, January 1, 1828. U.S. Chargé John Hamm reported to Washington that LeForest demanded $46,000 in reparations, which with interest had reached $56,000 by mid-1831. See USNA, State, Despatches, U.S. Ministers to Chile, Roll 3, Santiago, August 1, 1831. Also see PRO FO 16/10, John White, British Vice Consul, to Aberdeen, Valparaiso, December 24, 1829.

69. *Guardian* (Manchester), October 18, 1823.

70. PRO ADM 1/30, Maling to Captain of HMS *Esclair*, Valparaiso, July 9, 1825.

71. USNA, State, Despatches, U.S. Consuls, Valparaiso, Roll 2, Hogan to Sec. of State, Valparaiso, February 27, 1829.

72. PRO FO 16/12, White to Aberdeen, Valparaiso, January 14, 1830.

73. Ibid.

74. PRO ADM 1/35, Baker to George Elliot, HMS *Warspite*, Rio de Janeiro, March 14, 1831.

75. PRO ADM 1/36, Baker to Elliot, Rio de Janeiro, June 14, 1831.

76. Smith, *Great Britain and the Law of Nations*, 2:45–62, and Gordon Ireland, *Boundaries, Possessions, Conflicts in South America* (Cambridge, Mass., 1938), pp. 254–60.

77. Smith, *Great Britain and the Law of Nations*, 2:45–62.

78. PRO FO 204/Box 7, H. G. Ward to Canning, Mexico, May 20, 1826.

79. See, for example, PRO FO 61/12, Ricketts to Earl of Dudley, London, December 15, 1827. For one of the few expressions of concern about the possibility of Indians challenging the politically dominant elements, PRO FO 61/13, Thomas Willimott to Viscount Dudley, Lima, December 20, 1827.

80. *Quarterly Review* (London) 21 (January–April 1819): 430–33; *Weekly Register*, November 11, 1820, p. 169; September 22, 1821, p. 64; September 27, 1823, pp. 50–52; July 3, 1824, pp. 282–84; October 23, 1824, p. 114.

81. PRO FO 61/2, Rowcroft to Foreign Office, Lima, March 9, 1824; July 15, 1824; August 9, 1824. Also see Stevenson, *A Historical and Descriptive Narrative*, 1:306–7. For favorable views by United States agents see, for example, USNA, State, Despatches, U.S. Ministers to Brazil, Roll 3, Thomas Sumter, Jr., U.S. Minister to the Portuguese Court in Brazil, to their Excellencies, the American Ministers appointed to treat with Great Britain or to any American Minister in Europe, Rio de Janeiro, June 30, 1814, and USNA, State, Despatches, U.S. Consuls, Rio de Janeiro, Roll 1, Henry Hill to Adams, Rio de Janeiro, December 21, 1818.

82. PRO FO 61/2, Rowcroft to Foreign Office, Lima, August 15, 1824; PRO FO 18/34, Henry Wood to Canning, Guayaquil, February 28, 1826, in Humphreys, *British Consular Reports*, pp. 226–51.

83. PRO FO 15/4, Major General Todd, His Majesty's Superintendent, to José Tensillo, Belize, Honduras, February 1825. In this single communication of General Todd may be found nearly all the stereotypes of blacks current in Great Britain and the United States at the time.

84. PRO FO 18/84, W. Turner to Palmerston, Bogotá, October 7, 1831; Ricketts to Canning, Secret, February 18, 1826, Webster, *Britain and Independence*, 1:529–30.

85. PRO FO 6/17, Ponsonby to Canning, Buenos Aires, March 9, 1827; PRO FO 118/14, Ponsonby to Rear Admiral Otway, Buenos Aires, March 10, 1827.

86. PRO FO 6/13, Ponsonby to Canning, Buenos Aires, November 9, 1826, a copy.

87. PRO FO 6/3, Woodbine Parish to Canning, Buenos Aires, April 25, 1824.

88. "Notes on a Voyage to Carraccas [sic]," *Atlantic Magazine* 1 (May 1824): 52 ff.

89. PRO FO 61/2, Rowcroft to Canning (an enclosure), Lima, July 15, 1824. For favorable accounts of blacks as soldiers see chapter 2.

90. *Encyclopaedia Britannica*, 3d British ed., 1st American ed., 1798, s.v. "antediluvians."

91. Humphreys, *British Consular Reports*, p. 267.

92. PRO FO 61/11, C. M. Ricketts to Canning, Aboard H.M. transport *Egginton*, May 11, 1827. Also PRO FO 61/2, Rowcroft to Canning, Lima, August 15, 1824, which contains a long discourse on the various elements of the Peruvian population.

93. PRO FO 13/48, Fraser to Robert Gordon, Buenos Aires, April 13, 1828.

94. Luccock, *Notes on Rio de Janeiro and the Southern Part of Brazil*, p. 135.

95. Caldcleugh, *Travels*, 1:831.

96. Humphreys, *British Consular Reports*, p. 76.

97. PRO FO 61/2, Rowcroft to Foreign Office, Lima, August 15, 1824.

98. Humphreys, *British Consular Reports*, pp. 123–24.

99. PRO FO 18/52, Patrick Campbell to Lord Dudley, Bogotá, February 10, 1818.

100. J. P. Hamilton to J. La Planta (private), Bogotá, March 8, 1825, Webster, *Britain and Independence*, 1:385.

101. PRO FO 18/76, W. Turner to Lord Aberdeen, Bogotá, July 14, 1830.

102. PRO FO 118/17, Ponsonby to Dudley, Buenos Aires, August 27, 1827.

103. PRO FO 18/53, P. Campbell to Dudley, Bogotá, June 12, 1828.

104. PRO FO 18/75, W. Turner to Aberdeen, May 14, 1830, June 12, 1830.

105. PRO FO 204/Box 5, Mexico, March 25, 1826.

106. PRO FO 50/65, Richard Pakenham, British Chargé, to Palmerston, Mexico, March 1, 1831.

107. PRO FO 15/8, John O'Reilly, British Consul, Guatemala, to John Bidwell, Superintendent of the Consular Service, Guatemala, February 12, 1827.

108. PRO FO 61/2, John Rowcroft to Foreign Office, June 13, 1824.

109. PRO FO 61/14, Thomas Willimott to Dudley, Lima, March 20, 1828; PRO FO 18/76, W. Turner to Aberdeen, Bogotá, June 12, 1830, in which the writers elaborate on why ingrained corruption had encouraged and would continue to encourage the perversion of law.

110. PRO FO 61/16, Kelly to John Bidwell, Lima, July 9, 1829.

111. For the North American view of Latin American justice see chapter 3.

112. PRO FO 6/17, Ponsonby to Canning, Buenos Aires, March 9, 1827.

113. PRO FO 18/54, P. Campbell to Aberdeen, Bogotá, November 12, 1828. The document contains examples used by Campbell to support his assertion.

114. PRO FO 15/5, John O'Reilly to John Bidwell, Guatemala, August 3, 1826.

115. For provisions protecting Roman Catholicism see chapter 1 and later in this chapter.

116. See, for example, PRO FO 18/59, John Sutherland to John Bidwell, Maracaibo, January 2, 1828; PRO FO 6/8, Woodbine Parish to Canning, Buenos Aires, April 8, 1825; PRO FO 61/12, Ricketts to Dudley, London, December 15, 1827; PRO FO 18/68, J. P. Henderson to Aberdeen, Bogotá, February 21, 1829.

117. Wilkins B. Winn argues convincingly that the British wrung more liberal religious concessions from the Latin American governments than did the United States. See his "Issues of Religious Liberty in the United States Commercial Treaty with Colombia, 1824," *The Americas* 26 (1970): 291–301.

118. Great Britain, *British and Foreign State Papers, 1824–1825* (London, 1846), p. 36. This document may also be found in Edward Hertslet, *A Complete Collection of the Treaties and Conventions at the Present Subsisting between Great Britain and Foreign Powers*, 3 vols. (London, 1841), 2:48–49, and in Beaumont, *Travels in Buenos Ayres and Adjacent Provinces of the Rio de la Plata*, p. 268, where in a footnote the author adds that the treaty was sanctioned by the Argentine Congress in which there were eight individuals belonging to the secular clergy, with only two dissenting votes. The clergy's support of the treaty appeared in the *Missionary Herald* 21 (October 1825): 151–52, which also gives the dates that Great Britain signed similar treaties with eight of the Latin American states.

119. Canning made these points in a secret communication to Lionel Hervey, named Commissioner to Mexico, Secret, October 10, 1823, Webster, *Britain and Independence*, 1:436–38. Also see Canning to William à Court, October 18, 1822, and Frederick Lamb to Canning, Aranjuez, Spain, June 20, 1825, ibid., 2:390–93, 442–47.

120. PRO FO 6/16, Lord Ponsonby to Robert Gordon, Buenos Aires, January 4, 1827.

121. PRO FO 18/66, P. Campbell to Lord Aberdeen, September 13, 1829.

122. PRO FO 6/4, Parish to Canning, Buenos Aires, June 25, 1824. This document may also be found in Humphreys, *British Consular Reports*, pp. 1–25.

123. PRO FO 6/17, Ponsonby to Canning, Buenos Aires, March 19, 1827.

124. PRO FO 18/73, C. Fleeming to P. Campbell, Caracas, October 20, 1829.

125. Raguet to Clay, Rio de Janeiro, June 27, 1826, Manning, *Dip.Cor.*, 2:855–57.

126. For President Adams's views of the issue see his first and second "Annual Messages" (Richardson, *Messages and Papers*, 2:302, 2:354–55) and for President Jackson's proclamation of October 5, 1830, which in effect ended the controversy, see ibid., 2:497–99. Also see Jackson's second "Annual Message," ibid., pp. 501–4. George Dangerfield, *The Era of Good Feelings*, chap. 4, contains a highly readable account of the controversy. F. Lee Benns, *The American Struggle for the British West India Carrying Trade, 1815–1830* (Bloomington, 1923), treats in detail the legal and diplomatic issues.

127. Dangerfield, *The Era of Good Feelings*, p. 36, quoting figures from the House of Commons.

128. Humphreys, *British Consular Reports*, p. 35.

129. Great Britain, Parliament, *Acts and Papers* 34 (1831–32): 2007.

130. USNA, State, Despatches, U.S. Consuls, Buenos Aires, Roll 2, Forbes to Sec. of State, April 1, 1829.

131. Heman Allen to Sec. of State Clay, Valparaiso, April 4, 1826, manning, *Dip.Cor.*, 2:1112.

132. Humphreys, *British Consular Reports*, inserts following pp. 57, 137. Also see Dorothy B. Goebel, "British-American Rivalry in Chile, 1817–1820," *Journal of Economic History* 2 (1942): 190–202. For British influences in Chile other than economic see Jay Kinsburner, "The Political Influence of the British Merchants Resident in Chile during the O'Higgins Administration, 1817–

1823," *The Americas* 27 (July 1970): 26–39. Also see Goebel, "British Trade in the Spanish Colonies, 1796–1823," *American Historical Review* 43 (January 1938): 318.

133. PRO FO 6/3, Parish to Canning, April 25, 1831.

134. *Monthly Review* (London), 2d ser. 92 (October 1920): 48–49; PRO FO 61/2, Rowcroft to a Gentleman of Birmingham, Lima, August 22, 1824.

135. John Q. Adams recorded in his *Memoirs*, 5:153, that foreign missions were, of all the offices of the country, the most coveted and the most likely to terminate in disappointment. The *Aurora* considered overseas stations as "nothing more than sinecures, or the mere means by which the government rewards adherents or favorites, or bribes them for treachery to the public liberties and the happiness of the people," September 17, 1818.

136. See Introduction for a discussion of the British investment experience in the region. For an interesting sidelight on this topic see Webster, *Britain and Independence*, Appendix 2, 2:560, for a table entitled "Statement of the Loans Raised in England for the Service of the Late Spanish Colonies by Which Aid, Afforded Them in the Time of Their Extreme Need, They Have Achieved Their Independence." A footnote to the document reads, "Found in the papers of Lord Palmerston at Broadlands and printed by the kind permission of Lord Mount Temple."

137. For a different and interesting U.S. view of Canning see Clay's observations of him as recorded in H. U. Addington to Canning (Private and Confidential), Washington, May 2, 1825, Webster, *Britain and Independence*, 2:517.

138. Adams, *Memoirs*, 6:25.

139. Initially Whitehall had sought to guarantee itself a favored place in Latin America by obtaining special commercial concessions. The Treaty of 1810 with Portugal, for example, awarded Great Britain commercial privileges in Brazil. London, however, soon backed away from that approach in favor of open competition.

140. *Guardian* (Manchester), January 5, 1822.

141. Canning to Viscount Granville, January 21, 1825, Webster, *Britain and Independence*, 2:166–67. Also see PRO FO 61/8, C. Ricketts to Canning (Secret), Lima, July 14, 1825.

142. Smith, *Great Britain and the Law of Nations*, 1:151–52.

143. Adams, *Memoirs*, June 1822, 6:24–25.

144. Adams to Anderson, Washington, May 27, 1823, Manning, *Dip. Cor.*, 1:200.

145. Clay to Poinsett, Washington, March 26, 1825, Manning, *Dip. Cor.* 1:230.

146. It will be recalled that neither of the two envoys attended the Congress.

147. U.S. Congress, *Register of Debates of Congress*, 20th Cong., 2d sess., Appendix, pp. 41, 43, 44. For a full discussion of the U.S. position see Vernon G. Setser, *The Commercial Reciprocity Policy of the United States, 1774–1829* (New York, 1967).

148. Minister Poinsett in Mexico City believed that this jealousy should be cultivated as one strategy for at least postponing an invasion of the islands by either country. Poinsett to Clay, Mexico City, June 15, 1825, Manning, *Dip. Cor.*, 3:1626–27.

149. Logan, *No Transfer*, pp. 176–85, 190, 192.

150. Adams to Anderson, Washington, May 27, 1823, Manning, *Dip. Cor.*, 1:203.

151. Clay to Poinsett, Washington, March 26, 1825, Manning, *Dip. Cor.*, 1:231.

152. Clay to Everett, Washington, April 27, 1825, Manning, *Dip. Cor.*, 1:242–43.

153. Clay to Henry Middleton, Washington, May 10, 1825, Manning, *Dip. .Cor.*, 1:244–50; Logan, *No Transfer*, pp. 175–76. The *Times*, April 21, 1826, obtained a copy of the communication and carried lengthy excerpts from it along with editorial comment.

154. Salazar to Clay, December 30, 1825, U.S. Congress, *American State Papers, Foreign Relations*, 5:856.

155. Poinsett to Clay, Mexico City, February 1, 1826, Manning, *Dip.Cor.*, 3:1651–52.

156. Poinsett to Clay, March 8, March 18, 1826, Manning, *Dip.Cor.*, 3:1654–55, 1655. These communications also contain Poinsett's understanding of why Mexico was uninterested in peace with Spain. His analysis coincided with that of Clay as noted in his appeal to Alexander I; see earlier in the chapter.

157. PRO FO 72/275, Kilbee to La Planta, Havanah, September 23, 1823.

158. Ibid., October 20, 1823.

159. PRO FO 72/304, Kilbee to La Planta, Havanah, February 8, 1824.

160. Ibid., May 18, 1824.

161. Ibid., November 30, 1824.

162. Ibid., February 8, 1825.

163. Ibid., March 15, 1825.

164. Ibid., July 6, 1825.

165. See, for example, PRO ADM 1/277, Vice Admiral L. W. Halsted to J. W. Croker, Port Royal, Jamaica, August 24, 1825, in which Halsted noted that the Cuban population was in an unsettled state and that if "a Colombian force appeared off the S.E. with the smallest appearance of landing, an insurrection in all probability would take place," and "the island would be thrown into the greatest confusion and danger."

166. USNA, State, Despatches, U.S. Ministers to Mexico, Roll 1, Poinsett to Clay. Poinsett did not indicate what his response was to Mexican officials, but he suggested that the United States should take a hard line.

167. U.S. Congress, *Register of Debates of Congress*, "Instructions to Envoys to the Panama Congress," 20th Cong., 2d sess., Appendix, pp. 38–49. Also see President Adams's special message accompanying the transmission of documents requested by the House of Representatives in which he pointed out that the Cuban question was a major reason why the United States should be represented at Panama and warned that Mexico's and Colombia's designs on Cuba involved the danger of either a slave rebellion in the United States or the transfer of the Island to a European power. U.S. Congress, 19th Cong., 1st sess., 1826, p. 9.

168. U.S. Congress, *Register of Debates of Congress*, 19th Cong., 2d sess., April 6, 1826, p. 2062. Everett to Clay, Madrid, January 7, 1827, Manning, *Dip. .Cor.*, 3:2139–40.

169. Webster, *Britain and Independence*, 2:536–37.

170. Canning to Charles R. Vaughn (Secret and Confidential), February 8, 1826, Webster, *Britain and Independence*, 2:542–43.

171. Canning to Edward J. Dawkins, Webster, *Britain and Independence*, 1:406–9.

172. The evolution of the concept is best developed in Arthur P. Whitaker, *The Western Hemisphere Idea: Its Rise and Decline* (Ithaca, 1954).

173. See later in the chapter.

174. Patrick Mackie to Canning, London, November 20, 1823, Webster, *Britain and Independence*, 1:441.

175. See earlier in the chapter.

176. Canning to Dawkins, March 18, 1826, Webster, *Britain and Independence*, 1:403–5.

177. Ibid., 1:404–5.

178. Dawkins to Canning, London, October 15, 1826, Webster, *Britain and Independence*, 1:422–24.

179. *Weekly Register*, 17 (January 8, 1820): 306.

180. Adams to Hugh Nelson, U.S. Minister to Spain, Washington, April 28, 1823, in John Quincy Adams, *Writings*, ed. W. C. Ford, 7 vols. (New York, 1913–17), 7:373.

181. U.S. Congress, *Register of Debates of Congress*, 19th Cong., 2d sess., April 10, 1826, 2:2153.

182. Ibid., April 14, 1826, p. 3274.

183. Rattenbury, "Remarks," pp. 277–78; PRO FO 72/261, Kilbee to William Hamilton, Havannah, June 30, 1820; PRO FO 72/304, Kilbee to La Planta, Havana, February 6, 1824; *Weekly Register* 24 (April 5, 1823): 73.

184. *Weekly Register* 28 (August 6, 1825): 354; James M. Callahan, *Cuba and International Relations* (Baltimore, 1899), p. 17.

185. Jefferson to James Monroe, Monticello, April 27, 1809, Jefferson, *Writings*, 12:274–77.

186. Madison to William Pinkney, October 30, 1810, Madison, *Letters and Other Writings of James Madison*, 4 vols. (Philadelphia, 1865), 2:485–89. Also see Madison to the Senate and the House of Representatives, January 3, 1811, Richardson, *Messages and Papers*, 2:488.

187. See earlier in the chapter.

188. For a discussion of press reaction to the U.S. acquisition of East Florida see the detailed account in Logan, *No Transfer*, pp. 143–72.

189. The no-transfer principle is best handled in Logan, *No Transfer*.

190. Andrew Jackson, *Correspondence of Andrew Jackson*, ed. John S. Bassett, 7 vols. (Washington, 1926–35), 3:11–12.

191. Jackson to John C. Calhoun, August (no date), 1823, ibid., pp. 202–3.

192. Manning, *Dip.Cor.*, 1:185–86.

193. See earlier in the chapter.

194. Clay to James Brown, Envoy Extraordinary and Minister Plenipotentiary to France, October 25, 1825, Clay, *The Papers of Henry Clay*, 4:762–63.

195. See earlier in the chapter.

196. Adams to Hugh Nelson, April 28, 1823, *Writings*, 7:372–73. Also see Albert Weinberg, *Manifest Destiny* (Baltimore, 1935), pp. 59–70, 234–37.

197. U.S. Congress, *Register of Debates of Congress*, 19th Cong., 2d sess., 2:2064.

198. Goebel, "British Trade in the Spanish Colonies," pp. 302–3.

199. *Daily National Intelligencer*, October 28, 1826.

200. U.S. Congress, *Register of Debates of Congress*, 19th Cong., 2d sess., 2:2372.

201. PRO FO 72/304, Kilbee to La Planta. Also see Kilbee to La Planta, Havannah, January 5, 1824, in which Kilbee elaborated on the preemi-

nence of the United States in the commerce of Cuba and its dominance of the carrying trade.

202. See earlier in the chapter.

203. See "Extract" of a letter from Gray to Stratford Canning, Norfolk, Virginia, February 5, 1823; Stratford Canning to Admiral Rowley, Washington, February 7, 1823; Gray to Rowley, British Consulate, Virginia, undated, received March 24, 1823; Rowley to Bourchier, March 25, 1823; Rowley to Croker, Sec. of the Admiralty, Port Royal, Jamaica, March 31, 1823; manuscript copies of communications between President Monroe and Sec. of Navy Smith Thompson, all in PRO ADM 1/273. The contents of the above-mentioned manuscript copy had been printed as "Message of the President of the United States Transmitting Information in Relation to the Fortifying of Thompson's Island Usually Called Key West, Jan. 20, 1823," in *American State Papers, Naval Affairs* (Washington, 1823), 14:371. For a discussion of the importance of Key West to U.S. naval strategy see, for example, the remarks of Representative William A. Trimble (Ohio), in U.S. Congress, *Annals of Congress*, 17th Cong., 2d sess., December 20, 1822, pp. 435–36.

204. "Canning's Memorandum for the Cabinet, Dated November 15, 1822, Webster, *Britain and Independence*, 2:393–98.

205. Erskine to Canning, June 7, 1809, as cited in J. Fred Rippy, *Rivalry of the United States and Great Britain over Latin America, 1808–1830* (Baltimore, 1929), p. 74; Roy F. Nichols, *Advance Agents of American Destiny* (Philadelphia, 1956), pp. 47–48.

206. For reports on the existence of a secret group known as "Soles de Bolívar," whose precise object was unknown, and of an order called the "Black Eagles" with Mexican connections see PRO FO 72/304, Kilbee to La Planta, Havannah, February 8, 1825, and Kilbee to La Planta, March 15, 1825.

207. Adams, *Memoirs*, 6:70–73; Monroe to Madison, September 26, 1822, as noted in B. Perkins, *Casterleagh and Adams*, p. 308. Also see Whitaker, *United States and Independence*, pp. 400–402.

208. This topic is well handled in Lester D. Langley, *Struggle for the American Mediterranean*.

209. Adams to Randall, Washington, April 28, 1823, Manning, *Dip.Cor.*, 1:185–86.

210. Clay to Cook, March 12, 1827, Manning, *Dip.Cor.*, 1:282–84.

211. Everett to Clay, Madrid, December 12, 1827, Manning, *Dip.Cor.*, 3:2149–52.

212. Clay to Everett, April 12, 1826, Clay, *Papers*, 5:236–38.

213. PRO FO 72/261, Kilbee to William Hamilton, June 30, 1820.

214. Ibid.; also see references in note 203.

215. H. U. Addington to George Canning (Confidential), Washington, December 1, 1823, Webster, *Britain and Independence*, 2:505.

216. See the *National Register*, September 29, 1819, p. 210.

217. Adams, *Memoirs*, 6:69–74; Monroe, *Writings*, 6:192; Luxon, *Niles' Weekly Register*, p. 86.

218. Adams, *Memoirs*, 3:290.

219. As quoted in Dangerfield, *The Era of Good Feelings*, p. 281.

220. Canning to Lionel Hervey (No. 1 Secret), October 10, 1823, Webster, *Britain and Independence*, 1:433–36.

221. Great Britain, *Parliamentary Debates* (Lords), n.s., March 15, 1824, pp. 989, 992.

222. Canning to Frederick Lamb, August 1, 1825, Webster, *Britain and Independence*, 2:449.

223. PRO FO 72/304, Kilbee to La Planta, Havana, February 8, 1824.

224. U.S. Congress, *American State Papers, Foreign Relations*, 5:484–85.

225. Ibid.

226. U.S. Congress, 19th Cong., 1st sess., *Register of Debates*, May 26, 1826, 2:2636.

227. For correspondence between Porter and Grant between March 29 and April 24, 1824, and Porter to Sec. of Navy Southard, May 28, 1824, see U.S. Congress, *American State Papers, Foreign Relations*, 5:472–76.

228. Secretary of Navy Smith Thompson to President Monroe, dated December 28, 1822, "Message of the President . . . Transmitting Information in Relation to Fortifying Thompson's Island, Usually Called Key West, Jan. 20, 1823," Washington (1823).

229. See PRO ADM 1/278, Grant to Fleeming, July 16, 1827.

230. For evidence that the British claim was not accepted by all parties see Porter to Governor Vives, Havana, May 12, 1824, in which Porter noted that on a previous occasion Vives had asserted that Double-Headed-Shot Key belonged exclusively to Spain. U.S. Congress, *American State Papers, Foreign Relations*, 5:475–76.

231. PRO ADM 1/278, Grant to Fleeming, Bahama, July 16, 1827.

232. The Anguilla referred to by Fleeming was situated off the North Coast of Cuba and should not be confused with the resort island lying to the southeast of Puerto Rico.

233. PRO ADM 1/278, Fleeming to Croker, July 30, 1827.

234. PRO ADM 1/278, H. Hobson to Fleeming, Nassau, August 17, 1827.

235. Fleeming did not identify the source of the funds.

236. See PRO ADM 1/279, "Information gained privately respecting the Key Sal Banks from sources which can be depended on," signed Fleeming, August 26, 1828.

237. PRO ADM 1/279, Fleeming to Croker, Barham, Bermuda, August 26, 1828.

238. PRO ADM 2/1589, Croker to Fleeming, March 23, 1829. I failed to locate Fleeming's communication in which the admiral proposed in some way to lay claim to Key Sal in the name of Great Britain.

Chapter 5: Weighting the Determinants of Policy

1. D. Perkins, *The Monroe Doctrine, 1823–1826*, p. 86.

2. Barbara Tuchman, *Practicing History: Selected Essays* (New York, 1981), p. 289.

3. G. Almond, *The American People and Foreign Policy*, p. 72.

4. During the debates over the naming of delegates to the Panama Congress of 1826, the need to protect U.S. interests in any isthmian transit between the Atlantic and the Pacific arose and set off a debate that continued off and on for the remainder of the century. By the unpopular Clayton-Bulwer Treaty (1850) the United States and Great Britain agreed to cooperate in facilitating the building of a canal and bound themselves not to fortify or exercise exclusive control over such a transit. The issue was finally resolved by the Hay-Pauncefote Treaty (1901) by which Great Britain agreed to the United

States having a free hand in constructing, controlling, and fortifying an isthmian canal. After 1830, and thus beyond the scope of this study, British claims in Central America, for example, over the limits of the Mosquito Coast, Belize, and neighboring islands, led to indecisive diplomatic skirmishes between Washington and London without altering basic understandings on hemispheric issues between the two nations.

5. Even before the British government began closing consulates, the press in both England and the United States had begun warning of the consequences of relying on the new states as dependable markets or as trustworthy debtors. British and U.S. merchants agreed upon the media's assessment as they had earlier on how best to wring profits, if any, from weak and unstable Latin American markets.

Epilogue

1. Michael F. Jiménez, "Citizens of the Kingdom: Toward a Social History of Radical Christianity," *International Labor and Working-Class History*, No. 34 (Fall 1985): 4-8.

2. The following analysis of the Catholic Church in contemporary Latin America is based almost exclusively on Jiménez, ibid.; Paul E. Sigmund, "The Catholic Tradition and Democracy," *Review of Politics* 49 (1987), and "Christian Democracy, Liberation Theology, and Political Culture in Latin America," a paper presented at the Conference on Political Culture and Democracy in Developing Countries, Hoover Institution, Stanford, California, September 14–17, 1988; T. Sanders, "The Theology of Liberation: Christian Utopianism," *Christianity and Crisis* 33 (1973); Daniel H. Levine, "Religion and Political Conflict in Latin America" (Chapel Hill, N.C., 1986), and "Religion and Politics, Politics and Religion," *Journal of Inter-American Studies* 21, no. 1 (February 1979); and Michael Dodson, "Liberation Theology and Christian Radicalism in Contemporary Latin America," *Journal of Latin American Studies* 11:1 (May 1979), and "The Christian Left in Latin American Politics," *Journal of Inter-American Affairs* 21, no. 1 (February 1979). The issue of the *Journal of Inter-American Studies* containing the articles by Levine and Dodson also carried contributions by Renato Poblete, S.J., Roberto Calvo, Brian H. Smith, S.J., Sister Katherine Anne Gilfeather, M.M., and Margaret Crahan.

3. See especially Jiménez, "Citizens of the Kingdom."

4. See Hadley Cantril, ed., *Public Opinion, 1935–1946* (Princeton, N.J., 1951), p. 502, and John J. Johnson, *Latin America in Caricature* (Austin, 1980), p. 18.

5. *Gallup Opinion*, Rept. no. 22 (Princeton, 1968), and Johnson, *Latin America in Caricature*, p. 19.

6. Fredrick Merx, *Manifest Destiny and Mission in American History* (New York, 1963); chapters 2–8 contain good accounts of the debates as well as editorial comment on the subject in leading sectional newspapers.

7. Ibid., p. 161.

8. Ibid., p. 150.

9. See Bruce J. Calder, *The Impact of Intervention: The Dominican Republic during the U.S. Occupation of 1916–1924* (Austin, 1984), pp. xxvii ff., and Hans Schmitt, *The United States Occupation of Haiti, 1915–1934* (New Brunswick, N.J., 1971), esp. chap. 5, 6, 7.

10. Paul W. Drake, *The Money Doctor in the Andes: The Kemmerer Missions, 1923–1933* (Durham, N.C., 1989), p. 10.

11. Panama was later dropped from the Group when members determined that it had succumbed to the dictatorship of General Manuel Antonio Noriega.

12. Terry Carl, an address delivered during a conference on "The New Interdependence in the Americas: Challenges to Economic Restructuring, Political Redemocratization, and Foreign Policy," Stanford, California, June 5–6, 1989.

BIBLIOGRAPHICAL SOURCES

The individual chapters are generally well documented. The purpose here is to identify those sources, including many that did not find their way into the end notes but proved invaluable in the preparation of the volume.

Bibliographical Guides

The *Handbook of Latin American Studies* (Cambridge, Mass., 1936–47, Gainesville, 1948–78, Austin, 1979–); Samuel Flagg Bemis and Grace Gardner Griffin, *A Guide to the Diplomatic History of the United States, 1775–1921* (Washington, 1955); and Michael Meyer and Roger Trask, *A Bibliography of United States–Latin American Relations since 1810* (Lincoln, Nebr., 1968) are essential sources. Tom Jones, *South America Rediscovered* (Minneapolis, 1949), and Frank MacShane, *Impressions of Latin America: Five Centuries of Travel and Adventure by English and North American Writers* (New York, 1963) are major guides to firsthand accounts by foreign observers of the Latin American scene before, during, and immediately following the insurgencies. Carefully selected bibliographical references to various aspects of the independence wars and the political, economic, social, and cultural life of the new nations appear in volume 3, pages 841–919, of The *Cambridge History of Latin America*, ed. Leslie Bethell (Cambridge, England, 1985).

Primary and Modern Sources

The study rests primarily on the examination of microfilmed copies of State Department records in the United States National Archives, the Foreign Office and Admiralty Documents in the Public Record Office, Kew, England, printed records of the United States congressional and executive branches, the British Parliament and Foreign

Office, edited volumes of the writings, correspondence, and memoirs of major U.S. and British figures of the age, particularly John Quincy Adams, James Monroe, Richard Rush, Henry Clay, Robert Stewart Castlereagh, and George Canning, and the following newspapers and periodicals: *Daily National Intelligencer* (Washington), *Aurora* (Philadelphia), *Commercial Advertiser* (New York), *Times* (London), *Guardian* (Manchester), *Niles' Weekly Register* (Philadelphia), *North American Review* (Boston), *Quarterly Review* (London), *Scot's Magazine* (Edinburgh), and *Blackwood's Magazine* (Edinburgh), all of which are rich in political and social commentary on Latin America and on U.S.-British interests in the hemisphere.

Several studies by modern scholars can be profitably consulted by way of placing early hemispheric relations in a broader context and time frame than undertaken here. There is no better examination of the roots of Latin American independence movements than Peggy K. Liss, *Atlantic Empires: The Network of Trade and Revolution, 1713–1826* (Baltimore, 1983). Arthur P. Whitaker, *The United States and the Independence of Latin America, 1800–1830* (New York, 1964), contains excellent commentary on the role of the United States in the insurgencies. Samuel Flagg Bemis, *John Quincy Adams and the Foundations of American Foreign Policy* (New York, 1956), is the best general account of policy considerations undergirding U.S. diplomatic relations with Latin America and Great Britain during the years 1815–30.

Chapter 1: Domestic Factors I

The quantity so great, the quality of scholarship so impressive on the United States during its formative decades that it becomes a mere matter of preference as to what sources to include in a short bibliographical list. I suggest no more than a sampling of the published observations of foreigners, contemporaries, and modern scholars that elucidate aspects of the national experience that indirectly, but in important ways, influenced the U.S. response to developments in Latin America. Henry Commager, ed., *America in Perspective; The United States through Foreign Eyes* (New York, 1947), and Oscar Handlin, *This Was America: True Accounts of People and Places, Manners, and Customs, as Recorded by European Travelers to the Western Shore in the Eighteenth, Nineteenth and Twentieth Centuries* (Cambridge, Mass., 1949), are rich in snippets from the accounts of travelers from Britain and the Continent. Alexis C. de Tocqueville, however, is the one indispensable foreign observer of the United States scene. Charles Goodrich, *A History of the United States of America* (Hartford, Conn., 1823), was probably the most widely used history text-book during the 1820s. Samuel Perkins, *Historical Sketches of the United States from the Peace of 1815 to 1830* (New York, 1830), had the advantage of carrying the account through several critical years. The multivolume, edited writings of Presidents Jefferson, Madison, Monroe, John Quincy Adams, and Jackson and of the statesmen Richard Rush and Henry Clay are essential for understanding how national leaders saw their roles and responsibilities, the present and future of the Union, and its place in the Western world. Volumes one and two of James D. Richardson, ed., *A Compilation of the Messages and Papers of the Presidents, 1789–1908*, 11 vols. (New York, 1911), contain the major official papers of the executive branch through President Jackson's first term, ending in 1833.

Twentieth-century scholars provide the necessary in-depth analysis of the cultural and ideological evolution that the new nation underwent during the half century following independence from Great Britain. Studies that have, with good reason, stood the test of time include Vernon L. Parrington, *Main Currents in American Thought* (New York, 1927); Max Savelle, *Seeds of Liberty . . .* (New York, 1948); Gordon S. Wood, *The Rising Glory of America, 1760–1820* (New York, 1971); Howard Mumford Jones, *O Strange New World; American Culture: The Formative Years* (New York, 1964); Perry Miller, *The Life of the Mind in America . . .* (New York, 1964); Ralph Henry Gabriel, *The Course of American Democratic Thought . . .* (New York, 1940); Carl N. Degler, *Out of Our Past . . .* (New York, 1959); Stow Persons, *American Minds . . .* (New York, 1958); George Dangerfield, *The Awakening of American Nationalism, 1815–1828* (New York, 1965); Lewis Mumford, *The Golden Day: A Study in American Experience and Culture* (New York, 1926); Russel Blaine Nye, *The Cultural Life of the New Nation, 1770–1850* (New York, 1960); and Rush Welter, *The Mind of America, 1820–1860* (New York, 1975).

A good sense of the nation's remarkable economic growth before 1830 can be obtained from Curtis P. Nettels, *The Emergence of a National Economy, 1775–1815* (New York, 1962); Stuart Bruchey, *The Roots of American Economic Growth, 1607–1861; An Essay in Social Causation* (New York, 1965); Paul David, "The Growth of Real Product in the United States before 1840: New Evidence, Controlled Conjecture," *Journal of Economic History* 27 (June 1967): 151–97; Douglass C. North, *The Economic Growth of the United States, 1790–1860* (Englewood Cliffs, N.J., 1961); and Samuel Rezneck, "The Rise and Early Development of Industrial Consciousness in the United States, 1750–1830," *Journal of Economic and Business History* 4 (August 1932): 784–811. George R. Taylor, *The Transportation Rev-*

olution, 1815–1860 (New York, 1951), and H. Jerome Cranmer, "Canal Investment, 1815–1860," in Conference on Research Income and Wealth, *Trends in the American Economy in the Nineteenth Century* (Princeton) 24 (1960): 547–70, examine in some detail the surge in turnpike and canal construction following the War of 1812. Statistics appearing in any number of contemporary public documents and journals are supplemented and analyzed in the works of Jacques E. Barbier and Allan J. Kuethe, eds., *The North American Role in the Spanish Imperial Economy, 1760–1819* (Manchester, England, 1984); John H. Coatsworth, "American Trade with European Colonies in the Caribbean and South America, 1780–1812," *William and Mary Quarterly*, 3d ser., 24 (April 1967): 243–61; Peggy K. Liss, *Atlantic Empires: The Network of Trade and Revolution, 1713–1826* (Baltimore, 1983); J. R. Soley, "The Maritime Industries of America," in Nathanial S. Shaler, *The United States of America*, 2 vols. (New York, 1894), I:528–624; Worthy P. Sterns, "The Foreign Trade of the United States from 1820 to 1840," *Journal of Political History* 8 (1900): 34–57, 452–90; and Emory B. Johnson et al., *History of Domestic and Foreign Commerce of the United States*, 2 vols. (Washington, 1915). For British financial participation in the U.S. economic boom see Ralph W. Hidy, *The House of Baring in American Trade and Finance: English Merchant Bankers at Work, 1763–1861* (Cambridge, England, 1949), and Leland H. Jenks, *The Migration of British Capital to 1875* (New York, 1927).

The consequences of the trans-Appalachian movement were under constant review in the major newspapers and journals of the period. Nearly all the studies that treat economic expansion or domestic unease over slavery contain important material on the West. The national censuses beginning with that for 1790 document the population explosion in the West. Much information on the region appears in the congressional debates and executive papers in connection with relations with the various Indian nations and in reports of the War Department, which was charged with several responsibilities and duties not normally associated with the military. Of special interest because of their level of analysis are the studies of Ray A. Billington, *Westward Expansion: A History of the American Frontier*, 5th ed. (New York, 1982); Malcolm Rohrbough, *The Land Office Business: The Settlement and Administration of American Public Lands, 1789–1837* (New York, 1968); Henry N. Smith, *Virgin Land; The American West as Symbol and Myth* (Cambridge, Mass., 1950); Richard Slotkin, *Regeneration through Violence: Mythology of the American Frontier, 1600–1860* (Middletown, Conn., 1973); and Mary C. Young, "The

West and American Cultural Identity: Old Themes and New Variations," *Western Historical Quarterly* 1 (April 1970): 137–60.

The Roman Catholic Church and Catholic communicants were repeatedly faulted prior to 1830 without being prevented from making significant population gains in the nation. In fact, between 1815 and 1830 Catholics as a percentage of immigrants and of the total population increased. The number of bishoprics, places of worship, and activities among the Indian nations also increased impressively, and there was an evident trend toward the Church defending itself against Protestant attacks. The various Protestant sects propagandized from pulpits and in newspapers and journals. Especially active were the *New York Observer*, the *Baptist Missionary Magazine* (Boston), the *Missionary Herald* (Boston), the *Quarterly Register and Journal of American Education Society* (Andover, Mass.), *New England Galaxy* (Boston), and the *Christian Intelligencer and Eastern Chronicle* (Gardiner, Maine). The aggressive polemicist Bishop John England took it upon himself to lead the Catholic counterattack through his widely read and respected *United States Catholic Miscellany* (Charleston, S.C.).

The best of modern scholarship does not find religious controversy in the nineteenth century as threatening as it appeared to contemporaries. An excellent examination of early religious views can be found in Frank E. Manuel, *The Eighteenth Century Confronts the Gods* (Cambridge, Mass., 1959). Sidney E. Ahlstrom, *A Religious History of the American People* (New Haven, Conn., 1972), provides a good general introduction to the various religious sects during the early decades of the nineteenth century, but should be consulted along with Ernest L. Tuveson, *Redeemer Nation: The Idea of America's Millennial Role* (Chicago, 1968); Christopher Beam, "Millennialism and American Nationalism, 1740–1800," *Journal of Presbyterian History* 54 (Spring 1976): 182–99; John R. Bodo, *The Protestant Clergy and Public Issues, 1812–1848* (Princeton, 1954); William G. McLoughlin, *Revivals, Awakenings, and Reform: An Essay on Religion and Social Change in America, 1606–1977* (Chicago, 1978); M. J. Heale, "Humanitarianism in the Early Republic: The Moral Reformers of New York, 1776–1825," *Journal of American Studies* 2 (1968): 161–75; Ray Billington, *The Protestant Crusade, 1800–1860: A Study of the Origins of American Nativism* (New York, 1938); Merle E. Curti, *The American Peace Crusade* (Durham, N.C., 1929); and Paul Goodman, "Ethics and Enterprise: The Values of the Boston Elite, 1800–1860," *American Quarterly* 18 (Fall 1966): 437–51. They explore from different perspectives the challenges that the religious sects faced in an increasingly secularist society. The influence of religion on anthropology is unusually well handled by George W. Stocking, Jr., in his Introduction to James Cowles Prichard, *Researches into the Physical History of Mankind* (Chicago, 1973). Alice Fell Tyler, *Freedom's Ferment: Phases of American Social History to 1860* (Minneapolis, 1944), is weighted to the Catholic side. For the Catholic Church's activities among the Indians see John D. G. Shea, *History of the Catholic Church*, 4 vols. (New York, 1886–92); Gilbert J. Garraghan, *The Jesuits of the Middle United States*, 3 vols. (New York, 1938); and Robert F. Berkhofer, *The White Man's Indian: Images of the American Indian from Columbus to the Present* (New York, 1978).

Chapter 2: Domestic Factors II

Anglo-Americans of the early nineteenth century were profoundly race conscious and held alien peoples in low regard. Those traits come through clearly in the accounts of individuals who traveled to Latin America. As it turned out, British and French observers held much the same views as did Anglo-Americans. As a consequence public officials and the reading public had ready access to reports that confirmed their perceptions of the mixed population of Latin America as being of inferior quality.

A good introduction to how and on what basis Anglo-Americans have viewed aliens can be obtained from William Stanton's highly readable *The Leopard's Spots: Scientific Attitudes towards Race in America, 1815–1859* (Chicago, 1960); George Stocking, Jr., *Race, Culture, and Evolution* . . . (New York, 1968); Michael Banton, *Race Relations* (London, 1967); Harold R. Isaacs, *Scratches on Our Minds: American Images of China and India* (New York, 1958); Ronald T. Takaki, *Iron Cages: Race and Culture in Nineteenth-Century America* (New York, 1979); Pierre van den Berghe, *Race and Racism: A Comparative Perspective* (New York, 1967); Henri Baudet, *Paradise on Earth: Some Thoughts on European Images of Non-European Man*, trans. Elizabeth Wenthold (New Haven, Conn., 1965).

Perceptions of Spaniards and Portuguese can be traced to textbooks, journals, and the reports of public figures whose attacks upon Spain peaked during the decades that the Spanish court was charged with dalliance in dealing with issues over navigation of the Mississippi and the claims to the Floridas. Of the many textbooks that treated Spanish and Portuguese traits negatively, that of Jedidiah Morse, *The American Universal Geography*, first published as a one-volume work in 1789 and in a two-volume 7th edition in 1819, provided the most complete coverage. Images similar to those found in

Morse were nourished by such popular journals as the *Weekly Register* and the *North American Review*.

Numerous English and French authors and publicists writing with ill-concealed intent to discredit Spain by directing attention to its inhumane treatment of the Indians and its defense of the Inquisition evolved into what came to be known as the Black Legend. The corpus of literature on the Legend is well synthesized in Charles Gibson, *The Black Legend: Anti-Spanish Attitudes in the Old World and the New* (New York, 1971), and Benjamin Keen, "The Black Legend Revisited: Assumptions and Realities," *Hispanic American Historical Review (HAHR)* 49 (1969): 703–19; both well-documented studies that examine the legend from somewhat different perspectives. How differences with Spain over the navigation of the Mississippi and competing claims to the Floridas were used to keep alive negative images of Spaniards can be found throughout contemporary newspapers, journals, public documents, and the writings of major public figures. Philip C. Brooks in his *Diplomacy and the Borderlands Adams-Onis Treaty of 1819* (Berkeley and Los Angeles, 1939) brings the evidence together.

The negative view of the Spanish elite that circulated in Great Britain comes through clearly in C. K. Webster, *Britain and the Independence of Latin America, 1812–1830,* 2 vols. (London 1938), and manuscripts preserved in the Public Record Office, Foreign Office, files. Nancy Barker's *The French Experience in Mexico, 1821–1861: A History of Constant Misunderstanding* (Chapel Hill, N.C., 1979), and "The Factor of 'Race' in the French Experience in Mexico, *1821–1861*," *HAHR* 59 (1979): 64–80, leave no doubt that Frenchmen held Spaniards and their New World progeny in unusually low regard.

The race factor and perceptions of North American Indians have long attracted the attention of scholars, only a few of whom can be recognized here, to suggest the breadth rather than the depth of the intellectual endeavors. There is no better introduction to the field than Robert F. Berkhofer, Jr., *The White Man's Indian* . . . (New York, 1978), which is remarkable for its insights and documentation. The views of foreign travelers on white-Indian relations are summarized in Gary C. Stein, "And the Strife Never Ends: Indian-White Hostility as Seen by European Travelers to America, 1800–1860," *Ethnohistory* (Tempe, Ariz.) 20 (1973): 173–87. John G. E. Heckenwelder (1743–1823), Moravian missionary and government servant, and Henry Howe Schoolcraft (1803–1864), geologist, Indian agent, and superintendent of Indian Affairs (1836–41), although often criticized by contemporaries, probably did more than any other two early observers to add to our knowledge of Indian customs and Indian-white relations.

Their specialties were respectively the Indian nations of the Ohio Valley and the Algonquin tribes of the Great Lakes. For a suggestion of how one public figure struggled with the Indian "problem," see Lyman Parsons, "A Perpetual Harrow upon My Feelings: John Quincy Adams and the American Indian," *New England Quarterly* 46 (September 1973): 339–79. Important studies by modern scholars other than those by Berkhofer include Robert E. Bieder, *Science Encounters the Indian, 1820–1880* (Norman, Okla., 1986); Michael Rogin, *Fathers and Children: Andrew Jackson and the Subjugation of the American Indian* (New York, 1975); Roy W. Pearce, *Savagism and Civilization: A Study of the Indian and the American Mind* (Baltimore, 1965); Reginald Horsman, "Scientific Racism and the American Indian in the Mid-Nineteenth Century," *American Quarterly* 27 (May 1975): 152–68, and *Race and Manifest Destiny: The Origins of American Racial Anglo-Saxonism* (Cambridge, Mass., 1981); and the excellent article by Alden T. Vaughan, "From White Man to Redskin: Changing Anglo-American Perceptions of the American Indian," *American Historical Review* 87, no. 4 (1982): 917–53.

A number of studies have examined the role of Indian tribes in local and state economies, but few provide an overview of the subject. Francis Paul Prucha, *American Indian Policy in the Formative Years: The Indian Trade and Intercourse Acts, 1790–1834* (Cambridge, Mass., 1962), is probably the best introduction to the subject. Federal Indian policy has received considerable attention without the authors achieving a significant degree of agreement. The range of thinking on the subject can be gathered from Bernard Sheehan, *Seeds of Extinction, Jeffersonian Philanthropy and the American Indian* (Chapel Hill, N.C., 1973); Ronald N. Satz, *American Indian Policy in the Jacksonian Era* (Lincoln, Nebr., 1975); Francis Paul Prucha, "Andrew Jackson's Indian Policy: A Reassessment," *Journal of American History* 56 (December 1969): 527–39, and Mary E. Young, "Indian Removal and Land Allotment: The Civilized Tribes and Jacksonian Justice," *American Historical Review* 64 (October 1958): 31–45.

Hoxie N. Fairchild, *The Noble Savage: A Study in Romantic Naturalism* (New York, 1928); Roy Pearce, "The Significance of the Captivity Narrative," *American Literature* 19, no. 1 (March 1947): 1–20; and Louise K. Barnett, *The Ignoble Savage: American Literary Racism, 1790–1890* (Westport, Conn., 1975) provide thoughtful introductions to the Indian in United States literature.

Few topics of national interest have so attracted the attention of publicists, clergy, politicians, and scholars as have African slavery and the Afro-American in the larger white society. During the early decades of the nineteenth century those issues were explored amid a growing body of treatises by such individuals as Maupertius, Buffon, Blumenbach, Cuvier, Camper, White, Prichard, Lyell, Voltaire, and Kanes, whose findings and speculations fueled the debates over biblical chronology, monogenism and polygenism, environmentalism and hereditarianism. Some sense of the intensity of the debates can be obtained from *An Essay on the Causes of the Variety of Complexion and Figure in the Human Specie* (1st ed., 1787) by Samuel Standhope Smith, a monogenist and environmentalist and longtime president of Princeton University, and an extended reply to the *Essay* which appeared in the *American Review of History and Politics*, vol. 2 (Philadelphia, 1811); it challenged Smith's argument and came close to an explicit defense of Kanes's view of the multiple origins of man in *The Christian Herald and Seaman's Magazine* (Philadelphia), vols. 10 and 11 (1823–24), which ran several brief articles opposing slavery and explaining the degradation of blacks from an environmentalist position. Additional revealing material appeared in the *Weekly Register*, which carried on a campaign against slavery and the mistreatment of blacks; Thomas Jefferson's equivocal stand on blacks in his *Notes on the State of Virginia*; George M. Stroud, *A Sketch of the Laws Relating to Slavery in the Several States of the United States of America* (Philadelphia, 1827); and the often bitter exchanges in Congress over the many issues in which blacks figured. However, one finds in contemporary sources little that has not been extracted, synthesized, and interpreted from various perspectives in well-documented works by modern scholars, including Richard H. Popkin, "The Philosophical Basis of Eighteenth Century Racism," in *Studies in Eighteenth Century Culture: Racism in the Eighteenth Century*, ed. Harold E. Pagliaro (Cleveland, 1973); John C. Greene, *The Death of Adam: Evolution and Its Impact on Western Thought* (Ames, Iowa, 1959); Carl N. Degler, "Slavery and the Genesis of American Race Prejudice," *Comparative Studies in Society and History* 2 (October 1959): 49–65; Bentley Glass, Owsei Temkin, and William L. Straus, Jr., eds., *Forerunners of Darwin, 1745–1859* (Baltimore, 1959); Frederick M. Binder, *The Color Problem in Early National America as Viewed by John Adams, Jefferson, and Jackson* (The Hague, 1968); Winthrop Jordan, *White over Black: American Attitudes toward the Negro, 1550–1812* (Chapel Hill, N.C., 1968); John Hope Franklin, *From Slavery to Freedom: A History of Negro Americans*, 3d ed. (New York, 1967); George M. Fredrickson, *The Black Image in the White Mind . . .* (New York, 1971); Stanley Elkins, *A Problem in American Institutional and Intellectual Life* (Chicago, 1959); Leon Litwack, *North of Slavery: The Negro in the Free States, 1790–1860* (Chicago, 1961); and Ira Berlin, *Slaves without Masters: The Free Negro in the Antebellum South* (New York, 1975).

Early nineteenth-century editorials, sermons, political pronouncements, and tracts decrying racial mingling in the United States as socially taboo and biologically degenerating run into the hundreds if not thousands, but between then and now few serious in-depth studies have spoken directly to the subject. Indian-white comingling, which was not looked upon with the same degree of disapproval as that between blacks and whites, finds its way into Berkhofer's important studies at a number of points but he notes that conventional views of the social and biological consequences of such physical relationships is best sensed in the numerous and popular captivity novels, accounts of the experiences of the fur traders, missionary reports, and the records of local, state, and national legislative assemblies. Only when the nation's attention was directed to Texas (essentially a phenomenon of the 1830s) and contact with Mexicans proliferated were Anglo-Americans introduced to a literary genre intent on denigrating individuals of white-Indian descent. For commentary on that body of literature see David J. Weber, *Foreigners in Their Native Land* (Albuquerque, 1973) and Arnoldo De Leon, *They Called Them Greasers . . .* (Austin, 1983).

A considerable body of printed evidence shows that the dominant society of the early decades of the Union was passionately opposed to whites becoming sexually involved with blacks. But at the time a growing number of offspring from such relationships provided disturbing evidence that, despite social disapproval, black-white sexual relations were on the increase. Inquiry into the subject was hampered by two considerations in particular: the refusal of white society to accept a criterion that would have placed blacks and individuals of mixed racial origins in clearly defined racial categories and a social code that out of conviction or fear precluded rational discourse on the subject. Consequently except for a few individuals— among them Thomas Jefferson, who was much troubled over the political uncertainties of a large mulatto element in the population—the problem received relatively little analysis from contemporaries. Modern scholars, thus, have had to establish the views of the informed public toward persons of mixed descent from sermons of the Protestant clergy, and the laws, statutes, codes, court proceedings, and penitentiary records and to look to anthropologists to determine how science finally overtook the prevailing belief that racial crossing would lead to biological degeneracy. A few scholars, among them James Hugh Johnston, *Race Relations in Virginia & Miscegenation in the South, 1776–1860* (Amherst, Mass., 1970), and John Hope Franklin, *Color and Race* (Boston, 1968) have approached the subject head on.

Chapter 3: The Latin American Factor

For an overall view of how contemporaries viewed the new nations there are no better sources than the materials deposited in the United States National Archives and the published official documents identified in paragraph two of this bibliography complemented by the works of private individuals who wrote from personal experiences in Spain and the New World. In the last category Alexander von Humboldt, *Essay on the Kingdom of New Spain*, which had appeared in several different languages and editions between 1804 and 1830, is unequaled as a source book on the people, resources, and institutions of Spain's most prized colony. Often overlooked but of special interest because they appear to have encapsulated their contemporaries' perceptions of the new nations are Alexander Everett, *America or a General Survey of the Political Situation of the Powers of the Western Continent* (Philadelphia, 1827), and Henry Dunn, *Guatimala, or, the United Provinces of Central America in 1827–1828* (New York, 1828). Of the other authors publishing within the time span of this study the following, if not the best in all respects, collectively provide a better sampling of foreign views of the character and traits of the people than any other group of similar number. That all are British is explained by the fact that they were better observers, or at least reporters, than their Anglo-American counterparts. Members of the group and their publications are Alexander Caldcleugh, *Travels in South America during the Years 1819, 20, 21*, 2 vols. (London, 1825); Basil Hall, *Extracts of a Journal Written . . . in the Years 1820, 1821, and 1822*, 3d edition, 2 vols. (Edinburgh, 1824); John Luccock, *Notes on Rio de Janeiro and the Southern Parts of Brazil . . . from 1808 to 1818* (London, 1820); George Lyons, *Journal of a Residence . . . in . . . Mexico*, 2 vols. (London, 1828); John Miers, *Travels in Chile and La Plata . . .* , 2 vols. (London, 1826); William B. Stevenson, *A Historical and Descriptive Narrative of Twenty Years' Residence in South America*, 3 vols. (London, 1825); Henry G. Ward, a British agent in Mexico during the mid-1820s, *Mexico in 1827*, 2 vols. (London, 1828); J. A. B. Beaumont, *Travels in Buenos Ayres and the Adjacent Provinces of the Rio de la Plata* (London, 1828); and Maria Graham, *Journal of a Voyage to Brazil and Residence There, during Part of the Years 1821, 1822, 1823* (London, 1824).

Two books that appeared during the interwar years are of special interest: Lionel Cecil Jane, *Liberty and Despotism in Spanish America* (Oxford, 1929), an essentially intuitive and controversial interpretation of the nations at their inception, and Victor A. Belaúnde's wide-ranging and speculative *Bolívar and the Political Thought of the*

Spanish American Revolution (Baltimore, 1938). Important works of a more recent vintage include R. A Humphreys, *Tradition and Revolt in Latin America* (New York, 1969); John Lynch, *The Spanish American Revolutions, 1808–1826* (New York, 1973); and Tulio Halperin Donghi, *The Aftermath of Revolution in Latin America*, trans. Josephine de Bunson (New York, 1973).

Recent studies that speak directly to how the Latin American elites handled their race "problem" and also provide a number of different approaches to the subject are Charles R. Boxer, *Race Relations in the Portuguese Colonial Empire, 1415–1825* (Oxford, 1963); H. Hoetink. *The Two Variants in Caribbean Race Relations*, trans. Eva M. Hooykaas (London, 1967); Hoetink, *Slavery and Race Relations in the Americas: Comparative Notes on Their Nature and Nexus* (New York, 1973); Magnus Mörner, *Race Mixture in the History of Latin America* (Boston, 1957); and Robert Toplin, ed., *Slavery and Race Relations in Latin America* (Westport, Conn., 1974); John K. Chance, *Race and Class in Colonial Oaxaca* (Stanford, 1978); and Verena Martínez Alier's *Marriage, Class, and Color in Nineteenth-Century Cuba . . .* (London, 1974). Marta B. Goldberg, "La población negra y mulata de la ciudad de Buenos Aires, 1810–1840," *Desarrollo Económico* (April–June 1976), and George Reid Andrews, *The Afro-Argentines of Buenos Aires, 1800–1900* (Madison, 1980), using much the same data, reach different conclusions of how blacks fared in the postindependence capital of Argentina.

The 1820s were notable for the number of constitutions promulgated and discarded in Latin America. In them is found the intent of the constituent assemblies regarding the division of power among the executive, legislative, and judicial branches of the national government and between the provincial and municipal entities. Many of the constitutions, which are difficult to locate elsewhere, can be found in Great Britain, Foreign and State Papers. Commentary on how the nations, including the courts, were actually administered appears throughout the official documents and the accounts of the on-the-scene observers.

Among modern studies Charles Hale, *Mexican Liberalism in the Age of Mora, 1821–1853* (New Haven, Conn., 1968); Tulio Halperín Donghi, *Politics, Economics, and Society in Argentina in the Revolutionary Period* (Cambridge, England, 1975); and Simon Collier, *Ideas and Politics of Chilean Independence, 1808–1833* (London, 1976) are major contributions to the understanding of the ideological influences at work in the independence era. Volume 3 of *The Cambridge History of Latin America*, ed. Leslie Bethell (Cambridge, England, 1985), has articles by more than a dozen distinguished scholars who have used the most up-to-date research findings and who take an essentially sympathetic view of the trials and tribulations of the emergent nations.

Contemporaries nearly always treated the institutionalized armed forces and the ubiquitous caudillos within a political context and without pretense to objectivity. As a consequence the best analyses have been by modern scholars, only a few of whom have devoted sustained attention to the late colonial and early modern eras. Any meaningful list of works on the armed forces in the late colonial period would include Allan J. Kuethe, *Military Reform and Society in New Granada, 1773–1808* (Gainesville, 1978); Lyle McAlister, *The "Fuero Militar" in New Spain, 1764–1800* (Gainesville, 1957); and Christon Archer, *The Army in Bourbon Mexico, 1760–1810* (Albuquerque, 1977). Of works paying considerable attention to the immediate postindependence era the best are Robert L. Gilmore, *Caudillism and Militarism in Venezuela, 1810–1910* (Athens, Ohio, 1964); S. E. Finer, *The Man on Horseback: The Role of the Military in Politics* (New York, 1962); and Andrés M. Carretero, *Anarquía y caudillismo: La crisis institucional en febrero de 1820* (Buenos Aires, 1971). Charles E. Chapman, "The Age of the Caudillos . . . ," *HAHR* 12 (1932): 281–300, was among the first to call attention to the high price extracted from society for the very limited services provided by the caudillos.

The Roman Catholic Church had been a powerful force throughout the colonial era and remained so in the emerging states. Although the hierarchies in Spain and the Spanish colonies for the most part threw their weight to the side of the royalist cause during the insurgencies and following patriot victories tended to align with those elements devoted to the values inherited from Spain, the institution retained its hold on the public. The Church's reward for cooperation with the power elite was written in unmistakable terms in the constitutions of the new regimes. U.S. and British perceptions of the Church in Latin America come through clearly in the correspondence of agents posted throughout the area and in the attacks of British observers whose published accounts quickly found their way across the Atlantic. J. Lloyd Mecham, *Church and State in Latin America*, rev. ed. (Chapel Hill, N.C., 1966), is the standard secondary work on the subject, but Mary Watters, *A History of the Church in Venezuela, 1810–1930* (Chapel Hill, N.C., 1933), remains after a half-century a major contribution to our understanding of the Church as it related to the state.

Contemporary accounts of the economies of the new nations are uneven. Because bullion figured so significantly in trade and commerce and because several of the early observers of the economies traveled in Latin America on behalf of mining companies, the mining industry received considerable attention. Comments on the mining industry appear throughout the reports of official agents, but Alexander von Humboldt, *Political Essay on the Kingdom of New Spain*, 4 vols. (London, 1814), was the best early source available to the public. Joseph Andrews, *Journey from Buenos Ayres through the Provinces of Cordova, Tucumán, and Salta to Potosí...*, 2 vols. (London, 1927), and Alexander Caldcleugh, *Travels in South America...*, 2 vols. (London, 1825) are probably more suggestive of the dimensions of the problems the industry faced. In recent decades studies by Peter Bakewell, David Brading, and Doris Ladd on Mexico, and John Fisher on Peru, all based on primary sources, cast much light on the subject.

Foreigners were impressed with the extensive landholdings of the Catholic Church. Their accounts, however, contained few data with which readers could have formed other than superficial impressions of the Church's influence over the landholding systems or the national economies. This is not surprising if one appreciates the amount of painstaking research that went into Michael P. Costeloe's *Church Wealth in Mexico: A Study of the "Juzgado de Capellanias" in the Archbishopric of Mexico, 1800–1850* (London, 1967).

Anglo-Americans, acutely conscious of the confidence that their own society placed in the yeoman farmer, intuitively sensed that the sprawling private rural estates that dominated the Latin American countrysides, because of being self-contained and because of their illiquidity, would serve to brake agricultural development. But as in the case of reporting on the holdings of the Catholic Church, early accounts of private estates supplied little information to establish the degree to which they would influence political, economic, and social relationships. And modern scholarship has done little to enlighten the situation in respect to the early years of independence. Anyone interested in the subject must resort, for the most part, to books dealing with the colonial era. The most impressive work has been done on Mexico and Argentina: on the former by François Chevalier, *Land and Society in Colonial Mexico*, Foreword by Lesley Byrd Simpson, trans. Alvin Eustin (Berkeley and Los Angeles, 1963), and Enrique Florescano, *Origen y desarrollo de los problemas agrarios de México, 1500–1821* (Mexico, 1976), and Florescano, ed., *Haciendas, latifundios y plantaciones en América Latina* (Mexico, 1975), and the latter by Andrés M. Carretero, "Contribución al conocimiento de la propiedad rural en la provincia de Buenos Aires para 1830," *Boletín del Instituto de Historia Argentina* (Buenos Aires) 13, no. 22–23 (1970): 246–92, and Samuel Amaral, "Rural Production and Labour in Late Colonial

Buenos Aires," *Latin American Studies* 19, pt. 2 (1987): 235–78. The future disposition of the vast public lands the new states inherited from the colonial powers, for all intents, was not addressed. Yet today the extent of that inheritance is one of the better kept secrets of Latin America's past.

Chapter 4: The British Impact on United States–Latin American Relations

Latin America figured prominently in British diplomacy during the insurgencies and the years immediately following the colonies' separation from Spain and Portugal. Throughout the two-decade-long period London's motives in the region were twofold; first to use its influence in Madrid and Lisbon and the New World to create a balance of power in the Atlantic community and second to assure British capitalists, industrialists, and merchants a dominant role in the financial and commercial activities of the emergent countries. Of studies stressing the policy angle William Kaufmann, *British Policy and the Independence of Latin America, 1804–1828* (New Haven, Conn., 1951), is the most analytical and is especially good in the attention it pays to Britain's Latin American policies in their European context. For a British perspective on Britain's policies in Latin America there are no better sources than C. K. Webster's Introduction to his *Britain and the Independence of Latin America, 1812–1830*, Webster, 2 vols. (London, 1938); *The Foreign Policy of Castlereagh, 1815–1832* (London, 1925); Webster, "Castlereagh and the Spanish American Colonies," *English Historical Review* 27 and 30 (1912, 1915); Harold W. V. Temperley, "The Latin American Policy of Canning," *American Historical Review* 11 (1906): 779–97, which though skeletal is remarkably perceptive; and Gerald S. Graham and R. A. Humphreys, eds., *The Navy and South America, 1807–1823: Correspondence of the Commanders-in-chief on the South American Station* (London, 1962). Twentieth-century studies by H. S. Ferns, *Britain and Argentina in the Nineteenth Century* (Oxford, 1960); Alan K. Manchester, *British Preeminence in Brazil: Its Rise and Decline* (Chapel Hill, N.C., 1933); and Peter Winn, *El imperio informal británico en el Uruguay en el siglo XIX* (Montevideo, 1975), although of unequal quality, provide close-ups of British policies in countries where it exercised inordinate influence during their formative years.

Great Britain was clearly the dominant foreign economic force in the newly independent nations. Modern scholars have recognized that reality by nearly always examining U.S. penetration of the region in terms of its competing with England for the favor of the new regimes, but have examined British financial, industrial, and commercial activities without reference, or with only incidental reference, to the U.S. economic activities in the region. The following sources recognize that distinction. Studies that treat the U.S. economic efforts in the region within the larger U.S.-British context include J. Fred Rippy, *Rivalry of the United States and Great Britain over Latin America, 1808–1830* (Baltimore, 1929); R. A. Humphreys, "Anglo-American Rivalries and Spanish American Emancipation," *Royal Historical Society Transactions*, 5th ser., 16 (London, 1966): 131–56; E. J. Pratt, "Anglo-American Commercial and Political Rivalry on the Plata, 1820–1830," *HAHR* 11 (1931): 302–35; Watt Stewart, "The Diplomatic Service of John M. Forbes at Buenos Aires," *HAHR* 14 (1934): 202–18; Dorothy Burne Goebel, "British-American Rivalry in the Chilean Trade, 1817–1820," *Journal of Economic History* 2 (November 1942): 190–202; and Charles Salit, "Anglo-American Rivalry in Mexico, 1823–1830," *Revista de historia de América*, no. 16 (December 1943): 65–84. British economic interests in the new nations have received much scholarly attention. Works dealing primarily with British investments in the region include J. Fred Rippy, *British Investments in Latin America, 1822–1949* (Minneapolis, 1959); Leland H. Jenks, *The Migration of British Capital to 1875* (New York, 1927); D. C. M. Platt, *Finance, Trade, and Politics in British Foreign Policy* (Oxford, 1968); Peter Winn, *El imperio informal británico con el Uruguay en el siglo XIX* (Montevideo, 1975); and with British trade Judith Plow Williams, *British Commercial Policy and Trade Expansion, 1750–1850* (Oxford, 1972); Dorothy Burne Goebel, "British Trade to the Spanish Colonies, 1796–1823," *American Historical Review* 43 (January 1938); the indispensable *British Consular Reports on the Trade and Politics of Latin America, 1824–1826*, ed. R. A. Humphreys (London, 1940), Vera Blinn Reber's well-crafted *British Mercantile Houses in Buenos Aires, 1810–1880* (Cambridge, Mass., 1979), and D. C. M. Platt, *Latin America and British Trade, 1806–1914* (London, 1972).

Congressional debates along partisan lines over sending delegates to the Panama Congress of 1826 led to numerous derogatory remarks about the people and institutions of Latin America. George Canning took advantage of the situation in hopes of tightening Britain's already strong hold on Latin America. The case he made appears in C. K. Webster, *Britain and the Independence of Latin America, 1812–1830*, vol. 2 (London, 1938). Joseph B. Lockey, *Pan-Americanism: Its Beginnings* (New York, 1926), and Arthur P. Whitaker, *The Western Hemisphere Idea* (Ithaca, 1954), provide good general coverage of the issues involved. Pedro Gual of Colombia was the most influential Latin American delegate to the Congress. His distinguished career is sympathetically treated in Harold A. Bierck, *Vida pública de Don Pedro Gual* (Caracas, 1947).

Of all concerns over Latin America the disposition of Cuba, still in the possession of faltering Spain, had within it the greatest potential for shattering the modus vivendi that had permitted the two powers peacefully to pursue their interests in the region. A good sense of why the island was economically important can be gathered from Alexander von Humboldt, *Ensayo político sobre la Isla de Cuba*, trans. D. J. B. de V y M. (Paris, 1827); Dionisio Vives, *Quadro estadístico de la siempre fiel Isla de Cuba* (Havana, 1829), which appeared in English translation in the *American Quarterly Review* 7 (June 1830): 475–513. J. Freeman Rattenberry, "Remarks on the Cession of the Floridas to the United States of America and the Necessity of Acquiring the Island of Cuba by Great Britain," *The Pamphleteer* 25, no. 29 (London, 1819), presents a picture in which Cuba looms so large that His Majesty's Government should, if necessary, go to war to deny its acquisition by the United States. The reports of British Consul H. T. Kilbee, posted to Havana, deposited in the PRO FO file 72 and of British naval officers, assigned to the Caribbean, in PRO ADM 1 kept London well informed of developments that might adversely affect Great Britain's interest in the island. The U.S. early interests in Cuba may be traced in Roy Nichols, *Advance Agents of American Destiny* (Philadelphia, 1956); Joel R. Poinsett, *Notes on Mexico, Made in the Autumn of 1822* (Philadelphia, 1824); and William Ray Manning, *Early Diplomatic Relations between the United States and Mexico* (Baltimore, 1916), esp. chap. 5. The important role of Cuba in the formulation of the no-transfer principle and the Monroe Doctrine is well analyzed in John A. Logan, Jr., *No Transfer: An American Security Principle* (New Haven, Conn., 1961), and Dexter Perkins, *The Monroe Doctrine, 1823–1826* (Cambridge, Mass., 1927).

INDEX

Adams, John, on war with Great Britain, 112
Adams, John Quincy: on blockades, 120; on British and Latin America, 139, 140; dislike of George Canning, 185; fear of Latin American entanglements, 86–87; and importance of Cuba to United States, 153; opposition to early recognition of new states, 83; on privateering, 117; and religious liberty in Latin America, 26–27, 28; and Spanish administration in New World, 53
Alcedo, Antonio, quoted, 23
Alexander I, Czar, 142–43
Allen, Heman, on predominance of Great Britain in Latin America, 138
Amelia Island, 117
American Family concept, British opposition to, 151–53; reason for failure of, 151–53
American Quarterly Review, quoted, 8
Americans. See Anglo-Americans
Ames, Fisher, quoted, 71
Anderson, Richard Clough, Jr., U.S. Minister to Colombia, 29–30
Anglo-Americans: dependence of, on British publications, 12n.16; interest of, in racial types, 5, 6, 8; perceptions of non-Anglo-Americans by, 46
Anguilla Island, 165, 166
Anti-Catholicism: lack of influence on U.S.–Latin American relations of, 26–27; in United States, 21–23, 24.See also Catholic Church, in Latin America; Catholic Church, in United States

Anticlericalism, 133
Appleby, Joyce O., 10
Araucanian Indians, 62
Arce, José, 110
Armed forces: changing role of, 93–94; civilian fear of, 95–96; political role of, 95; violence of, 92–93
Atlantic Magazine, on blacks in Venezuela, 67
Aurora, 52
Authoritarianism, prevalence of, in Latin America, 3
Ayacucho, Battle of, 111

Beaumont, J. A. B., 57; quoted, 63
Beck, Theodoric, and promotion of industry, 12
Bemis, Samuel Flagg, 6
Benton, Thomas Hart, on Haiti, 76–77
Black Legend: British literature on, 48, 49; political uses of, in England and France, 49; uses of, in United States, 50
Blacks, in Latin America: British views of, 130–31; character of, in Peru, 130; consequences of participation in Independence Wars by, 89; demographic preponderance of, in tropics, 66–67; enfranchisement of, 90; favorable impressions of, 67; fear of, by elites, 90; foreign portrayal of, 67–70; importance of, as soldiers in insurgent armies, 67–69; and Indian laborers compared, 130; North American negative images of, 68; praised as laborers, 67; status of, 63–64; treatment of, 68

Blacks, in United States: British opposition to, 120–23; discrimination against, 63–65, and legislation and courts, 65; perception of, 64–66

Blockades, U.S. and British opposition to, 118–23

Bodo, John R., 10

Bolívar, Simón: and Catholic Church, 99, 100; complaints of lack of U.S. support, 82; on interracial mixing, 71; and monarchy, 33–34, 42

Bolivian constitution of 1826, provisions for a strong executive, 34–35

Boves, Thomas, blacks in army of, 67n.122

Brazil: acceptance of monarchy in, in Latin America, 34; corruption in, 54–55; independence movement in, 54–55; Lord Ponsonby on monarchy in, 37; master-slave relations in, 68

British: blacks as seen by, 136–37; Creoles as seen by, 132–33; preeminence of, in Latin America, 134–55. See also Great Britain

British legion, 115

British West Indies, trade controversy, 137

Bureaucrats, conservatism and incompetence of, 97–98

Cairns, W. B., 10, 12

Caldcleugh, Alexander, on master-slave relations in Brazil, 68

Calhoun, John C., on importance of Cuba to United States, 156

Campbell, Patrick, in praise of monarchy, 135–36

Canals, development of, 14

Canning, George: dislike of John Quincy Adams, 185; on importance of monarchy in Brazil, 37; on monarchism in Latin America, 36–37

Carroll, Charles, 22

Catholic Church, in Latin America: British castigation of, 133–34; conservatism of, 3, 25–26; corruption within, in Brazil, 55; Creole domination of, 99; as interpreter of social value system, 3; legal status of, 100–101; low regard for clergy of, 26; negative U.S. views of, 25–26; political

role of, 99, 100, 101; Protestant disdain of, 26; real estate holdings of, 25–26; religious monopoly of, 133; social role of, 99–101

Catholic Church, in United States, 21; anticlerical literature, 23; declining resentment toward, 22; growth of membership in, 23, 212n.50; influence of, in U.S.–Latin American policy, 173–75; links to monarchism of, 23; official support of missions of, 28–29; opposition to, 22–23, 24–25; and secularism, 22; treatment of, by government, 28

Caudillos: basic conservatism of, 97; as political phenomenon, 96–98. See also Armed forces

Cherokee Nation, 60

Chile, irresponsibility of government of, 123

Chiloé, island of, French interest in, 128–29

Chocano, José Santos, quoted, 88

Church and state, separation of, 2, 30

Clay, Henry: as champion of insurgent cause, 83; concern of, over French interest in Cuba, 127; displeasure with Bolivar, 39; distrust of Great Britain of, 112; on importance of Cuba, 156; low regard for Indians, 59; on republicanism in Latin America, 38

Colombia, and Cuba, 141

Commerce and industry: changing views toward in Anglo-America, 12–13; growth of, in Anglo-America, 11, 12

Connecticut Observer, 23

Cook, Captain James, 8

Creoles: British view of, 132–33; changing North American views of, 56–57; character of, 55–58; composition of, 55; cultural values of, 92–93; elite status of, 92–93; as heirs of Spain and Portugal, 55; political role of, 93; portrayal of, in literature, 57–58; as viewed by Britain and United States, 56–58

Cuba: British interest in, 159, 161–62; early U.S. interest in, 154–55; favorable geographical position of, 163; fear of Colombia in, 144; geopolitical importance of, 4–5; Great Britain on U.S. interest in, 147–48, 159–60; importance of, in U.S.–British relations, 140–49, 153, 155, 157, 159–64; importance of remaining under Spain, 160–61; importance of, to United States, 154–56; independence for, advantages and disadvantages of, 163–64; interest of, in joining United States, 158–59; Mexican and Colombian threats to and interest in conquest of, 75–76, 140–45; negotiations on future of, 127; pirate bases in, 118; reasons left to Spain, 160–64; U.S.–British agreement on future of, 146–47; U.S. concern over possible invasion of, by Mexico and Colombia, 141–45; U.S. fear of race war in, 145–46; U.S. interest in islands and keys off north shore of, 164–67; U.S. opposition to annexation of, by United States, 160–61; U.S. policy on future of, 156, 158–60; U.S. trade with, 157; U.S. warning to France about, 156

Daily National Intelligencer, 52, 113
Dawkins, Edward J., British agent at Panama Congress, 152–53
Dickens, Charles, 12
Dorrego, Manuel, 111

Economics, Latin American: British influence on, 107–8; lack of independence of, 101; role of land in, 101–3
Edwards, Martha L., 10
Ethnocentrism, 6; in United States, 45–46
Europeans, perceptions of, in United States, 2
Everett, Alexander H.: on Colombian and Mexican threats to Cuba and Puerto Rico, 143; on Spanish character, 47

Fajardo, Puerto Rico, 116
Falkland Islands, British occupation of, 129
Fitch, John, 12
Fleeming, Vice Admiral Charles: concern of, over U.S. interest in Cuban islands and keys, 164–67; on Latin American opposition to monarchical government, 136
Forbes, John M., 109

Foreign Enlistment Act, violations of, 115
Foreign policy, U.S., public participation in, 74
France: competition for influence in New World, weaknesses in, 124–25; interest in Chiloé Island of, 126–29; promotion of monarchy in Argentina, 35; promotion of monarchy in Peru, 35–36; U.S. and British actions toward, to checkmate in Latin America, 124, 126
Francia, Dr. (José Gaspar Rodríguez), anti-Catholic view of, 26
Franklin, Benjamin: on industry, 12; view of blacks, 64
French fleet in Caribbean, U.S. and British reactions to, 126–27
Fuero Militar, 95
Fueros, ecclesiastical, 100
Fulton, Robert, 13–14

Gage, Thomas, contribution to Black Legend literature, 49
Gamarra, Augustín, 91
Gauchos, 72
Gold, declining production of, 104
Great Britain: commercial treaty of, with Argentina, 134–35; concern for friendship of United States, 167–69, distrust of, in United States, 112–13; impact on U.S.–Latin American relations, 180–86; importance of United States to, 167–68; influence of, in Portugal, 54; investment experience of, in Latin America, 19–20; no growth policy, 161–63; opposition to American Family concept idea, 151–53; preeminence of, in Latin America, 4–5; preference for monarchy in Latin America, 135–36; role in independence movements, 4; role as mediator between Spain and its colonies, 114–15; use of force to protect agents, 123–24
Griffin, Charles, 6
Guerrero, Vicente, 91, 110

Haiti, 114; control of San Domingo of, 110–11; race factor in recognition of, 75; Thomas Hart Benton's discourse on, 76–77

Hakluyt, Richard, 49
Hall, Francis, and patriotism of black soldiers, 68
Harrison, William Henry, 109
Henderson, James, on Bolívar favoring monarchy, 37
Hidalgo Affair, 124
Hidalgo y Costilla, Miguel, 99
Hill, Henry, U.S. Consul, attack on character of Brazilian mixed races, 72
Hogan, Michael, on antiforeignism of Chilean government, 123
Hughes, H. Stuart, 9
Humboldt, Alexander von, 8; on blacks, 66

Immigrants, importance of, 2
Indians, in Latin America: and agriculture, 63; Anglo-American compassion for, 61–62; Anglo-American images of, 62–63; as base of social pyramid, 61–62; British view of, 130; compared with North American Indians, 62–63; consequences of independence wars on, 89; contribution of, during colonial era, 61; and mining, 63; mistreatment of, by mixed races, 90–91; plight of, 88–89; political role of, 89; unfavorable character of, 63
Indians, in United States: as allies of France and Great Britain, 58–59; failure to contribute to the economy, 59–60; Madison's attack on, 221n.80; treatment of, 60–61
Irregular armies. See Armed forces; Caudillos
Isolationism, U.S. tendency toward, 3
Iturbide, Augustín, 39

Jackson, Andrew: on importance of Cuba, 156; and invasion and public defense of Florida, 51
Jefferson, Thomas: and anti-Catholicism, 22–23; on U.S. superiority and future, 45
Jesuits: U.S. midwest missions of, supported by War Department, 28–29; views of, in United States, 23
Jones, Howard Mumford, 11
Juan, Jorge, low regard for mestizos, 72

Key West, 158
Kilbee, Henry T., British Consul in Cuba: on Cubans, 160; reports of, 143–44; on U.S. interest in Cuba, 160

Land: distribution of, by Crown, 102; illiquidity of, 102–3
Larned, Samuel, on role of minerals in economy, 104–5
Latin America: Anglo-American knowledge of, 80; authoritarianism in, 110–11; capital illiquidity in, 102–3; condition of, at independence, 3; conditions favoring U.S. recognition of, 82–85; corruption of courts of law in, 98–99; dependence on minerals of, 104–5; disunity in, 87–88; early U.S. interest in, 80–81; economic conditions in, 101–10; experiences similar to those in United States, 79–80; fiscal mismanagement in, 20; foreign adventurers in, 80; Iberian inheritance, 3; implications of instability in, 110–13; influence of, on U.S. policy to 1830, 175–77; investment practice of, 108; lack of investment capital for development of, 103; poor prospects for, 4; presumed nonappreciation of U.S. actions, 86; provincialism in, 3; recognition of certain states by United States, 85; social conditions in, at independence, 87–88; support of insurgents from, by Baltimore, 81; trade and commerce in, Britain and, 136–39; trade and commerce in, U.S. policies concerning, 140
Latrobe, Benjamin, 12
Lavalle, Juan, 111
Le Forest, Charles A., French agent in Chile, 36, 127–28
Leopold Association in Vienna, 23
List, Frederick, 13
Lockey, Joseph Byrne, quoted, 37
López Fuentes, Gregorio, 88
"Lowell Girls," 13
Luccock, John, on Brazilian mixed races, 131

Madison, President James, on importance of Cuba to United States, 154–55

Maling, Captain Thomas, 35
Malvinas, Las, 129. *See also* Falkland
Islands
Manchester Guardian, on free trade, 136
Manifest Destiny, 44–46
Marines, British use of, to protect
agents, 124
Mestizos, Anglo-American prejudices
against, 71–73. *See also* Mixed races
Mexico: British influence in, 87; early
U.S. threats to, 87; interest in Cuba,
141
Military. *See* Armed forces
Miller, Douglas, 10
Miller, Samuel, on economic develop-
ment in United States, 12
Miscegenation, Anglo-American preju-
dices against, 70–71; *Encyclopedia
Britannica* quoted on, 131
Missions. *See* Jesuits
Mixed races, 90–92; anti-foreignism of,
92; aspirations of, 91–92; British
view of, 131–32; character of, 70–73;
Creole distrust of, 92; importance of,
in postindependence era, 90–91; political influence of, 53; social, economic, and political roles of,
91–92; U.S. prejudices against,
70–72
Monarchy, in Latin America, 32–41;
British preference for, 135–36; British
prospects for, as seen by George Canning, 36–37; conditions favoring, 33;
failure of predicted, 136; French promotion of, 35–36, 42–43, 125–26;
influence of, on U.S. policy, 170–73;
U.S. acceptance of, 39
Monroe, President James, on republicanism in Latin America, 38; reasons
of, for delaying recognition of new
states, 84
Monroe Doctrine, 115; enunciated, 85;
reception of, in Europe and Latin
America, 86
Morelos y Pavón, José María, 99
Morse, Jedidiah, quoted, 45–46
Most favored nation policy, 139

Nationalism, growth of, in United
States, 3
Native Americans: compared with civi-
lized tribes of Latin America, 58–59;
perceptions of, 58–63. *See also* Indi-
ans, in United States
Nativism, 23–24
Neutrality, U.S. and British policy on,
114–16
New York Advertiser, 8
New York Observer, 8
Newspapers: importance of, in United
States, 7; public interest in, 7–8
Niles, Hezekiah, 1
*Niles' Weekly Register. See Weekly
Register*
North America, confidence of, in re-
publicanism, 2
North American Review: quoted, 13,
52; on Spanish character, 47
Nye, Russel Blaine, 11

O'Higgins, Bernardo, 122
Otway, Admiral R. W., 123–24

Páez, José, 91
Panama Congress of 1826: British op-
position to American Family concept
at, 151–53; British position on Cuba
at, 147–48; debates over sending dele-
gates to, 57, 86
Parish, Woodbine, British chargé: on
monarchy, 136; request of, for marine
protection, 124
Paulding, Kirke, 13
Pedro I (Brazil), 11; abdication of, 111
Perceptions: defined, 5; importance of,
7; importance of, in international
relations, 9, 73–75; racial, and U.S.–
Latin American relations, 74–77,
177–79
Perkins, Dexter, 6
Pinckney Treaty, 16, 50
Piracy, 116–17
Pirates, 116. *See also* Privateering
Plato's Republic, quoted, 99
Poinsett, Joel R.: agent to Chile and
Argentina, 83; anti-Catholic view of,
25
Polignac, Prince: support of Catholi-
cism in Latin America, 36; warned
by Great Britain, 125
Ponsonby, Lord: on irresponsibility of
Brazilian government, 123; on mon-
archy in Latin America, 135
Portales, Diego, 100

Porter, Commander David: confrontation of, with Spanish office in Puerto Rico, 118; court-martial of, 118

Portugal: British influence in, 54; dependence on Great Britain, 54–55; Inquisition in, 54; religious fanaticism in, 53

Portuguese, character of, 53–55

Prieto, General Joaquín, 111

Privateering: agreement on, by United States and Great Britain, 116–17; President Monroe's concern about, 118–19; U.S. objection to, 83

Privateers: United States and Great Britain's opposition to, 116–20; use of, by Great Britain, 116

Protestant missions, lack of, in Latin America, 31–32

Protestantism: British protection of, in commercial treaties, 134–35; importance of, 21

Provincialism, 95–96

Public land policies: changes in, 16; revenues from, 18

Puerto Rico, pirate bases in, 118. See also Cuba

Pueyrredón, Juan Martín, preference for monarchism, 35

Racism, 5

Raguet, Condy, 136; affronts Brazilian government, 121

Reciprocity, 140

Religious liberty, provided for, in treaties between United States and Latin America, 29–31

Removal Act of 1830, 61

Republicanism in Latin America: Anglo-American confidence in, 44–45; Great Britain's acceptance of, 41–42; importance of, to United States, 38–39; preference for, 33, 39–41

Richmond Enquirer, 57

Roman Catholicism. See Catholic Church, in Latin America; Catholic Church, in United States

Rosas, Juan Manuel, 111

Rowcroft, Thomas, on black character, 130

San Martín, José: and monarchy, 33; victories of, over royalists in Chile and Peru, 82

Santa Cruz, Andrés de, 91

Santander, Francisco de Paula, 111

Santo Domingo, occupation of, by Haiti, 111

Secularism: rise of, in United States, 27–28; U.S. trend toward, 2–3, 11

Southern United States, economic growth in, 15

Spain: Catholic fanaticism in, 48; cruelty of Spanish soldiers, 52; differences with United States, 50–51; importance of, as trading partner, 51; inability to defend Cuba, 142–43; U.S. perceptions of, 46–49; possibility of war with United States, 50; U.S. agents' views toward, 52–53

Spanish character, 46–53

Sprague, Charles, on importance of "American independence," 45

Stereotypes. See Perceptions

Sucre, Antonio de, 111

Technology, rapid development of, in United States, 12–13

Ticknor, George, on Spanish character, 46

Times (London), on privateering, 119–20

Toqueville, Alexis de, 21; on North American patriotism, 45

Toussaint L'Ouverture, 114

Travel literature, importance of, 8

Treaty of Ghent, 112; issues carried over from, 84

Treaty of Metheun, 37

Tudor, William, 109

Turner, Frederick Jackson, 10

Turnpikes, development of, in United States, 12, 14

Two-sphere concept. See Monroe Doctrine

Ulloa, Antonio de, low regard for mestizos, 72

United States: agents in Latin America, quality of, 108–10; areas of agreement with Great Britain, 114–29; borrowing from Great Britain, 17–19;

commercial treaties with Latin America, 29–31; domestic factors in U.S.–Latin American relations, 179–81; early relations with, 50–51; efforts to promote republicanism in Latin America, 38–39; factors contributing to disunity in, 10; growth of international trade, 15; industrial development in, 11; infrastructural development in, 13–15; interest in acquiring Mexican territory, 87; interest in islands and keys off Cuban Coast, 164–67; low regard for Spanish officials, 51; naval squadrons of, 120; neutrality laws of 1817 and 1818, 81; possibility of war with Spain, 50; prosperity in, 30, 45; recognition of new states in Latin America, 85; response to Mexican and Colombian threats to Cuba, 140–44; technological development in, 12, 13; territorial expansion of, 16–17

Uruguay, independence of, 111; character of, 132

Vaughn, Minister Charles R., on U.S. views of Cuba and Puerto Rico, 146–47
Victoria, Guadaloupe, on invasion of Cuba, 144

War, and resolution of international issues, 112, 113
War of 1812, influence on United States, 1–2
Ward, H. G., on Mexican character, 130; on monarchy in Mexico, 37
Wars of independence, Latin American, British participation in, 115
Webster, Daniel, on importance of Cuba, 153
Weekly Register: cited, 113; on British interest in Cuba, 153
Western United States, demographic growth in, 16–17; influence on U.S.–Latin American relations, 17
Westward expansion, 15–17
Whitaker, Arthur P., 6, 11
White Legend, 218n.21
Whitney, Eli, 13

Designed by Martha Farlow

Composed by BookMasters, Inc., in Trump Medieval

Printed by BookCrafters, Inc., on 50-lb. BookText Natural and bound in Holliston Roxite A